TAKING SIDES

Clashing Views in

Management

SECOND EDITION

Selected, Edited, and with Introductions by

Marc D. Street
Salisbury University

and

Vera L. Street
Salisbury University

Contemporary Learning Series

A Division of The McGraw-Hill Companies

To my most magnificent wife, Vera.
You are my reason, my inspiration, my motivation

Photo Acknowledgment
Cover image: The McGraw-Hill Companies/John Flournoy

Cover Acknowledgment
Maggie Lytle

Printed on Recycled Paper

Preface

He who knows only his side of the case knows little of that. His reasons may have been good, and no one may have been able to refute them. But if he is equally unable to refute the reasons on the opposite side he has no ground for preferring either opinion.

—John Stuart Mill[1]

The United States criminal system is adversarial in nature; two sides with incompatible goals meet in front of a judge and jury in order to determine the fate of an individual charged with a crime. Underlying this process is the presupposition that truth can be reached through the presentation of conflicting viewpoints. This book, the second edition of *Taking Sides: Clashing Views in Management,* is predicated on this very same presupposition. Each of the debates presented here mimics the courtroom: There are two opposing sides, each vigorously presenting its evidence and questioning their opponents case; there is a judge, the reader, who considers the relative merits of each side, hopefully maintaining objectivity while searching for truth; and there is a verdict, signaling victory for one side and conviction for the other.

This text consists of 18 debates on controversial issues in the field of business management. Each issue consists of opposing viewpoints presented in a pro and con format. It is your role as judge to give each side a fair and unbiased hearing. This will be a difficult task, for each of the authors of the 36 articles is an expert and defends his or her position with great vigor. To help in your task, we suggest that you ask difficult questions, make notes on troubling points, and interact with the material. Most importantly, if you have a preconceived opinion about an issue, force yourself to look critically at the side you support. This, too, is difficult to do; it's much easier to find the weaknesses in the opposing side than in your own. But doing so helps protect against self-deception and, frequently, strengthens your original belief. And, perhaps most importantly, it makes you think!

Organization of this book   Each issue starts with an *introduction*, which sets the stage for the debate as it is argued in the yes and no selections. The *postscript* follows the selections and provides some final observations and comments about the topic. The postscript also contains *suggestions for further reading* on the topic that should prove beneficial in the event you are still undecided. Keep in mind that the selections represent only two possible viewpoints on a topic; there may well be other positions on these subjects beyond the two in the book. Relevant Internet site addresses (URLs) have been provided

---

[1]M. Neil Browne and Stuart M. Keeley, *Asking the Right Questions,* 6th ed., Prentice Hall, 2001.

for your benefit and can be found on the page immediately preceding the part openers. Finally, at the back of the book is a list of all the *contributors to this volume*. Biographical information on the philosophers, economists, social commentators, educators, political analysts, and other experts who contributed articles can be found here.

We'd like to present a final word on this most recent edition of the text. Those familiar with the first edition will notice that we have made several significant changes to this second version. First, we dropped three topics that proved to be either somewhat inaccessible or not overly controversial to our students and readers. Second, we have updated three topics carried over from the first edition with newer articles by different authors; this, we think, contributes to the overall "newness" of this edition. Finally, and perhaps most significantly, we have added four new, topical issues. Two of these—the illegal immigration and Social Security reform issues—were test driven by the first author in several of his undergraduate classes with resounding success. Students found both topics to be very controversial, topical, and compelling. It is our sincere hope that you too find the topics here to be not only controversial, but interesting and educational as well. We thank you for your interest in our work!

Acknowledgments   We would like to thank our University of South Florida, St. Petersburg undergrad and graduate students for their comments, feedback, and topic and article suggestions. We would also like to extend a special thanks to our wonderful editor at McGraw-Hill, Jill Peter. As was the case with the first edition, her calmness, professionalism, and flexibility were of incalculable value in the ultimate completion of this book. Once again, thank you Jill! Finally, we'd like to thank our family and friends for their continued support and encouragement. Thanks to you all!

Contents In Brief

Contents

Robert D. Hay and Edmund R. Gray believe that corporations should be
held accountable for more than profit maximization. Their argument is
based on stakeholder theory and is presented in the form of an historical
account of the evolution of managerial thinking on this important topic. In
answering "no" to this question, Alexei Marcoux presents a frontal
attack on stakeholder theory. Consistent with the views of Nobel
Laureate Milton Friedman, Marcoux argues that the very nature of
stakeholder theory is immoral and can only lead to disastrous results for
all involved.

Larry Gross contends that downsizing violates the psychological and
social contracts implicit in the employer-employee relationship since
there is an implied sense of job security afforded the employee as long
as he or she is productively advancing the goals of the organization.
Downsizing productive employees is a clear violation of this contract
and, therefore, immoral. Professor Joseph Gilbert analyzes the ethicality
of downsizing through the application of three prominent approaches to
the study of ethics: utilitarianism, rights and duties, and justice and
fairness. Gilbert concludes that, with one notable exception, downsizing
is an ethically valid and morally responsible corporate behavior.

Ethics scholar Chris Provis examines bluffing within the context of labor negotiations and concludes that it does indeed constitute unethical behavior. Bluffing, he argues, is deception and therefore, unethical, regardless of whether it occurs in or out of the negotiation process. University of California, Santa Barbara philosopher Fritz Allhoff presents a clever and unique defense of bluffing in business negotiations. The central tenet in Allhoff's position is that certain roles that we are required to assume allow us to morally justify behaviors that might otherwise be considered immoral.

Legal scholar Robert B. Thompson presents Manne's argument on insider regulation. Thompson then provides us with an analysis of the status and relevance of Manne's position three decades after the publication of his seminal text. UCLA professor of law Stephen Bainbridge does not accept Manne's arguments. Bainbridge believes that insider trading ultimately causes inefficiency in the markets and, therefore, must be subject to regulation.

In an article calling for the end to affirmative action, African American social commentator Dr. McWhorter draws on his experiences as a previous supporter of affirmative action while providing numerous insightful observations. Judith Appelbaum, speaking before the SUNY, Binghamton, argues that discrimination in the workplace is still very much with us today. And, since affirmative is needed to combat ongoing discrimination, it's still needed today.

Human resource management scholars Ying-Tzu Lu and Brian H. Kleiner believe that workplace drug testing does not inherently violate employee privacy rights. They suggest that workplace drug testing can lead to increased firm profitability, primarily as a result of increased worker productivity. *Reason* magazine senior editor Jacob Sullum argues that not only is drug testing invasive and insulting, but that it has no real bearing on job performance.

Society for Human Resource Management human resource expert Nancy Lockwood discusses several important benefits that result from workplace diversity. Included among these is the possibility of increased organizational productivity and profitability. The opposing view is presented by social critic Roger Clegg, who attacks the notion that pursuing diversity for its own sake is a wise strategy regardless of whether it occurs in the workplace or in the educational system.

Stephen J. Rose and Heidi I. Hartmann, scholars at the Institute for Women's Policy Research, argue in their 2004 study that discrimination is still the main reason for the persistence in the gender gap. Naomi Lopez, director of the Center for Enterprise and Opportunity at the Pacific Research Institute in San Francisco, provides evidence that the wage gap is a function of several different variables beyond gender discrimination. She concludes her analysis with the observation that we may never reduce the wage gap entirely and that such an outcome is not necessarily undesirable.

Political consultant and Social Security expert Dr. James Morrison presents an argument supporting Social Security reform and shows how it would be extremely beneficial to American business, particularly small business. The con side of this debate is provided by two important members of The Century Foundation: vice president Greg Anrig, Jr. and senior fellow Bernard Wasow. Their article consists of 12 reasons why privatizing Social Security is bad for business and bad for the country.

Sarah Anderson and John Cavanagh argue that outsourcing is a real threat to the economic health of the United States and provide several suggestions as to the types of governmental actions necessary to keep American jobs from moving overseas. Included in their discussion is an analysis of the views of the two 2004 presidential candidates, John Kerry and George W. Bush. Dr. Daniel Drezner argues that the controversy surrounding outsourcing is not new and that its current form is more hype than substance. He shows how outsourcing is actually economically beneficial to America, despite the warnings of critics. Dr. Drezner also asserts that the concept of outsourcing is consistent with a solid understanding of free-market capitalism and an appreciation of traditional American principles and values.

Lisa Newton believes that the typical U.S. CEO should not receive ten or more times the annual pay of CEOs in other industrial countries. She also points out, in no uncertain terms, that CEOs are only partly responsible for the ultimate success of their organization and the accompanying increase in shareholder wealth. Ira Kay and Steven Rushbrook believe that U.S. CEOs are entitled to whatever levels of pay they receive. They argue from a free-market perspective where labor, like every other business input, is subject to free-market forces. They also provide a discussion on the incredible amount of wealth U.S. CEOs have created for their shareholders.

Actual testimony taken from a congressional hearing just prior to the vote on the act itself is presented in this article. Included are comments from the authors of the act, Paul Sarbanes (D-MD) and Michael Oxley (R-OH). Cato Institute senior fellow Alan Reynolds provides his audience with a scathing indictment of the mind-set and philosophy beyond the creation of the act in his argument that Sarbanes-Oxley was not a positive reaction to the call for corporate governance change.

Scholars William T. Robinson and Sungwook Min provide results of a study indicating that the advantages from being first outweigh the risks of implementing the strategy. William Boulding and Markus Christen take a contrary position and argue that first-moving is not necessarily a wise strategy, presenting evidence from their own research that, in the long-run, first-movers actually experience performance disadvantages.

Clayton M. Christensen and Michael E. Raynor argue that firms are subject to pressures to continually grow from sources both inside and outside of the organization. Business scholars Jim Mackey and Liisa Välikangas cite many interesting statistics to support the view that lasting growth is elusive and unrealistic and, thus, not necessary to define a firm as successful.

In his review of *The Skeptical Environmentalist,* David Pimentel disagrees with Lomborg's optimistic assessment. He also accuses Lomborg of selectively presenting advantageous data while simultaneously ignoring evidence that is damaging to his position. Denis Dutton, professor of philosophy at the University of Canterbury in New Zealand, agrees with

Lomborg that the environment is much better off than the environmentalists would have us believe.

Issue 16. Should U.S. Corporations Be Allowed to Hire Illegal Aliens? 310

Rob Paral, a research fellow with the Immigration Policy Center, believes that the pluses of hiring illegal immigrants outweigh the minuses. Fred Dickey disagrees. In a detailed exposé on immigration published in the *Los Angeles Times,* reporter Dickey maps out his case against the use of illegal immigrants in the American workforce.

Issue 17. Is Economic Globalization Good for Humankind? 332

Foreign policy expert Murray Weidenbaum, in a reprint of a speech he delivered in 2001, promotes his "yes" response by systematically presenting, and then debunking, the most common "myths" surrounding globalization. He believes that globalization is a force for positive change. Professor Herman Daly feels that increasing globalization requires increases in political, social, and cultural integration across borders as well. The outcome is a loss of national identity for the countries involved as power is transferred from traditional domestic sources—i.e., governments, domestic businesses, local enterprises—to transnational corporations.

Issue 18. Are Global Sweatshops Exploitative? 350

The first article, written by scholars Richard Appelbaum and Peter Dreier, chronicles the rise of the grassroots, college campus, anti-global sweatshops movement in the late 1990s. Columnist and social commentator Radley Balko argues that sweatshops are not exploitative. His article presents several additional points frequently offered in defense of globalization in general, and sweatshops in particular.

Introduction

Controversial Issues in Management

This introduction consists of four sections, each of which briefly discusses a different area of business management. Each section provides important information about a specific management area and, in so doing, sets the stage for the debate topics that comprise the four parts of this book. This essay is organized in a manner paralleling the presentation of the debate topics in the text: business ethics is discussed in the first section, organizational behavior and human resource management in the second, strategic management in the third, and environmental and international management-related issues in the final section.

Business Ethics and Management

Many business ethics scholars analyze this complex management topic at two levels. The macro-level involves issues broad in nature and relevant for analysis at the organizational level. In this text, we limit our discussion to a specific macro-level issue, albeit a critically important issue. This topic concerns the degree of moral responsibility an organization has to the society in which it functions. At the micro-level of analysis, business ethics is concerned primarily with the ethical decision-making process of individuals in the workplace. Both of these levels of analysis are expanded on briefly below.

Macro-level Analysis: Corporate Social Responsibility vs. Profit Maximization

Twenty-five years ago, corporate America measured success by the creation of shareholder wealth. Companies that increased shareholders' wealth were successful, and those that didn't, were not. In the early years of the new century, determining corporate success is a much more complicated affair. The traditional *shareholder theory* of profit maximization has been replaced with a new method of defining corporate success known as *stakeholder theory.*

Stakeholder theory and social responsibility. This approach to defining corporate success differs dramatically from the traditional shareholder approach. In this view, a stakeholder is any entity that contributes resources to the firm and therefore, has a "stake" in the firm's survival. A typical list of an organization's stakeholders includes customers, employees, management, suppliers, shareholders, partners, governments, and society at large. Each stakeholder determines organizational performance independent of the others and, since each stakeholder has contributed different resources, each is likely to use different criteria by which to evaluate performance. This can lead to situations where one set of stakeholders is pleased with firm performance while another feels the firm has performed very poorly.

An important implication of stakeholder theory is that managers have obligations that go beyond profit maximization since they are concerned with satisfying the needs of all of its stakeholders. Thus, those firms that do not place the interests of one set of stakeholders above the rest are acting in a *socially responsible* manner, whereas firms that stick to the traditional emphasis of maximizing profit with disregard of other stakeholder interests are irresponsible and immoral.

Shareholder theory and profit maximization.   Standing in complete contrast to the current trend towards stakeholder-driven social responsibility is the traditional economic advocacy of shareholder theory. Advocates of free-market capitalism believe that the only responsibility an organization has is to maximize profits for its shareholders. They point out that shareholders own the companies in which they invest, not employees, customers, suppliers, or other stakeholders. Their investment subjects them to the risks and rewards associated with ownership and, therefore, entitles them to expect management to act in accordance with their wishes. If, for example, management acts against shareholder interests by spending profits for a social program rather than increasing dividends, they have, in effect, stolen from the owners of the firm. Thus, it is not surprising that most free-market advocates view stakeholder theory as promoting behaviors and outcomes that are both illegal and immoral.

Micro-level Analysis: Ethical Decision Making

At the micro-level of analysis, business ethics is the study of the influences and processes involved in individual ethical decision making (EDM). The primary focus is to identify those factors that affect an individual's decision to act morally (or not) at the workplace. Understanding these factors is of prime importance for managers, not only to understand their own ethical behavior, but that of their employees as well. Over the years, EDM scholars have developed many different models of ethical behavior but, despite these efforts, there is currently no dominant model accepted by all. However, scholars have managed to identify several factors that appear to be predictive of ethical behavior. We briefly discuss these next.

Personal characteristics.   Research has shown that individuals who score high on *Machiavellianism* are more likely to act unethically than those who score low. Machiavellianism is a personality trait best described with the adage, "the ends justify the means." High Machs, as they are known, are more concerned with reaching their goals than in the manner in which they achieved them. *Locus of control* measures the extent to which an individual feels that luck, fate, or forces beyond his control are primarily responsible for what happens to him in life. Individuals who strongly believe this to be the case (known as externals) are much more likely to engage in unethical behavior than are individuals who strongly disagree with this view (known as internals). *Gender* has also been shown to predict ethical behavior. All things equal, females are much more likely to act ethically than are males.

Situational characteristics.   EDM scholars have noted that several characteristics of the ethical decision situation play a role in whether an individual acts morally or not. One of the strongest predictors is the *likelihood of getting caught*; the greater it is, the lower the probability of unethical behavior. Peer behavior also plays a significant role in ethical behavior. An individual is more likely to act unethically if his/her peers are acting unethically. This is known as *differential association*—basically we tend to do what our peers do. Finally, the probability of unethical behavior increases if the *costs* of getting caught acting unethically are perceived as being less than the *benefits* from doing so.

Business Ethics and Taking Sides

The first portion of this book consists of four debates, one at the macro and three at the micro-levels of analysis. We have already looked at background information about the corporate social responsibility vs. profit maximization controversy; Issue 1 frames this organizational-level topic in a debate format and presents articles supportive of each side.

The second issue in Part 1 involves the popular corporate strategy of downsizing. Increasingly, U.S. firms are adopting the view that reducing costs through labor force reductions—downsizing—should not be reserved only for desperate firms on the edge of bankruptcy. But what about the human element involved? When employees are factored into the equation, does the moral aspect of the decision to downsize become more obvious?

Issue 3 examines an old, but still relevant, business behavior: bluffing. It's an age-old question—is it morally acceptable to bluff during negotiations? We present contrasting responses to this interesting topic.

Issue 4 presents a debate that has simmered beneath the surface of corporate America for two decades but is now enjoying a resurgence of sorts. Thanks to the Martha Stewart affair earlier in the decade, the topic of insider trading has received renewed attention, both in the popular press and in academic circles. Our concern here is with its legality; specifically, we ask if insider trading should be illegal in the first place.

Organizational Behavior and Human Resource Management

Organizational Behavior Basics

According to a leading introductory textbook, organizational behavior (OB) is concerned with the "study of what people do in an organization and how that behavior affects the performance of the organization" (Stephen P. Robbins, *Organizational Behavior*, Prentice Hall, 2001). Some business scholars (including the author of this introduction) refer to OB as "psychology in the workplace";

an apt description given that much of what we know about human behavior at work is based on the application of knowledge generated by the psychological sciences. This is really not surprising considering that the main goal of OB is to generate knowledge about human behavior as a means to improving organizational effectiveness.

The value of OB to the practicing manager.   The field of organizational behavior has value for managers to the extent that it can positively affect important organizational outcomes. And although OB scholars study many different aspects of workplace behavior, a core group of four critically important outcomes has received the most research attention over the years.

U.S. corporations lose billions of dollars each year as a result of employees failing to report to work. Loss of labor hours is only part of the cost; *absenteeism* frequently upsets the flow of work and results in operational inefficiencies. Fortunately, OB scholars know quite a bit about what causes absenteeism and how it can be reduced. For example, research consistently shows that females tend to be absent more frequently than males, primarily because of family-related concerns (pregnancy, raising children, etc.). As a result of this finding, many managers reduce the impact of absenteeism by allowing female employees greater flexibility in their work schedules.

Turnover occurs when an employee, voluntarily or not, permanently leaves the organization. Like absenteeism, turnover is extremely costly to employers, affecting productivity and upsetting the flow of work. By some conservative accounts, turnover costs can run as high as \$15–20,000 per employee. Understanding why an employee leaves an organization is a terrifically complicated process; nevertheless, OB scholars have made inroads here as well. For example, research shows that the more an employee is committed to the organization and its goals, the less likely he/she is to leave.

A third important outcome is *job satisfaction*. This is one of the most studied variables in organizational behavior, a fact attesting to its importance in the workplace. OB scholars have established, for example, that organizations with highly satisfied workers have lower absenteeism and turnover rates and higher levels of productivity than do organizations whose employees are less satisfied with their jobs. So, what can managers do to increase job satisfaction? Research suggests four ways: provide mentally challenging work, fair and equitable rewards, supportive working conditions, and supportive colleagues.

The fourth important outcome is *productivity*. OB scholars have studied this variable from the perspective of the organization as well as the employee. We've already seen that at the organizational level, job satisfaction, absenteeism, and turnover have been shown to impact organizational productivity. At the individual level, the belief is that the more motivated an individual is, the more productive he or she is likely to be. The OB literature contains many different models of workplace motivation, each offering managers various suggestions as to how they can motivate their employees.

Other OB topics of interest to managers.   Organizational behavior has much to say about other issues of interest to managers beyond those discussed above.

Personality researchers are concerned with, among other things, identifying the various components of personality and exploring whether some personality traits are predictive of success on the job. Another important area of research involves *decision making*. This multifaceted field offers many different theories about how humans make decisions and offers managers much insight into the factors that lead to poor decision making and how to avoid them. Over the last 25 years, *work teams* have become an important work unit at most major corporations in America. As a result, many OB scholars study work group dynamics and processes and have learned much about what differentiates an effective work team from an ineffective one. One of the oldest areas of OB research concerns *leadership and the use of power and politics* in the workplace. Despite the large body of research on this topic, OB scholars have a less than impressive record of providing useful insights and suggestions to practicing managers about how to develop, identify, or create effective leaders in the workplace.

Human Resource Management Basics

Human resource management (HRM) is the design and implementation of formal systems that utilize human resources to accomplish organizational goals (Mathis and Jackson, *Human Resource Management*, South-Western Thompson, 2003). Although the fields of organizational behavior and human resource management are both conducted primarily at the individual level of analysis, HRM is a much more practical area of management than is OB. It is only a slight stretch to describe OB as a field characterized by theories and concepts while laws, regulations, and formal systems characterize HRM.

Typical HRM functions. Virtually every major U.S. corporation has an HR department that is in charge of managing several interlinked activities concerning the firms' employees. Although it varies from firm to firm, in general HR managers are responsible for at least seven different human resource functions: HR planning, equal employment opportunity compliance, staffing, human resource development, compensation, health and safety concerns, and employee/management relations.

    Human resource planning involves anticipating and responding to the forces that will affect the supply of and demand for employees. For example, firms that are growing usually have a need for more employees; HR managers are responsible for determining how many are needed, where they are needed, and when they are needed. *Equal employment opportunity* (*EEO*) compliance affects every aspect of HR management and has become the single most important area of HR management over the last two decades. It is absolutely imperative that managers are aware of the requirements of affirmative action and the necessity of developing a diverse workforce. Firms that are oblivious—or worse, ignore—the dictates of EEO risk severe damage to their reputations and will likely face costly legal proceedings.

    Staffing consists of three HR functions: job analysis, recruiting, and selecting. Job analysis tells HR managers what workers do and provides the basis for recruiting qualified applicants to apply for open positions. Selecting is the process of choosing from among the group of qualified applicants. *Human resource development* is concerned with such activities as new employee orientation, skills training, career development, career planning, and evaluating employee performance. *Compensation* is another crucial HR function and, along with pay and incentives for good performance, includes the distribution of employee benefits. HR managers help develop wage and salary systems, incentive and bonus plans, and competitive benefits packages.

Complying with federal safety regulations, dealing with drug-related issues, and managing workplace security, particularly in a post–911 America, are a few of the challenges involved in the *health and safety* HR function. Last, but certainly not least, is the HR function that monitors the *relationship between employees and management*. There has been a dramatic increase in the number of lawsuits brought by disgruntled employees who believe their rights to privacy, for example, have been violated by inappropriate corporate policies. Courts have been very receptive to such accusations; consequently, it is critical that the HR department develops, updates, and communicates organizational policies so that all parties involved know what is expected.

OB, HRM, and Taking Sides

Two of the five debates in this part involve the topic of discrimination: Issue 5 wonders if affirmative action has outlived its usefulness, while Issue 8 asks if the persistent wage gap between men and women is due to discrimination or to some other factors. The sixth debate involves the question of whether employee drug-testing is a wise corporate strategy, particularly in light of the seemingly obvious concerns about privacy rights. In today's EEO-driven work environment, much is made about the supposed benefits of maintaining a diversified workforce. Issue 7 takes this topic head-on and questions whether striving for and/or maintaining workplace diversity are worthwhile corporate goals or not. One of the first topics raised by President Bush at the beginning of his second term in office was the issue of Social Security reform. Bush, his supporters, and many Libertarians believe that if Social Security is to avoid bankruptcy, some form of privatization-based reform is needed. The last debate in this part of the text examines this topic and wonders if Social Security reform would be beneficial to American business interests.

Strategic Management

Strategic Management Basics

While OB and HRM are primarily concerned with understanding, motivating, and managing individual employees in the workplace, the focus of strategic management is on the organization as a whole. As you might expect, the basic unit of strategic management is a *strategy*. At its most basic, a strategy is a plan designed to achieve a specific goal. In the business world, strategic management refers to the process of effectively developing and executing the collection of plans designed to achieve the organization's goals. Typically, the goals of the organization reflect the overall purpose of the company as spelled out in the firm's mission statement. In most large companies, top-level executives and managers are responsible for the development of the organization's strategies, while mid-level managers and supervisors are typically in charge of making sure the strategies are implemented successfully. Thus, the executives are involved in *strategy formulation,* while the managers and supervisors are concerned with *strategy implementation.*

SWOT Analysis as a source of strategy formulation.   So far so good, but where do the strategies come from in the first place? Perhaps the most frequent method used by executives to develop strategies is a SWOT analysis. In this procedure, the organization identifies its strengths, weaknesses, opportunities, and threats. Once this information has been gathered, top management develops plans of attack that (a) capitalize on the firm's strengths, and (b) allow the organization to take advantage of available opportunities. Management must also be careful, however, to (a) try and counter potential threats from the external environment (such as competitors), (b) while also avoiding spending excessive resources on weak areas. Thus, the most effective strategies are those that support the mission of the organization by taking advantage of the firm's strengths and opportunities and minimizing the effects of threats and weaknesses. In an ideal world, the firm can turn its strengths into a *sustained competitive advantage.* This occurs when an organization is able to consistently outperform its competitors even though the competitors have tried to reduce its advantage by duplicating the firm's sources of strength.

Levels of strategies.   Many corporations in the United States and abroad conduct business in more than one industry and/or in more than one market. Consequently, they have a need for more than one level of strategy. When top management develops plans and sets goals for the overall corporation, it is engaging in *corporate-level strategy* development. When top management chooses a specific set of strategies for a particular business or market, it is engaging in *business-level strategy* development.

Types of strategies.   There are several different models for identifying the major strategic approaches available to organizations when conducting business-level strategy development. One of the most popular approaches is Michael Porter's three generic strategies framework. Firms that attempt to distinguish themselves from competitors by virtue of the quality of their products or services are using a *differentiation* strategy. Other firms try to achieve success by keeping costs of production lower than their competitors, thus employing a *cost leadership strategy.* Still other firms will concentrate their efforts on a specific geographic region or market, employing what Porter calls a *focus strategy* approach.

At the corporate-level of strategic development, perhaps the most important question concerns the extent and nature of *diversification.* Diversification refers to the number of distinct businesses an organization is involved in and the degree to which they are related to each other. Some companies, such as WD-40, make just one product and are not concerned with strategic issues of diversification; theirs is a single-product strategy. Others, like General Motors for example, are involved in literally hundreds of businesses. Firms such as GM need to make corporate-level strategic decisions about the nature and type of diversification they should employ. *Related diversification* occurs when the organization runs several different businesses that are linked to each other in some manner. RJR Nabisco, for example, has numerous different businesses that share the same distribution mechanism—your local grocery store. The main advantage of implementing a related diversification strategy is that it reduces the firm's dependence on a specific business, thereby lowering its economic risk. *Unrelated diversification* is a strategy in which the organization's multiple businesses do not share any obvious links. During the 1980s, this was a favored approach of many large nonfinancial corporations interested in establishing themselves in the securities industry. Sears, for example, adopted an unrelated diversification strategy when it bought Dean Witter, as did GE when it purchased Kidder Peabody. Interestingly, research strongly suggests that unrelated diversification is not a sure road to success, which probably accounts for why its popularity as a corporate-level strategy has waned in recent years.

Strategic Management and Taking Sides

Part 3 of your text contains issues particularly relevant to the topic of strategic management. For many U.S. firms, an increasingly popular and effective cost control method is outsourcing. While moving domestically expensive operational functions to a country with lower wage rates may reduce costs, many have argued that it is an unpatriotic strategy and should not be condoned. You can decide for yourself when you read Issue 10.

In recent years, the business and news media have portrayed numerous examples of U.S. CEOs receiving millions of dollars in salary and benefits while their organizations were posting losses, laying off workers, and, in some instances, declaring bankruptcy. As a result of the public outrage generated by these accounts, the question of top-level management compensation has taken on greater importance in the field of strategic management. We address this topic in Issue 11, where we ask, "Are U.S. CEOs Overpaid?"

The next issue in Part 3 concerns the Sarbanes-Oxley Act of 2002. This legislation was designed to address the numerous violations of corporate governance rules and procedures top-level executives committed during the wave of scandals that affected corporate America over the last half-decade. Like the question of CEO pay, this too is a "hot" topic in strategic management, and provides us with Issue 12: "Corporate Governance Reform: Is Sarbanes-Oxley the Answer?"

New to this edition is the debate over the often-employed corporate strategy of first-to-market leadership. Common financial wisdom tells us that firms will take extraordinary risks only if extraordinary gains from success are possible. Given that adopting a "first-mover" strategy is a common in corporate America, we would expect experience to show that doing so results in superior financial returns. But not so fast—interestingly, research on this topic is anything but unequivocal. In Issue 13, we present the question of whether a first-mover strategy is a successful strategy and invite you to decide for yourself.

The last issue in Part 3 presents an intriguing, though seldom discussed, question: must firms grow in order to be considered successful? As you interact with this debate, try to avoid adopting the seemingly obvious "of course!" perspective before you've read both sides of the argument; you might be surprised at your final answer.

Environmental and International Management Issues

Over the last quarter century, two managerial challenges have grown in importance so dramatically that executives in corporate America have no alternative but to take them into account when formulating organizational strategy. The first of these challenges originates in the conflict between an organization's need to be financially successful and society's expectations that it conduct its business in a socially responsible manner. More specifically, U.S. organizations now face the difficult challenge of maintaining financial success while recognizing obligations to protect and maintain the world's physical environment. The second major challenge also involves competitive pressures. U.S. firms need to develop successful responses to the threats and opportunities resulting from the tremendous increase in international competition and the expansion of global markets that has occurred over the last twenty-five years.

The Environmental Challenge

As noted in the ethics section of this introduction, the corporate social responsibility (CSR) doctrine holds that organizations have obligations to society that extend beyond merely maximizing profit for their shareholders. For example, an important obligation of every firm, according to the CSR perspective, is to conduct business in a way that, at a minimum, is respectful of the natural environment. The history of business in America is full of stories of companies carelessly polluting rivers and streams, pumping tons of soot and chemicals into the air, cutting down and destroying millions of acres of forest and wetlands, and causing ecological disasters such as the Exxon *Valdez* oil spill. Not surprisingly, CSR advocates—primarily environmentalist groups— have applied tremendous public pressure on U.S. corporations to act responsibly towards the environment. The federal government has responded to the decades of environmental neglect by passing numerous laws forcing corporations to regulate their environmentally damaging behaviors. And although many major corporations have responded to the challenge, the constant stream of ominous reports on the decline of the earth's environment indicate that there is still much to be done.

For managers, the problem is that complying with all the laws and regulations, as well as conducting their business operations in a socially responsible manner, can be very costly. Firms often spend millions of dollars bringing their operations into compliance with federal laws and regulations, thus diverting funds that would normally go to profitable projects. Clearly, then, twenty-first-century managers in corporate America face a difficult challenge: conducting their business operations in a manner respectful of the environment while successfully responding to the rapidly increasing levels of competition both domestically and abroad.

The International Challenge

In the early 1980s, the U.S. lighting industry was dominated by the General Electric corporation. GE's reign as the major player in the field came under serious attack, however, when Westinghouse, its major domestic competitor, sold its lamp operations to the huge Dutch conglomerate, Phillips Electronics. Virtually overnight, GE's competitive picture changed and they found themselves suddenly on the defensive. In response, GE went global; they bought a Hungarian electronics firm and entered into a joint venture with Hitachi in order to break into the Asian markets. In 1990, GE generated less than 20 percent of its lighting sales from abroad; today the number is closer to 50 percent. (This information taken from, Gary Dressler, *Management*, Prentice Hall, 2001).

GE's experiences are not uncommon, nor are they unique to American firms. In response to the tremendous growth of competition from international firms, corporations all over the world have embraced the idea of globalization by extending sales and/or production operations to markets abroad. Globalization offers firms many advantages: access to new sources of cheap labor; access to new sources of highly skilled labor; access to established markets; and access to emerging markets (China, Russia, and India, for example). These advantages come with a cost, however; globalization, by its very definition, means greater competition. Thus, a second critical challenge facing U.S. managers is responding successfully to the tremendous growth of competition from international firms, both here and abroad.

Environmental Management, International Management, and Taking Sides

An underlying assumption of the environmental movement in the United States and abroad is that the health of the planet is deteriorating and that business activity is primarily responsible. But is this assumption true? Issue 15 provides two radically different responses to this important question.

The next debate involves one of the most important and controversial social issues of our time and its impact on corporate America. Very few dispute that the growing number of illegal aliens poses a serious problem to the United States and is likely to be an important political, social, and economic issue for the foreseeable future. In Issue 16, we ask whether U.S. firms should be allowed to tap into this reservoir of labor legally. Passions run high when this topic is raised, so it's no surprise that the two articles presented here come to completely different conclusions.

A growing number of countries around the world have embraced the idea of globalization as a means of raising the standard of living for their citizens. But despite the fact that much evidence attests to the economic benefits that accrue as a result of globalization, there are those that question whether globalization on the whole is a positive occurrence. Issue 17 provides two competing answers to the question, "Is Economic Globalization Good for Humankind?"

The final issue in this book concerns a specific outcome of the globalization movement, the emergence of global sweatshops. For many Third World countries, an abundance of cheap labor is the only competitive resource they have to offer. Numerous multinational firms have moved some of their domestic production operations overseas in order to take advantage of the lower labor costs. To globalization advocates, "sweatshops" are a natural step in the economic growth of the country; to members of the anti-globalization movement, it's exploitation. One thing is certain—the question, "Are Global Sweatshops Exploitative?" inspires passionate answers on both sides of the debate.

On the Internet . . .

The W. Maurice Young Centre for Applied Ethics

The mission of the centre is to bring moral philosophy into the public domain by advancing research in applied ethics, supporting courses with a significant ethical component, and acting as a community resource.

http://www.ethics.ubc.ca/about.htm

U.S. Securities and Exchange Commission

The primary mission of the U.S. Securities and Exchange Commission (SEC) is to protect investors and maintain the integrity of the securities markets. This site has information on all things securities investing related, including the following link on the SEC's stance on insider trading.

http://www.sec.gov/investor/pubs/insidertradingguide.htm

The Ludwig von Mises Institute

Named after famed economist Ludwig von Mises, the institute works to advance the Austrian School of economics by defending the market economy, private property, sound money, and peaceful international relations, while opposing government intervention as economically and socially destructive. Check this Web site for insightful comments on corporate social responsibility, downsizing, and insider trading.

http://www.mises.org/

The Adam Smith Institute

The Adam Smith Institute is the UK's leading innovator of market economic policies. Named after the great Scottish economist and author of *The Wealth of Nations*, its guiding principles are free-markets and a free society. Many social issues, such as downsizing are covered here.

http://www.adamsmith.org/about/

PART 1

Ethical Issues for Managers

*A*n *old saying holds that business ethics is an oxymoron. For years, the generally accepted view on morality and business was that they don't mix, that business is a game played by a different set of rules. To act morally was to act weakly. And in the business arena, weak firms were dead firms.*

Well, things certainly change. In today's business arena, firms are finding that immoral behavior can prove fatal. Thanks to the plethora of scandals on Wall Street in the 1980s and the massive corporate scandals of the past 10 years, the field of business ethics is enjoying unprecedented influence and popularity. The issues in this part of the book involve ethical questions that are important to many managers in corporate America.

- Do Corporations Have a Responsibility to Society that Extends Beyond Merely Maximizing Profit?

- Is the Corporate Strategy of Downsizing Unethical?

- Is Bluffing During Negotiations Unethical?

- Should Insider Trading Be Legalized?

ISSUE 1

Do Corporations Have a Responsibility to Society That Extends Beyond Merely Maximizing Profit?

YES: Robert D. Hay and Edmund R. Gray, from "Introduction to Social Responsibility," in David Keller, man. ed., *Ethics and Values: Basic Readings in Theory and Practice* (Pearson Custom Publishing, 2002)

NO: Alexei M. Marcoux, from "Business Ethics Gone Wrong," Cato Institute (July 24, 2000)

ISSUE SUMMARY

YES: Robert D. Hay and Edmund R. Gray believe that corporations should be held accountable for more than profit maximization. Their argument is based on stakeholder theory and is presented in the form of an historical account of the evolution of managerial thinking on this important topic.

NO: In answering "no" to this question, Alexei Marcoux presents a frontal attack on stakeholder theory. Consistent with the views of Nobel Laureate Milton Friedman, Marcoux argues that the very nature of stakeholder theory is immoral and can only lead to disastrous results for all involved.

$\mathbf{T}$oday business students are taught that organizations have responsibilities that extend beyond merely trying to maximize profits for their shareholders. The traditional "shareholder" theory of profit maximization has been replaced with a new perspective: stakeholder theory. This theory asserts that organizations have responsibilities to all groups that are affected by the ultimate success and survival of the firm. An organization is responsible not only to its shareholders, but to its employees, customers, suppliers, community, local governments, and all other stakeholders who are affected by its existence. On the surface, this approach seems to be for the better; after all, wouldn't concern for the interests of those impacted by the organization cause the company to act in a manner that makes each better off? Well, as is often the case in management, the answer is not clear-cut. Many business scholars and successful business leaders argue that stakeholder theory is both immoral in its premises and damaging in its practice. Thus, we have a controversy for you to consider: Do corporations have a responsibility to society that goes beyond maximizing profit?

Those who answer in the affirmative usually provide a two-pronged response—the first based on stakeholder theory and the second on practical observations and assertions. Stakeholder theory argues that the manager's job is to balance interests among the various groups with a stake in the company's survival. Consequently, management's obligations have been expanded beyond focusing primarily on financial gain for shareholders to include satisfying the needs and concerns of all of its stakeholders. Organizations that recognize this expansion and act on it accordingly are said to be acting in a socially responsible manner, whereas firms that stick to the traditional emphasis of increasing share price as priority one are deemed irresponsible and immoral. The second prong in the "yes" response consists of more practical arguments. One point often raised is that since corporations are the source of many problems in society—pollution, corruption, discrimination, etc.—they should be required to resolve those problems. After all, the community in which the corporation resides is a legitimate stakeholder of the firm. Another argument holds that organizations frequently have financial resources and, therefore, are in position to use the money for social good and not only for increasing the power and wealth of the firm.

On the other side of the debate, the strongest and most consistent defender of shareholder theory has been economist and Nobel Laureate Milton Friedman. In his anti-stakeholder approach, Friedman argues that shareholders—not employees, customers, or suppliers—own the companies in which they invest and, consequently, have the legal right to expect management to comply with their desires (which is usually to maximize the value of their investments). Consider the example of a corporation whose management, without shareholder consent, wants to use some of the company's profits on its local community by contributing to the creation of a park project. If management chooses to reduce profit distribution to its shareholders and spend it on the project, they have acted both immorally and illegally since they have, in effect, stolen from the shareholders. If they choose to pay shareholders out of profit and instead finance the project by reducing labor costs, the employees will suffer. If they choose to avoid antagonizing shareholders and employees and contribute to the park by raising product prices, they will hurt their customers and possibly price themselves out of the market. Thus, according to Friedman, doing anything other than increasing shareholder wealth is tantamount to theft, is immoral, and is ultimately self-defeating for the organization.

In the "yes" selection that follows, Robert D. Hay and Edmund R. Gray argue for the stakeholder theory that is presented in the form of an historical account of the evolution of managerial thinking on this important topic. The "no" article is written by Alexei Marcoux and represents a frontal attack on stakeholder theory. Consistent with Friedman's views, he attempts to show that the very nature of stakeholder theory is immoral and can only lead to disastrous results for all involved.

Robert D. Hay and
Edmund R. Gray

YES

Introduction to Social Responsibility

It was Jeremy Bentham, late eighteenth century English philosopher, who espoused the social, political, and economic goal of society to be "the greatest happiness for the greatest number." His cardinal principle was written into the Declaration of Independence as "the pursuit of happiness," which became a societal goal of the American colonists. Bentham's principle was also incorporated into the Constitution of the United States in the preamble where the goal was stated "to promote the general welfare."

The economic-political system through which we in America strive to achieve this societal goal emphasizes the economic and political freedom to pursue individual interests. Adam Smith, another English political economist of the late eighteenth century, stated that the best way to achieve social goals was as follows:

> Every individual is continually exerting himself to find out the most advantageous employment for whatever capital he can command. It is his own advantage, indeed, and not that of the society, which he has in view. But the study of his own advantage naturally, or rather necessarily, leads him to prefer that employment which is most advantageous to the society. . . .
>
> As every individual, therefore, endeavors as much as he can both to employ his capital in the support of domestic industry, and so to direct that industry that its produce may be of the greatest value, every individual necessarily labours to render the annual revenue of the society as great as he can. He generally, indeed, neither intends to promote the public interest, nor knows how much he is promoting it. By preferring the support of domestic to that of foreign industry, he intends only his own security; and by directing that industry in such a manner as its produce may be of the greatest value, he intends only his own gain, and he is in this, as in many other cases, led by an invisible hand to promote an end which was not part of his intention. Nor is it always the worse for the society that it was no part of it. By pursuing his own interest he frequently promotes that of the society more effectually than when he really intends to promote it. I have never known much good done by those who affected to trade for the public good. It is an affectation, indeed, not very common among merchants, and very few words need be employed in dissuading them from it.

From BUSINESS AND SOCIETY, 2nd Ed. by Robert D. Hay and Edmund R. Gray, pp. 198–205, Pearson Custom Publishing, 2002. Copyright © 2002 by Thomson Learning. Reprinted by permission.

Adam Smith's economic values have had an important influence on American business thinking. As a result, most business people for the first hundred and fifty years of our history embraced the theory that social goals could be achieved by pursuing individual interests.

By 1930 American values were beginning to change from that of the individual owner ethic to that of the group or social ethic. As part of this changing mood, it was felt that Smith's emphasis on owner's interests was too predominant at the expense of other contributors to a business organization. Consequently, a new philosophy of management took shape which stated that the social goals could be achieved by balancing the interests of several groups of people who had an interest in a business. It was stated by Charles H. Percy, then president of Bell and Howell, in the 1950s as follows:

There are over 64 million gainfully employed people in the United States. One half of these work directly for American corporations, and the other half are vitally affected by business directly or indirectly. Our entire economy, therefore, is dependent upon the type of business management we have. Business management is therefore in many respects a public trust charged with the responsibility of keeping America economically sound. We at Bell & Howell can best do this by keeping our own company's program on a firm foundation and by having a growing group of management leaders to direct the activities of the company.

Management's role in a free society is, among other things, to prove that the real principles of a free society can work within a business organization.

Our basic objective is the development of individuals. In our own present program we are doing everything conceivable to encourage, guide, and assist, and provide an opportunity to everyone to improve their abilities and skills, thus becoming more valuable to the company and enabling the company to improve the rewards paid to the individual for such additional efforts.

Our company has based its entire program for the future on the development of the individual and also upon the building of an outstanding management group. This is why we have emphasized so strongly the supervisory training program recently completed by all Bell & Howell supervisors, and why we are now offering this program to others in the organization training for future management responsibilities.

But a company must also have a creed to which its management is dedicated. I hope that we can all agree to the following:

We believe that our company must develop and produce outstanding products that will perform a great service or fill a need for our customers.

We believe that our business must be run at an adequate profit and that the services and products that we offer must be better than those offered by competitors.

We believe that management must serve employees, stockholders, and customers, but that we cannot serve the interests of any one group at the undue expense of the other two. A proper and fair balance must be preserved.

We believe that our business must provide stability of employment and job security for all those who depend on our company for their livelihood.

We believe that we are failing in our responsibility if our wages are not sufficiently high to not only meet the necessities of life but provide some of the luxuries as well. Wherever possible, we also believe that bonus earning should be paid for performance and output "beyond the call of duty."

We believe that every individual in the company should have an opportunity for advancement and growth with the organization. There should be no dead-end streets any place in an organization.

We believe in the necessity for constantly increasing productivity and output. Higher wages and greater benefits can never be "given" by management. Management can only see that they are paid out when "earned."

We believe in labor-saving machinery. We do not think human beings should perform operations that can be done by mechanical or electronic means. We believe in this because we believe in the human dignity and creative ability of the individual. We are more interested in the intellect, goodwill, initiative, enthusiasm, and cooperativeness of the individual than we are in his muscular energy.

We believe that every person in the company has a right to be treated with the respect and courtesy that is due a human being. It is for this reason that we have individual merit ratings, individual pay increases, job evaluation, and incentive pay; and it is why we keep every individual fully informed—through The Finder, through our annual report, through Family Night, and through individual letters—about the present program of the company and also about our future objectives.

We believe that our business must be conducted with the utmost integrity. We may fight the principle of confiscatory taxation, but we will pay our full share. We will observe every governmental law and regulation, local, state, and national. We will deal fairly with our customers, we will advertise our product truthfully, and we will make every attempt to maintain a friendly relationship with our competitors while at the same time waging the battle of free competition.

Some business leaders, on the one hand, preach the virtues of the free enterprise, democratic system and, on the other hand, run their own business in accordance with autocratic principles—all authority stemming from the top with little delegation of responsibility to individuals within the organization. We believe in democracy—in government and in our business.

We hope that every principle we believe in is right and is actually being practiced throughout the company as it affects every individual.

Then in the late 1960s American business leaders began to take another look at the problems of society in light of the goal of "the greatest happiness for the greatest number." How could people be happy if they have to breathe foul air, drink polluted water, live in crowded cities, use very unsafe products, be misled by untruthful advertising, be deprived of a job because of race, and face many other problems? Thus, another philosophy of management emerged. It was voiced by several American business leaders:

Business must learn to look upon its social responsibilities as inseparable from its economic function. If it fails to do so, it leaves a void that will quickly be filled by others—usually by the government. (George Champion, Chase National Bank, 1966.)

I believe there is one basic principle that needs to be emphasized more than ever before. It is the recognition that business is successful in the long term only when it is directed toward the needs of the society. (Robert F. Hansberger, Boise Cascade, 1971.)

The actions of the great corporations have so profound an influence that the public has come to judge them not only by their profit-making record, but by the contribution of their work to society as a whole. Under a political democracy such as ours, if the corporation fails to perceive itself and govern its action in essentially the same manner as the public at large, it may find itself in serious trouble. (Louis B. Lundborg, Bank of America, 1971.)

With these remarks we can see that there has been a shift in managerial emphasis from owners' interests to group interests, and finally, to society's interests. Managers of some American businesses have come to recognize that they have a social responsibility.

Historical Perspective of Social Responsibility

The concept of the social responsibility of business managers has in recent years become a popular subject of discussion and debate within both business and academic circles. Although the term itself is of relatively recent origin, the underlying concept has existed as long as there have been business organizations. It rests on the logical assumption that because the firm is a creation of society, it has a responsibility to aid in the accomplishment of society's goals. In the United States concepts of social responsibility have moved from three distinct phases which may be labeled Phases I, II, and III.

Phase I—Profit Maximizing Management

The Phase I concept was based on the belief that business managers have but one single objective—maximize profits. The only constraint on this pursuit was the legal framework within which the firm operated. The origin of this view may be found in Adam Smith's *Wealth of Nations*. As previously noted, Smith believed that individual business people acting in their own selfish interest would be guided by an "invisible hand" to promote the public good. In other words, the individual's drive for maximum profits and the regulation of the competitive marketplace would interact to create the greatest aggregate wealth for a nation and therefore the maximum public good. In the United States this view was universally accepted throughout the nineteenth century and the early part of the twentieth century. Its acceptance rested not only on economic logic but also on the goals and values of society. America in the nineteenth and first half of the twentieth centuries was a society of economic scarcity; therefore, economic growth and the accumulation of aggregate wealth were primary goals. The business system with its emphasis on maximum profit was seen as a vehicle for eliminating economic scarcity. In the process employee abuses such as child labor, starvation wages, and unsafe working conditions could be tolerated. No questions were raised with regard to using up the natural resources and polluting streams and land. Nor was anyone really concerned about urban problems, unethical advertising, unsafe products, and poverty problems of minority groups.

The profit maximization view of social responsibility also complemented the Calvinistic philosophy which pervaded nineteenth and twentieth century American thinking. Calvinism stressed that the road to salvation was through hard work and the accumulation of wealth. It then logically followed that a business person could demonstrate diligence (and thus godliness) and accumulate a maximum amount of wealth by adhering to the discipline of profit maximization.

Phase II—Trusteeship Management

Phase II, which may be labeled the "trusteeship" concept, emerged in the 1920s and 30s. It resulted from structural changes in both business institutions and in society. According to this concept, corporate managers were responsible not simply for maximizing the stockholders' wealth but rather for maintaining an equitable balance among the competing claims of customers, employees, suppliers, creditors, and the community. In this view the manager was seen as "trustee" for the various contributor groups to the firm rather than simply an agent of the owners.

The two structural trends largely responsible for the emergence of this newer view of social responsibility were: (1) the increasing diffusion of ownership of the shares of American corporations, and (2) the development of a pluralistic society. The extent of the diffusion of stock ownership may be highlighted by the fact that by the early 1930s the largest stockholders in corporations such as American Telephone and Telegraph, United States Steel, and the Pennsylvania Railroad owned less than one percent of the total shares outstanding of these companies. Similar dispersion of stock ownership existed in most other large corporations. In such situations management typically was firmly in control of the corporation. Except in rare circumstances, the top executives were able to perpetuate themselves in office through the proxy mechanism. If an individual shareholder was not satisfied with the performance of the firm, there was little recourse other than to sell the stock. Hence, although the stockholder's legal position was that of an owner—and thus a principal-agent relationship existed between the stockholder and the managers— the stockholder's actual position was more akin to bondholders and other creditors of the firm. Given such a situation it was only natural to ask, "To whom is management responsible?" The "trusteeship" concept provided an answer. Management was responsible to all the contributors to the firm—that is, stockholders, workers, customers, suppliers, creditors, and the community.

The emergence of a largely pluralistic society reinforced the logic of the "trusteeship" concept. A pluralistic society has been defined as "one which has many semi-autonomous and autonomous groups through which power is diffused. No one group has overwhelming power over all others, and each has direct or indirect impact on all others. From the perspective of business firms this translated into the fact that exogenous groups had considerable impact upon and influence over them. In the 1930s the major groups exerting significant pressure on business were labor unions and the federal government. Today the list has grown to include numerous minority, environmental, and consumer groups among others. Clearly, one logical approach to such a situation is to consider that the firm has a responsibility to each interested group and that management's task is to reconcile and balance the claims of the various groups.

Phase III—Quality of Life Management

Phase III, which may be called the "quality of life" concept of social responsibility, has become popular in recent years. The primary reason for the emergence of this concept is the very significant metamorphosis in societal goals which this nation is experiencing. Up to the middle part of this century, society's principal goal was to raise the standard of living of the American people, which could be achieved by producing more goods and services. The fact that the U.S. had become the wealthiest nation in the world was testimony to the success of business in meeting this expectation.

In this process, however, the U.S. has become what John Kenneth Galbraith calls an "affluent society" in which the aggregate scarcity of basic goods and services is no longer the fundamental problem. Other social problems have developed as direct and indirect results of economic success. Thus, there are pockets of poverty in a nation of plenty, deteriorating cities, air and water pollution, defacement of the landscape, and a disregard for consumers to mention only a few of the prominent social problems. The mood of the country seems to be that things have gotten out of balance—the economic abundance in the midst of a declining social and physical environment does not make sense. As a result, a new set of national priorities which stress the "Quality of life" appear to be emerging.

Concomitant with the new priorities, societal consensus seems to be demanding that business, with its technological and managerial skills and its financial resources, assume broader responsibilities—responsibilities that extend beyond the traditional economic realm of the Phase I concept or the mere balancing of the competing demands of the sundry contributors and pressure groups of the Phase II concept. The socially responsible firm under Phase III reasoning is one that becomes deeply involved in the solution of society's major problems.

Personal Values of the Three Styles of Managers

Values are the beliefs and attitudes which form one's frame of reference and help to determine the behavior which an individual displays. All managers have a set of values which affect their decisions, but the values are not the same for each manager; however, once values are ingrained in a manager, they do not change except over a period of time. It is possible to group these values into a general pattern of behavior which characterizes three styles of managers—the profit-maximizing style, the trusteeship style, and the "quality of life" style of management.

Phase I Managers

Phase I, profit-maximizing managers have a personal set of values which reflects their economic thinking. They believe that raw self-interest should prevail in society, and their values dictate that "What's good for me is good for my country." Therefore, Phase I managers rationalize that making as much profit as is possible would be good for society. They make every effort to become as efficient as possible and to make as much money as they can. To them money and wealth are the most important goals of their lives.

In the pursuit of maximum profit the actions of Phase I managers toward customers are reflected in a *caveat emptor* philosophy. "Let the buyer beware" characterizes decisions and actions in dealing with customers. They are not necessarily concerned with product quality or safety, or with sufficient and/or truthful information about products and services. A profit-maximizing manager's view toward employees can be stated as, "Labor is a commodity to be bought and sold in the marketplace." Thus, chief accountability lies with the owners of the business, and usually the Phase I manager is the owner or part owner of the organization.

To profit maximizers technology is very important. Machines and equipment rank high on their scale of values, therefore, materialism characterizes their philosophy.

Social values do not predominate the thinking of Phase I managers. In fact, they believe that employee problems should be left at home. Economics should be separate from societal or family concerns. A Phase I manager's leadership style is one of the rugged individualist—"I'm my own boss, and I'll manage my business as I please." Values about minority groups dictate that such groups are inferior, so they must be treated accordingly.

Political values are based on the doctrine of laissez faire. "That government is best which governs the least" characterizes the thinking of Phase I managers. As a result anything dealing with politicians and governments is foreign and distasteful to them.

Their beliefs about the environment can be stated, "The natural environment controls one's destiny; therefore, use it to protect your interests before it destroys you. Don't worry about the physical environment because there are plenty of natural resources which you can use."

Aesthetic values to the profit maximizer are minimal. In fact, Phase I managers would say, "Aesthetic values? What are they?" They have very little concern for the arts and cultural aspects of life. They hold musicians, artists, entertainers, and social scientists in low regard.

The values that a profit-maximizing manager holds were commonly accepted in the economic textbooks of the 1800s and early 1900s although they obviously did not apply to all managers of those times. It is easy to see how they conflict with the values of the other two styles of management.

Phase II Managers

Phase II, trusteeship managers have a somewhat different set of values. They recognize that self-interest plays a large role in their actions, but they also recognize the interests of those people who contribute to the organization—the customers, employees, suppliers, owners, creditors, government, and community. In other words, they operate with self-interest plus the interests of other groups. They believe that "What is good for my company is good for the country." They balance profits of the owners and the organization with wages for employees, taxes for the government, interest for the creditors, and so forth. Money is important to them but so are people, because their values tells them that satisfying people's needs is a better goal than just making money.

In balancing the needs of the various contributors to the organization, Phase II managers deal with customers as the chief providers of revenue to the firm. Their values tell them not to cheat the customers because cheating is not good for the firm.

They are concerned with providing sufficient quantities of goods as well as sufficient quality for customer satisfaction. They view employees as having certain rights which must be recognized and that employees are more than mere commodities to be traded in the marketplace. Their accountability as managers is to owners as well as to customers, employees, suppliers, creditors, government, and the community.

To the trusteeship-style manager, technology is important, but so are people. Innovation of technology is to be commended because new machines, equipment, and products are useful to people to create a high standard of living. Materialism is important, but so is humanism.

The social values held by trusteeship managers are more liberal than those held by profit maximizers. They recognize that employees have several needs beyond their economic needs. Employees have a desire for security and a sense of belonging as well as recognition. Phase II managers see themselves as individualists, but they also appreciate the value of group participation in managing the business. They view minority groups as having their place in society. But, a trusteeship manager would add: "Their place is usually inferior to mine; they are usually not qualified to hold their jobs but that's not my fault."

The political values of Phase II managers are reflected in recognizing that government and politics are important, but they view government and politics as necessary evils. They distrust both, recognizing that government serves as a threat to their existence if their firms do not live up to the laws passed since the 1930s.

The environmental beliefs of trusteeship managers are stated as follows: "People can control and manipulate their environment. Therefore, let them do it for their own benefit and incidentally for society's benefit."

Aesthetic values are all right to the trusteeship manager, but "they are not for our firm although someone has to support the arts and cultural values."

Phase III Managers

In contrast to profit maximizers and trustee managers, "quality of life" managers believe in enlightened self-interest. They agree that selfishness and group interests are important, but that society's interests are also important in making decisions. "What's good for society is good for our company" is their opinion. They agree that profit is essential for the firm, but that profit in and of itself is not the end objective of the firm. As far as money and wealth are concerned, their set of values tells them that money is important but people are more important than money.

In sharp contrast to *caveat emptor* in dealings with customers, the philosophy of Phase II managers is *caveat venditor*, that is, let the seller beware. The company should bear the responsibility for producing and distributing products and services in sufficient quantities at the right time and place with the necessary quality, information, and services necessary to satisfy customers' needs. Their views about employees are to recognize the dignity of each, not treating them as a commodity to be bought and sold. Their accountability as managers is to the owners, to the other contributors of the business, and to society in general.

Technological values are important but people are held in higher esteem than machines, equipment, computers, and esoteric products. A "quality of life" manager is a humanist rather than a materialist.

The social values of "quality of life" managers dictate that a person cannot be separated into an economic being or family being. Their philosophy is, "We hire the whole person including any problems that person might have." Phase III managers recognize that group participation rather than rugged individualism is a determining factor in an organization's success. Their values about minority groups are different from the other managers. Their view is that "A member of a minority group needs support and guidance like any other person."

The political values of "quality of life" managers dictate that government and politicians are necessary contributors to a quality of life. Rather than resisting government, they believe that business and government must cooperate to solve society's problems.

Their environmental beliefs are stated as, "A person must preserve the environment, not for the environment's sake alone, but for the benefit of people who want to lead a quality life."

As far as aesthetic values are concerned, Phase III managers recognize that the arts and cultural values reflect the lives of people whom they hold in high regard. Their actions support aesthetic values by committing resources to their preservation and presentation.

Alexei M. Marcoux  **NO**

Business Ethics Gone Wrong

It arose from the scandals that plagued Wall Street during the 1980s: a growing public support for business ethics as an object of study and teaching in America's colleges and universities. Business ethics courses are offered (and often, for business majors, required) in ever-increasing numbers. The ranks of the academy swell with professors whose principal vocation is teaching and writing in business ethics. Philanthropists endow chairs in business ethics faster than universities can fill them.

Although deriving and explaining the ethical norms that support and lubricate a well-functioning market economy are worthwhile tasks, the intellectual fashion in business ethics is quite a different matter. For among business ethicists there is a consensus favoring the stakeholder theory of the firm—a theory that seeks to redefine and reorient the purpose and the activities of the firm. Far from providing an ethical foundation for capitalism, these business ethicists seek to change it dramatically.

Shareholders and Stakeholders

Stakeholder talk is rampant. In Great Britain, Tony Blair's Labour Party came to power promising Britons a "stakeholder society." Perhaps capitalizing on the trend, Yale law professors Bruce Ackerman and Anne Alstott argue for a far-reaching overhaul of the American tax and welfare systems in their recent book, The Stakeholder Society. But stakeholder theory, as it has emerged in business ethics, is different.

Stakeholder theory is most closely associated with R. Edward Freeman, Olsson Professor of Applied Ethics at the University of Virginia's Darden School. The theory holds that managers ought to serve the interests of all those who have a "stake" in (that is, affect or are affected by) the firm. Stakeholders include shareholders, employees, suppliers, customers, and the communities in which the firm operates—a collection that Freeman terms the "big five." The very purpose of the firm, according to this view, is to serve and coordinate the interests of its various stakeholders. It is the moral obligation of the firm's managers to strike an appropriate balance among the big five interests in directing the activities of the firm.

This understanding of the firm's purpose and its management's obligations diverges sharply from the understanding advanced in the shareholder theory of the firm. According to shareholder theorists such as Nobel laureate economist Milton Friedman, managers ought to serve the interests of the firm's owners, the shareholders. Social obligations of the firm are limited to making good on contracts, obeying the law, and adhering to ordinary moral expectations. In short, obligations to nonshareholders stand as sideconstraints on the pursuit of shareholder interests. This is the view that informs American corporate law and that Friedman defends in his 1970 New York Times Magazine essay, "The Social Responsibility of Business Is to Increase Its Profits."

Corporate Social Responsibility and Stakeholder Theory

Stakeholder theory seeks to overthrow the shareholder orientation of the firm. It is an outgrowth of the corporate social responsibility (CSR) movement to which Friedman's essay responds. According to CSR, the firm is obligated to "give something back" to those that make its success possible. The image of the firm presented in CSR is that of a free rider, unjustly and uncooperatively enriching itself to the detriment of the community. Socially responsible deeds (such as patronizing the arts or mitigating unemployment) are necessary to redeem firms and transform them into good citizens.

One wonders, however, why firms are obligated to give something back to those to whom they routinely give so much already. Rather than enslave their employees, firms typically pay them wages and benefits in return for their labor. Rather than steal from their customers, firms typically deliver goods and services in return for the revenues that customers provide. Rather than free ride on public provisions, firms typically pay taxes and obey the law. Moreover, these compensations are ones to which the affected parties or (in the case of communities and unionized employees) their agents freely agree. For what reasons, then, is one to conclude that those compensations are inadequate or unjust, necessitating that firms give something more to those whom they have already compensated?

Stakeholder theory constitutes at least something of an advance over CSR. Whereas CSR is fundamentally antagonistic to capitalist enterprise, viewing both firm and manager as social parasites in need of a strong reformative hand, stakeholder theory takes a different tack. Rather than offer stakeholder theory as a means of overthrowing capitalist enterprise, stakeholder theorists profess to offer theirs as a strategy for improving it. As Robert Phillips of the University of Pennsylvania's Wharton School writes, "One of the goals of the stakeholder theory is to maintain the benefits of the free market while minimizing the potential ethical problems created by capitalism."

On the theory that "you'll catch more flies with honey than with vinegar," stakeholder theorists ostensibly praise corporate leaders and maintain that firms are social institutions and their managers are community leaders. Given appropriate latitude, firms and managers are disposed to serve the social good. Corporate law and the market for corporate control, however, preclude firms and managers from following their inclinations and serving their social missions. Stakeholder theory seeks to free both firm and manager from their exclusive attention to the narrow, parochial concerns of shareholders so that they can focus on a broader set of interests.

But although the diagnosis of the problem with capitalist enterprise is (at least, on the face of it) different from that advanced in CSR, the stakeholder theorists' remedy is largely the same: the elevation of nonshareholding interests to the level of shareholder interests in formulating business strategy and policy. The stakeholder-oriented manager is admonished to weigh and balance stakeholder interests, trading off one against another in settling on a course of action. Stakeholder theorists seek a reorientation of the corporate law toward the interests of stakeholders and the insulation of managers from the market for corporate control.

Problems

Whatever the appeal of the stakeholder theory's inclusiveness of and sensitivity to the myriad interests that affect and are affected by firms, there are several powerful reasons to resist the theory's adoption and embodiment in a reformed corporate law.

Equity Capital.   Because it undermines shareholder property rights, stakeholder-oriented management denigrates and discourages equity investment. In the stakeholder-oriented firm, equity investors bear the same downside risks that they bear in the traditionally governed, shareholder-oriented firm. The upside potential of their investment, however, is diminished significantly; for in distributing the fruits of the firm's success, equity investor interests are only some among many to be considered and served. In short, when the firm loses, shareholders lose; when the firm wins, shareholders might lose anyway if other interests are deemed to be more weighty and important.

Stakeholder-oriented management effectively eliminates issuing shares as a means of financing the firm's growth and new ventures. By diminishing the orientation of the firm toward shareholder interests, stakeholder-oriented management will presumably lead investors to discount sharply the value they attach to shareholdings. So stakeholder-oriented management essentially entails a near-exclusive reliance on debt as the fuel of expansion.

But the problems do not stop there. Debtholders, whether banks or bondholders, typically use equity holdings, returns to equity, and appreciation in the market price for shares as signals of financial health, and hence as mechanisms for pricing debt capital. Widespread or legally mandatory adoption of stakeholder-oriented management threatens to undermine well-established, stable, and efficient market norms for pricing capital in favor of a regime under which capital is more costly for firms to acquire because investment (whether in the form of equity or debt) is an inherently riskier proposition. That, in turn, threatens prospects for economic growth, stable employment, and the liquidity of financial markets. In short, stakeholder-oriented management promises poorer, static, risk-averse firms and hence a poorer, static, risk-averse economy. Stakeholder-oriented management is contrary to the interests of the very stakeholders it is intended to help.

Managerial Accountability.   People recoil in horror at corporate officers' and directors' salaries, perks, and other bonuses that at times bear no relation to the performance of the firms they manage. This sorry state of affairs results from the confluence of a number of recent trends in corporate law that make it more difficult for shareholders to discipline self-serving managers:

The decline of the ultra vires doctrine (under which shareholders could sue managers for embarking on projects contrary to the corporate purpose).

The emergence of so-called corporate constituency statutes (which permit managers to consider and appeal to a broader range of interests in determining how and whether to fend off a takeover bid—and thereby hamper the smooth operation of the market for corporate control).

The expansive reading given to the business judgment rule (which shields some managerial actions from substantive review by courts) by the Supreme Court of Delaware—where many firms are incorporated.

But whatever the impediments to disciplining self-serving managers under current law and public policy, they pale in comparison with those promised by stakeholder-oriented management (and a stakeholder-oriented corporate law). Whereas under the current corporate law much self-serving managerial behavior is recognizably self-serving but shielded from substantive review, under stakeholder-oriented corporate law such behavior would be considerably more difficult even to detect, as well as to deter.

It would be more difficult to detect because all but the most egregious of self-serving managerial behavior will coincide with the interests of some stakeholding group, and hence the self-serving manager may point to the benefited and burdened stakeholders and argue that, in his estimation, this was the optimal way to balance competing stakeholder interests. Absent a powerful principle of balanced distribution of the benefits of the firm (something stakeholder theorists have been notoriously slow to sketch), stakeholder theorists must acquiesce in self-serving managerial action that can plausibly be said to accomplish some sort of balance among competing stakeholder interests. That point is made with admirable clarity by Frank Easterbrook and Daniel Fischel in their 1991 book, The Economic Structure of Corporate Law: "A manager told to serve two masters (a little for the equity holders, a little for the community) has been freed of both and is answerable to neither. Faced with a demand from either group, the manager can appeal to the interests of the other."

Self-serving managerial action would be more difficult to deter under stakeholder-oriented corporate law because stakeholder theory anticipates that good-faith stakeholder-oriented managerial actions will serve some interests and frustrate others in pursuit of an overall balance of interests. Therefore, stakeholder-oriented corporate law must provide protections to managers at least as extensive as those afforded under current business judgment rule doctrine—lest managers be the perpetual object of derivative lawsuits brought by shareholders, employees, customers, suppliers, or communities who believe that their interests were unfairly or improperly weighed and balanced. Between the ability of managers to justify their self-serving behavior in terms of the balanced pursuit of stakeholder interests, on the one hand, and the protections that a stakeholder-oriented corporate law must afford to managers if firms are to be managed at all, on the other hand, the accountability of managers for their actions must necessarily suffer.

Interest-Group Politics.   Because stakeholder-oriented management anticipates the weighing and the balancing—and hence often the frustrating—of competing interests, it promises to make the boardroom (populated, per Freeman, by representatives of all stakeholding groups) the site of wasteful, inefficient interest-group politicking. That is, the corporate boardroom will be transformed from a forum in which economically rational strategies are adopted in pursuit of added value into one in which legislative and bureaucratic political maneuvering will be the order of the day. Surprisingly, stakeholder theorists recognize and, apparently, welcome this. In a 1998 issue of Business Ethics Quarterly, communitarian thinker Amitai Etzioni is comforted by the thought that there "is no reason to expect that the politics of corporate communities would be any different from other democratic systems."

One can scarcely imagine how firms, whose resources are far more limited than are those of governments (and unsupported by the taxing power), can remain viable if their decision procedures are characterized by the strategic bargaining, logrolling, and other wasteful tactics that are the hallmark of democratic politics. If a camel is a horse designed by a committee, then what misshapen beast is a firm shaped by the strategic interactions of its stakeholder representatives?

Small Victories

The market economy, the liberty it safeguards, and the prosperity it secures are threatened not, as in the recent past, by firebrands who seek to abolish it, but by more modest tinkerers who seek to "improve" it in the name of myriad social concerns. Defending the market economy from this attack requires more than cataloging the defects of alternative economic systems and the merits of markets. It requires a principled defense of the shareholder-oriented firm—the basic productive institution on which the market economy is constructed.

Despite its worrisome implications, stakeholder-oriented management and its accompanying rhetoric encounter little systematic opposition in philosophy departments, business schools, or boardrooms. The costs of complacency about that state of affairs are potentially high. For although they have so far failed to bring wholesale change to the corporation and the law that governs it, stakeholder-oriented activists have won important piecemeal victories. The passage of corporate constituency statutes in several states has weakened the market for corporate control and, hence, the property rights of shareholders. Federal plant-closing legislation has legitimized among policymakers the idea that firm managers ought to be responsive to a multiplicity of interests. Corporate mission statements in which stakeholders and their interests feature prominently—whether adopted earnestly or as cover for self-serving managers— serve to further legitimize the subordination of shareholder interests to other concerns. If the market economy and its cornerstone, the shareholder-oriented firm, are in no danger of being dealt a decisive blow, they at least risk death by a thousand cuts.

Business Ethics Reconsidered

Too often the free-market response to the changes sought by stakeholder-oriented business ethicists has been to denigrate the role of ethics in business—as if stakeholder-oriented reforms are the inevitable consequence of injecting concern for ethics into business. But the partisans of stakeholder theory are not spokespeople for ethics; they are spokespeople only for a particular conception of ethics—and a particularly flawed conception, at that. The manifold failings of stakeholder theory should not be taken to reflect poorly on the project of business ethics; rather, they reflect poorly on stakeholder theory itself.

Defenders of the free market, limited government, and the rule of law must articulate an alternative business ethics, one that recognizes and provides reasoned argument for the moral merit of the shareholder-oriented firm. Norms of honesty, integrity, and fair play, rather than an albatross around the neck of the free market, are a central, if neglected, part of the story of the success of the shareholder-oriented firm. In short, shareholder-oriented firms are not merely wealth-enhancing, they are good.

POSTSCRIPT

Do Corporations Have
a Responsibility to Society
That Extends Beyond Merely
Maximizing Profit?

Advocates of the shareholder approach generally believe that free-market capitalism is the best mechanism for addressing social problems. They argue that the free market, guided by Adam Smith's invisible hand and based on the view that organizations exist to maximize shareholder wealth, will provide the necessary incentives for solving problems society considers important. Some organization, driven by the desire to maximize shareholder wealth first and foremost, will provide a solution and reap its just rewards. In this scenario, all parties involved are better off when the company concerns itself with trying to make as much money as it can for its shareholders and does not distract itself with the claims of other groups with which it interacts. Critics point out that this scenario fails to take into account the issue of time. Consider a situation where a community has a pollution problem that, for whatever reason, cannot be solved by current pollution-control technology. Free-market advocates would argue that someone (or company) will invent the necessary technology since doing so will result in large financial gains. Maybe so, say the critics. But what if it takes 10 years for the technology to be developed? What happens to the community in the meantime? The point is that situations occur where the time lag between the onset of a problem and its solution can be too long to let the corporations ignore the concerns of other stakeholders while they search for a profit-maximizing solution.

Alexei Marcoux provided a direct attack on stakeholder theory in his article. But even if you did not find his arguments convincing, there is much potential for trouble if corporations become too involved in the concerns of their stakeholders. One possible problem is conflict of interest: Managers could play one group of stakeholders against another. Another problem concerns the concentration of power that might result. Do we really want corporations making decisions and wielding even more power than they currently have in community affairs, for example?

We conclude, then, that both sides of this interesting and topical debate have powerful arguments on their side. Where do you stand on this issue? Should the only purpose of an organization be to maximize profit, or do other stakeholders have a legitimate claim to the fruits of the organizations' success?

Suggested Readings

Thomas Donaldson, Patricia H. Werhane, & Margaret Cording, *Ethical Issues in Business: A Philosophical Approach* (7th ed.). Prentice Hall, 2002.

R. Edward Freeman, Fixing the ethics crisis in corporate America. *Miller Center Report*, Fall 2002.

Milton Friedman, The social responsibility of business is to increase its profits. *The New York Times Magazine*, September 13, 1970.

Samuel Gregg, "Stakeholder" theory: What it means for corporate governance. *Policy*, Winter 2001, vol. 17, no. 2. The Center for Independent Studies. http://www.cis.org.au/Policy/winter01/polwin01-7.htm

David Henderson, The case against corporate social responsibility. *Policy*, Winter 2001, Vol. 17, No. 2. The Center for Independent Studies. http://www.cis.org.au/policy/winter01/polwin01-6.pdf

ISSUE 2

Is the Corporate Strategy of Downsizing Unethical?

YES: Larry Gross, from "Downsizing: Are Employers Reneging on Their Social Promise?" *CPCU Journal* (Summer 2001)

NO: Joseph T. Gilbert, from "Sorrow and Guilt: An Ethical Analysis of Layoffs," *SAM Advanced Management Journal* (vol. 65, 2000)

ISSUE SUMMARY

YES: Larry Gross contends that downsizing violates the psychological and social contracts implicit in the employer–employee relationship since there is an implied sense of job security afforded the employee as long as he or she is productively advancing the goals of the organization. Downsizing productive employees is a clear violation of this contract and, therefore, immoral.

NO: Professor Joseph Gilbert analyzes the ethicality of downsizing through the application of three prominent approaches to the study of ethics: utilitarianism, rights and duties, and justice and fairness. Gilbert concludes that, with one notable exception, downsizing is an ethically valid and morally responsible corporate behavior.

Corporate downsizing is the strategic action of reducing the size of an organization's workforce in the hope of achieving greater efficiency and productivity through the reduction in labor costs. Although academic discussion of the concept can be traced back to the 1950s, it wasn't until the early 1980s that the idea of downsizing as a strategic tool found expression in the marketplace of corporate America. The accelerated growth of international and global competition during the decade of the 1980s forced American businesses to reduce costs and focus on increasing organizational efficiency. An obvious way to quickly lower costs and trim waste is to reduce the size of the workforce. This line of thinking, coupled with the growing competitive pressures, proved irresistible to thousands of corporations of all size and financial condition. The result? Millions of employees were laid off as corporate America embraced the notion of downsizing as a valuable managerial weapon. By the time the 1990s were over, the acceptance of downsizing as an effective and dependable arrow in the corporate quiver was complete.

Although top management has expectations about the impact downsizing will have on their labor costs, they are typically much less concerned about the impact on the employees affected by the decision. An important moral question arises when we view downsizing from the perspective of the employee— namely, does the corporation have the moral right to downsize in the first place? In other words, is downsizing unethical? Most frequently, those answering "no" base their position on a stakeholder approach to business ethics. This approach argues that businesses have obligations that extend beyond merely maximizing shareholder wealth to include any entity or individual that is impacted by the organization's activities. Consider the following statement from Larry Gross, author of the "yes" position of this Taking Sides debate: "Downsizing is driving a breach in the corporation's social responsibility not only to the employees who lose their jobs, but also to the others who remain . . . That same breach of promise on the part of these companies also affects the society where they do business" (*CPCU Journal,* 2001, vol. 54, no. 2, p. 113). Gross also contends that downsizing violates the psychological and social contracts implicit in the employer–employee relationship since there is an implied sense of job security afforded the employee as long as he or she is productively advancing the goals of the organization. Downsizing productive employees is a clear violation of this contract and, therefore, immoral. As you read this article, ask yourself if you would feel the sense of violation Gross refers to if you were to fall victim to downsizing at your job.

Professor Joseph Gilbert, in the "no" selection for this debate, analyzes the ethicality of downsizing through the application of three prominent approaches to the study of business ethics: utilitarianism, rights and duties, and justice and fairness. According to Gilbert, an important element in this analysis involves understanding the motivation behind the decision to downsize. He argues, for example, that a moral analysis of an organization that reduces labor costs as a last-ditch effort to avoid bankruptcy and the resultant loss of all jobs will yield a different conclusion than an analysis of a highly successful organization that downsizes in a proactive, aggressive effort to increase its profits. Gilbert further suggests that it makes sense to view the motivations for downsizing as existing on a continuum: At one end is the corporation that lays off workers to avoid closing, at the other is the profitable organization that downsizes to further increase profits, and somewhere in the middle is the company that downsizes to forestall potential problems. To further complicate the matter, the results of the analysis may differ depending on which of the three approaches are used.

After conducting this analysis, Gilbert concludes that, with the exception of successful firms that lay off employees primarily to further increase profits, downsizing is an ethically valid and morally responsible corporate behavior. Keep Gilbert's conclusions in mind next time the media report that another major corporation has laid off thousands of its workforce. Was the company's survival in doubt, or was the downsizing the apparent effort of top management to make a good situation even better?

YES

Larry Gross

Downsizing: Are Employers Reneging on Their Social Promise?

. . . The phenomenon of downsizing, which is advertised to create financial and operational efficiencies in the modern corporate environment, has impacted millions of employees over the last several years. In the first half of 1996, the number of job cuts increased by 28 percent from the year before, resulting in 100,000 layoffs in January 1996 alone. The list of corporations that had made significant cuts included all types of industries including communications, technology, and manufacturing as well as insurance.

There was a resurgence in the number of job cuts in the last six months of 2000 due to companies looking to dilute the impact of a projected economic slowdown. In December 2000, U.S. corporations announced 133,173 layoffs, a 203 percent increase over November's total according to a report by Challenger, Gray, and Christmas, an international outplacement firm. This number of reductions represented the highest number of job cuts ever recorded since the survey began in 1993, and this was only the fourth time that the number of layoffs totaled more than 100,000 in one month. These job reductions crossed over all industry sectors, and included a major health insurer who cut 5,000 jobs as part of restructuring plan to improve profit.

The trend in the increase of downsizing activity is predicted to continue due to companies taking action to compensate for the loss of market share and sharp drops in profitability expected from a slowing economy, according to John Challenger, chief executive of Challenger, Gray, and Christmas. He observes, "Companies are jumping in to make decisions to get their costs in line now and not wait."

Many companies in the insurance community, both large and small, adopt downsizing as a business strategy. Downsizing, which may be proposed for any number of objectives, including cost management, always results in reduced staff. This is critical because reducing staff is downsizing's real objective, contrary to any of the stated objectives that attempt to rationalize it. One irony about the downsizing trend is that those released are not the newest employees. Long-term employees, especially middle managers who may have given 10 to 30 years in service to the company, are often discharged. Many of those who fall into that category are unable to find employment that allows them to use their current skill sets or to maintain their lifestyle. A study by the

American Society for Training and Development indicated that onethird of the displaced managers over 35 years old find jobs that pay less than they previously earned. These victims of downsizing often need five years to get back to their former pay level.

Corporate downsizing has posed an even more serious dilemma than the individual situations suggest. Downsizing is driving a breach in the corporation's social responsibility not only to the employees who lose their jobs, but also to the others who remain either as an employee or with a vested interest in the company's future. That same breach of promise on the part of these companies also affects the society where they do business.

There is a fallacy inherent in downsizing. Organizations that undergo this type of change do not appear to be better off than they were before they implemented the process.

Downsizing does not appear to be in the best long-term interest of the corporation, its employees, or its shareholders. In fact, there is considerable evidence in this regard.

As a result, it is important to understand downsizing's key objectives in order to evaluate whether its stated goals are met. One definition states that downsizing is "a set of activities . . . undertaken on the part of management, designed to improve organizational efficiency, productivity, and or competitiveness. It represents a strategy that affects the size of the firm's workforce and its work processes."

Atwood cites that existing research describes the attributes of downsizing as intentional; it usually involves, although is not limited to, reductions in personnel; it focuses on improving efficiency of the organization; and it also affects work processes intentionally or unintentionally.

Reviewing the financial results for companies engaged in significant downsizing during the early 1990s, one study cited that the massive job cuts rarely lead to strong sustained gains in the affected company's stock over the long term. Where median share prices initially rose six months after downsizing by 8 percent, they slid to a 26 percent loss within three years. In another study, only 21 percent of the firms surveyed reported that they achieved satisfactory shareholder return on investment as a result of downsizing, and 46 percent found that reducing head count did not reduce expenses to the degree that had been anticipated. In the same study, only 32 percent increased profits to anticipated levels and only 22 percent of the downsized companies saw the increase in productivity they expected.

In some cases, no effective increase in stock prices occurred even in the short term. In 1995 the Times Mirror Company reported third and fourth quarter losses coincident with the elimination of more than 2,000 jobs. It blamed the losses on the cost of huge layoffs, downsizing, and closures aimed at saving money in the long run.

A report by the Wyatt Company, a national management consultant firm, stated that only 12 percent of downsized companies increased market share, 9 percent improved product quality, and just 7 percent increased innovation. Despite various actions taken by management at these firms to downsize, the data indicated that many had experienced unexpected and undesirable outcomes.

In a four-year study examining 30 firms in the automotive industry, the data revealed "very few organizations in the study implemented downsizing in a way that improved their effectiveness. Most deteriorated in terms of predownsizing levels of quality, productivity, effectiveness, and the 'dirty dozen,' e.g., conflict, low morale, loss of trust, rigidity, scapegoating." Ellen Bayer, global human resources chief for the American Management Association, states, "We've found that in both the long and short term, growing companies tend to outperform downsized firms-especially in such areas as employee morale and turnover rates." These financial effects of downsizing are directly impacted by the fact that the downsizing process is the wrong choice from an ethical perspective. Downsizing is in direct conflict with the Stakeholder Approach to corporate social responsibility. This approach emphasizes accountability to a larger constituency that has significant interest in the corporation's well-being and long-term survival. This infers that purely market-driven ethical decision-making can only capture a short-term benefit without regard for the viability of the organization in the environment it operates.

In fact, the short-term advantages of downsizing only benefit a very small segment of the organization, if at all. The downsizing process indicates a rationalization of action based on a corporate application of psychological egoism. Employees are sacrificed for the apparent benefit or survival of the larger corporation, which is considered an entity in itself that is worthy and capable of self-interest. This "culture of narcissism" represents the acceptance of a business environment where corporations have only one objective, profit, which is in contrast to the need to keep the triangular interests of shareholders, management, and employees in balance.

In a 1999 case study of downsizing that was used by a hospital to address a $16 million budget shortfall, the report cited that within two years almost every reduced position was back in place. The study suggested that the organization never asked whether the projected cost saving was worth the turmoil and impact on productivity and whether better options should have been evaluated by the organization instead.

The fact that downsizing is a bad decision for all affected is coupled with a level of responsibility that the corporation has to two key environments—the employees affected and the society in which the corporation operates. People who are productive employees with years of tenure and education lose their jobs, with seemingly little regard for the disruption of their lives by the corporations that employed them. The financial impact is obvious, but what about the psychological and social implications this action caused?

Despite the absence of a written contract, employees have an implied agreement from their employers in return for their effort to advance the corporation's goals. This includes a promise of protection and safety through wages, benefits, and good working conditions. While the assumption of the implicit psychological contract that assured lifetime job security may no longer hold, a new contract in which employees are more autonomous and self-reliant has taken its place. In the new employment relationship, trust is established through this contract that represents the obligations between the employee and the organization and is based on a normative approach of trust. In this approach employees see trust as an ethical relationship explained in terms of shared ideals and values. This obligation matches Lawrence Kohlberg's Social Contract Legalistic Orientation, a stage of moral reasoning that creates a socio-legal obligation that exists without statutory support. Downsizing violates the promise this relationship creates.

Employees expect that all parties will honor their explicit and implicit obligations. Distrust occurs when these obligations are not met or when the parties have different expectations regarding the obligations. When downsizing is employed as an organizational strategy, it focuses on economic goals over the promotion of commitment, and, as a result, the employees view the strategy with distrust.

The further impact of this breach of the promise is evident anecdotally. John A. Challenger notes, "It may be unrealistic to expect intense loyalty on the part of the worker when in many instances the employer cannot promise in return. The current spate of mergers in the banking, media, utilities, and other industries, major re-engineering efforts, and downsizings all have weakened the ties that spur employee commitment and productivity."

The lack of the corporation's initiative to protect its employees causes the individual workers to suffer. Employees are devastated by the emotional aspect of downsizing, which rocks their self-esteem and self-confidence. They see themselves valued solely as an expense item of the corporation and believe that if that's the way it is, why bother? Frederick Reichheld, a corporate strategy consultant and expert in loyalty practice states, "The great betrayal of American workers is the failure of companies to let them know how much value they are creating, versus how much they are costing."

A 1996 survey commissioned by the American Management Association demonstrated the physical toll to employees by downsizing and restructuring through evidence that the number of both occupational and nonoccupational disability claims increased significantly during these periods. These increases were also found to occur not only to employees whose jobs were being eliminated but also among those who remained employed. These remaining employees suffered distress from several sources: threat of job loss, job description changes, added responsibility due to the layoff of co-workers, salary freezes or cutbacks, and forced relocation, among others. In a 1997 European study, the authors found a significant association between downsizing and medically certified sick leave where the rate of absenteeism was 2.3 times greater after major downsizing.

Downsizing also causes a conflict for those managers who are charged with the decisions of who to let go and the implementation of the downsizing process when they recognize the implied agreement exists. Based on the ethics standard that is applied, the individual manager is forced to decide between what is his or her responsibility to the corporation's will and survival and the promise of security that he or she offers on behalf of the corporation in return for the employee's productivity. Because downsizing often results in almost explosive change, there is little time for the manager to come to terms with this inconsistency or to distance him- or herself from the result. When faced with this task, many decide to leave the company rather than deal with the stress of the conflict. Other managers defer the dilemma to upper management instead of implicating themselves.

The breach of promise to society is perhaps the most serious implication of all because everyone is hurt as a result. The rationale that corporations use to describe the benefits of a particular "cost management" effort appear to be flawed-not only in terms of its return to the corporation, but to the society in which it operates as well. The continuous implementation of restructuring efforts that did not appear to have focus are evidence of this rationale, which continues to cause damage to employees' lives and the corporation itself. The reduction of the work force for the singular purpose of reduced costs/more profits breaches the integrity the corporation has in relation to the quality of its contribution to the overall health of society. A profit-oriented approach simply leads to a restriction of the corporation's definition of a goal and an indifference to the means by which these goals are pursued.

Loss of perspective hinders a corporation's ability to compete in the marketplace because it diminishes the corporation's sensitivity to the needs and preferences of customers. Nash writes, "One cannot achieve market sensitivity or organizational cooperation by working on the assumption that your own way of doing things and your profit are necessarily more compelling than anything else."

Feldman and Liou in their article "Downsizing Trust," indicate that the call for principled implementation of downsizing strategies has become a current theme in management literature. They state that the term leadership based on the ideals of trust and power has replaced the word management. Trust has become the new foundation of leadership, replacing authority, and focusing on the reciprocal relationship between leaders and followers. Reciprocity in this relationship refers to a mutual loyalty and commitment between leaders and followers based on truth and honesty. This accounts for the fact that organizational leaders acknowledge that the social contract exists between the employee and the organization and that the organization must honor the contract.

This concept points to new strategies for staff reduction based on organizations approaching it with a quality focus, which requires them to change their fundamental assumptions about people, organizations, and management. This strategy embodies the issue of trust between the employee and the organization. It recognizes the need for empowerment of the individuals who work there and their need to strive to maintain pride in their work and the continuous improvement of all aspects of work within the organization. In this scenario, the organization is responsible for providing training, opportunity, and responsibility for decision making in tandem with accountability, mutual respect, and trust.

In the future, companies must do everything in their power to provide training or placement for employees who may lose their jobs because of the normal dynamics of change that is inherent in any system that requires a destabilizing element to allow organizations to shift away from the status quo. Companies must also pay serious attention to the transition experienced by employees remaining within the organization. This is necessary to provide the protection factor that is implied in the employee/employer relationship.

A well-designed and consistent communications plan is key to any effort designed to successfully assist an organization through change. Communication must be provided, and it should be proactive so that information can be shared early in the process. In a 1995 survey, 65 percent of the responding organizations ranked "gaps in communication channels" as the number one negative factor experienced after restructuring. A well-designed communication plan breaks down barriers and helps people accept the change. An additional study found that insufficient communication from top management might result in middle managers not supporting or even sabotaging new initiatives.

T. Quinn Spitzer, CEO of Kepner-Tregoe, an international consulting firm, states, "There is no new social contract. The companies that always had one still do; the companies that never had one are more inclined to talk about it." Spitzer contends there are four dimensions to this responsibility that have been misapplied over the years:

1. Culture—Organizations will run their businesses with the idea that an employee is at least as important as the investor and the customer.
2. Skill building—Organizations will give employees the skill sets needed to do their jobs; workers have the reciprocal responsibility of self-reliance.
3. High performance work environment—Organizations will offer a hospitable workplace and reward systems that allow opportunity for excellence. For their part, workers must have some control over their destiny and must perform.
4. Employment security—This is considered as a paramount concern rather than employment for life. Organizations will be mindful of job security in decision making, instead of laying off as an initial strategic response to business downturns.

Recent management literature reviews the evolution of a work/life initiative, where action to benefit the individual is directly linked to business strategy such as flexible work scheduling. This results in a change in perspective from a human-cost to a human—investment approach when evaluating the benefit to the organization. Specifically, it allows a corporation to measure the value of a work/life procedure and balance it in terms of organizational efficiencies. As part of the process, the intervention and related investments are defined in terms of the broadest group of stakeholders and its measurable return in terms of the company's business strategy.

Lee Perry, professor of strategy and organizational behavior at the Marriott School of Management, believes that by using technology and redeploying people based on comprehensive process analysis, the reduction-in-staff aspect of restructuring may be mitigated. He states, "Managers are using a machete when they should be using a scalpel." He suggests, "If organizations could bring the goals of business and society together, what would it look like?"

There is a definite correlation between the need to do what is "right" and a successful business enterprise. From my observations about downsizing, I also see that the definition of that term is the result of a cooperative understanding of the employer, employee, and the other stakeholders to make sure all interests are addressed. The reality is that although we cannot escape the dynamics of change, we cannot allow it to serve as an excuse to act unethically. As Edward B. Rust Jr., chairman and CEO of State Farm Insurance Company, stated, "Mutuality of trust makes it far less difficult to go through the changes that the marketplace places on us." We must confirm our responsibility to each other through how we face these types of situations, whether we act as individuals or as the conscience of our corporations.

Joseph T. Gilbert  **NO**

Sorrow and Guilt: An Ethical Analysis of Layoffs

Closing the office door, looking straight into an employee's face, and telling him that he no longer has a job is not an easy task. When that employee's performance has been satisfactory or even exemplary, it is even more difficult for a manager to terminate him or her. Yet, this happens hundreds of thousands of times when companies decide to reduce the size of their workforce by layoffs. From the stock market's point of view, such a decision is usually a good thing—a company's stock price often rises on the day that a layoff decision is announced. From top management's point of view, such a decision can seem to be the best, or even the only one, available to solve serious problems that the top manager must address. From the point of view of the managers or supervisors assigned to deliver the news to individuals about to be terminated, the decision often produces sorrow or guilt, or both. From the point of view of the terminated employees, shock, disbelief, and anger are among the typical reactions. . . .

Since layoffs cause suffering, sorrow is an appropriate emotion. Is guilt appropriate, and if so on whose part? In other words, is moral or ethical wrong involved in layoffs?

This article focuses on the decision to conduct layoffs and the subsequent decision about which employees will be laid off. . . . We will argue that in some circumstances, laying off some employees is the ethical thing to do, and managers who fail to do so are guilty of unethical conduct. In other circumstances, no ethical defense of layoffs can be found, and managers who decide on layoffs in these circumstances are guilty of unethical acts. In a wide range of circumstances in between, there are ethical arguments for and against layoffs. For these cases, we show how ethical reasoning can be applied to assist managers in determining the morally right thing to do.

One common definition of an act with ethical or moral consequences is that such an act involves decisions freely taken that will have positive or negative consequences for others. Layoff decisions clearly fall within this definition. Our analysis will employ the three major approaches often used in writing and teaching about managerial ethics: utilitarianism (the greatest good for the greatest number), rights and duties, and justice and fairness. . . .

Ethical Analysis: The Basic Tools

To determine whether a decision, such as downsizing, or an action, such as laying off an employee, is ethical, managers have certain analytical techniques available to them. While these techniques are not as widely known as statistical analysis or flow charting, they are gradually becoming part of a manager's standard tool kit. Business schools are placing more emphasis on ethics, partly because of the large number of clearly unethical business practices exposed during the 1980s.

Most business school textbooks and courses on ethics take the same basic approach to analyzing the morality or ethics (we use the words interchangeably in this article) of business decisions. The three most commonly accepted approaches draw on the work of moral philosophers dating back more than two thousand years to Plato and Aristotle. While these philosophers were not familiar with corporations or computers, they did think long and deeply about issues of morality. The fact that their writings are still read and discussed indicates that they have something worthwhile to say.

Ethics is the branch of philosophy that deals with the morality of human decisions and actions, and business ethics deals with them in a business setting. These dry-sounding definitions point to the link between the best work of some deep moral thinkers and particular decisions or actions taken by managers in a contemporary business setting. . . .

Utilitarianism.   One approach to determining the morality of a decision or action is utilitarianism, which holds that a moral decision or action is one that results in the greatest good for the greatest number of people. The philosophers most commonly identified with this view are two nineteenth century Englishmen, Jeremy Bentham and John Stuart Mill. The assumption of this approach is that pleasure causes happiness and pain takes it away. Since pleasure and the happiness it causes are the ultimate good for humans, the act that causes the greatest pleasure or happiness for the greatest number of people is the morally good act. This view also assumes that people live in communities and must take this fact into account in deciding on the moral rightness of what they do. While this view may sound simplistic, it is often called upon in business settings to justify or condemn certain actions. We will examine the issue further, but it is common to justify layoff on the basis that terminating 500 people will save the company from bankruptcy and hence preserve the jobs of 2,500 others.

Rights and duties.   A second approach to ethical analysis is to examine the issues of rights and duties. The basic position here is that individuals have rights, either as humans, as citizens of a given country or state, or as occupants of a particular position. These right rights confer duties on others, and the morality of a given decision or act can be determined by an analysis of these rights and duties. The philosopher most commonly associated with this view is Immanuel Kant. While issues of rights and duties may sound more philosophical and less mathematical than that of determining the greatest good for the greatest number, it is not necessarily so. My right to personal comfort may be outweighed by your right to live. My duty to my family may be outweighed by my duty to serve my country in time of war. Once again, calculation enters into many, but not all, ethical decisions. Few people would question that humans have a basic right to life, and that random killing is morally wrong. A somewhat different question, related to layoffs, is whether workers have a right to their jobs, and therefore, managers have a duty not to lay them off.

Justice and fairness.   The third basic approach involves issues of justice and fairness. While some would treat justice and fairness as issues within the first two approaches, others maintain that they constitute a third approach. Both utilitarianism and rights and duties have been criticized for being unfair in certain cases. In some situations, you may not have a clear right to your job, and it may not be clear that maintaining your job serves the greatest good of the greatest number, but does not seem fair for you to be terminated when you have been performing well and earning both praises and raises. In the United States, we tend to equate justice with legality, but there are situations where an action that is legal does not seem fair or just. As with the previous two approaches, calculation sometimes enters into considerations of justice and fairness, because it may be impossible in a given situation to be fully fair to everyone involved. The philosopher whose work is most often cited on issues of justice and fairness is John Rawls, a professor at Harvard University.

With this brief summary of the three most common approaches to analyzing issues of managerial ethics, we now turn to the issue of layoffs. . . . There are a variety of reasons why managers may choose to layoff employees. An ethical or moral analysis of layoffs requires that we identify some of these reasons.

At one extreme is the situation where a company ceases operation, either at the choice of its owners or because of bankruptcy. In this case, obviously, all employees lost their jobs, but this is not usually referred to as a layoff. A similar situation, but not as drastic, occurs when a company is in serious danger of going out of business, and reducing labor costs through layoffs is the only apparent alternative. We will refer to such situations as layoffs to save the company. In other situations, layoffs are a preventative measure. In such cases, managers analyze their company's competitive situation, see that it is deteriorating and that labor costs are a significant factor, and move to reduce these costs before the company reaches the life or death stage. We will refer to this category as layoffs to improve the company.

In still other situations, layoffs are conducted to improve an already good situation. Here it is the judgment of managers that while the company is not deteriorating, greater profits could be achieved by reducing labor costs. Such layoffs may come about in mergers or acquisitions. Here two companies become one, and frequently plants or offices are closed and their employees laid off to reduce duplication. These layoffs are also conducted to reduce labor costs, but the motivating factor (or at least the precipitating factor) is the merger or acquisition.

Another circumstance in which layoffs are conducted to improve an already good situation involves outsourcing. The theory of core competency, popular in current strategy literature, suggests that a company can perform best by identifying its core competency, concentrating its efforts and its employees on performing core functions, and contracting with other companies to perform other functions. In practice, this can lead to layoffs if a company decides to stop performing certain functions and not to employ those people who formerly carried them out. We will categorize these situations (mergers, acquisitions, and outsourcing) as layoffs to change the company. The three categories of layoffs that we have identified (to save, to change, or to improve the company) are not mutually exclusive, but they are sufficiently different to provide a basis for further discussion.

Utilitarianism and Layoffs

On the face of it, deciding the morality of a decision or action by counting may seem strange. Yet it is an approach to decision-making that is frequent in everyday life and in the business world. . . .

When a manager terminates an employee who has done nothing wrong, it can scarcely be argued that this is good for the employee. Whether the action is called downsizing, rightsizing, outplacement, or some other term, the terminated employee had a job yesterday and now does not. . . .

The utilitarian argument focuses on obtaining the greatest happiness or good of the greatest number. Happiness is also the goal in other systems of ethics, dating back to Aristotle in the fourth century, B.C. This basis for deciding on moral acts makes some intuitive sense. Most people would probably agree that is morally better, in general, to make people happy than to make the unhappy, to being them pleasure rather than to bring them grief. What the utilitarian argument maintains is that it is not enough to consider the happiness or unhappiness of a single individual. Attention must be focused on the sum of happiness or grief resulting from a decision or action. Thus, the terminated employee receives pain rather than pleasure from his termination. The manager who conducts the face-to-face interview terminating the employee is likely to suffer grief rather than happiness as a result of the termination interview. If there is any moral justification for this action, it must lie in a greater sum of happiness coming to a larger number of others. An echo of this approach can be heard in the stakeholder analysis approach to issues of business strategy.

This line of reasoning is strengthened if the company, and hence the jobs of employees who are not laid off, can only be saved by reducing the labor force. If this is the case, then the happiness or pleasure of employment for all those who remain justifies the pain of those laid off and those managers who conduct the termination interviews. Further justification can be found in the happiness of stockholders, bondholders, and others who would be hurt by the company's bankruptcy. Given this situation, the utilitarian approach would clearly condone the layoffs as the moral thing to do. But how can we be sure that we are dealing with layoffs to save the company rather than to improve it.

Resolving this issue is not easy. When a company is in serious trouble, there is usually a perceived need to act quickly. Thoughtful consideration of all available alternatives is not likely to occur. Competing by price reductions only worsens a company's financial situation unless there are accompanying cost reductions. Competing by improving the present products or services, or introducing new and better ones, is often not a short-term possibility. Competing by greatly increased marketing efforts is costly, and if the company is already in financial trouble, costly solutions do not appear practical. Reducing staff can be done quickly, and there is ample precedent for such a decision. . . . While not an attractive alternative, a U.S. company in financial trouble can seek protecting by entering Chapter 11 bankruptcy, reorganizing its finances, and continuing as a going concern. As an alternative to layoffs, this solution may postpone the action, but often companies in Chapter 11 bankruptcy reduce staff as part of their reorganization before emerging from bankruptcy. So layoffs are still carried out, and the negative consequences of bankruptcy are added to the mix. In a utilitarian analysis, such a scenario is apt to result in greater unhappiness for more people (suppliers, creditors, shareholders) than would occur with layoffs alone.

In the final analysis, the only way to know for sure whether a company was in a situation of either conducting layoffs or going out of business is to wait and see. Yet it is cold comfort to managers or employees to find out after the fact that layoffs were needed to save the company and that, as a result of inaction, all jobs have been lost. Some uncertainty is inevitable regarding the question of whether the situation involves saving or improving the company. The luxury of waiting for definite answers is simply not available. Hence, we suggest a decision rule which says that if, in the judgment of senior management at the time the layoff decision is made, the situation was one of saving the company, it should be treated as such for purposes of ethical analysis.

Another possibility is that layoffs are not the only step between the present situation and a company's closing, but are seen as a way of dealing with deteriorating performance (layoffs to improve the company). In this case, it is more difficult to conclude that the unhappiness of those laid off and of managers who conduct the terminations is outweighed by a greater good for a greater number of people as a result of the company's improved performance. The unhappiness is clear, the greater good and those who benefit from it is less clear. In this category of layoffs, the further the situation deviates from a clearcut choice between layoffs and the company's closing, the less compelling the utilitarian argument becomes. However, top managers, by their positions, are charged with the future as well as the present well-being of the company. They are responsible for being proactive as well as reactive. In a situation where layoffs now can prevent a crisis later, choosing layoffs can be the best decision for the greatest number.

In the case of layoffs to improve already adequate performance (layoffs to change the company), the decision might bring happiness to managers whose compensation is tied to company performance through stock options or bonus plans, and to stockholders if the resulting improvements in performance cause the stock price to rise. However, in many cases companies conducting layoffs to improve performance do not attain the hoped-for results. Even if the results are achieved, unhappiness comes not only to the workers laid off and their managers, but also to many of the workers who remain. They face increased workloads and uncertainty about their own future with the company. Further, the families of those laid off also suffer pain. Workers at competing companies, observing the layoffs carried out by their rival may well suffer pain at the prospect that their own company will lay them off to maintain competitive. Thus, by a utilitarian analysis, it is by no means clear that layoffs to improve a company's position are always moral. . . .

The second question concerns how many and which employees are to be laid off. A utilitarian analysis emphasizes the impact of these choices (how many and who) on the results to be obtained. For the choices to be moral, the unhappiness caused must be offset by a greater sum of happiness for others resulting from the company's improved performance. . . .

If the reason for layoffs is to reduce labor costs, then it seems clear that laying off highly paid employees will reduce cost most. Older employees with greater seniority are normally more highly paid than newer and younger employees. A utilitarian analysis would note that older employees may suffer a greater degree of pain, since they often have a more difficult time finding new jobs than younger employees. Where negotiated contracts between labor and management prevail, unions typically negotiate as part of the contract that any layoffs occurring during the contract period will be based on reverse seniority, with the newest workers being laid off first. Another factor to be considered in a utilitarian analysis is that employees who perform their jobs best provide the most good to the company. Following this approach, the poorest performers should be laid off. However, many companies do not document performance in a way that can serve as a ground for determining layoffs on merit. Others do not choose to follow such an approach, even if they are able to.

A utilitarian approach concludes that layoffs are sometimes ethical, but some circumstances involving the desire to change a company, this approach finds that layoffs are not ethical. This approach emphasizes a consideration of human as well as financial factors and a concern for balancing the unhappiness which such actions bring to some participants with the benefits that result to others. The utilitarian approach does not assume that the company's financial situation is paramount, but does consider that greater good may come to a larger number of people, and that the unhappiness resulting from layoffs, might be morally justified by an analysis of the whole situation. It further considers that, if layoffs are to occur, the basis for deciding who will be laid off is also open to moral analysis.

Of the three approaches to ethical analysis used in this article, utilitarianism is the least abstract. Because major corporate decisions are so often based on impersonal analysis of financial considerations, the utilitarian approach adds an important perspective to those decisions.

Rights, Duties, and Layoffs

Much of philosophy deals with what it means to be human. There is general agreement that humans have a right to live, and that they have this right not because of their citizenship in one or another country, or because of their membership in a religion, or because of their occupation or position in life. If humans have a right to live, then they have a duty not to randomly take each other's lives. In general, rights imply duties. This is obvious with a little thought. If

I have a right to privacy, you have a duty not to invade my privacy. If I have a right to free speech, you have a duty not to silence me.

In addition to rights that people may have simply by reason of being human, other rights are conveyed to all or some citizens of a country. In the United States, citizens who are at least 18 and are not felons have a right to vote. Not all humans have this right, but citizens of some countries have it. Rights can also be granted to citizens of a state or province. Citizens can also have duties by virtue of their status as citizens. . . .

A third group of rights consists of those a person may have by virtue of their positions in a company or agency. A supervisor may have the right to sign company checks for up to $5,000, while the chief financial officer may have the right to sign for up to $5 million. A police officer has the right to apprehend and jail a suspect, while ordinary citizens do not. These rights can be very powerful in practice. The central point is that a person has these rights not as a human or as a citizen, but by virtue of occupying a certain position.

It is important in conducting an ethical analysis to distinguish legal rights and duties from moral rights and duties. They often overlap: most people agree that random killing is both legally and morally wrong. However, they are not always identical. In the not-so-distant past, it was illegal to drive over 55 miles per hour in the U.S., but one could argue that it was not morally wrong. If legal and moral rights and duties are always identical, then a change in the legal speed limit results in a change in the moral rightness of driving at a certain speed. A further argument against identity of legal and moral rights and duties lies in the source of laws. In the U.S., federal laws that apply to all citizens are made by Congress. Many people are uneasy with the idea of Congress as their source of moral right and wrong.

The law in the U.S. as to whether an employer can terminate an employee at will (for any reason or no reason) varies from state to state. Federal law prohibits termination for some reasons (age, gender, disability). In cases where a labor-management contract determine wages and conditions of work, grounds for termination are usually specific and limited. Whatever rights to a job an employee has under such agreements come from the employee's membership in a group covered by the negotiated contract. Applying a rights and duties approach to the ethical analysis of layoffs, it appears that the central question is whether an employee has a moral right to his or her job, and whether supervisors then have a corresponding moral duty not to determinate that employee until he or she forfeits that right.

Upon reflection, it is clear that an employee does not have an absolute right to retain a job. An employee who shoots his boss or is caught embezzling large amounts of money does not have a right to keep a job. A more limited question involves the right of an employee to keep a job as long as he or she is performing it satisfactorily. It is difficult to see the basis of such a right. As indicated, some rights come from our status as humans. . . . With some few exceptions, U.S. employees do not have legal rights (rights as a citizen) to keep their jobs as long as they perform well. Some countries do provide such rights; others provide less legal job protection than the U.S. The third source of rights is from status in an organization, but the general status of employee does not in and of itself seem to confer the right to keep a job. . . .

The moral analysis of layoffs in terms of rights and duties requires an emphasis on the individual. What a manager may or may not morally do is determined by examining the rights of the individual employee. If the manager has a duty to retain the employee the duty results from the employee's right. If the manager is free to determine whether the employee keeps or loses a job, and can morally make either decision, in terms of this analysis the manager has that freedom because the employee does not have a right which constrains the manager's freedom. This part of the analysis, then, concludes that under a rights and duties approach, managers are not morally prohibited from conducting layoffs.

Managers have duties by virtue of their positions as manager. Top managers have a duty to act in the best interests of their company and its stakeholders; a wealth of literature on agency theory analyzes the manager's role as an agent for the owners or stockholders of a company. In the extreme case that characterizes our first category, where layoffs provide the only means to save the company, one could argue that top managers have a duty to do what is best for the company, and that in this case conducting layoffs is best. This approach leads to the conclusion that managers sometimes have a duty to conduct layoffs, and that failure to act on this duty would be unethical.

It is considerably less clear whether managers have a duty to conduct layoffs to improve or to change their company. Because such attempts in the past have often failed to improve performance, it makes sense to ask whether managers have a duty to take steps that might fail. The discussion of rights and duties leads to the conclusion that managers have a right to conduct layoffs in these situations (since employees do not have an overriding right to keep their jobs); it is much harder to prove that they have a duty to do so. If they have a right to conduct layoffs to improve or change the company, then under this method of analysis, it would not be unethical to do so. Particularly in the case of layoffs to change the company, when performance is already good, it does not appear that a credible arguments can be made for a managerial duty to conduct lay-offs. . . .

Fairness, Justice, and Layoffs

. . . A philosophical approach tries to remove the level of analysis from what an individual perceives to be fair and just, and to prescribe some rules and guidelines that can be applied across many situations. Many philosophers, beginning with Plato discuss justice as involving a sense of proportion. The just reward for a heroic deed is greater than for a minor, inconsequential action. The punishment for murder is greater than for petty theft. An unjust consequence (reward or punishment) is one that is out of proportion to the action that triggers it. Justice, in most philosophical analyses, also involves a sense of consistency. If certain actions are judged worthy of reward or punishment, each person who performs the action should, in justice, receive the same reward or punishment. This idea is sometimes expressed in the statement that those similarly situated should receive similar treatment. . . .

Applying this analysis to the question of layoffs, it appears that a central question is that of the fairness to the laid-off employee. Since the employee has, by our earlier definition of the situation, performed well and done nothing to trigger termination, it does not appear that there is a proportion between the action (termination) and the preceding behavior (satisfactory performance). It also does not appear that the principle of consistency is followed, since some employees who have performed well lost their jobs, while others who have performed similarly remain employed.

An approach that is sometimes taken in the name of fairness is to lay off a certain percentage of employees "across the board." In practice, this means that each division or department or region must lay off some percentage of its employees. This does not solve the problem of fairness or consistency but merely shifts it to a lower level of decision-maker. Under this approach, the head of each unit must still decide which employees will keep their jobs and which will lose them. A disadvantage of this approach is that it disconnects layoff decisions from improving the company's performance, since it is rare that all units are equally overstaffed or equally important in their contribution to the company's overall performance.

Viewed from the perspective of the social system or the whole company, the discussion of fairness changes. In the extreme case, where failure to reduce labor costs by conducting layoffs results in the company's closing, all employees lose their jobs. . . .

As the cause for layoffs deviates from the clearcut case where they represent the only way to avoid the company's closing, the argument from fairness when the system is viewed as a whole becomes weaker. Layoffs taken as a proactive step to forestall problems management foresees are less clearcut but still defensible. If layoffs are conducted to increase the profits of an already profitable firm, it is unlikely that a person behind Rawls' veil of ignorance would consider the system allowing this to be just.

Would it be fair and just if the employees laid off were those with the least seniority or those who, while performing adequately, did not perform as well as others who retain their jobs? From the point of view of the system, seniority or merit present arguably consistent bases for deciding who loses their job and who keeps it. We should note, however, that relative seniority is much easier to establish than relative merit in performance. From the point of view of the individual, although these approaches attain some consistency, the problem of lack of proportion remains. . . .

Of the two approaches, merit would appear to be more defensible, since it ties the goal of layoffs (improved company performance) to the judgment of which individuals should suffer layoffs (those who contribute least to the company's performance). Seniority might be defensible if there is not sufficient evidence to use merit. The defense of seniority would lie in the fact that it is measurable and might be seen as a proxy for individual performance in the sense that employees with more experience will, in general, contribute more to the company's performance than those with less experience. . . .

The fairness and justice approach requires an emphasis on more than just the individual, who is the center of the rights and duties approach. Questions of fairness and justice address issues of proportion and consistency, but within a narrower setting than that addressed by the utilitarian approach. Of the three methods for ethical analysis, then, utilitarianism takes the widest view, considering the greatest good of the greatest number, whoever and wherever they might be. A major criticism of this approach is that it neglects important individual concerns. The rights and duties approach, as we have noted, centers on the individual, and looks out from the individual's rights to those on whom these rights impose duties. The fairness and justice approach considers both the individual and the social system within which he or she operates. The major focus of this approach is limited to a company or agency or possibly a community.

Comments and Conclusion

We have applied the three basic theories commonly used in managerial ethics to analyze the issue of the morality of layoffs. The views of these three basic theories generally coincide. In the extreme case where layoffs are the only way to save a company, the utilitarian approach finds the decision to conduct layoffs to be moral, because the layoffs generate the greatest good for the greatest number. The rights and duties approach sees the action of layoffs in the same situation to be moral because employees do not have absolute rights to their jobs. However, this view also requires that layoffs be conducted in a fair and just manner, because employees do have a right to be treated fairly. Finally, the justice and fairness approach, does not find layoffs to be moral, because they lack proportionality between the individual's behavior (good performance) and the resulting action (termination of employment). However, when the focus is changed from fairness to each individual to fairness in the total system, layoffs are justified—at least when the alternative is that all employees lose their jobs. Since all the individuals involved are part of the system, a reasonable argument can be made that the system view is the more appropriate one to be used here. Given that layoffs are to be conducted, this approach finds seniority or merit to be moral bases for determining who will lose jobs and who will keep them.

In the opposite extreme case, where layoffs are proposed in an attempt to change a company that is already performing well and does not appear to be in danger, none of the three approaches supports the conclusion that such layoffs are ethical. In this situation, the greatest good for the greatest number is not achieved. While employees do not have rights to their jobs, managers do not have a duty to conduct such layoffs. Finally, justice and fairness are not served. . . .

POSTSCRIPT

Is the Corporate Strategy of Downsizing Unethical?

Predicting the future is always difficult. However, when it comes to business, one thing seems certain: Global competition is here to stay and is likely to become even more intense in the foreseeable future. As a result, U.S. firms will continue to be exposed to intense competitive pressures from both domestic and international businesses. As a means of reacting to these pressures, we also expect downsizing to remain a popular strategic initiative for reducing labor costs and increasing organizational efficiency. But as the two articles in this debate make clear, the popularity of downsizing does nothing to address the basic moral question of whether or not downsizing is immoral.

Larry Gross argues that downsizing—under all conditions—is immoral. The basis of his view is that laying-off workers violates important aspects of the employer–employee relationship as well as ultimately harming society itself. There may be trouble with this view, however. Consider this observation by Frank Navran: "The truth is that unless an organization was designed expressly and overtly for the purpose, it is not in business to provide employment. Jobs are the by-product of successful organizational endeavors, not their intended output" ("The Ethics of Downsizing," *The Ethics Resource Center*, 1996). The first responsibility of an organization is, like that of an individual, to act in a manner that is life-sustaining. From this perspective, downsizing is not inherently unethical, despite Gross's protestations.

John Gilbert argues downsizing is not immoral in most instances, depending on the health of the organization at the time of the layoffs. According to Dr. Gilbert, the only time downsizing is unequivocally immoral is when the organization is profitable, its prospects for the future bright, and it chooses to reduce its workforce primarily to increase immediate profit levels. Critics might assert that this is the motivation behind the majority of layoffs by huge U.S. firms over the last twenty or so years. After all, giant corporations such as GE, IBM, and Merrill Lynch have never really been in danger of going out of business, but each has engaged in aggressive, large-scale downsizing initiatives. It's hard to believe that these actions were motivated by much more than keeping stock prices high and increasing overall shareholder wealth.

This is a topic that invites passionate responses on both sides of the debate. Hopefully, the articles presented here provided you with some insight about the topic and alternative ways in which to view and think about the morality of downsizing.

Suggested Readings

James K. Glassman, Thank you American business men. *American Enterprise Institute Magazine,* March 2000.

C. Jenkins, Downsizing or dumbsizing: The restructuring of corporate America. *Brigham Young Magazine,* 51, 1997.

V. Mabert and R. Schmenner, Assessing the roller coaster of downsizing. *Business Horizons*, 1997, issue 49, volume 4: pp. 45–53.

Ian Maitland, The upside of downsizing. *The Star Tribune,* 1996. www.startribune.com/stonline/html/special/leaky/mait07.html

Frank J. Navran, The ethics of downsizing. *Ethics Resource Center*, 1996, article ID #17. www.ethics.org

John Orlando, The fourth wave: The ethics of corporate downsizing. *Business Ethics Quarterly,* April 1999.

ISSUE 3

Is Bluffing During Negotiations Unethical?

YES: Chris Provis, from "Ethics, Deception and Labor Negotiation," *Journal of Business Ethics* (Kluwar Academic Publishers, The Netherlands, 2000)

NO: Fritz Allhoff, from "Business Bluffing Reconsidered," *Journal of Business Ethics* (Kluwar Academic Publishers, The Netherlands, 2003)

ISSUE SUMMARY

YES: Ethics scholar Chris Provis examines bluffing within the context of labor negotiations and concludes that it does indeed constitute unethical behavior. Bluffing, he argues, is deception and therefore unethical, regardless of whether it occurs in or out of the negotiation process.

NO: University of California, Santa Barbara philosopher Fritz Allhoff presents a clever and unique defense of bluffing in business negotiations. The central tenet in Allhoff's position is that certain roles that we are required to assume allow us to morally justify behaviors that might otherwise be considered immoral.

In 1968, business scholar Albert Carr published an article in the *Harvard Business Review* entitled, "Is business bluffing ethical?" In this paper, now a classic of its kind in the field of business ethics, Carr argued that "most bluffing in business might be regarded simply as game strategy—much like bluffing in poker, which does not reflect on the morality of the bluffer." He noted that in other areas of life we expect people not to always be truthful, and we typically do not condemn them for doing so. In criminal trials, for example, no one expects the accused to tell the truth when he claims his innocence. "Everyone from the judge down takes it for granted that the job of the defendant's attorney is to get his client off, not to reveal the truth; and this is considered ethical practice" (Carr, 1968). The essence of Carr's argument is based on his view that ethics of business are different from the ethics of morality or religion. Carr's article both reflected, and supported, the dominant perspective on the relationship between business and ethics at that time; namely, that business exists outside the normal bounds of ethical scrutiny. Therefore, behaviors such as bluffing—immoral in non-business settings—are "fair game" and not immoral in the business world.

Much has changed in the study and practice of business ethics since the publication of Carr's seminal article. The view that business is a human activity exempt from moral considerations no longer holds sway. The business scandals of the 1980s and 1990s focused much attention on corporate malfeasance and contributed mightily to the current intensive scrutiny of the behavior of American executives. Now, in the early part of the twenty-first century, the dominant view holds that corporations—and the executives who run them—have moral obligations to society beyond their traditional financial obligations to shareholders. Given the dramatic shift in how society views its relationship with the business community, it makes sense to ask whether attitudes toward bluffing in business transactions have changed as well. So, with that background, we present two articles with different answers to the question, is bluffing during business negotiations unethical?

Ethics scholar Chris Provis examines bluffing within the context of labor negotiations and concludes that it does indeed constitute unethical behavior. The basis of his analysis is the assertion that "other things being equal, it is wrong to deceive others or conceal information from them if doing so is likely to affect their actions and harm their interests." Bluffing, he argues, is deception and therefore unethical, regardless of whether it occurs in or out of the negotiation process. Thus, we are subject to the same degree of moral scrutiny in negotiations as we are in any other social interaction. "Negotiation," he writes, "is not a world set apart from our usual interactions with one another." Despite its rather simplistic charm, Provis's argument is not new. Many scholars past and present have rejected this analysis. So, to further bolster his position, he examines, and then rejects, the traditional arguments that the negotiation process, by its very nature, is a unique activity and cannot be subject to the same moral constraints as other forms of human behavior.

University of California, Santa Barbara philosopher Fritz Allhoff presents a clever and unique defense of bluffing in business negotiations. His argument rests on two very important papers supporting the legitimacy of bluffing: the afore-mentioned work of Albert Carr and a 1993 article by Thomas Carson. He examines the papers one at a time, pointing out the important points of each. And although he feels that both papers make positive contributions, he too concludes that both fail to convince the reader of the moral legitimacy of bluffing. Thus, the stage is set for Allhoff to present his unique argument.

The central tenet in Allhoff's position is that certain roles that we are required to assume "make acts permissible [or impermissible, or obligatory] that would otherwise be impermissible." He provides various non-business examples to show the validity of this "role-differentiated morality" before turning his attention back to bluffing in negotiations. As you read this article, do you accept his concept of role-differentiated morality? And if so, do you agree with his conclusion that bluffing is ethical?

YES

Ethics, Deception and Labor Negotiation

. . . There has been widespread emphasis on the importance of trust amongst parties to the employment relationship. Trust seems to be bound up with ethical action, but there is some question about what is ethical in bargaining, particularly where deception and bluffing are concerned. Because it is possible for cooperative bargainers to be exploited, some writers suggest that deceptive behavior is an established practice that is ethical and appropriate. There are several problems about that view. It is questionable how clear and uniform such a practice has been, even amongst experienced negotiators; in many cases an appearance of bluffing can be explained as exchange of concessions where claims were genuine but parties make sacrifices in order to reach agreement. . . . Deception cannot be justified as self-defense on the basis of a presumption that others will try to deceive us, since it is not reasonable to make a general presumption to that effect, and it is questionable to what extent bluffing and deception are necessary for self-defense, since there other techniques available by which parties can guard themselves against exploitation. Several factors explain why some writers endorse deception, including failure to make some important distinctions amongst different types of strategies.

Clearly, the discussion requires some basic assumptions about what is ethical and what is not. In particular, it is assumed here that other things being equal it is wrong to deceive others or conceal information from them if doing so is likely to affect their actions and harm their interests. There is room for further discussion of that assumption, but the following analysis is intended to pursue some of its implications rather than to defend it. The intention here is to suggest that negotiation is not somehow different, that we are subject to the same ethical constraints in negotiation as we are in other social interaction. Claims that negotiation is different are often based on claims about conventions and accepted practices and the need for self-protection, but those claims will be called into question. The view put here is that even though deception may sometimes be ethical (to prevent harm to others, perhaps), it is not especially so in negotiation. Negotiation is not a world set apart from our usual interactions with one another. . . .

From *Journal of Business Ethics*, Vol. 28, 2000, pp. 145–158. Copyright © 2000 by Kluwer Academic Journals. Reprinted by permission.

Deception, Bluffing and the Practices of Negotiation

It has been contended by some authors that there is an accepted practice of parties' bluffing when they state their "reservation prices": the least they will accept or the most they will yield. An example is Carr's article "Is Business Bluffing Ethical?", where he suggested that

> Most executives from time to time are almost compelled, in the interests of their companies or themselves, to practice some form of deception when negotiating with customers, dealers, labor unions, government officials, or even other departments of their companies. By conscious misstatements, concealment of pertinent facts, or exaggeration—in short, by bluffing—they seek to persuade others to agree with them.

Carson and his colleagues have written similarly that

> There can be no doubt that bluffing is an important bargaining tool. It can be employed to create impressions of enhanced strength as well as to probe the other party to find out the level of its critical sticking points.

"Bluffing" may seem a relatively innocuous tactic. Sometimes, the term may be used to refer just to exaggerated claims. However, it often goes beyond this to the case where a negotiator tries to convince the other party falsely that no further concessions can be made. Then, bluffing involves deception about what a bargainer is able or willing to accept, and there seems to be no clear line between that case and simple exaggerated claims, since sometimes it is just by exaggerated claims that a negotiator tries to produce a false impression. As Carr's statement implies, general acceptance of bluffing may be taken to imply acceptance of "conscious misstatements," "concealment of pertinent facts," "exaggeration" and presumably of other similar tactics. Many negotiators would think twice about some of these maneuvers. Nevertheless, bluffing is widely defended in academic literature. In fact, however, I shall argue that negotiators may bluff less often than many writers suggest: an appearance of bluffing sometimes results from the dynamics of concession exchange.

There can be no doubt that deception and bluffing are tactics which negotiators sometimes use. However, there is a question about how often they do so. It has been suggested that this is related to the degree of experience and sophistication of the negotiators. In his 1993 paper, Carson suggests that it is amongst "hardened and cynical negotiators" that statements about intentions or settlement preferences are not warranted to be true. Friedman and Shapiro say that "experienced labor negotiators expect that opponents will hide information and try to build up false perceptions about their limits and determination." They imply that MGB trainers may need to refrain from advocating openness and honesty because doing so can make them appear naïve.

It is certainly plausible that experienced negotiators are attuned to nuances in statements of position, and allow for them in what they say. As an example, we may take Ann Douglas' transcript of the Atlas case, where the mediator comments at one point "see—if you went in there now and started to talk about a 35-hour week, you're dealing with experienced negotiators and they'd m—immediately read something that might not be there." It is also plausible to suggest that experienced negotiators are discreet at the outset of a negotiation. Earlier in that transcript, professionals show great mirth at the story of an error made by the president of a company in disclosing the company's real position in a negotiation.

However, it is questionable to what extent these examples confirm that negotiators generally practice "deception." Neither sensitivity to what other negotiators may infer, nor discretion at the outset of negotiation, amounts to deceptive conduct, and there are other accounts which paint pictures of honesty. Dufty recounts the comment of a union official who referred to employer representatives as "four honest men who called a spade a spade and laid their cards on the table and got down to business." Douglas' Atlas transcript elsewhere suggests that professional negotiators may condemn deception and concealment: for example, the union negotiator at one point expresses concern and anger that in a previous negotiation his management counterparts gained an advantage by such tactics:

> They gave us the same business last time in here—in this same room, cried the blues all over the place . . . And immediately after the reopening negotiations were over, decentralization announcement is made in November. (Pause) So they're—they're in no position to give us that, "We're playin' nice and fair and square with you boys and girls."

Some well-known historical figures and some recent writers with wide experience of negotiation in other areas have advocated honesty rather than deception. Nyerges says that "honesty is unconditional" and that "a good negotiator should resist the temptation to be dishonest when dealing with a partner whose honesty is questionable." Williams reports a research project on the negotiating behavior of attorneys. It found that a significant majority used a cooperative approach rather than a competitive approach with an exaggerated opening position. There is evidence that while experienced negotiators may do better than naïve negotiators, that results not from deception or bluffing, but by their making more different proposals that they would find satisfactory. Overall, the actual behavior of negotiators does not present a clear, uniform picture. However, the evidence does suggest that deception is less consistent than often contended.

People's beliefs that deceptive behavior is widespread may be partly the result of a self-fulfilling prophecy. By acting deceptively in anticipation of deceptive behavior by others, we tend to elicit the sort of deceptive behavior we anticipate. This dynamic has been documented for competitive behavior in Prisoners' Dilemma situations in general, and it seems likely to apply to deceptive behavior in particular. We have noted that some experienced negotiators advocate honesty rather than deception, and this suggests that there is not a general practice of deception. However, the possibility of a self-fulfilling prophecy could explain why some people think there is.

Conventions, Practices and Concession Exchange

Even though those points cast some doubt on it, the idea persists that it is both usual and ethical to use tactics like bluffing, exaggeration and distortion. The idea that tactics like these are ethical is supported with the claim that in such negotiation "some statements are *expected* to be untrue while others are not." On this view, a union statement that it will not settle for less than a 5% wage increase might be acceptable because the management negotiators know that the true figure is something less, and the union negotiators intend them to know. Carr suggested that there is no lying, or no deception, in negotiation, because people are interpreting one another's statements differently than usual. He quotes British statesman Henry Taylor's comment that "falsehood ceases to be falsehood when it is understood on all sides that the truth is not expected to be spoken." A series of writers about negotiation have suggested that much of the deception that occurs is ethically sound because the deceptive statements in question are not taken seriously and are not expected to be.

Now it is true that inferences may depend on context, as well as on the way the negotiator makes the statement. There may be some negotiations where all parties are aware that others are not committed to the positions they are stating, just as people may not be committed to what they say in many other situations, ranging from jokes to role plays. But a number of writers generalize beyond that. Carson says that "it is not expected that one will speak truthfully about one's negotiating position," while Strudler claims that "at the outset of the negotiation, both parties would know that they can expect lies." He says that "deception is a signaling and symbolic device," and that "the conventions of deception are often clear."

However, it seems too strong to say that the conventions are clear, in labor relations at least. If I bluff by saying that 10% is as high as I can go, then as Carson and his colleagues suggest, "even if I don't *expect* you to believe that 10% is my final position, I probably still *hope* or intend to deceive you into thinking that I am unwilling to offer as much as 12%." Still, it could be that there was at least an accepted norm which permitted deception in negotiation, so that listeners would not make all the same inferences they might outside of the negotiation context. Carr rests his argument on the analogy with games like poker, where bluffing and deception are sanctioned by the rules of the game. The implication is that even though each party may really be trying to deceive the other, each also knows that the other party is trying to do that. On this view, bluffing and similar tactics are genuine efforts to mislead, but they are not unethical since other negotiators can be expected to anticipate them and will be on their guard accordingly.

Perhaps this sort of idea lies behind the contention by Carson and his colleagues that "no one familiar with standard negotiating practices is likely to take at face value statements which a person makes about a 'final offer.'" It could also be what Lewicki had in mind when he went so far as to suggest that

> In fact, bargainers are *expected* to bluff in negotiation; if they did not inflate their desired objective and make concessions toward that goal, they would be accused of bargaining "unfairly" . . .

Self-Defense, Fairness, and Alternatives to Deception

. . . The point can be stated as one about fairness. People commonly enter into games at which they have some capacity and skill. However, where wages and conditions are determined by negotiation, that is not a game that people can ignore. Haggling and bluffing in some voluntary bargaining over the price of a carpet in an oriental bazaar may be enjoyable and satisfying for both parties, particularly if they do have a shared understanding of what they are about, but the situation is different if they have no choice but to participate, if they are bargaining over their livelihood, and if one party has more skill or power than the other. In that situation, tactics of bluffing and deception may be quite unfair.

Dees and Cramton's point is too strong as a general proposition, that in the absence of trust and reciprocity one is entitled to use otherwise immoral practices. However, we may still be inclined to feel that because we expect bluffing and deceptive practices from others, we are entitled to protect ourselves, and that means trying to deceive them in turn. However, there remain two major difficulties with that view. First, it is not reasonable to presume that other negotiators always try to deceive us. Second, even where we are uncertain about others' honesty, there are other strategies for us to use in response than trying to deceive them.

As to the first point, we have already raised some questions about whether there is a general practice of attempted deception amongst negotiators, and those can be supplemented by some general considerations. There is evidence that "the disposition to employ deception as a tactic is influenced by a wide variety of factors." These factors include individual differences, the relationship between the parties, what is at stake, and so on. Since there are many factors that affect whether another party will try to deceive us, and since there are at least some occasions where the other party will try to be honest, it seems reasonable to suggest that there is an obligation on us to try to discern whether the other party is trying to deceive us on any particular occasion. There is evidence that individuals differ in their levels of generalized interpersonal trust, and at the same time it is clear that there are significant differences in negotiators' expectations of one another as a result of differences in linguistic background and cultural norms.

Since there are differences amongst individuals and situations, prudence suggests that we ought to take account of these detailed differences so far as we can, and ethical requirements point in the same direction. If we simply act on the basis of some blanket assumption that "people always do it," we run two risks: the risk of obtaining a less satisfactory agreement than we might otherwise, and the ethical risk that we may disadvantage another party who is being more frank and open than we realize. The overall implication is that we ought not act on any general assumption about others' lack of honesty or openness.

It is true, however, that we have only limited ability to detect others' attempts at deception. To decide quickly that the other is being honest can often carry significant risk. On the other hand, to be deceptive because of the mere possibility of deception by the other party may do them an injustice and may wreck any possibility of cooperation and trust. Is there a way out of that dilemma?

Fortunately, there are well-documented strategies that we can use to guard against deception by others without leaving ourselves too wide open. These tend to revolve around "indirect communication," including possibilities of fractional concessions and other indirect communication. Fractional concessions allow each party to take small initial risks which can grow into a process of reciprocal exchange resulting in agreement. A small concession may elicit one in return from the other party, by the process of 'reciprocity' mentioned above; this may allow another in response, and so on. Neither party risks a great deal more than the other at any particular point. Further, the concessions may have a communicative function. As well as inducing concessions in response, the willingness to make appropriate concessions can communicate willingness to cooperate, and information about one's interests and preferences. This can be supplemented by verbal interchange, and by other processes of indirect communication, which may include hints, non-verbal behavior and other "back-channel" communication. These can be used independently as well as in conjunction with concession exchange. Indirect communication allows each party to make offers or put suggestions which are ambiguous and therefore disavowable if the other does not respond, but which allow increasingly clear communication if both parties wish that to occur.

Conclusion

Indirect communication requires some experience and skill, and one implication is that for negotiation to be both ethical and effective parties may need to have appropriate skills as well as good intentions. The ability to send and comprehend quite subtle verbal and non-verbal messages may be an important part of the process, and lack of those skills can inhibit trust and cooperation just as much as dishonest intentions may. That fact may go together with others to help account for the idea that dishonesty and deception are widespread in negotiation. The theme of this paper is that deception and bluffing are less common in labor negotiations than is contended in some literature, that they ought to be considered less ethical than suggested by that literature, and that they are less necessary than implied in that literature.

In explaining why those views are held, the fact that a lack of communication skill can look like dissimulation goes part of the way to account for them. Processes of self-fulfilling prophecy may also help to explain those views: deceptive bargainers may elicit deceptive behavior in response to their own and so confirm their expectations. Another relevant factor is that the process of concession exchange can seem to be one in which parties move from false positions to real positions. A better account of the process recognizes that the parties are likely to have been making genuine exploratory claims which they then give up piece by piece in exchange for others doing so, in order to reach an agreement. Alternatively, it may be a process in which they clarify or revise their preferences. But in neither case need it involve deliberately misleading the other party.

Another part of the explanation why some writers report and endorse deceptive behavior may be a failure to make significant distinctions. "Bluffing," "concealment," "distortion," "deception," "conscious misstatements," "hiding information" and "lies" can be distinguished from actions that are often appropriate or necessary. If questioned by police, I may not lie to them, but I have a right to remain silent, and fundamentally the same distinction is available to negotiators. To decline to inform people about something is not necessarily to deceive them about it. How much a negotiator is obliged to tell another will depend on circumstances. For example, it may depend how the other party's interests are affected, and on their relative power. In many cases, we may be able to adopt the strategy Adler and Bigoness draw from Fisher and Ury, that "a principled negotiator need not disclose information or intentions so long as the negotiator makes clear that he or she is withholding information and is doing so for good reasons." Sometimes, there will be good reasons; sometimes, there will not. But there are much more likely to be good reasons for doing that than for lying or distortion.

There can be debate on how to apply some of the terms referred to above: for example, does "withholding information" amount to concealment? Does "bluffing" always involve deception, or only sometimes? It would be easy to become enmeshed in purely semantic disputes over matters like those. The answer may depend on details of the case. But it seems clear that not all of the dispute is a semantic one, and we can generalize to some extent. Strategies of "indirect communication" involve some withholding of information, but they do not involve "distortion," "deception" or "conscious misstatements." Negotiators who try deliberately to deceive others about their own intentions for the sake of pursuing their own advantage will generally be doing something unethical, even if they rationalize it as protecting themselves against possible exploitation, since there are usually other strategies of self-protection available. In practice there will be hard cases, as there are in many ethical matters. However, they can be made easier by taking care over detail, and not being misled by questionable ideas about how common deceptive practices are. Failure to analyze the various different sorts of tactics available can encourage behaviors which are unethical and which are inimical both to sound agreements and to good relationships between parties.

Fritz Allhoff

 **NO**

Business Bluffing Reconsidered

1. Introduction

Imagine that I walk into a car dealership and tell the salesperson that I absolutely cannot pay more than $10,000 for the car that I want. And imagine further she tells me that she absolutely cannot sell the car for less than $12,000. Assuming that neither one of us is telling the truth, we are bluffing about our reservation prices, the price above or below which we will no longer be willing to make the transaction. This is certainly a common practice and, moreover, is most likely minimally prudent—whether our negotiating adversary is bluffing or not, it will always be in our interest to bluff. Discussions of bluffing in business commonly invoke reservation prices, but need not; one could misrepresent his position in any number of areas including the financial health of a company poised for merger, the authority that has been granted to him by the parties that he represents, or even one's enthusiasm about a project. The goal of bluffing is quite simple: to enhance the strength of one's position during negotiations.

Bluffing has long been a topic of considerable interest to business ethicists.[1] On the one hand, bluffing seems to bear a strong resemblance to lying, and therefore might be thought to be *prima facie* impermissible. On the other, many people have the intuition that bluffing is an appropriate and morally permissible negotiating tactic. Given this tension, what is the moral standing of bluffing in business? The dominant position has been that it is permissible and work has therefore been done to show why the apparent impermissibility is either mismotivated or illusory. Two highly influential papers have taken different approaches to securing the moral legitimacy of bluffing. The first, by Albert Carr, argued that bluffing in business is analogous to bluffing in poker and therefore should not be thought to be impermissible insofar as it is part of the way that the game is played. The second, by Thomas Carson, presented a more subtle argument wherein the author reconstrued the concept of lying to require an implied warrantability of truth and, since business negotiations instantiate a context wherein claims are not warranted to be true, bluffing is not lying.

I think that both papers are on the right track to the solution to the problem, but that both authors' positions are problematic. In this paper, I will consider the arguments of both Carr and Carson, and I will present my criticisms of their ideas.

From *Journal of Business Ethics*, Vol. 45, 2003, pp. 283–289. Copyright © 2003 by Kluwer Academic Journals. Reprinted by permission.

Drawing off of their accounts, I will then develop my own argument as to why bluffing in business is morally permissible, which will be that bluffing is a practice that should be endorsed by all rational negotiators.

2. Albert Carr

Carr's article is somewhat informal and therefore lacks clear and rigorous argumentation. His thesis, however, is that business is a game, just like poker, and that bluffing is permitted under the rules of the game. To strengthen the analogy between business and poker, he points out that both business and poker have large elements of chance, that the winner is the one who plays with steady skill, and that ultimate victory in both requires knowledge of the rules, insight into the psychology of the other players, a bold front, self-discipline, and the ability to respond quickly and effectively to opportunities presented by chance.[2]

Even if we grant Carr that there are no morally relevant disanalogies between poker and business, which seems dubious, he still has a problem by trying to legitimize bluffing on the grounds that it is permitted by the rules of the game.[3] As Carson has pointed out, Carr seems somewhat confused as to how we determine the rules of the game.[4] In some passages, Carr seems to think that convention determines the rules, whereas in others he seems to think that the law delineates boundaries and all acts within those boundaries are permissible. Regardless, neither of these standards can help to establish the moral legitimacy of bluffing.

The reason is that either one of these moves would violate a long standing principle in moral philosophy, dating back to David Hume, that one cannot reason from what is the case to what ought to be the case.[5] There have been numerous conventions, such a discrimination, that have nevertheless been immoral. And there have also been numerous practices, such as slavery, that have been legally sanctioned but that are also immoral. Facts about the way that the society operates or about the way that the law is, can not be used to derive values. The two supports that Carr gives for the moral permissibility of bluffing are precisely the sorts of considerations that are patently disallowed in moral philosophy.

Carr hints at, but does not discuss, a potentially more promising notion, that of consent. Certainly bluffing in poker, and most likely bluffing in business, is a practice to which all involved parties consent, which is more than can be said for other conventions. But since the fact-value divide makes convention wholly irrelevant, consent would have to do the entirety of the work, and not merely be used to identify a special kind of convention. This is clearly not what Carr has in mind, and I do not propose to read it into his argument. Furthermore, I still do not think that consent alone establishes permissibility. Just as I may consensually enter a poker game knowing full well that bluffing might happen, I may consensually travel to a dangerous neighborhood knowing full well that a crime against me might happen. Since my consent in the latter case does not provide moral license for the act against me, consent can similarly not be used to legitimize bluffing in the former.

3. Thomas Carson

Carson approaches the problem from a different direction, though he arrives at more or less the same conclusion. His strategy is to deny that bluffing is a form of lying and, in order to make this argument, he takes issue with the conventional idea that lying is a false statement made with the intent to deceive and proposes instead that "a lie is a false statement which the 'speaker' does not believe to be true made in a context in which the speaker warrants the truth or what he says."[6] Bluffing is certainly lying on the traditional definition; the bluffer's statement is false and it is intended to deceive. But Carson thinks that his definition of lying excludes bluffing. Why? He argues that the second requirement, the warrantability of truth, is largely absent in negotiations. There are some claims made during negotiations that convention dictates to be warranted as true, such as claims to have another offer on the table. If I were to claim that I had another offer while I did not, this would be a lie because it would satisfy both parts of Carson's requirements. Claims about reservation prices, however, do not carry implied warrantability of truth—as a matter of fact, nobody *ever* takes such claims to be literally true. Carson therefore thinks that bluffing is not lying and should therefore not hold the moral disapprobations that we confer on lying.

There are, I think, two problems with Carson's defense of bluffing. The most obvious one is that, even if bluffing is not lying, it does not follow that it is morally permissible. It might be wrong for some other reason. For example, we might want to distinguish between lying and other kinds of deception which are still morally objectionable. Imagine that I leave my children home for the weekend and tell my oldest son that his girlfriend is not allowed in the house. If I call home to ask my younger son what my older son is doing and am told "he is talking to his friend Robert," this might be strictly and literally true only because his girlfriend is in the kitchen getting something to drink and is currently unavailable for conversation. The answer, though true and not a lie, is deceptive insofar as it masks a fact that my younger son knows to be salient. Or I might ask my older son directly whether his girlfriend is in the house and he truthfully answers no because she is still in transit to the house. Again, this answer is not a lie, but is deceptive. If we find such behavior morally objectionable, which many of us would, then the absence of lying alone does not secure moral license. And if it is not morally objectionable, some argument has to be given as to why; it certainly not intuitively obvious that all non-lying deceptions are morally permissible. Therefore, the most that Carson's argument can establish is that bluffing does not carry the same *prima facie* wrongness that lying does, not that it is morally permissible, which is his desired conclusion.

The second problem is that Carson's account still requires the same dependence convention that caused trouble for Carr. Carson admits that he will not pursue specific guidelines to determine whether a context involves implied warrantability of truth, but the examples that he gestures at are suggestive of conventionality playing a strong role.[7] For instance, he says that statements made in negotiations between experienced negotiators are understood to be not warranted as true. But this is only the case because it is a matter of convention; we could easily imagine another society wherein negotiators do not bluff, but are honest about their reservation prices. We have already seen why convention alone cannot provide any reason to think that a practice is morally permissible.[8] To say it another way, we can meaningfully ask whether a practice is morally permissible *despite* its being conventional. A defense of bluffing must extend beyond mere conventionality and into the realm of moral philosophy, else it is doomed to violate the fact-value divide.

4. Bluffing, Role-Differentiated Morality, and Endorsement

I will now develop what I think is the correct solution to the problem of bluffing in business. As I said earlier, I think that both Carr and Carson start off on the right track, but then go wrong for the reasons that I have presented.[9] In particular, both authors appeal to games in order to argue for the permissibility of bluffing in business; Carr uses a poker analogy and Carson argues that claims made during bluffing are similar to claims made during the game of Risk. But the problem that both authors have is that they infer moral legitimacy from the rules of their games, and this inference cannot be made. What we need is not an appeal to convention, but rather a moral argument that legitimizes bluffing within those games and that can be extended to bluffing in business.

One way that we could get this is to invoke what has become known as role-differentiated morality. Conventional wisdom within ethics has held that ethical rules are universal, and that everyone should be bound by the exact same moral laws. But work in professional ethics has recently come to challenge this idea.[10] These applications have come most auspiciously in legal ethics, where legal ethicists have often sought to defend ethically objectionable practices of lawyers (such as discrediting known truthful witnesses and/or enabling perjurious testimonies) on the grounds that the lawyer's role, that of zealous advocate, carries different moral rules than non-lawyer roles.[11] Though the applications have certainly been controversial, the underlying idea, role-differentiated morality, has garnered wide support.

Put simply, role-differentiated morality suggests the following three claims:

1. Certain roles make acts permissible that would otherwise be impermissible.
2. Certain roles make acts impermissible that would otherwise be permissible.
3. Certain roles make acts obligatory that would otherwise not be obligatory.

In this paper, I do not wish to provide an extended defense of the plausibility of role-differentiated morality; this has been done by other authors (including the two I cited above), and I do not feel that I have anything of value to add. What I will say in defense of the idea here is that it has tremendous intuitive resonance, as I think can be clearly shown through examples. In support of the first claim, we might say that soldiers fighting a just war are morally permitted to kill, whereas ordinary civilians are not. In support of the second claim, we could suggest that college professors should not have sexual relationships with their students (nor bosses with their subordinates), regardless of the act being consensual. In support of the third claim, we might claim that parents have special obligations to their children, such as providing for them and caring for them, that non-parents would not have towards the same child. I think the self-evidence of these examples gives strong support for the notion of role-differentiated morality.

Now, we can return to bluffing and ask whether some roles should allow for its moral permissibility.[12] I think that it is pretty clear that yes, some roles do allow for bluffing, while others definitely do not (though it remains, for now, an open question under which one bluffing in business falls). Some roles clearly do not morally permit bluffing. For example, consider a relationship between a husband and a wife. They have duties to each other to be honest and not to manipulate each other to secure advantages in negotiation. We might even want to say that negotiating, which is a necessary precondition for bluffing, is not the sort of activity in which husbands and wives should partake. Negotiating assumes conflicting aims of the negotiators and pits them against each other as adversaries, whereas husbands and wives should, ideally, share the same goals and cooperate. When disagreements do occur (such as on how much to pay for a new house), they should not negotiate against each other to determine their collective reservation price but rather should debate the issue and build a consensus as a unified front. I think that husband or wife is a role in which bluffing is not morally permissible,[13] but there are others, such as any fiduciary role wherein one is morally bound to be fully open with another.

There are, on the other hand, roles under which bluffing *is* morally permitted. Both Carr and Carson suggested that bluffing is permitted in games, and I think that they are exactly right. But they got the reason wrong, convention alone cannot deliver moral permissibility. Whatever justifies bluffing in these cases needs to have moral, rather than merely descriptive, force. I think that the key to these cases is that the players involved in the game actually *endorse* the practice of bluffing; people play these games for fun, and bluffing makes the games much more fun. If bluffing did not exist in poker, and everyone's bet merely reflected the strength of their hands, there would be no game at all since the final results would all be made apparent. Thus, insofar as anyone even wants to play poker in a meaningful way, he is committed to endorsing the practice of bluffing. Bluffing in Risk is similarly explained; bluffing adds an exciting (though in this case non-essential) element to the game to which players are attracted. If this were not the case, we would certainly expect a proliferation in strategy games in which there were no bluffing via diplomacy, and this is certainly not what we see. Bluffing, in some games, is a welcome feature in which participants actually want to be involved.

Is endorsement a moral feature? Absolutely. Imagine that my son takes $20 out of my wallet. There could be two scenarios leading up to this act. In one, he asks me for the money and I endorse his taking it (to pay the delivery-person for pizza, let's say) and, in the other, he does not ask and instead takes it without my permission. Obviously he acted permissibly in the first scenario and impermissibly in the second, and it was my approval, or endorsement, of his actions that is the *only* morally relevant difference. Therefore, endorsement carries with it the moral force to legitimize certain acts (or practices), and I think that it is precisely what is necessary to legitimize bluffing in games.[14]

I hope to have established both the plausibility of role-differentiated morality and that bluffing is permitted in some roles, but not in others. I can now return to my central aim and ask under which category bluffing in business falls. I think that bluffing in business is permissible for the same reason that it is permissible in games, namely that the participants endorse the practice. To explain why, let us return to the example with which I started. When I go to the car dealer with a reservation price of $12,000, what that means is that, all factors considered, that car has to me a utility marginally greater than the $12,000 does. *Ex hypothesi,* I am already willing to spend the $12,000; if that were the best that I could do, I would accept the offer. Any price that I can achieve below $12,000 would obviously be an improvement on the situation. Bluffing and negotiating are the mechanisms wherein I can achieve a final sale at a price beneath my reservation price and, insofar as any rational agent would welcome that end, he should also endorse its means.

Furthermore, other than bluffing, I cannot think of another reasonable procedure for the buyer to lower the sale price below my reservation price (or for the seller to raise the sale price above his reservation price). I might, for example, try to do so by force or threats, but these are obviously immoral. I might also make outright lies, such as to assert that the dealer across town has already guaranteed me a lower price. As Carson has already argued, this seems seriously immoral. So I think it is quite reasonable to suppose not only that the prospective buyer would endorse bluffing, but that there are no other reasonable alternatives.

One response to my position might be that bluffing does help the individual but that in negotiations there is not one, but two bluffers, and that the addition of the second cancels out all advantage to the first. Therefore, bluffing would should not actually be endorsed, since it yields no expected improvement, and maybe even eschewed on the grounds that it takes time and energy. However, I do not see how the addition of another bluffer really changes anything. If the car dealer will go as low as $10,000 and I will pay as high as $12,000, then we would both agree to (and, *ex hypothesi,* be happy with) any transaction at any price between and including $10,000 and $12,000. Assuming that the reservation price of the buyer is higher than the reservation price of the seller, the issue is not whether the two parties will come to mutually agreeable terms, the question is just what those terms will be. Ideally, each party would like to be able to bluff while having his opponent's position be transparent, but since that is obviously not a possibility, both should welcome bluffing as an opportunity to improve their positions.

It is also interesting to note that, without bluffing, the idea of negotiations itself almost (though not quite) becomes incoherent. Suppose that bluffing were not practiced, but that parties merely met and announced their respective reservation prices. I tell the car dealer that I will give him $12,000 for the car and she tells me that he will take as little as $10,000 for the car. Now what? I do not even know how to settle on a transaction price other than to do something arbitrary such as splitting the reservation window in half and settling at $11,000. This seems like the wrong answer for a number of reasons. Such resolutions could be inefficient (i.e. not Pareto optimal), not utilitarian, unfair to those who negotiate well, etc.[15] Negotiating is, I think, an essential part of business. To reach a transaction price, it makes the most sense for the buyer to start low and the seller high, and to reach some agreement in the middle. By announcing reservation prices, we would be creating a system that I find less attractive and, furthermore, would give the participants every reason to transgress and to bluff.

Finally, I think that there really is a lot of merit in the analogies between business negotiating and games (despite the criticisms by Koehn and others). But I would go further than claiming that it is *like* a game, it seems to me that it *is* a game. Perhaps this is not true in the sense that negotiators are drawn to their work because they find it amusing, this is false in a wide number of cases and I certainly do not mean to trivialize many serious negotiations. But if two parties come to the negotiating table and the reservation price of the buyer is higher than the reservation price of the seller, then we already know that, *ceteris paribus*, the transaction will occur and, furthermore, it will occur at a price to which both parties are amenable. It seems to me that the occurrence of the transaction and the satisfaction of the parties is what is really important, where the price falls within the reservation window just determines what each party gains (in terms of money not spent or extra money earned) *in addition to* a mutually beneficial transaction. Whether the stakes are millions of dollars or not, the parties are still merely trying to secure money that they would otherwise be satisfied without.

Notes

1. The first important paper was Albert Carr's "Is Business Bluffing Ethical?" *Harvard Business Review* January/February 1968, pp. 143–153. John Beach later reflects upon the treatment that the topic received in the years since Carr's publication (though Beach is somewhat critical of this response). See his "Bluffing: Its Demise as a Subject unto Itself," *Journal of Business Ethics* 4 (1985), pp. 191–196. Then, Thomas Carson reconsiders Carr's classic treatment of the subject and proposes an alternative conception of business bluffing; see "Second Thoughts about Bluffing," *Business Ethics Quarterly* 3(4) (1993), pp. 317–341. There are also numerous other examples within the literature, though I take these to be the most important.

2. Carr (1968), p. 72.

3. Daryl Koehn has, for example, argued that the analogy between business and poker is quite weak; he takes nine features that exist in games and argues that few, if any, of these exist in business. For the sake of argument, I am willing to grant Carr's analogy; I think that, even with this analogy, he is unable to secure the conclusion that he desires. See Koehn's "Business and Game-Playing: The False Analogy," *Journal of Business Ethics* **16** (1997), pp. 1447–1452. Norman Bowie also argued against the legitimacy of adversarial models (such as poker) as proper characterizations of bargaining and negotiating. See his "Should Collective Bargaining and Labor Relations Be Less Adversarial?." *Journal of Business Ethics* 4 (1985) 283–291. Robert S. Adler and William J. Bigoness also challenge adversarial models in their work and find Carr's poker analogy to

be flawed. See "Contemporary Ethical Issues in Labor-Management Issues in Labor-Management Relations," *Journal of Business Ethics* **11** (1992), pp. 351–360.

4. Carson (1993), 324–325.

5. *A Treatise of Human Nature,* ed. P. H. Nidditch, 2nd ed. (Oxford: Oxford University Press, 1978) III.I.i.

6. Carson (1993), p. 320. I assume that speaker is placed in scare quotes in order to allow for the possibility of non-verbal lying, such as when someone gives false directions by pointing in the wrong direction without saying anything. This definition results partly from earlier work by Carson and a criticism that he consequently received from Gary Jones. To trace through this, start with Thomas Carson, Richard Wokutch, and James Cox's "An Ethical Analysis of Deception in Advertising," *Journal of Business Ethics* **4** (1985), pp. 93–104. Jones's criticism can be found in "Lying and Intentions," *Journal of Business Ethics* **5** (1986) 347–349. And, finally, Carson's response is in "On the Definition of Lying: A reply to Jones and Revisions," *Journal of Business Ethics* **7** (1988), pp. 509–514.

7. Carson (1993), pp. 321–322.

8. And, in an interesting recent article, Chris Provis argues that bluffing (or, more precisely, deception) is not as ubiquitous in business as everyone often assumes; he thinks that the appearance of bluffing can often be accounted for by genuine concessions. If Provis is correct, then Carson's reliance on conventionality is empirically flawed. Or, as I argue, the reliance on convention is conceptually flawed (in order to secure moral permissibility). So, either way, the approach will not work. See Provis's "Ethics, Deception, and Labor Negotiation," *Journal of Business Ethics* **28**(2) (2000), pp. 145–158.

9. As I have indicated, other authors have also criticized the two approaches. What I have tried to do however, is be as charitable as possible: to grant all of their assumptions (the analogies, the adversarial nature of negotiating, Carson's definition of lying, etc.) and then aspired to show that they still cannot, even on their own terms, secure their desired conclusions.

10. An especially good and influential article is Richard Wassterstrom's "Lawyer's as Professionals: Some Moral Issues," *Human Rights Quarterly* **5**(1) (1975).

11. Monroc H. Freedman, "Professional Responsibility of the Criminal Defense Lawyer: The Three Hardest Questions," *Michigan Law Review* **27** (1966).

12. This step of my argument might be overly pedantic, and I might fare just as well if I skipped it and went directly to arguing for bluffing in business contexts specifically. However, I do think that it is an important part of the conceptual framework that I want to establish.

13. This is obviously not to say that husbands or wives cannot bluff in business situations, just that a husband cannot bluff *qua* husband nor a wife *qua* wife. The husband or wife who bluffs in business is not bluffing *qua* husband or *qua* wife, but rather *qua* businessperson.

14. John Rawls has argued that it is not morally permissible sell oneself into slavery (i.e., *even if* I endorsed the sale, it is still immoral). See his *Theory of Justice* (Cambridge: Harvard University Press, 1971). This poses an interesting objection to my idea that endorsement alone suggests *prima facie* permissibility. There are two ways that I could respond. First, I could disagree with Rawls and argue that any decision made by free and rational agents should be honored (so long as it did not harm others), that to do otherwise would show lack of respect for the being's rational nature. I am personally inclined towards this view, though I know that many are not. The other way that I could go would be to argue that Rawls' point merely indicates that people cannot voluntarily give up their rights and that consenting to being bluffed is not problematic

since we do not have the moral right to be told the truth. I think that either of these responses could be profitably developed, though I will not do so here.

15. The "Split-the-Difference" theory of negotiating is discussed by Roger Bowlby and William Schriver in their "Bluffing and the 'Split-the-Difference' Theory of Wage Bargaining," *Industrial and Labor Relations Review* **31**(2) (January 1978), pp. 161–171. Their discussion, however, is quite empirical and numerical rather than normative.

References

Adler, R. S. and W. J. Bigoness: 1992, 'Contemporary Ethical Issues in Labor-Management Relations,' *Journal of Business Ethics* **11**.

Beach, J.: 1985, '"Bluffing" its Demise as a Subject unto Itself,' *Journal of Business Ethics* **4**.

Bowie, N. E.: 1985, 'Should Collective Bargaining and Labor Relations Be Less Adversarial?,' *Journal of Business Ethics* **4**.

Bowlby, R. L. and W. R. Schriver: 1978, 'Bluffing and the "Split-the-Difference" Theory of Wage Bargaining,' *Industrial and Labor Relations Review* **31**(2).

Carr, A.: 1968, 'Is Business Bluffing Ethical?' *Harvard Business Review* (January/February).

Carson, T. L.: 1993, 'Second Thoughts about Bluffing,' *Journal of Business Ethics* **3**(4).

Carson, T. L.: 1988, 'On the Definitions of Lying: A Reply to Jones and Revisions,' *Journal of Business Ethics* **7**.

Carson, T. L., R. E. Wokutch and J. E. Cox, Jr.: 1985. 'An Ethical Analysis of Deception in Advertising,' *Journal of Business Ethics* **4**.

Freedman, M.: 1966, 'Professional Responsibility of the Criminal Defense Lawyer: The Three Hardest Questions,' *Michigan Law Review* **27**.

Hume, D.: 1978, *A Treatise of Human Nature* (2nd ed.). P. H. Nidditch (ed.). (Oxford University Press, Oxford).

Jones, G. E.: 1986, 'Lying and Intentions,' *Journal of Business Ethics* **5**.

Koehn, D.: 1997, 'Business and Game-Playing: The False Analogy,' *Journal of Business Ethics* **16**.

Post, F. R.: 1990. 'Collaborative Collective Bargaining: Toward an Ethically Defensible Approach to Labor Negotiations,' *Journal of Business Ethics* **9**.

Provis, C.: 2000. 'Ethics, Deception, and Labor Negotiation,' *Journal of Business Ethics* **28**.

Rawls, J.: 1971. *A Theory of Justice* (Harvard University Press, Cambridge).

Wasserstrom, R.: 1975, 'Lawyer's as Professionals: Some Moral Issues,' *Human Rights Quarterly* **5**(1).

POSTSCRIPT

Is Bluffing During Negotiations Unethical?

One of the central questions inherent in the business negotiation process concerns the morality of using deception (i.e., bluffing) as a means of achieving one's goals. The traditionally accepted view held that business is an activity akin to a game and, as such, is played according to its own set of rules. From this perspective, bluffing during negotiations not only falls within the rules of the game, but constitutes accepted, reasonable behavior as well. In recent years, however, the belief that business plays by a different set of rules from the rest of society has been overthrown and replaced with a new perspective. The dominant viewpoint now demands much greater corporate responsibility and accountability to society on the part of executives and their firms. Managerial behavior is subject to much greater moral scrutiny now than at any other time in American history. It's not surprising, then, that the moral legitimacy of bluffing as a common business behavior has come under question in recent years.

The first of the two articles presented here argued that the original justifications for the moral legitimacy of bluffing are deficient. Scholar Chris Provis, in his reassessment of the long-standing dominant viewpoint, rejects the suggestion that business is analogous to a game in which the rules not only allow, but encourage, bluffing as a legitimate behavior. He also rejects the contention that bluffing is necessary as a form of negotiating self-defense: If I don't bluff, I'll be at a major disadvantage since my opponents will. As you read Provis's article, did you find his arguments to be persuasive?

In the second article, philosopher Fritz Allhoff argues that bluffing is morally permissible when individuals are acting in certain roles, such as a negotiator. He also contends that reasonable people will want to allow for bluffing in the negotiation process. Indeed, he states that without bluffing, "the idea of negotiations itself almost (though not quite) becomes incoherent." How about Allhoff's clever attempt at justifying bluffing? Do you feel his argument is sound?

Suggested Readings

Albert Carr, Is business bluffing ethical? *Harvard Business Review,* January/ February, 1968.

Thomas L. Carson, Second thoughts about bluffing. *Journal of Business Ethics*, vol. 3, no. 4, 1993.

T. L. Carson, R. E. Wokutch, and J. E. Cox Jr., An ethical analysis of deception in advertising. *Journal of Business Ethics*, vol. 4, 1985.

F. Flores and R. C. Solomon, Creating trust. *Business Ethics Quarterly*, vol. 8, no. 2, pp. 205–32, 1998.

F. R. Post, Collaborative collective bargaining: Toward an ethically defensible approach to labor negotiations. *Journal of Business Ethics*, vol. 9, 1990.

ISSUE 4

Should Insider Trading Be Legalized?

YES: Robert B. Thompson, from "Insider Trading, Investor Harm, and Executive Compensation," *Case Western Reserve Law Review* (Winter 1999)

NO: Stephen Bainbridge, from "Why Regulate Insider Trading?" *Tech Central Station* (September 8, 2004)

ISSUE SUMMARY

YES: Legal scholar Robert B. Thompson presents Manne's argument on insider regulation. Thompson then provides us with an analysis of the status and relevance of Manne's position three decades after the publication of his seminal text.

NO: UCLA professor of law Stephen Bainbridge does not accept Manne's arguments. Bainbridge believes that insider trading ultimately causes inefficiency in the markets and, therefore, must be subject to regulation.

In October 2004, domestic diva and multimillionaire Martha Stewart began serving her prison sentence for obstructing justice during an investigation into alleged insider trading activities. Although Stewart was not convicted of insider trading, her trial, and the investigation that preceded it, placed the topic of insider trading on the front of business publications and newspapers across America. Interestingly, a number of observers—typically those defending Stewart—questioned whether insider trading should be considered a criminal activity in the first place. And, although the Stewart case drew much attention to the topic in the public domain, the regulation of insider trading has received considerable attention in the academic and legal professions in recent years. Indeed, since 1997, legal commentaries have seen print at the rate of about one per month.

The first systematic justification for regulating insider trading is typically attributed to the work of H. L. Wilgus in 1910. Wilgus, a legal scholar, argued from an appeal to fairness and morality perspective. In an article published in the *Michigan Law Review,* he concluded that insider trading was morally distasteful (Jonathan R. Macy, "Securities Trading: A Contractual Perspective," *Case Western Reserve Law Review*, Winter 1999) Wilgus's writings first drew attention to the topic of insider trading; shortly thereafter, other legal scholars joined him in condemning the action in moral terms. (*Note:* Insider trading, as we know it today, was not illegal at this time.)

The move to regulate insider trading gained momentum in the aftermath of the stock market crash of 1929 and the depression that immediately followed. The public increasingly viewed governmental intervention as a necessary step in order to safeguard investors and restore public confidence in the securities markets. The views of Wilgus and others like-minded found fertile ground during the congressional hearings held in 1933 and 1934. These hearings ultimately led to the Securities Act of 1933 and the Securities Exchange Act of 1934, both of which contained provisions outlawing insider trading. These provisions were justified on two grounds, both of which were promulgated and defended by Wilgus and his supporters. The first defense is that insider trading is an abuse of information because the individual uses, for personal gain, information intended strictly for corporate ends. The second justification argues that it is inherently unfair for an individual to act on information he or she has access to but those with whom he or she is dealing does not (the general public, for example, when the insider is buying or selling stock).

The dominant view that insider trading is immoral and should, therefore, be subject to regulation went unchallenged until the publication of two seminal works by Henry Manne in 1966. Manne, now dean emeritus of the George Mason University School of Law, astounded the legal profession, the securities industry, and the federal government with the publication of his book, *Insider Trading and the Stock Market.* Drawing on work in economics and employing a property rights–based perspective, Manne's highly analytical approach argued for the abolition of insider trading laws. In so doing, he noted that, among other things, the congressional hearings of 1933 and 1934 "resulted in the practical adoption of many of the ideas of Wilgus and Bearle [an important legal scholar of the time] without any concrete explanation for their blanket acceptance" (Macey, 2004, p. 269). Manne's desire to examine the ideas of Wilgus played to a wider audience—solidified his position as the most important and serious critic of insider regulation—when he published *In Defense of Insider Trading* in the *Harvard Business Review* later that same year.

The following selections provide us with two different reponses to the question, should insider trading be legalized? The "yes" article is by legal scholar Robert B. Thompson, who distills Manne's argument into three main attacks on insider regulation. Thompson then provides us with an analysis of the status and relevance of Manne's position three decades after the publication of his seminal text. UCLA professor of law Stephen Bainbridge also addresses Manne's position. But while Thompson concludes that Manne's position is still very much valid today, Bainbridge cannot accept his arguments. Bainbridge, in direct contrast with Manne, believes that insider trading ultimately causes inefficiency in the markets and, thus, must be subject to regulation.

YES

Robert B. Thompson

Insider Trading, Investor Harm, and Executive Compensation

The core questions in most law school classes change little from year to year even as the contexts in which those questions are raised and the answers which are provided sometimes move dramatically to reflect cutting-edge adaptations and changing regulatory policy. Insider trading has been one of those core questions in corporate and securities law since the early 1960s when the Securities and Exchange Commission's decision in In re Cady, Roberts & Co.[1] propelled Rule 10b-5 into the center of the debate over the regulation of such conduct. With the publication of Henry Manne's book Insider Trading and the Stock Market five years later defending this practice,[2] the issue was joined in a way that still shapes how courts and writers frame the topic. This essay addresses insider trading at the turn of the century by looking at three key assertions from Manne's 1966 book: (1) there is no coherent theory explaining regulation of insider trading;[3] (2) there is no significant injury to corporate investors from insider trading;[4] and (3) insider trading constitutes the most appropriate device for compensating entrepreneurs in large corporations.[5] Each of the parts which follow this introduction identifies the underlying premise for each assertion, the flourish with which Dean Manne presented it, the extent to which it has shaped debate over the last thirty-three years, and its place in the current discussion.

I. The Absence of a Coherent Theory

Manne's book opens with chapters devoted to the assertion that "in the literature on insider trading almost no careful analysis of the subject exists."[6] In discussing the traditional legal approach and opinions from courts, commentators, and legislative hearings, Dean Manne's language was somewhat mild compared to the other topics addressed later in the book and he was ecumenical in suggesting that arguments on both sides were "disappointing"[7] and "conclusionary."[8] His underlying premise was that the existing doctrines based on morality or "it's just not right" provided no foundation for determining regulation of insider trading, but that economic analysis could.[9]

On this point Jon Macey's opening paragraph. "The same, of course, is true today"[10] is very apt. Commentators regularly assail the incoherence of the law of insider trading[11] terming it problematic,[12] if not "seriously flawed."[13]

From *Case Western Reserve Law Review*, Vol. 50, No. 2, Winter 1999, pp. 291–304. Copyright © 1999 by Case Western Reserve Law Review. Reprinted by permission.

Since the Supreme Court's 1997 decision in United States v. O'Hagan,[14] legal commentaries have been appearing at an average of around one a month.[15] As summarized by former SEC commissioner Roberta Karmel, "despite the large number of articles discussing insider trading, a general consensus among commentators has not developed as to why insider trading is unlawful."[16]. . . .

It seems fair to say that after almost forty years of judicial and academic efforts to develop a coherent theory to explain federal insider trading regulation, the literature is no more coherent than it was in 1966.

II. Shareholders as a Whole Are Not Hurt by Insider Trading

The second assertion, the focus of the middle part of Manne's book, is that no significant injury to corporate investors results from insider trading.[17] The subtext here is one of efficiency of markets.[18] Insider trading makes the market more efficient by moving the price in the right direction. An event or information that alters the value of the company and its stock will create a gap between the stock's current value and what it will trade for once the market has incorporated the new information.

Time-function traders, whose trading decisions are based on reasons beyond a change in price, benefit by receiving a better price as compared to what they would have received absent the insider trading. The premise is that they would have traded anyway (and before the disclosure of the new information and the accompanying change in price), and therefore would have absorbed the entire gap related to the change in value. The time-function trader benefits by whatever amount toward the new price the insider trader causes the price to move.

In contrast, price-function traders, whose trading decisions are motivated by a change in price, can be disadvantaged as compared to where they would have been absent the insider trading. Absent the change in price caused by the insider trader entering the market, the price-function traders would not have traded and presumably still would have had their shares when the information was later announced and the price changed in response to that announcement. If this group is further segmented to focus on long-term investors rather than short-swing traders, and the lens is widened to focus on all such traders over time and not just those in a particular stock and a particular time, the magnitude of the loss defined this way gets considerably smaller. Indeed, Dean Manne does not hold back in how he describes this risk: "de minimis . . . almost infinitesimally small . . . [and] so small as to be unworthy of serious concern."[19]

On this point, the impact of Manne's work is substantial. The challenge to show investor harm has been difficult and complex.[20] Despite explicit congressional action authorizing a cause of action for those who trade contemporaneously with an insider,[21] private enforcement of insider trading is small and the heavy lifting has been left to the SEC and the Justice Department. Professor Donald Langevoort has concluded that the addition of section 20A to the Securities Exchange Act of 1934 makes "private rights of action by marketplace traders something of relatively small practical importance in the world of insider trading enforcement."[22]

In the wake of the Private Securities Litigation Reform Act of 1995,[23] private actions for insider trading have taken on more importance as allegations of that conduct commonly are used as a way to meet the heightened pleading standards now required for securities class actions.[24] Insider trading is one of the two most common factors cited in securities class action complaints as evidence of particularized facts necessary for a pleading to survive the heightened standards required by the 1995 Act.[25] Yet, that statistic overstates the importance of private action for insider trading. Plaintiffs usually seek to use insider trading by individuals to reach not the traders, but the corporation that made false or incomplete disclosures. Based on data in the Stanford Securities Class Action Clearinghouse database, less than 10% of the cases alleging insider trading include a count seeking private relief under section 20A.[26] The thirty-seven complaints in the database as of June, 1999 that include a count based on section 20A reduce to only fifteen transactions because of multiple filings; there was no indication of recovery by that date for any of those lawsuits.[27]

There appears to be little, if any, overlap between those private cases and the insider cases brought by the government, which average around fifty per year.[28] Of the fifteen companies for which insider trading was alleged as part of a securities class action, all but one allege selling after inaccurate reports or that bad news was withheld or covered up.[29] For the government suits, the dominant setting is trading on the basis of good news, such as in advance of tender offers.[30] It may be that enforcement of insider trading might evolve into a division of responsibility with indirect private enforcement taking a stronger relative role where the insider's action is to cover up bad news. It is more likely that the relative unimportance of private enforcement in insider trading will continue.

Given the lack of observable direct insider trading harm to individual traders, the debate over insider trading has moved in a different direction. Professors Jon Macey and David Haddock adapted the S graphs from the middle portion of the Manne book to illustrate that direct costs of insider trading are borne first by market professionals and then passed along to market participants through higher spreads and trading costs.[31] They pursued this to a public choice explanation of regulation. Michael Dooley's work suggests similar conclusions,[32] as do Dean Manne's later writings about the SEC.[33]

The Supreme Court's current approach to insider trading regulation takes yet another approach to investor harm. In O'Hagan, there is no mention of individual harm in specific transactions. Rather, the focus is on harm from a decrease in public confidence in the market. This could be related to the harm to price function traders that was explicitly part of Manne's economic calculation. He discussed price function traders who might not otherwise have traded but who are induced to trade by the price effect from insider trading that moves the price off what the price function traders otherwise thought was the correct market price. The O'Hagan reasoning assumes traders will be pushed in the opposite direction—to put their money in a mattress or at least be less inclined to trade because of insider trading.[34] The focus, however, is not on the harm incurred from the foregone trade; such claims would not be easily susceptible to proof and would be difficult to calculate under the usual measures of damages. Instead of identifying individual loss in a specific transaction, the harm is the loss of market confidence and resulting loss of liquidity in the market generally.[35]

Dean Manne took on the investor confidence argument in his response to the critics of his book. He pointed to evidence in the 1920s and thereafter that "the public has never shown any signs of losing confidence in the stock market because of the existence of insider trading."[36] But it is difficult to separate and empirically test factors that would show such a connection. For example, similar national regimes under which one country banned insider trading and the other did not, or findings on liquidity before and after a change in the regulation of insider trading, cannot be easily isolated from other factors so as to observe the effect of insider trading. In the face of such challenges, with harm being so diffuse and difficult to measure, economics loses some of its relative advantage to politics as an explanatory tool for why we have government regulation.

In such a setting, understanding regulation may require not just the rational choice economics that is at the core of Manne's work, but also the learning of behavioral economics and cognitive psychology. Even if there is no loss or little individual effect as a result of insider trading, investors may still want the conduct regulated. There may be a parallel to preferences revealed in various experimental settings of the ultimatum game. In the ultimatum game, two parties are given a sum of money to divide. One of the parties is to propose the division; the other can then choose either to accept or reject. If accepted, the parties get to keep the proceeds as divided; if rejected, neither gets anything. Traditional rational choice economics and game theories based on similar assumptions of self-interested behavior would predict a small amount to be offered to the second party (so that the second party would be better off than if there were no transaction) but the disproportionate portion to the first party. Instead of such a split, many experiments find "offers typically average about 30–40 percent of the total, with a 50–50 split often the mode. Offers of less than 20 percent are frequently rejected."[37] Thus in some settings, players depart from the equilibrium predicted by rational self-interest and instead propose a division that is closer to equal sharing.[38] Similarly, shareholders may prefer to limit insider trading even if the harm is not immediately visible. Part of the attraction of the investor confidence argument for insider trading is likely a manifestation of the choices said to be evidenced by the outcome of the ultimatum game.

III. Insider Trading As Executive Compensation

The third assertion, and the one that provoked most of the uproar in the 1960s, was that insider trading constitutes the most appropriate device for compensating entrepreneurs in the large corporation. Again, Professor Macey has captured the underlying core of Manne's contribution and how it focused the debate on insider trading as a matter of intra-firm contract and private ordering; what Macey terms "an applied executive compensation problem."[39] Manne's description was a bit more dramatic, asserting that insider trading "may be fundamental to the survival of our corporate system"[40] and that those pressing for a rule banning insider trading "may inadvertently be tampering with one of the wellsprings of American prosperity."[41]

On this assertion, Manne's analysis has not changed the legal result. Our corporate system has both survived and prospered in the last third of the twentieth century even as insider trading has become more regulated. The rest of the world has moved more in the direction of regulating insider trading rather than away from it.[42]

The executive compensation aspect has faltered in part because there has not been widespread acceptance of Manne's assertion that:

> Information is not a free good, and we should not assume, without more information than we now possess, that its distribution is generally capricious, arbitrary, random, or uncontrolled. Rational, self-serving individuals will not blithely and willingly allow information of tremendous value to pass freely to individuals who have no valid claim upon it. The safer assumption is that individuals with the power to control the flow of valuable information do so rationally and allocate it in a market-like system of exchange. . . .[43]

Yet except perhaps for Raymond Dirks, who was an entrepreneur of sorts and for whom the Supreme Court found no legal liability,[44] the defendants in the visible insider trading cases have not been entrepreneurs—the group for whom the compensation was seen as necessary. More illustrative is the lawyer, James O'Hagan, for whom takeover information provided a needed source of funds,[45] or Keith Loeb in the Chestman case,[46] two generations and one marriage removed from the entrepreneur. Despite Manne's recognition of leakage within the rational economic model,[47] and despite the possible distortions of the defendant pool because we no longer have a basis to test a control group in which insider trading is permitted,[48] the dominance of defendants like O'Hagan and Loeb continue to act as a drag on Manne's executive compensation argument.

More fundamentally, executive compensation has changed in a way that makes this prong of the insider trading argument less compelling. At the time of writing his book in 1966, Manne based part of his assertion for insider trading as executive compensation on his comparative analysis of the various alternatives for compensating entrepreneurs. Salary, bonus, profit-sharing plans, and stock options failed to meet the conditions for appropriately compensating entrepreneurs. Since 1966, changes in insider compensation have come closer to filling the need that Manne described. Not only has there been growth in executive compensation generally, but there is a richer array of forms that are regularly used.[49] The experience of venture capital financing has produced compensation agreements aimed directly at compensating start-up entrepreneurs and balancing their return with others who contribute to the enterprise. Options need not require that money already be invested, as concerned Manne in 1966, and there is a greater willingness to make differential awards that permit payment for entrepreneurial services.[50]

These various forms of compensation have some advantages over insider trading as entrepreneurial compensation. First, they seem less likely to reward the wrong people. Defining the target group is direct, although not perfect; information leakage is less likely. Second, this compensation is not secret, which makes it easier to monitor. The Securities and Exchange Commission requires extensive periodic disclosure of executive compensation for all public companies and also when companies are selling securities;[51] disclosure that was enhanced by extensive changes made in 1992.[52] In addition, these other forms of compensation typically require a corporate governance process prior to their initial availability, such as action by the directors or shareholders,[53] as opposed to insider trading, which is triggered by the insider's actions. Compensation is often a volatile issue and has been so for much of this century.[54] Currently, executive compensation is higher than in past periods,[55] and higher in the United States than in other countries.[56] In that setting, the disclosure and governance framework that governs non-insider trading compensation likely has a comparative advantage as compared to insider trading as compensation.

IV. Conclusion

The three central assumptions that Henry Manne used to present his defense of insider trading in 1966 remain as relevant signposts in the debate over regulation more than three decades later. There still is no coherent analytical approach to this topic, although we have been through several, sometimes-conflicting approaches during that period. Economics, particularly the property rights approach that flowed from Manne's work, has contributed to a richer understanding of insider trading and became especially influential in judicial doctrine at the beginning of this decade. To date, there has been no effective answer to the lack of investor harm as defined by Manne. Instead, the focus has shifted back to the larger and more amorphous harm to collective investors. Manne's two challenges to defects in the then-existing attacks on insider trading have fared better than the positive justification put forward for permitting insider trading. The argument that executive compensation in the form of insider trading is needed to facilitate entrepreneurial activity was a difficult argument to make in 1966 and has receded in its impact since then.

Notes

1. Securities Exchange Act of 1934 Release No. 8-3925, 40 S.E.C. 907 (Nov. 8, 1961). Federal regulation of insider trading existed prior to 1961 under section 16 of the Securities Exchange Act of 1934, 15 U.S.C. §78p, but the reach of that statute extended only to a limited set of insiders (officers, directors, or 10% shareholders) who engaged in two transactions, both buying and selling, within a six-month period for companies whose shares are traded in a national market. Under Rule 10b-5, the reach of regulation has been extended beyond these statutory insiders to include tippees, constructive insiders and misappropriators with only one transaction required for any security, not just those listed or traded on a national exchange.

2. HENRY G. MANNE, INSIDER TRADING AND THE STOCK MARKET (1966) [hereinafter INSIDER TRADING].

3. See id. chs. 1–3.

4. See id. chs. 4–7.

5. See id. chs. 8–10.

6. Id. at 15.

7. Id. at 5 (describing the position of Robert Walker in a 1923 article opposing regulation).

8. Id. at 5, 10 (describing arguments of Professor H.L., Wilgus in a 1910 article supporting regulation and in the House Report accompanying the Securities Exchange Act of 1934).

9. See id. at 15; see also id. at 46 ("There is in today's literature, however, very little analysis helpful to a court or a legislature asked to resolve the issues posed by the Texas Gulf Sulphur case.").

10. Jonathan R. Macey, Securities Trading: A Contractual Perspective, 50 CASE W. RES. L. REV. 269, 269 (1999).

11. See James D. Cox, Insider Trading and Contracting: A Critical Response to the "Chicago School," 1986 DUKE L.J. 628, 634 (asserting that aggressive enforcement of insider trading "without a coherent, let alone articulated, philosophy of regulation is one of the most unsettling aspects of the federal securities laws").

12. See Paula J. Dalley, From Horse Trading to Insider Trading: The Historical Antecedents of the Insider Trading Debate, 39 WM. & MARY L. REV. 1289, 1293–94 (1998).

13. See Jill E. Fisch, Start Making Sense: An Analysis and Proposal for Insider Trading Regulation, 26 GA. L. REV. 179, 184 (1991).

14. 521 U.S. 642 (1997).

15. See, e.g., Stephen M. Bainbridge, Insider Trading Regulation: The Path Dependent Choice Between Property Rights and Securities Fraud, 53 SMU L. REV. [Graphic Character Omitted] (1999); Victor Brudney, O'Hagan's Problems, 1997 SUP. CT. REV. 249; Dalley, supra note 12; Fisch, supra note 13; Donna Nagy, Reframing the Misappropriation Theory of Insider Trading Liability: A Post-O'hagan Suggestion, 59 OHIO ST. L.J. 1223 (1998); Richard W. Painter et al., Don't Ask, Just Tell: Insider Trading After United States v. O'Hagan, 84 VA. L. REV. 153 (1998); Alan Strudler & Eric W. Orts, Moral Principle in the Law of Insider Trading (1999) (unpublished manuscript, on file with author).

16. Roberta S. Karmel, Outsider Trading on Confidential Information—A Breach in Search of a Duty, 20 CARDOZO L. REV. 83, 83 (1998).

17. See INSIDER TRADING, supra note 2, at 182.

18. What is presented here as a subtext that insider trading promotes efficient market may be distinct from the injury to investors rationale if insider trading makes the market more efficient but shareholders are nonetheless injured. See STEPHEN BAINBRIDGE, SECURITIES LAW: INSIDER TRADING 128–36 (1999).

19. Id. at 110.

20. See William K.S. Wang, Trading on Material Nonpublic Information in Impersonal Stock Markets: Who is Harmed, and Who Can Sue Whom Under SEC Rule 10b-5?, 54 S. CAL. L. REV. 1217 (1981) (discussing the difficulty of identifying a victim of insider trading).

21. See 15 U.S.C. §78t-1 (1994). This section was originally enacted as the Insider Trading and Securities Fraud Enforcement Act of 1998.

22. Donald C. Langevoort, INSIDER TRADING: REGULATION, ENFORCEMENT AND PREVENTION, in 18 SEC. L. SER., 9–17 (1998).

23. See 15 U.S.C. § 78a (1995) (codifying, as amended, the Private Securities Litigation Reform Act of 1995, Pub. L. No. 104–67, 109 Stat. 737 (1995)).

24. Section 21D(b)(2) of the 1934 Act added by the 1995 Reform Act requires that plaintiff in any private action for money damages "state with particularly facts giving rise to a strong inference that the defendant acted with the required state of mind." 15 U.S.C. § 78u-4.

25. See Joseph A. Grundfest & Michael A. Perino, Securities Litigation Reform: The First Year's Experience (John M. Olin Program in Law & Economics, Working Paper No. 140) (reporting that more than half of securities class actions claims filed in the year after the 1995 Act included allegations of insider trading) (Feb. 1997) (on file with author).

26. See Federal Court Securities Class Actions (visited June 10, 1999) <http:// securities.stanford.edu/complaints/complaints.html>. There were 761 cases in the database on that date, but only thirty-seven list section 20A. See id. Grundfest and Perino note that more than half of them mention insider trading. See Grundfest & Perino, supra note 47, at iii.

27. See Federal Court Securities Class Actions (visited June 10, 1999) <http:// securities.stanford.edu/complaints/complaints.html>.

28. The Annual Reports of the SEC show the number of insider trading prosecutions around fifty per year during the 1990s.

29. That complaint was filed in Susser v. Florida Panthers Holdings, Inc., No. 97-6084 1997) (S.D. Fla. 1997), available in Stanford Securities Class Action Clearinghouse database, (visited June 10, 1999) <http://securities.stanford.edu/ complaints/ floridap/ 97cv06084/001.html> (alleging that defendants who were officers and directors covered up good news in order to buy shares at a bargain price).

30. See Lisa K. Meulbroek, An Empirical Analysis of Illegal Insider Trading, 47 J. FIN. 1661, 1678 (1992) (stating that 79% of all insider information is takeover related).

31. See David D. Haddock & Jonathon R. Macey. A Coasian Model of Insider Trading, 80 NW. U. L. REV. 1449, 1452–54, 1469 (1987).

32. See Michael P. Dooley, Enforcement of Insider Trading Restrictions, 66 VA. L. REV. 1 (1980) (measuring harm to investors and finding none).

33. See, e.g., Henry G. Manne, Insider Trading and the Law Professors, 23 VAND. L. REV. 547, 554 (1970); Henry G. Manne, Insider Trading and Property Rights in New Information, 4 CATO J. 933, 937–943 (1985).

34. See United States v. O'Hagan, 521 U.S. 642, 658 (1997) ("[I]nvestors likely would hesitate to venture their capital in a market where trading based on misappropriated nonpublic information is unchecked by law.").

35. See Victor Brudney, Insiders, Outsiders, and Informational Advantages Under the Federal Securities Laws, 93 HARV. L. REV. 322, 356 (1979) ("[S]ome investors will refrain from dealing altogether, and others will incur costs to avoid dealing with such transactors or corruptly to overcome their unerodable informational advantages.").

36. Henry G. Manne, Insider Trading and the Law Professors, 23 VAND. L. REV. 547, 577 (1970). For a current statement of that view, see BAINBRIDGE, supra note 40, at 155 ("The loss of confidence is further undercut by the stock market's performance since the insider trading scandals of the mid-1980s. . . . One can but conclude that insider trading does not seriously threaten the confidence of investors in the securities markets.").

37. Colin Camerer & Richard H. Thaler, Anomalies: Ultimatum, Dictators and Manners, J. ECON. PERSP., Spring 1995, at 209–10 (1995).

38. This behavior is sometimes discussed in the context of reciprocity norms. See, e.g., Jon D. Hanson & Douglas A. Kysar, Taking Behavioralism Seriously: The Problem of Market Manipulation, 74 N.Y.U.L. REV. 630, 680–81 (1999)

("Reciprocity norms manifest themselves in numerous ways, most of which seem relevant to the market context. For example, individuals are often more willing to cooperate with those actors they feel are behaving cooperatively or fairly. On the other hand, individuals will often refuse to cooperate with others who are being uncooperative. Moreover, individuals are often willing to sacrifice to hurt others who are being unfair.") (citations omitted). See also Jennifer Arlen, Comment: The Future of Behavioral Economic Analysis of Law, 51 VAND. L. REV. 1765, 1776 (1998) ("[R]isk of perceived unfairness is greater that it might at first seem because people tend to have a self-serving assessment of what is fair.").

39. Jonathan R. Macey, Insider Trading, Henry Manne and Academic Life, 50 CASE W. RES. L. REV. 269, 281 (1999).

40. INSIDER TRADING, supra note 2, at 110.

41. Id.

42. In part, the preference may reflect an association with American prosperity of that period. More specifically it may reflect the efforts of American regulators. See also David D. Haddock, Academic Hostility and SEC Acquiescence: Henry Manne's Insider Trading, 50 CASE W. RES. L. REV. 313, 316–17 (1999) (discussing the status and evolution of government regulation of insider trading).

43. INSIDER TRADING, supra note 2, at 158.

44. See Dirks v. SEC, 463 U.S. 646, 665 (1983).

45. See United States v. O'Hagan, 521 U.S. 642, 648 (1997) (affirming O'Hagan's disbarrment and reversing his theft conviction resulting from an insider transaction).

46. See United States v. Chestman, 947 F.2d 551, 555 (2d Cir. 1991) (en banc), cert. denied, 503 U.S. 1004 (1992).

47. See INSIDER TRADING, supra note 2, at 169 (discussing possible information leakage but dismissing it as unimportant).

48. As Manne observed in discussing the economics of partial enforcement, "the absence of the more highminded participants from a segment of the securities field makes it that much more lucrative and attractive for those we least want to encourage." Henry G. Manne, Insider Trading and the Law Professors, 23 VAND. L. REV. 547, 555 (1970).

49. See generally John Balkcom & Roger Brossy. Executive Pay-Then, Now, and Ahead, 22 DIRS. & BDS., Fall 1997, 55, 58 (noting that "trends in executive pay have gone far to align the interests of the managers and the shareholder").

50. See INSIDER TRADING, supra note 2, at 140.

51. See 17 C.F.R. §§ 229.401–05 (1999) (republishing as administrative rules, SEC Regulation S-K).

52. See Securities Act of 1933 Release No. 33-6962, 52 SEC Docket 1961, 1963 (Oct. 16, 1992) (requiring new disclosure as to options and stock appreciation rights and requiring disclosure of the relationship between compensation and corporate performance designed to "furnish shareholders with a more understandable presentation of the nature and extent of executive compensation").

53. See generally Balkcom & Brossy, supra note 71, at 61.

54. See, e.g., Rogers v. Hill, 289 U.S. 582 (challenging the compensation program of the American Tobacco Company); Salary $12,000, Bonus $1,623,753, THE LITERARY DIGEST, Aug. 9, 1930, at 10 (publishing the annual compensation of the president of Bethlehem Steel).

55. See generally GRAEF S. CRYSTAL, IN SEARCH OF EXCESS: THE OVERCOMPENSATION OF AMERICAN EXECUTIVES 27 (1966) (explaining that executive pay was around thirty-five times the pay of the average manufacturing worker in 1974 and 120 times the average pay two decades later).

56. See, e.g., DEREK BOK, THE COST OF TALENT: HOW EXECUTIVES AND PRO-
     FESSIONALS ARE PAID AND HOW IT AFFECTS AMERICA 95 (1993) (showing
     that American levels of corporate compensation are not replicated in other
     industrial nations); Deborah Orr, Damn Yankees, FORBES, May 17, 1999, at
     206 (noting average U.S. chief executive's pay still far outpaces the rest of the
     world because of long term-incentives like stock options, which while
     common here, are rarer abroad).

Stephen Bainbridge  **NO**

Why Regulate Insider Trading?

The Washington Post recently reported on the considerable attention the SEC and Justice Department are devoting to enforcement of the insider trading laws. Who can forget the recent high profile case against Martha Stewart, which is only the very tip of a large iceberg? Is this a useful expenditure of government resources?

Henry Manne's 1966 book *Insider Trading and the Stock Market* stunned the SEC and corporate law academy by daring to propose the deregulation of insider trading. Manne argued that insider trading benefits both society and the firm in whose stock the insider traded. First, he argued, insider trading causes the market price of the affected security to move toward the price that the security would command if the inside information were publicly available. If so, both society and the firm benefit through increased price accuracy. Second, he posited insider trading as an efficient way of compensating managers for having produced information. If so, the firm benefits directly (and society indirectly) because managers have a greater incentive to produce additional information of value to the firm.

Although I have tremendous respect for Manne's daring in proposing such provocative arguments, I'm afraid I don't buy either one. As to the first, Manne argued (correctly) that both firms and society benefit from accurate pricing of securities. The "correct" price of a security is that which would be set by the market if all information relating to the security had been publicly disclosed. But while U.S. securities laws purportedly encourage accurate pricing by requiring disclosure of corporate information, they in fact do not require the disclosure of all material information. Where disclosure would interfere with legitimate business transactions, disclosure by the corporation is usually not required unless the firm is dealing in its own securities at the time.

Manne argued insider trading is an effective compromise between the need for preserving incentives to produce information and the need for maintaining accurate securities prices. Suppose, for example, that a firm's stock currently sells at fifty dollars per share. The firm has discovered new information that, if publicly disclosed, would cause the stock to sell at sixty dollars. If insiders trade on this information, the price of the stock will gradually rise toward but will not reach the "correct" price. Absent insider trading or leaks, the stock's price will remain at fifty dollars until the information is publicly disclosed and then rapidly rise to the correct price of sixty dollars. Thus, insider trading acts as a replacement for public disclosure of the information, preserving market gains of correct pricing while permitting the corporation to retain the benefits of nondisclosure.

The problem with this argument is that insider trading affects stock market prices through what is known as "derivatively informed trading." First, those individuals possessing material nonpublic information begin trading. Their trading has only a small effect on price. Some uninformed traders become aware of the insider trading through leakage or tipping of information or through observation of insider trades. Other traders gain insight by following the price fluctuations of the securities. Finally, the market reacts to the insiders' trades and gradually moves toward the correct price. But while derivatively informed trading can affect price, it functions slowly and sporadically. Given the inefficiency of derivatively informed trading, the market efficiency justification for insider trading loses much of its force.

As for Manne's second argument, insider trading in fact appears to be a very inefficient scheme for compensating corporate managers. Even assuming a change in stock price that accurately measures the value of the innovation, the insider's "compensation" from insider trading is limited by the number of shares he can purchase. This, in turn, is limited by his wealth. As such, the insider's trading returns are based, not on the value of his contribution to the corporation, but on his wealth.

Another objection to the compensation argument is the difficulty of restricting trading to those who produced the information. Where information is concerned, production costs normally exceed distribution costs. As such, many firm agents may trade on the information without having contributed to its production.

A related objection is the difficulty of limiting trading to instances in which the insider actually produced valuable information. In particular, why should insiders be permitted to trade on bad news? Allowing managers to profit from inside trading reduces the penalties associated with a project's failure because trading managers can profit whether the project succeeds or fails. If the project fails, the manager can sell his shares before that information becomes public and thus avoid an otherwise certain loss. The manager can go beyond mere loss avoidance into actual profit making by short selling the firm's stock.

In sum, the arguments for deregulating insider trading are not very persuasive. But that doesn't answer the question, why do we regulate insider trading? Efficiency-based arguments for regulating insider trading (as opposed to those grounded on legislative intent, equity, or fairness) fall into three main categories: (1) insider trading harms investors and thus undermines investor confidence in the securities markets; (2) insider trading harms the issuer of the affected securities; and (3) insider trading amounts to theft of property belonging to the corporation and therefore should be prohibited even in the absence of harm to investors or the firm. Only the latter proves very persuasive.

There are essentially two ways of creating property rights in information: allow the owner to enter into transactions without disclosing the information or prohibit others from using the information. In effect, the federal insider trading prohibition vests a property right of the latter type in the party to whom the insider trader owes a fiduciary duty to refrain from self-dealing in confidential information. To be sure, at first blush, the insider trading prohibition admittedly does not look very much like most property rights. Enforcement of the insider trading prohibition admittedly differs rather dramatically from enforcement of, say, trespassing laws. The existence of property rights in a variety of intangibles, including information, however, is well-established. Trademarks, copyrights, and patents are but a few of the better known examples of this phenomenon. There are striking doctrinal parallels, moreover, between insider trading and these other types of property rights in information. Using another's trade secret, for example, is actionable only if taking the trade secret involved a breach of fiduciary duty, misrepresentation, or theft. Likewise, insider trading is only unlawful if the use of the information involves a breach of fiduciary duty by the insider.

The rationale for prohibiting insider trading is precisely the same as that for prohibiting patent infringement or theft of trade secrets: protecting the economic incentive to produce socially valuable information. As the theory goes, the readily appropriable nature of information makes it difficult for the developer of a new idea to recoup the sunk costs incurred to develop it. If an inventor develops a better mousetrap, for example, he cannot profit on that invention without selling mousetraps and thereby making the new design available to potential competitors. Assuming both the inventor and his competitors incur roughly equivalent marginal costs to produce and market the trap, the competitors will be able to set a market price at which the inventor likely will be unable to earn a return on his sunk costs. Ex post, the rational inventor should ignore his sunk costs and go on producing the improved mousetrap. Ex ante, however, the inventor will anticipate that he will be unable to generate positive returns on his up-front costs and therefore will be deterred from developing socially valuable information. Accordingly, society provides incentives for inventive activity by using the patent system to give inventors a property right in new ideas. By preventing competitors from appropriating the idea, the patent allows the inventor to charge monopolistic prices for the improved mousetrap, thereby recouping his sunk costs. Trademark, copyright, and trade secret law all are justified on similar grounds.

This argument does not provide as compelling a justification for the insider trading prohibition as it does for the patent system. A property right in information should be created when necessary to prevent conduct by which someone other than the developer of socially valuable information appropriates its value before the developer can recoup his sunk costs. Insider trading, however, often does not affect an idea's value to the corporation and probably never entirely eliminates its value. Legalizing insider trading thus would have a much smaller impact on the corporation's incentive to develop new information than would, say, legalizing patent infringement.

The property rights approach nevertheless has considerable justificatory power. Consider the prototypical insider trading transaction, in which an insider trades in his employer's stock on the basis of information learned solely because of his position with the firm. There is no avoiding the necessity of assigning the property right to either the corporation or the inside trader. A rule allowing insider trading assigns the property right to the insider, while a rule prohibiting insider trading assigns it to the corporation.

From the corporation's perspective, legalizing insider trading likely would have a relatively small effect on the firm's incentives to develop new information. In some cases, however, insider trading will harm the corporation's interests and thus adversely affect its incentives in this regard. This argues for assigning the property right to the corporation, rather than the insider.

Those who rely on a property rights-based justification for regulating insider trading also observe that creation of a property right with respect to a particular asset typically is not dependent upon there being a measurable loss of value resulting from the asset's use by someone else. Indeed, creation of a property right is appropriate even if any loss in value is entirely subjective, both because subjective valuations are difficult to measure for purposes of awarding damages and because the possible loss of subjective values presumably would affect the corporation's incentives to cause its agents to develop new information. As with other property rights, the law therefore should simply assume (although the assumption will sometimes be wrong) that assigning the property right to agent-produced information to the firm maximizes the social incentives for the production of valuable new information.

Because the relative rarity of cases in which harm occurs to the corporation weakens the argument for assigning it the property right, however, the critical issue may be whether one can justify assigning the property right to the insider. On close examination, the argument for assigning the property right to the insider is considerably weaker than the argument for assigning it to the corporation. As we have seen, Manne argued that legalized insider trading would be an appropriate compensation scheme. In other words, society might allow insiders to inside trade in order to give them greater incentives to develop new information. As we have also seen, however, this argument founders because insider trading in fact is an inefficient compensation scheme.

The economic theory of property rights in information thus cannot justify assigning the property right to insiders rather than to the corporation. Because there is no avoiding the necessity of assigning the property right to the information in question to one of the relevant parties, the argument for assigning it to the corporation therefore should prevail.

None of this is to say that the precise set of rules the SEC has adopted is ideal. To the contrary, as I detailed in my book on insider trading, there are serious problems with a number of features of the current enforcement regime. As to the basic question of whether we ought to regulate insider trading, however, economic efficiency commands an affirmative answer.

POSTSCRIPT

Should Insider Trading Be Legalized?

In addition to the Martha Stewart case, in virtually all of the major corporate scandals at the turn of the century—Enron, Global Crossing, Tyco Corporation, World-Com—insider trading was identified as a major source of illegal activity. A natural outcome of this has been a revival of the debate over the moral and legal status of insider trading. Most observers have adopted the traditional viewpoint of insider trading as morally heinous behavior and deserving of criminal prosecution. But a growing chorus of dissenters have resurrected the work of Henry Manne and offered it as justification for legalizing insider trading. Although much of this dissention is rooted in academia, Manne's views are becoming known to a wider audience.

In a recent interview with syndicated talk radio show host and social commentator Larry Elder, Henry Manne reiterated his belief that insider trading should be legalized. In so doing, he highlighted an often neglected aspect of his earlier position. Manne contends that, independent of the economic, legal, or moral arguments against regulation, the reality is that insider trading is virtually impossible to detect and enforce: "That's, of course, why they didn't indict Martha Stewart for insider trading. The SEC does not win many of the cases they bring, and they don't bring many. It's really very interesting to wonder what kind of law is this that it is so difficult to prove that you've got a case" (Elder, "Legalize Insider Trading," *Capitalism Magazine*, September 24, 2004). He suggests that the SEC would be well advised to spend its time and money in other pursuits.

Regardless of whether enforcement is feasible or not, the fact is that most of the public, and virtually all of the political powers, are supportive of continued regulation of insider trading activities. In fact, a significant portion of the massive, landmark Sarbanes-Oxley Act of 2002 on corporate governance specifically addresses the issue of insider trading. Thus, whether you agree with Manne's viewpoint or not, there can be no debating that the current socio-political environment is characterized by the view that insider trading is harmful, immoral, illegal, and therefore, subject to governmental regulation.

Suggested Readings

Stephen M. Bainbridge, Insider trading: An overview. *Encyclopedia of Law and Economics*, 2000.

Andrew Bernstein, The injustice of insider trading laws. *The Ayn Rand Institute*, July 12, 2004. http://www.aynrand.org/site/News2? page=News Article&id=9559

Larry Elder, Legalize insider trading. *Capitalism Magazine,* September 24, 2004. http://www.capmag.com/article.asp?ID=3933

Jonathan R. Macey, Securities trading: A contractual perspective. *Case Western Reserve Law Review*, vol. 50, no. 2, Winter 1999, p. 269.

On the Internet . . .

About.com: Affirmative Action

This site provides a myriad of links to help you understand the controversial topic of Affirmative Action as well as information on any current developments and reform initiatives.

http://racerelations.about.com/od/affirmativeaction/

Workplace Fairness

Workplace Fairness is a nonprofit organization that brings together employers, workers, policymakers, and others to ensure and promote fairness in the workplace and employment relationships.

http://www.nerinet.org/

Partnership for a Drug-Free America

This Web site has much information on drug use by young adults as well as many links to related sites. Also features an updated news resource link.

http://www.drugfreeamerica.org/Home/
default.asp?ws=PDFA&vol=1&grp=Home

Institute for Women's Policy Research

"The Institute for Women's Policy Research (IWPR) is a public policy research organization dedicated to informing and stimulating the debate on public policy issues of critical importance to women and their families."

http://www.iwpr.org/

The Heritage Foundation

The Heritage Foundation is a research and educational institute whose mission is to formulate and promote conservative public policies based on the principles of free enterprise, limited government, individual freedom, traditional American values, and a strong national defense.

http://www.heritage.org/

PART 2

Organizational Behavior and Human Resource Management

*A*ffirmative *Action has been with us for several decades. There can be no question that it has helped in obtaining more and better opportunities for minorities and females during this time. But, as some critics claim, has it become outdated? Do we still need it? Companies have the right to protect themselves from harm and to ensure a safe and drug-free workplace. But employees also have a right to privacy. Given this inherent conflict, perhaps* not *testing is a wise policy? In the late 1950s, women made about 40 percent less than did males. In 2003, the male-female wage gap has only shrunk to 25 percent. Is discrimination still responsible for this difference? Part 2 explores these and other important questions for managers.*

- Has Affirmative Action Outlived Its Usefulness in the Workplace?

- Is Workplace Drug Testing a Wise Corporate Policy?

- Is Diversity in the Workplace a Worthwhile Goal for Corporations?

- Is Gender Discrimination the Main Reason Women Are Paid Less than Men?

- Would Reforming Social Security Be Good for American Business?

ISSUE 5

Has Affirmative Action Outlived Its Usefulness in the Workplace?

YES: John H. McWhorter, from "The Campus Diversity Fraud," *City Journal* (Winter 2002)

NO: Judith C. Appelbaum, from "Affirmative Action: End It or Defend It?" *National Women's Law Center,* Speech at State University of New York at Binghamton (November 2, 2000)

ISSUE SUMMARY

YES: In an article calling for the end to affirmative action, African American social commentator Dr. McWhorter draws on his experiences as a previous supporter of affirmative action while providing numerous insightful observations.

NO: Judith Appelbaum, speaking before the SUNY, Binghamton, argues that discrimination in the workplace is still very much with us today. And, since affirmative is needed to combat ongoing discrimination, it's still needed today.

One of the most important outcomes of the 1960s civil rights movement in America was the concept of affirmative action. In the workplace, affirmative action can be defined as the "process in which employers identify needs and take positive steps to create and enhance opportunities for protected class members [i.e., minorities and females]" (Mathis & Jackson, *Human Resource Management*, Thompson South-Western Publishers, 2003). For most private companies, implementing an affirmative action program is a voluntary decision. However, in addition to all state and federal government agencies, those businesses that contract government work are required by law to maintain affirmative action programs in their workplace. One of the effects of these requirements has been to increase the diversity of the workforce in corporate America. And while many people feel this is a positive result, there are many others who are, both in principle and in practice, vigorously opposed to the concept of affirmative action. Many of its detractors argue that it has accomplished its goals and is, at best, no longer needed and, at worst, damaging to the American social fabric. Supporters contend that affirmative action has not yet met all its goals and is still very much needed in the workplace. The debate over the legitimacy and effectiveness of affirmative action is characterized by strong passions on both sides and represents one of the most important social issues of the early twenty-first century.

One of the reasons for the intensity surrounding this issue is that there are several compelling arguments on each side of the debate. Let us consider a couple of important points in defense of affirmative action. Proponents believe that many of the current differences in racial and gender success in the workplace can be attributed to the effects of discrimination built up over many years. These effects cut both ways: Women and minorities suffer unfair employment treatment while males and nonminorities have received, in effect, preferential treatment. Not surprisingly, supporters of affirmative action argue that it is needed to overcome the effects of past discrimination. A second argument rests on the observation that social ills like crime, drug abuse, and low educational attainment levels are most likely to occur among those at the lowest level of the socioeconomic ladder, a rung that consists primarily of minorities. Since economic disparities will be reduced as a result of the increased employment and economic opportunities provided by affirmative action, social problems such as these could be expected to decline, thereby benefiting all members of our society.

The other side of the debate also has several strong points you should be aware of when thinking about affirmative action. An important consideration is the concept of reverse discrimination. Like it or not, the fact is that when we give preferential treatment to any group of individuals we necessarily discriminate against other groups. Critics of affirmative action argue that this occurs frequently, is reverse discrimination (usually against males and nonminorities), and note that this position requires adopting a "two wrongs make a right" viewpoint. Another line of reasoning against affirmative action involves the recognition that the overwhelming majority of nonprotected class members have nothing to do with past discrimination—indeed, many were not even alive at the time—and yet it is exactly these individuals who are penalized by affirmative action programs. Opponents argue that it is patently unfair, unjust, and immoral for these individuals to be penalized for discrimination that occurred in the past and in which they played no part.

In the two selections that follow, the question of whether affirmative action has outlived its usefulness in the workplace is addressed. The yes selection, an exceptionally well-written and cogent article, is presented by Manhattan Institute Senior Fellow, John H. McWhorter, Ph.D. Dr. McWhorter is an African American social commentator who admits to changing his initial support of affirmative action to his current belief that it is bad for both protected class members and society at large. The no side of this debate is provided by Judith C. Appelbaum, vice president and legal director at the National Women's Law Center in Washington, D.C. In a speech presented at the State University of New York, Binghamton, Ms. Appelbaum covers important ground in her defense of affirmative action in the workplace. Of particular note is her argument that affirmative action is (and was) intended to "counteract ongoing discrimination." And since, she argues, discrimination is still occurring at the workplace, affirmative is still needed as a counterweight. Do you find her argument persuasive?

YES

John H. McWhorter

The Campus Diversity Fraud

In September, the Georgia Supreme Court ruled that the crude "black bonus" in the University of Georgia's admissions policy wasn't what the U.S. Supreme Court's 1978 *Bakke* decision meant when it allowed colleges to take "diversity" into account in admissions decisions. Let's hope that this decision spells the beginning of the end for the "diversity" argument in college admissions. It has been, from the start, an argument shot through with duplicity and bad faith. It is a craven, disingenuous, and destructive canard, antithetical to interracial harmony and black excellence—and racist besides.

The diversity imperative now so powerful on campus arose almost by chance, springing from a remark Justice Lewis Powell made in his concurrence in the *Bakke* decision. Allan *Bakke* had charged the medical school at the University of California at Davis with discrimination for twice turning him down, despite his high grades and admissions-test scores, while routinely admitting black students with C averages and poor admissions-test scores. The court found that quota systems like Davis's were unconstitutional, but Powell's opinion hedged slightly, asserting that it was appropriate for schools to base their admissions decisions upon a quest for a "diverse student body." Powell's statement provided a justification that universities, including the University of Georgia, quickly seized upon as a cover for admitting black students with significantly lower qualifications than those of white or Asian students. Instead of ending campus affirmative action, *Bakke* became its license.

White guilt is a dangerous and addictive drug, and for 20-plus years the *Bakke* decision has supported stricken higher-education administrators in their habit. Meanwhile, the diversity shibboleth has taught a generation of young Americans that black students are more important for their presence in promotional brochure photographs than for their scholastic qualifications—an essentialization now as rife among black as among white students. This message ultimately perpetuates the very underperformance that has made the fig-leaf diversity notion necessary.

The very term "diversity" craftily overshoots the actual goal in question. Mormons, paraplegics, people from Alaska, lesbians, Ayn Randians, and poor whites exert little pull on the heartstrings of admissions committees so committed to making college campuses "look like America." The diversity that counts is brown-skinned minorities, especially African Americans.

Affirmative action at its inception in the late 1960s, when college administrators supposed that blacks' low representation on campuses was simply a matter of discrimination, meant nothing more than opening the doors and providing some remedial help where needed. But these efforts to bring in qualified blacks ran up against the uncomfortably small number of such people in an America just past legalized segregation. Faced with those who were admitted, university professors, not surprisingly, proved unequal to the task of undoing the effects of 14 years of poor preparation in the basic skills necessary for college course work. Meanwhile, the triumph of the separatist belief in black America that scholastic achievement was a "white" endeavor rather than an American one further decreased the numbers of black students qualified for top schools, and it holds down their numbers to this day.

As a result, though Justice Powell doubtless had intended his diversity imperative to play out as a mere thumb on the scale, giving the edge to a brown-skinned candidate where his qualifications were equal to a white-skinned one's, brute quota systems quickly came to reign on selective campuses. After my first year at Rutgers University, where I earned my bachelor's degree in the mid-1980s, it was painfully clear to me that the black students were generally a rung below the general preparation and performance level of the white ones. Certainly there were excellent black students—but they were exceptions rather than the rule. Even as a teenager unconcerned with social policy or admissions procedures, I couldn't but notice that black students had gotten in under some kind of quota system.

Rutgers top brass long maintained that race was used as just one of many factors, as the *Bakke* decision had directed. But a few years after I graduated, a student working in the admissions office blew the whistle, revealing that black students were put into a special pool and admitted according to significantly lower criteria than other students. Nor was Rutgers unique. Similar disclosures have emerged in school after school, including the University of California, the University of Texas, the University of Michigan, and, most recently, the University of Georgia. Even in their pro–affirmative action manifesto, *The Shape of the River,* William Bowen and Derek Bok admit—and painstakingly document—that this practice has been routine in selective universities across the nation for 30 years.

At the University of California at Berkeley, where I teach, the quota system was as obvious on the ground as it had been at Rutgers in the 1980s. One older white professor, an avowed leftist, confided in me that since the early 1970s black students had done badly in his classes so often that he had found himself viewing any black student who appeared on the first day of class as a potential problem. A white remedial-composition tutor observed that he had worked with so many minority students hopelessly underprepared for Berkeley-level work that he had found himself questioning the wisdom of racial preferences, despite his leftist persuasion. Professors across the country have expressed similar views to me.

Many would dismiss such observations as bias and stereotyping. The facts are otherwise. Stephan and Abigail Thernstrom note in *America in Black and White* that black Berkeley students who enrolled in 1988 had an average

SAT score below 1,000, compared with white students' average of over 1,300. The highest quartile of black SAT scores in this class clustered at the bottom quarter of the SAT scores of all students. The high school grade average among black students was B-plus, rather than the straight-A average required of white students. Nor was this a mere Berzerk-ley aberration: in 1992, the gap in average SAT scores between black and white entrants was 150 points at Princeton, 171 at Stanford, 218 at Dartmouth, and 271 at Rice.

Graduation rates reflect this gulf in preparation. The Thernstroms document that, of the black students who entered Berkeley in 1988, 41 percent did not graduate, while only 16 percent of their white classmates did not. Bowen and Bok report that, at 28 top universities, black students in the class of 1989 were about three times more likely to drop out than white students.

Many ascribe these higher dropout rates to financial pressures rather than to the sharp deficits in high school grades and SAT scores. But the burden of proof is upon such people to identify just why grades and scores would *not* correlate significantly with a student's chances of finishing college. Few have any problem seeing a causal link here when it comes to white students.

The argument that grades and scores are irrelevant to assessing a candidate defies both logic and experience. Consider the SAT. No one would argue that a student with a perfect SAT score is only a possible good match for Harvard or that a student with an abysmal SAT score was prime Harvard material. Precisely what, then, leads to the conclusion that SAT scores in between have no predictive power? In fact, as the Thernstroms show, graduation rates for black students who started at Berkeley in 1988 closely tracked their SAT scores: students with lower SATs were correspondingly less likely to get their degrees. Bowen and Bok acknowledge that SAT scores actually *overpredict* black students' college performance—that is, black students do less well than their scores would predict, not better.

Faced with such hard facts, diversity fans have asserted that leadership skills, helping to put together the high school yearbook, and spunk are as relevant to assessing a student's scholastic potential as . . . well, how they did academically in high school or how they scored on standardized tests. But aren't leadership skills and spunk equally prevalent among white students? Surely, blacks aren't innately perkier than whites. College-admissions committees that cheerily emphasize such extra-academic factors in evaluating black applicants basically are saying that blacks can't compete in the truly decisive arena: the classroom. In the name of diversity, black students find themselves patronizingly exempted from serious competition.

Can we justify this exemption from standards by saying that it leads to a larger good? Supporters of campus diversity have made three broad arguments to this effect. The first is that bending the admissions rules to ensure diversity helps foster an interracial fellowship that all students will carry with them into society after they graduate. I tried to hold on to this idea for years, but in the end it just doesn't wash.

In truth, "diverse" college campuses are among the most racially balkanized places in America. Separate black fraternities and sororities thrive. They first emerged in the early twentieth century, when white fraternities and sororities didn't welcome black applicants. Today, black Greek organizations are thoroughly unenthusiastic toward *whites*. Reinforcing this separatism, some universities host all-black graduation ceremonies—the idea, apparently, being that one's achievement is less a human or American one than a black one. In addition, black students typically cluster in their own section of the dining hall, throw their own parties, have their own theme houses, and leave college with a separatist ideology that they often didn't hold when they first arrived. Interracial fellowship this is not.

Nor is one likely to find much interracial camaraderie in African-American studies classes. Supporters of such classes say that they help blacks learn about their rich heritage, but in practice, they often double as exercises in stoking hatred of the White Man. At Stanford, I was a teaching assistant in a predominantly black class on Black English. In itself, the subject encompasses much more than mere street slang—extending to grammatical structure, literature, and educational issues. Yet, class discussion devolved into visceral dismissal of whites so often that one white student complained to the professor that he felt any opinions he ventured beyond genuflections to black victimhood were unwelcome—and he was right. When, in a course I taught at Berkeley on the history of black musical theater, a female white student observed that rap lyrics were misogynistic, several black students dressed her down so vehemently that they left her in tears.

Confronted with such racial enmity, white students understandably start shunning blacks. John H. Bunzel documents in *Race Relations on Campus: Stanford Students Speak Out* that white Stanford students who endured constant vague accusations of racism from black students often became less interested in interracial outreach than they had been as freshmen—a trend I've noticed on other campuses where I've taught or visited.

For the black student who doesn't toe the separatist line but really seeks interracial fellowship, university life can be uncomfortable. Blacks quickly discover that black authenticity means hunkering down behind a racial barricade, glaring angrily at the symbols of white "hegemony" that supposedly surround them, and believing that they are eternal victims in their own land. Edgy conversations with other black students who question the authenticity of one's own "blackness" become a regular feature of life. Bunzel reports that black Stanford students told him they were expected to "talk black, dress black, think black, and certainly date black." A black student who joins a traditionally white frat or sorority will face accusations that he or she is a self-hating sellout. A black acquaintance once told me that the overwhelming hostility she met with during her college years from black students scornful of her white friendships was far worse than any white racism she experienced at the time.

Scratch the surface, it seems, and diversity really means maintaining one's separatist missiles at the ready. After black University of California regent Ward Connerly helped launch an ultimately successful campaign to outlaw racial preferences in U-Cal admissions a few years back, some black locals formed a committee called "Citizens Against Ward Connerly." At one event, a committee representative joked, "Ward Connerly wants the University of California to be all vanilla—and I don't like vanilla." She sought audience approval, but given that at least half of her listeners were white, all she got was some nervous laughter. She quickly backtracked, adding, "I like to have some mix-ins—chips, nuts." Her initial remark, though, revealed the truth: the people so furiously committed to campus diversity aren't interested in a color-blind America. Their real goal is to ensure that the privileges of a college education don't distract black students from the urgent task of keeping the fires of black alienation burning.

Since the notion that diversity encourages interracial bonding is so patently false, its defenders frequently make a second, somewhat different, argument. Racial preferences in admissions, they maintain, are crucial in order to ensure, if not fellowship, then at least *exposure* to different ethnic and racial groups, teaching a valuable lesson about the many equally valid viewpoints in a multicultural society. This view received official *imprimatur* in Powell's *Bakke* concurrence, where the justice asserted that universities would benefit from selecting "those students [i.e., dark-skinned minorities] who will contribute most to the robust exchange of ideas."

Given that *Bakke* concerned a medical school, just how being black qualifies one to make especially vigorous observations about surgical incisions and metabolic pathways is unclear, but never mind. The real, if implicit, assumption behind the exposure idea is that whites will learn about—and learn to respect—blacks from the other side of the tracks, whom they supposedly find so alien, despicable, and threatening. But in practice, what white students often learn at a university that lets in blacks under the bar is that blacks may not be as sharp as whites. It's difficult to imagine how even the most well-intentioned white students could have avoided such a conclusion at Rutgers when I studied there in the 1980s.

More fundamentally, the "exposure" argument rests on a falsehood: that black students typically come from disadvantaged circumstances, unfamiliar to their white classmates. In fact, at selective schools, inner-city blacks have been vanishingly rare since the late 1960s, when a handful of top schools briefly—and unsuccessfully—experimented with admitting unqualified urban blacks to see if they could cope. But among black students in the last class admitted to Berkeley under the old racial preferences regime, more than 65 percent came from households earning at least $40,000 a year; the parents of 40 percent earned at least $60,000 yearly. Of blacks admitted in 1989 to the 28 selective universities that Bowen and Bok survey, just 14 percent came from homes earning $22,000 or less.

Precisely what traits do middle-class black kids display that a white student must learn about so that he won't wash out in the management job he starts after graduation? I've found that middle-class black students asked to list a few such traits usually draw a blank. Even if many blacks from the 'hood *did* show up at selective schools, however, why would learning about their cultural traits be vital to white students' education? In African-American studies courses on the same campuses, blacks regularly—and rightly—decry the stereotype that all African Americans are poor. Surely a firsthand, four-year tutorial in the vibrancy of ghetto life would simply reinforce that stereotype. Poverty is a tragedy, not a life-style.

If neither the hope for greater interracial harmony nor the idea of whites learning from blacks justifies diversity policies, there is, finally, the moral argument that blacks deserve compensation for their tragic history. Centuries of disenfranchisement and segregation bar most blacks from really qualifying for top schools, affirmative action's defenders charge, so it's the right thing to do to let them in through the back door. "How, without racial preferences, can we make up for the fact that whites benefited from socially ingrained preferences for centuries?" furiously asked one black man at a talk I gave recently. Harvard sociologist Nathan Glazer, reversing his longtime opposition to race-based admissions, claims that whites "owe" blacks due to past injustices. For all their sincerity, however, people like Glazer don't understand that this tit-for-tat defense of racial preferences bars the only path that can lead us beyond our racial dilemmas.

It's indisputable that historical disenfranchisement has left many blacks ill equipped to compete even when ladders to success beckon, as they do today—partly because of the economic and social obstacles to achievement that disadvantaged status entails and, even more, because long-term oppression helped create a black cultural identity opposed to mainstream success. For blacks to rise to the top, they must learn skills and cultivate new attitudes. Those who've grown up under conditions that don't offer direct paths to accomplishment have the task—unfair, but hardly limited to blacks—of discovering the knack of turning lemons into lemonade, as oppressed groups in America have done for centuries. A group that believes that mainstream achievement is inauthentic will have to refashion its self-conception if it is ever to get ahead in the only society it will ever call home.

Lowered standards are antithetical to both of these vital goals. A fundamental tenet of economics and psychology is that most people will do their best only if they have the incentive to do so. Lowered standards have robbed blacks of that incentive. One can only learn to ride a bicycle by mastering the subtle muscular poise of the endeavor oneself; as long as the training wheels remain on, one isn't really riding the bike.

The point here isn't moral but logical: black students will only reach their full potential if the affirmative-action safety net is withdrawn and they're required to strive for excellence. Perhaps the most sobering reality black Americans face today is that even our tragic history cannot exempt us from this hard truth of the human condition. Asian students have never had the illusion that there was any path up other than showing their best stuff, come hell or high water, which is why so many of them excel. Students, though, who daily hear the message, "You only have to do pretty well to get into a top school" will—a few naturally gifted stars excepted—only do pretty well. To elevate diversity over true excellence condemns black students to mediocrity and is, quite simply, racist.

To call today's university administrations racist may seem a bit strong. Yet what else should we make of university officials' apparent belief that blacks are the only group in American history incapable of overcoming social and historical obstacles? So troubled is University of California president Richard Atkinson by the fall in black and Hispanic admissions to his flagship

Berkeley and UCLA campuses since the end of racial preferences in the system that he has proposed eliminating the SAT from admissions requirements altogether.

Never mind that, after the overturning of preferences, black admissions fell only on these two top campuses, rising at several other UC schools; and that the University of California is now trying diligently to prepare minority students in middle and high schools throughout the state to submit competitive dossiers to UC. Atkinson is so skeptical that the new race-blind regime will ever bear fruit that he doesn't consider it worth waiting to see what *might* happen over time. Instead, all he sees is the "re-segregation" that black and Latino faculty and administrators and their white fellow travelers warned about when the battle over preferences was raging. Implicitly, he seems to think that Berkeley and UCLA are the only California colleges worth attending, so that black students who don't get into them have no choice but to fail.

This is offensive nonsense. Sure, over the past few years, many black kids who would have gone to Berkeley under the old system now attend UC Santa Cruz, UC Davis, or other solid second-rank schools. But so what? They're much more likely to thrive on these campuses than if they found themselves, unprepared, at legendarily demanding Berkeley and UCLA. And isn't Atkinson's conviction that the new system re-creates the era of Orville Faubus strangely dismissive of California's non-elite state schools for the man entrusted with their stewardship?

Equally important, under the new race-blind system, black students know that they are as qualified academically as other students on campus. Armed with a confidence based on reality, black students will be more comfortable in white company and less likely to compensate for feelings of inferiority by retreating to their own section of the dining hall.

Affirmative-action supporters retort that under-qualified black students must be admitted to top schools, because the prestige of such institutions and the connections one makes attending them are essential to success in later life. This claim doesn't stand up to the slightest scrutiny. Journalist James Fallows notes in a recent piece in *The Atlantic* that "the four richest people in America, all of whom made rather than inherited their wealth, are a dropout from Harvard, a dropout from the University of Illinois, a dropout from Washington State University, and a graduate of the University of Nebraska." Top universities, he adds, rarely show up on the résumés of congressmen, Nobel laureates, industry leaders, and even U.S. presidents. As for blacks, Stephan and Abigail Thernstrom show that, of today's African-American congressmen, army officers, recent Ph.D.s, MacArthur Foundation genius-award winners, and top business officials, only a tiny sliver attended elite colleges.

None of this is rocket science. Every college administrator knows that diversity is really a code word for "at least 5 percent black faces with a good sprinkling of Latinos," and that this outcome is attainable only through quotas. Racial preferences continue to receive protection from the diversity fig leaf. It's a powerful rhetorical weapon. The question, "Aren't you in favor of diversity?" today means, "Don't you like black people?"—and nothing chills most thinking white Americans more than the fear of being deemed racist. At the same time, many blacks cheer preferences under the misguided impression that racism is the only possible cause of unequal performance, and thus they remain blind to the importance of the perseverance and individual initiative that will truly succeed in fostering black excellence.

A university culture truly committed to erasing the sins of the past would champion diversity in its true sense, infusing its discourse on race with a range of views wider than variations on victimhood. Since 1978, diversity has served as a flimsy and evasive perversion of justice. It has helped no one, least of all black students. It's high time we swept it into the dustbin of history.

Judith C. Appelbaum

 **NO**

Affirmative Action: End It or Defend It?

Thank you very much; I'm pleased to be here today to address this important topic. As you heard, the title of my talk poses the question, "Affirmative Action: End It, or Defend It?" My view is strong and unequivocal: we ought to *defend* it, and that is what I will undertake to do this afternoon. In fact, I am going to try to show that *ending* affirmative action, at this time in our nations history, would be a serious mistake.

Let me start by addressing a preliminary question that may be on some peoples' minds: is affirmative action already dead, or fairly close to it? The answer is, in general, no. To be sure, in some places, and for some purposes, affirmative action is now being eliminated. The voters in California in 1996 approved a ballot initiative, Proposition 209, that amended the states constitution to prohibit state government affirmative action programs. Washington State voters passed a similar ballot measure in 1998. And the U.S. Court of Appeals for the Fifth Circuit—the federal appellate court with jurisdiction covering Texas, Louisiana, and Mississippi—held in 1996 in a case called *Hopwood v. Texas* that public institutions of higher learning may not use race in higher education admissions.

But the U.S. Supreme Court has *not* held that all affirmative action is unconstitutional or impermissible. The Court's 1978 decision in *University of California v. Bakke,* upholding the consideration of race in college admissions decisions to ensure a diverse student body, is still the law of the land that is, everywhere except in the Fifth Circuit, where the judges on the *Hopwood* panel decided to ignore *Bakke.* In the most recent affirmative action case decided by the Supreme Court, in 1995, the Court ruled that government race-based affirmative action programs must be subjected to "strict scrutiny" under the constitution, to ensure that they are narrowly tailored to serve a compelling government interest, but the Court did not completely rule out the use of these programs when that test is met. Indeed, in that case (called *Adarand Constructors v. Pena*) which involved a federal program that creates an incentive for companies working on federal highway projects to subcontract with qualified minority- and women-owned businesses the Supreme Court sent the case back down to the lower courts, and just last month the U.S. Court of Appeals for the 10th Circuit (out in Denver) concluded that that particular program *does* in fact meet the "strict scrutiny" test and upheld it.

Speech at the State University of New York at Binghamton, November 2, 2000. Copyright © 2000 by National Women's Law Center. Reprinted by permission.

Also on the "good news" side of the ledger for affirmative action, efforts to copy the California and Washington State anti-affirmative action ballot measures have not gotten off the ground in other states, like Florida. In fact, to my knowledge, there are no anti-affirmative action measures on any ballots across the country in this month's elections. And proposed federal legislation to end all affirmative action, nationwide, has been successfully blocked in Congress by affirmative action supporters.

That said, there's no question that affirmative action is under severe attack. Legislative and ballot measures seeking to end it undoubtedly will continue to spring up. Challenges to affirmative action continue to be launched in the courts as well; there are cases pending right now seeking to ban the use of race as a factor in the admissions process at the University of Michigan and the University of Georgia, for example. And while the Supreme Court, as I said, has not completely ruled out the use of affirmative action, the "strict scrutiny" standard is a difficult one to satisfy, and even that degree of acceptance of affirmative action is precarious: some Justices on the Court (Scalia, Thomas) have made it clear that they do not believe *any* affirmative action can be justified, *ever.*

In a nutshell, affirmative action in the U.S. today is alive (if not entirely well) and continues to be widely practiced, but there is no doubt that it is taking a beating and that the threats to eliminate it are real.

So why should we worry about this state of affairs? Why *is* it important that affirmative action be retained?

As an affirmative action defender, let me start by saying that if the case could be made that race and sex discrimination have been eradicated in our country, and that we now live in a society that truly offers equal opportunity for all, then maybe it *would* be time to dismantle affirmative action. Is that the case?

Let's look at a few facts.

- The bipartisan Glass Ceiling Commission reported, in 1995: that African American men and women comprise less than 2.5% of total employment in the top jobs in the private sector in this country; that only 5% of the senior managers in the nations largest companies are female; and that virtually all of these women are white. And maybe even more striking, the Commission found that the following "stereotypes"—I'll call them prejudices—are commonplace in corporate America:
  - That women, of whatever race or national origin: don't want to work, aren't tough enough, are unwilling or unable to make decisions, are too emotional, are not sufficiently aggressive, are too aggressive, and are too passive.
  - That African American women: are incompetent, educationally deficient, aggressive, militant, hostile, lazy, sly, untrustworthy.
  - That African American men: are unqualified, unpredictable, hostile, undisciplined, lazy, violent.
  - The Commission found equally appalling stereotypes about Hispanics, Asians, and others as well.
- Then there's the wage gap. The latest figures show that the average woman who works full time, year round, earns 72 cents for every dollar the average man earns. An African American woman earns just

63 cents and a Hispanic woman earns 52 cents for each dollar that a white man earns. And several studies show that a large portion of the wage gap persists when you hold constant such factors as family responsibilities and choice of careers—leaving discrimination as the only explanation.

- There's also the volume of complaints filed at the EEOC—in fiscal year 1999, there were over 28,000 charging race discrimination and almost as many charging sex discrimination.

- Another measure of discrimination in the workplace is found in something called "audit studies" a method of testing for the existence of discrimination by matching equally qualified pairs of men and women (or candidates of different races) to apply for the same openings, and comparing their success. A series of these audits have found that African American applicants fare worse than whites, and women worse than men. A similar approach was used in a study—one of my favorites—that examined the effects of audition screens on the hiring of orchestra musicians—screens that prevented the judges from seeing the musicians gender. The use of these screens was found to increase a female musicians chances of selection significantly.

- Then, of course, there's case after case in the courts and reported in the newspapers. I am going to mention just a couple of examples that are included in a piece you can find on the National Women's Law Center's web site. The piece is called "Sex Discrimination in the American Workplace: Still a Fact of Life," and it summarizes a sampling of sex discrimination cases involving unequal pay for equal work, sexual harassment, and discrimination in hiring, promotions and job assignments, in workplaces of every type, in every part of America. Here are just three examples:

  - Example one. A federal court found that Lucky Stores, a grocery store chain in California, discriminated against women in promotions and hiring. Notes from a meeting attended by store management included comments such as "men do not want competition from women," "women don't have as much drive to get ahead," "the crew won't work for a black female," "[it is] impossible [to] . . . find qualified women." A teenaged boy who joined the company was given training opportunities that his mother, a cash register operator at Lucky for 21 years, had never had. The company eventually settled, paying some 12,000 women employees $107 million.

  - Example two. A number of female employees of Boeing Company sued the aerospace giant alleging that it discriminated against women employees in pay, promotions, and other workplace benefits. They claim, for example, that women assigned to "skill" departments were often asked to sweep the floors or clean up after the male workers. The suit follows a Labor Department settlement in which Boeing agreed to pay over $4.5 million to resolve claims that the company underpaid women and minorities.

  - Example three. Last year, the city of Concord, California agreed to settle the sex discrimination and harassment claims of eight female employees of the local police department for $1.25 million. The women alleged that they were denied training opportunities, were forced to jump extra hurdles to apply for promotions, received poor assignments, were refused back-up cover by male officers in the field, were propositioned for sex by other officers, and were told by a supervisor, "women do not belong in police work, they really belong at home, cooking and taking care of the house and children."

These examples, by the way, are not from ancient history; they are all from the last few years.

Finally, on the subject of race discrimination in America today, let me refer you to a September 2000 report by the U.S. State Department to the United Nations on our country's progress in meeting our obligations under the international Convention on the Elimination of All Forms of Racial Discrimination. This report describes how much work remains to be done to eliminate racial discrimination in this country, citing, for example, the brutal murder of James Byrd in Texas in 1998, discriminatory highway traffic stops (so-called "racial profiling"), continued discrimination in employment, housing, the criminal justice system, and access to capital and credit, and segregation in our nations schools. The report also notes that while overt discrimination may be less pervasive in this country than it was a few decades ago, there remain many subtle forms of discrimination based on ignorance and stereotyping that continue to restrict and limit equal opportunity in the United States as my recitation of both racial and gender stereotypes from the corporate world, a few moments ago, also shows.

Taking all of this together, we can hardly conclude that race and sex discrimination are relics of the past. But it is then fair to ask, what does this have to do with affirmative action?

It has everything to do with affirmative action because affirmative action is a set of tools used to *counteract ongoing discrimination,* and even prevent it. It consists of measures that open doors so that everyone has a fair chance to compete. In the employment arena, affirmative action includes recruitment and outreach efforts to include qualified women and minorities in the talent pool when hiring decisions are made, as well as employers efforts to analyze their own workforce to see how they're doing in hiring and promoting qualified female and minority employees, and their use of flexible goals and timetables to measure their own progress toward doing better. In education, affirmative action includes taking race or national origin into account to achieve a diverse student body, as well as programs to prepare and motivate female students for study in traditionally all-male fields. In the area of business opportunities, affirmative action means policies that encourage government agencies to do business with qualified minority-owned or female-owned businesses.

Let me give you just one actual example of affirmative action in practice, from a case that made it to the Supreme Court in 1987, *Johnson v. Transportation Agency of Santa Clara County.* The case is best known for the Court's decision upholding an employers affirmative action plan that included flexible goals and timetables. But the facts of the case illustrate how, when the deck starts out stacked against a woman trying to move into a non-traditional job, affirmative action makes a difference. A male and female employee of a county transportation agency, with substantially equal qualifications, Paul Johnson and Diane Joyce, applied for a promotion to road dispatcher. No woman ever before had held that position. Three male supervisors interviewed the two candidates—including one supervisor who had previously given Diane Joyce a hard time (derided her as a "skirt-wearing person")—and they recommended the man. That could have been the end of the matter. But the employer then looked at the records it kept as part of its affirmative action plan and found that of 238 skilled craft positions, *zero* were held by women. The employer took that into account, and Diane Joyce ended up with the promotion. Last time I checked, she was still successfully performing that job. Without affirmative action, she never would have had the chance she deserved.

It's important to understand that what happened in the *Johnson* case before application of the employer's affirmative action plan is what happens every day. Supervisors making hiring or promotion decisions rarely engage in the purely objective, scientific exercise that is sometimes imagined. They are human beings making subjective judgment calls, and these judgments are inevitably influenced by the natural tendency we all have to feel most comfortable with people like ourselves. The Glass Ceiling Commission's report is replete with illustrations of how such feelings of "kinship" or "chemistry" contribute to holding women and minorities back. Sociology Professor Barbara Reskin at Harvard also has written about this phenomenon.

Before leaving the *Johnson* case, I want to note that it also illustrates what affirmative action is *not*. It is not quotas or blind hiring by the numbers, which is unlawful, and it is not handouts for the unqualified. Diane Joyce was fully qualified, and the affirmative action plan that helped her did not set a quota-like numerical requirement; it simply enabled the employer to take the previous exclusion of women into account. That's why the Supreme Court upheld the use of affirmative action in the *Johnson* case.

You don't have to take my word for it that affirmative action, properly used, does not sacrifice merit or lower standards. In a study published in the most recent issue of the Journal of Economic Literature, a publication of the American Economic Association, two respected economists provide a lengthy review of over 200 serious studies of affirmative action. They conclude not only that affirmative action has made a positive difference for women and minorities, but also that it has not lowered performance in the workplace. And a study of affirmative action in higher education, set forth in a book by prominent educators Derek Bok and William Bowen called *The Shape of the River,* concluded that Black students who benefited from affirmative action at highly selective colleges did very well, by every measure: they went on to graduate, earn advanced degrees, and succeed in their chosen fields.

It is also clear that affirmative action has a positive impact not just on its immediate beneficiaries, but on others as well, and in many ways produces important benefits for all of us, for our society as a whole.

Affirmative action programs that help women and members of racial or ethnic minorities advance in the workplace are helping their families make ends meet.

Diversity in our student bodies improves the learning process for everyone, as the Supreme Court recognized in the *Bakke* decision. Experts in education and learning have found that a diverse university student body has far-ranging and significant benefits for all students, non-minorities and minorities alike. For example, students educated with a diverse set of peers are found to learn better and think in more complex ways, and they are also better prepared to participate more fully in our pluralistic society. The experts report that at a time in life when social and political attitudes are being shaped, and are heavily influenced by contacts with peers, the exposure of college students to members of different racial and ethnic groups can have a positive life-long impact on ones openness to different perspectives and the ability to thrive in a diverse world after college.

The Bok and Bowen study I mentioned a moment ago describes another benefit of affirmative action in higher education: the minority graduates they tracked went on to become community leaders, unusually active in civic affairs and social service activities, thereby benefiting the communities in which they lived.

Enrollment and scholarship programs that promote diversity in professional schools indirectly serve the public in dramatic ways, too. For example, the advancement of women in medical science has been accompanied by increased attention to womens health issues and expanded research in those areas. And research has shown that female and minority doctors have a much greater likelihood of treating traditionally under-served patient populations, such as the poor and members of minority groups.

Communities benefit from affirmative action in myriad other ways. The racial integration of law enforcement lessens tensions between minority communities and the police. Studies indicate that the increased presence of women in police forces and the criminal justice system improves the handling of domestic violence cases. These changes have benefited women, children, and all other members of the family and community who are affected by violence in the home.

Affirmative action programs also expand the talent pool for employers to draw on, and many companies report that a diverse workforce improves the bottom line. Indeed, in a case now pending that challenges the use of race as a factor in admissions decisions at the University of Michigan and its law school, General Motors and a long list of other Fortune 500 companies filed a "friend of the court brief" in support of the University, explaining why the success of American businesses depends on safeguarding the freedom of academic institutions to select diverse student bodies, as well as on the companies own efforts to create diverse workplaces. As General Motors put it, "Only a well educated, highly diverse workforce, comprised of people who have learned to work productively and creatively with individuals from a multitude of races and ethnic, religious, and cultural backgrounds, can maintain America's global competitiveness in the increasingly diverse and interconnected world economy."

Interestingly, at one time in our history it was said that "What's good for General Motors is good for America." Personally, I don't think *that's* always true. But I do believe that GM is right when it says affirmative action is good for GM . . . and good for America. And many others agree; General Colin Powell, for example, has said that "affirmative action is good for America."

One final comment. Because affirmative action has been prohibited in a few parts of the country as a result of ballot measures and lower court decisions, as I said at the outset, we actually have some direct evidence of what happens when affirmative action is ended. In California, after Proposition 209, there has been a significant decrease in the admission of Blacks, Hispanics, and Native Americans at the University of California at Berkeley and UCLA, two flagship UC campuses. And at the University of Texas Law School, in the wake of the 1996 *Hopwood* decision, there were only five African Americans among the 433 students in the class of 2000, seven in the class of 2001, and seven in the class of 2002 which means that for three years in a row, the percentage of African Americans in the entering class has been *lower than in the fall of 1950, the first year that school was desegregated and forced to admit African Americans.* Of course, it's too soon to measure the impact this resegregation will have on the school, the legal profession it shapes, or the larger community but from everything we know about the benefits of affirmative action, we can assume this is a giant step backwards.

So to those who argue we should *end* affirmative action, I would say: do you really want to jeopardize the important gains affirmative action has brought, and turn back the clock? I respectfully submit that we are all better off—far better off—defending, not ending, affirmative action.

POSTSCRIPT

Has Affirmative Action Outlived Its Usefulness in the Workplace?

In the 1960s, America was a society polarized across racial lines. Dr. Martin Luther King, in his famous "I have a dream" speech, presented his vision of an American society where skin color plays no role in securing economic and social opportunities. His hope was that harmony between the races would be possible if all were afforded the same opportunities to succeed. And, although he did not live long enough to see its emergence, there can be no doubt that King's civil rights activities helped pave the way for the development of affirmative action as an important vehicle for promoting a more diverse American workplace. But in a cruel twist of fate, it seems that affirmative action has given rise to the very scenario it was intended to alleviate. Consider these comments from Dr. Onkar Ghate, a widely respected resident fellow at the influential Libertarian think tank, the Ayn Rand Institute: "The consequence of the spread of racial quotas [i.e., affirmative action] and multiculturalist ideas hasn't been harmony, but a precipitous rise in racial hatred throughout America, particularly in the classroom and the workplace."

But is abandoning affirmative action the answer? Ms. Appelbaum, in the "con" side of this debate, makes an interesting argument for the continued use of affirmative action in the workplace. She bases her view on evidence that discrimination is still occurring in the workplace even now, some 40 years or so after Dr. King's speech. In her article, Appelbaum marshals evidence showing that racial and sexist stereotypes are still pervasive and points out that the male-female wage gap has yet to disappear. In the face of continued discrimination in the workplace, it would be foolish and wrong to discard affirmative action. To those that do, she asks: ". . . do you really want to jeopardize the important gains affirmative action has brought, and turn back the clock? I respectfully sumit that we are all better off—far better off—defending, not ending, affirmative action."

Suggested Readings

Affirmative Action and Diversity Project, The affirmative action and diversity project: A webpage for research, 2004. http://aad.english.ucsb.edu/

Dinesh D'Souza, *The End of Racism*. Free Press, 1995.

Joe R. Feagin and Hernan Vera, *White Racism: The Basics*. Routledge, 1995.

Marie Gryphon, The affirmative action myth. The Cato Institute, July 10, 2004. http://www.cato.org/dailys/07-10-04.html

Edwin A. Locke, What we should remember on Martin Luther King day. The Ayn Rand Institute, January 14, 2002. http://www.aynrand.org/site/News2?page=NewsArticle&id=7903&news_iv_ctrl=1076

News press release, MLK day: King's colorblind dream is being destroyed. The Ayn Rand Institute, January 10, 2001. http://www.aynrand.org/site/News2?page=NewsArticle&id=7637&news_iv_ctrl=1221

Philip F. Rubio, *A History of Affirmative Action.* University Press of Mississippi, 2001.

ISSUE 6

Is Workplace Drug Testing a Wise Corporate Policy?

YES: Ying-Tzu Lu and Brian H. Kleiner, from "Drug Testing in the Workplace," *Management Research News* (vol. 27, no. 4/5, 2004)

NO: Jacob Sullum, from "Urine—or You're Out: Drug Testing Is Invasive, Insulting, and Generally Irrelevant to Job Performance. Why Do So Many Companies Insist on It?" *Reason* (November 2002)

ISSUE SUMMARY

YES: Human resource management scholars Ying-Tzu Lu and Brian H. Kleiner believe that workplace drug testing does not inherently violate employee privacy rights. They suggest that workplace drug testing can lead to increased firm profitability, primarily as a result of increased worker productivity.

NO: *Reason* magazine senior editor Jacob Sullum argues that not only is drug testing invasive and insulting, but that it has no real bearing on job performance.

In the workplace, substance abuse costs employers tens of millions of dollars every year as a result of the increased levels of absenteeism, work-related accidents, health care costs, and theft. The U.S. Department of Labor reports that 70 percent of illegal drug users are employed, a number exceeding 10 million workforce members (Mathis & Jackson, *Human Resource Management,* Thompson South-Western, 2003, p. 527). It's not surprising, then, that employers across the country have adopted various types of drug-testing policies as a way of fighting back. The federal government entered the battle with the passage of the Drug-free Workplace Act of 1988. This act requires all government agencies and firms with governmental contracts to take action towards eliminating drugs from the workplace.

Despite society's apparent acceptance of drug testing at work, there is considerable opposition to the policy of testing employees. Central to the opposition's position is the issue of employee privacy rights. Notwithstanding the indisputable fact that corporations have a right to protect themselves, critics of workplace drug testing fear that it infringes on employee privacy rights. Critics also point to studies that call into question the degree to which employee productivity is truly affected by workplace drug use. Given these criticisms, it seems fair to ask, as we do in this debate: Is workplace drug testing a wise corporate policy?

Concerns about employee privacy comprise a continuum of viewpoints: At one end are those who are against drug testing in the workplace under any and all circumstances. They typically invoke a rights-based argument in contending that individual rights always trump organizational rights. America is a country founded on the belief in the supremacy of individual rights and, since drug testing violates an individual's right to privacy, organizations should not be allowed to implement them under any conditions.

At the opposite end are the pro-testing advocates. The view here is that organizations, often owners of private property and as much legal citizens as are individuals, have a right to protect themselves. Inasmuch as they can be held accountable for the moral and legal violations committed by their employees, they should be allowed to exercise reasonable control over the workplace. Given the tremendous damage drug abuse can cause an organization, drug testing is clearly a reasonable activity.

Perhaps the most commonly accepted view, representing the midpoint of our continuum, is that corporations should hold employee privacy as an important corporate principle. Testing can be done, but all effort should be made to protect employee privacy throughout the process and it should be implemented only in cases with reasonable grounds for suspicion. Thus, determining employee drug use is fair game only when there is evidence that it results in undesirable behaviors such as lower productivity or increasing the likelihood of safety violations.

Before you read the following articles and develop your own opinion, some facts should be presented. It is important to know that the courts have consistently sided with the rights of corporations to test employees provided there was no evidence of discrimination in its implementation nor unwarranted targeting of individuals for testing. Courts have been particularly supportive of drug testing when the job in question is of a sensitive nature. The fact that workplace drug testing is legal accounts in large measure for its widespread use by employers. Recent surveys of major American corporations indicate that nearly 90 percent of the firms use some form of drug testing in the workplace. Almost all firms surveyed use the tests as part of the applicant process and eliminate from consideration those individuals who failed (Gray & Brown in *Perspectives in Business Ethics*, 2nd ed. McGraw-Hill, 2002, p. 433). Thus, workplace drug testing is both legal and widespread; but the question remains, does that make it right?

Human resource management scholars Ying-Tzu Lu and Brian H. Kleiner believe that workplace drug testing, when conceived with foresight and implemented correctly, does not inherently violate employee privacy rights. Indeed, they conclude that workplace drug testing ultimately leads to increased firm profitability, primarily as a result of increased worker productivity. On the other hand, *Reason* magazine senior editor Jacob Sullum is adamantly against workplace drug testing. Sullum argues that not only is drug testing invasive and insulting, but that it has no real bearing on job performance. His clearly articulated view is that drug testing certainly does not constitute wise corporate policy.

YES    Ying-Tzu Lu and Brian H. Kleiner

Drug Testing in the Workplace

Introduction

Drug use in the workplace costs businesses $75 billion to S100 billion each year, according to the federal Labor Department (Rosen, 2000), so it is a very serious problem in the business world and has negative impacts on business. Those workers who use drugs in the workplace will significantly affect workplace safety, productivity and profitability. Compared with the non substance-abusing workers, substance-abusing workers have higher rate of absenteeism, higher health care and compensation claim costs, and more on-the job injuries (May, 1999). Moreover, the National Safety Council reported that 80 per cent of those injured in serious drug-related accidents at work were not the drug abusing employees but innocent co-workers and others (Ferraro, 2000). In addition to these problems, workers who do not abuse drugs may also experience lowered morale. Therefore, it is very important for the company to have effective drug testing programmes to combat these problems and to help achieve a drug-free workplace.

In order to have effective drug testing programmes, employers need to know when they can implement drug testing programmes to avoid liability because more and more lawsuits are involved in drug testing issues. In deciding when to test, employers need to consider six considerations: public versus private employees; union versus non-union employees; employees' job responsibilities; employee morale; evaluating the evidence of the workplace drug problem; and state or local legislation regulating drug testing. Under these six considerations, there are certain types of options for the company to implement a drug testing programme, including the discussion of the legality of each option under certain situations.

When to Test

More and more companies are aware of the importance of drug testing and formulate their own drug testing policies. However, more and more companies which have drug testing policies involve in the legal issues. Therefore, in order to avoid legal issues, employers need to decide when to test employees for drug testing. To decide when to test, employers have six considerations (De-Cresce, 1989).

From *Management Research News*, vol. 27, no. 4/5, 2004, pp. 46–53. Copyright © 2004 by Emerald Group Publishing Ltd. Reprinted by permission.

1. Whether the employer is a public entity.
2. Whether the employees to be tested arc unionised.
3. Whether the responsibilities of the employees implicate public safety or raise other special considerations.
4. Whether a drug testing programme may have an adverse impact on loyal and dedicated employees.
5. Whether there is evidence of an existing drug problem among employees to be tested.
6. Whether there is any state or local legislation restricting drug testing in the employment context.

Public versus Private Employees

The legal considerations for public and private employers in the drug testing area are quite different. Public employers have more hurdles than private employers because of The Fourth Amendment. The Fourth Amendment provides that "The right of the people to be secure in their persons, houses, papers, and effects, against unreasonable searches and seizures, shall not be violated, and no Warrants shall issue, but upon probable cause, supported by Oath or affirmation, and particularly describing the place to be searched, and the persons or things to be seized" (DeCresce, 1989). Since The Fourth Amendment can only apply to government-required drug testing, private employers have more latitude to test than public employers do. For public employees in a "safety-sensitive" position, public employers can screen for illegal substances only if they have a reasonable suspicion. Under the case of Capua v. City of Plainfield (DeCresce, 1989), the firefighters are required to submit a urine sample without reasonable suspicion or probable cause. Therefore, the court verdict that the testing was unlawful based on the city's violation of the Fourth Amendments. However, for private employees, private employers can test them for drugs at will unless they are protected by a collective bargaining agreement that limits drug testing. In brief, private employees have less protectable privacy rights in the workplace than public employees.

Union versus Non Union Employees

Unionised employers who need to obey the collective bargaining agreement have more hurdles than non union employers do. For example, unionised employers may not unilaterally establish a random-testing programme without notifying the union or will be required to decide when to test employees is "reasonable" unless they have an agreement with the union (Bahls, 1998). If the company unilaterally impose a random-testing programme the programme will violate the collective bargaining agreement. However, private non union employers may not have to prove that their drug testing programmes are reasonable. Thus, private non unionised employees have little legal weapon to oppose the implementation of drug testing because they do not have the protections offered by a collective bargaining agreement. However, this does not mean that private non union employers should adopt aggressive policies allowing drug testing at any time for any reason. They also need to follow the state law or common law otherwise they will be held illegal for the implementation of drug testing.

Employees' Job Responsibilities: Safety and Public Image

In deciding when to test, it is very important for employers to consider the degree of safety risk posed by drug use on the job and who will be tested. For example, employers should test employees involved in safety-sensitive jobs or those in which drug abuse might jeopardise public safety. Consider the case of Webster v. Motorola Inc. (Bryan, 1998). Two employees sued Motorola Inc. after the company instituted a urinalysis testing programme. The plaintiffs claimed this to be an excessive invasion of privacy. One of these plaintiffs was required to drive a company vehicle 20,000 miles per year. The court ruled that public safety out-weighed his right to privacy. The other plaintiff was a technical writer whose job could not harm public safety and whose right to privacy out-weighed any benefit from drug testing. Therefore, it is more defensible for Motorola Inc. to test an employee who drives a company vehicle than it is to test an employee who performs various administrative duties. As a result, any drug testing policy must be tailored according to the responsibilities of the employees. The validity of the policy will depend upon its reasonableness as applied to the employees tested. Thus, employers should consider different approaches toward different groups of employees.

Employee Morale

Drug testing programmes often have negative impacts on employees morale. When employers ask for drug testing, many employees may find that they are very humiliated to be required to urinate into a bottle. They may think that employers do not trust them so ask them to take drug testing. Moreover, since drug test can only show the presence of drugs, employees may perceive that employers use drug testing to know their off-duty conducts and intrude into their private lives. They will feel it is none of the employer's business about their off-duty conducts. Employers should consider whether off-duty conducts would affect the workplace and public safety (Flynn, 1999). If off-duty conducts will not affect the workplace and public safety, the company would have a claim for invasion of privacy for implementing the drug testing. Furthermore, the company will lose loyal and dedicated employees. Therefore, the company should be very careful of the drug testing policy which regulate employees' time away from the company.

Evaluating the Evidence of the Workplace Drug Problem

In deciding when to test, employers should provide a rationale testing. Employers should have reasonably suspects on employees whom are using drugs on the job or reporting to work in an impaired condition. This is so-called "reasonable suspicion."

The employer must have a reasonable basis for believing that an employee is using drugs or reporting to work under the influence of drugs before requiring a drug test. Moreover, the employer's suspicion must be individualised to the particular employees to be tested. The employer can not think that other employees in the same department are using drugs. It will be unlawful to ask all employees in the same department to submit to drug test because of the particular case. The employer can point to evidence through supervisors' observations of physical characteristics or reports of on-the-job use or possession. However, it is very important in reasonable-suspicion testing to make sure supervisors are well trained to understand signs of potential drug abuse. Supervisors should not look for just one sign to give reasonable suspicion of drug use but look for signs, as many as possible. Consider the case of Scott Wilson v. City of White Plains (Scott Wilson v. City of White Plains, 2000). After the city received the anonymous letter for reporting to work under the influence of drugs, Wilson was dismissed from his job as a firefighter for the City of White Plains because of the positive drug testing result. He filed a lawsuit that there is no reasonable suspicion for a drug test. However, the court found that before the test were administered, a commissioner evaluated Wilson and found that his eyes were watery and that he was having difficulty focusing. In addition, he had a history of chronic absenteeism. Therefore, the finding of reasonable suspicion was supported by far more than just the anonymous letter. The city was lawful to order an employee to submit to a drug test on reasonable suspicion of drug use. However, under the case of Craslawsky v. The Upper Deck Company (Craslawsky v. The Upper Deck Company, 2000), a manager at a baseball card publisher suspected that an employee had been drinking and asked her to take a drug test. The employee sued and claimed the violation of privacy and no reasonable suspicion. The court agreed that the manager exercised poor judgement in demanding the test.

State or Local Legislation Regulating Drug Testing

There are both state and federal laws that impact drug testing in the workplace. When employers want to implement the drug testing policy, they need to consider whether they violate the state or federal law. Many states have drug testing laws that determine what an employer can and can not do. It is important for employers to ensure that the testing rules and procedures established are in compliance with state regulation. For example, the Iowa drug testing law prohibits random tests (Fogarty, 1998). Therefore, it is unlawful for employers in Iowa to have random test for employees in a safety-sensitive position. Employers also should notice the new legislation on drug testing. For instance, Iowa might pass stronger privacy protections of drug testing bill (Fogarty, 1998). Employers in Iowa should be very careful to prepare to check whether their drug testing policies conflicts with the new bill. If the existing policy conflicts with the new bill, the employer should revise the policy to avoid the liability.

Testing Options

Under above six considerations, there are certain types of testing options for the company to implement its drug testing policies (Fay, 1991). In addition to discuss certain types of testing options, the legality of each options under certain situations is also included in the following discussion.

Pre-Employment Testing

The most common form of drug testing is pre-employment testing. Pre-employment screening can generate information that can help prevent hiring an illicit drug user. Pre-employment screening of job applicants for substance abuse is usually legal (Meiners, 1997). Courts have consistently upheld the legality of requiring a pre-employment drug test as a condition of employment. However, employers must be sure that prospective employees have been given notice of pre-employment testing and all applicants are treated similarly. It is unlawful to treat a particular person differently from other applicants. If an employer refuses to hire someone who used to be addicted, employers can be subject to a lawsuit under the ADA (the American With Disabilities Act). Employers just can refuse to hire someone with a history of drug abuse if they can show that the employee poses a "direct threat" to others (Lin, 1999). However, current illegal drug abusers are not protected under the ADA. Therefore, employers are lawful to refuse to hire someone who is a current illicit drug user. In addition, even though applicants produce the samples in private, it is also unlawful to have someone watching while they provide samples. This will be an excessive invasion of privacy.

Random Testing

There are two types of random testing: Discretionary random testing and Systematic random testing. Under a discretionary random testing policy, employers require employees to submit to a drug test at any time for good reason, bad reason, or no reason at all. Most court decisions have indicated that pure random testing is unreasonable and unlawful. Systematic random drug testing is the unannounced testing of a percentage of employees who have been selected for testing by a random selection method. The advantage of this policy is that employers can apply this policy in a fair manner. Therefore, most companies use this type of random drug testing rather than discretionary random testing. Random drug testing will be upheld when in a safety-sensitive environment and announced in advance as a condition of employment (Meiners, 1997). Random drug testing for employees who are not in safety-sensitive positions is going to be much more difficult because there is the argument that the employer has violated the right to privacy. Therefore, for the company with random drug testing to all employees to avoid liability, random drug testing should be tailored to the responsibilities in each category of employees. To employees in a safety-sensitive position, the company should have random drug testing once or twice a year. To employees in a non safety-sensitive position, the company should have random drug testing once every three years. It might be unlawful for the company to have the same random drug testing policy to all employees in different positions. For the company with random drug testing to only employees in a safety-sensitive position, it is unlawful to have random drug testing to employees in a non safety-sensitive position. Under the case of Gonzalez v. Metropolitan Transportation Authority (Hatch, 1999), Denise worked for the Los Angeles Metropolitan Transportation Authority as a bus dispatcher and was required to submit a random urine testing. He sued for the test was unreasonable because he did not occupy a "safety-sensitive" position. The court agreed that it is unlawful to have random testing to employees in the Gonzalezs' positions.

Reasonable Cause Testing

Substance tests given because of "reasonable suspicion" of improper usage are most likely to be upheld when there is an announced policy of such tests and when safety is an issue (Meiners, 1997). If there is no announced policy of such tests, it might be unlawful for the company to require employees to submit to a test. In addition, testing an employee because someone reported that the employee was seen in the company of drug users is less likely to be upheld unless the person is in a position of sensitivity or safety.

Periodic Testing

Periodic testing usually occurs in connection with an annual physical examination. Since this policy usually provide advance notice, the court has upheld this form of testing. Providing advance notice can undermine the claim for invasion of privacy because employees know they need to submit drug testing during an annual physical examination when they take the job. However, sufficient warning may also enable drug abusing employees to beat the system. Therefore, this policy is not as effective as other policies.

Postaccident Testing

Postaccident testing usually occurs after an industrial accident. This policy requires not only the perpetrator but also the victim to submit to drug tests. Drug tests after accidents have been upheld because the public safety issues generally outweigh the employer's right to privacy. This is probably the most defensible form of testing without cause because the accident means that safety has been threatened. An accident happens to give an employer reason to check to see if it happened because of drugs. Under the case of Harrison v. Eldim, Inc, (Harrison v. Eldim, Inc., 2000), Donavan Harrison had worked at Eldim Inc. for three months when he suffered a deep cut on his thumb. His job included using a corrugator to cut metal into strips. He was required to perform a drug test. He sued saying that the drug test was unreasonable and constituted an invasion of privacy. The court said his work at Eldim was sufficiently dangerous that he risked serious injury to himself and to others if he used the machine while under the influence of drugs. Therefore, the drug test was not unreasonable and an invasion of privacy. In addition, employers have a legal obligation to investigate whether the employee himself caused the accident. If the employer never makes the effort to investigate, the employer may be negligent and subject to damages.

Conclusion

Drug testing programmes should be applied consistently and legally follow the state or federal law. When employers want to implement a drug testing programme, they should consider whether the employee is in a safety-sensitive position or whether there is "reasonable suspicion" employees who, are using drugs on the job or reporting to work in an impaired condition. Once the employer is aware of the legality of his action, they can perform the drug testing programme very effectively and provide a drug-free workplace and a safe working environment. Furthermore, the employer will have higher profitability because the worker would have higher productivity, higher morale, lower rate of absenteeism, lower health care and compensation claim costs, and less on-the job injuries.

References

Bahls, J. E. (1998, Mar). "Dealing with drugs: Keep it legal." *HR Magazine* [Online], 43:4, pp. 104–116. Available: ABl/Inform [2000, June 6].

Bryan, L. A. (1998, Oct). "Drug testing in the workplace." *Professional Safety* [Online], 43: pp. 10, 28–32. Available: ABI/Inform [2000, June 6].

"Craslawsky v. The Upper Deck Company." (2000, May). *Workplace Substance Abuse Advisor* [Online]. Available: Lexis-Nexis [2000, June 21].

DeCresce, R., Mazura, A., Lifshitz, M., and Tilson, J. (1989). *Drug Testing In The Workplace.* Chicago, ASCP Press.

Fay, J. (1991). *Drug Testing.* Stoneham, Butterworth-Heinemann.

Ferraro, E. F. (2000, Jan). "Is drug testing good policy?" *Security Management* [Online], 44:1, 166. Available: ABI/Inform [2000, June 6].

Flynn, G. (1999, Jan). "How to prescribe drug testing." *Workforce* [Online], 78: 1, 107–109. Available: ABI/Inform [2000, June 6].

Fogarty, T. A. (1998, Jan 9). "Drug testing again on Agenda." *Des Moines Register* [Online]. Available: ABl/lnform [2000, June 6].

Harrison v. Eldim, Inc. (2000, Apr 26). *Workplace Substance Abuse Advisor* [Online]. Available: Lexis-Nexis [2000, June 21].

Hatch, D. D. (1999, Jul). "Drug-testing rationale must be on individual basis." *Workforce* [Online]. Available: ABI/Inform [2000, June 6].

Lin, G. R. (1999, Nov). "Keep out!" *Credit Union Management* [Online]. Available: ABI/Inform [2000, June 6].

May, D. (1999, Apr). "Testing by necessity." *Occupational Health & Safety* [Online], 68:4, pp. 48–51. Available: ABI/Inform [2000, June 6].

Meiners, R. E., Ringleb, A. H., and Edwards, F. L. (1997). *The Legal Environment of Business.* pp. 531–534. St. Paul. West Publishing Company.

Rosen, L. (2000, Apr 2). "How firms handle workers' drug tests." *San Francisco Examiner* [Online], J-5. Available: ABI/Inform [2000, June 6].

"Scott Wilson v. City of White Plains. (2000, May)." *New York Law Journal* [Online], p. 29. Available: Lexis-Nexis [2000, June 21].

Jacob Sullum

 **NO**

Urine—Or You're Out

In 1989 the U.S. Supreme Court upheld a drug test requirement for people seeking Customs Service positions that involved carrying a gun, handling classified material, or participating in drug interdiction. Justice Antonin Scalia dissented, calling the testing program an "immolation of privacy and human dignity in symbolic opposition to drug use." Scalia noted that the Customs Service policy required people to perform "an excretory function traditionally shielded by great privacy" while a monitor stood by, listening for "the normal sounds," after which "the excretion so produced [would] be turned over to the Government for chemical analysis." He deemed this "a type of search particularly destructive of privacy and offensive to personal dignity."

Six years later, Scalia considered a case involving much the same procedure, this time imposed on randomly selected athletes at a public high school. Writing for the majority, he said "the privacy interests compromised by the process of obtaining the urine sample are in our view negligible."

Last March [2002] the Supreme Court heard a challenge to a broader testing program at another public high school, covering students involved in any sort of competitive extracurricular activity, including chess, debate, band, choir, and cooking. "If your argument is good for this case," Justice David Souter told the school district's lawyer, "then your argument is a fortiori good for testing everyone in school." Scalia, who three months later would join the majority opinion upholding the drug test policy, did not seem troubled by that suggestion. "You're dealing with minors," he noted.

That factor helps explain Scalia's apparent equanimity at the prospect of subjecting every high school student to a ritual he had thought too degrading for customs agents. But his nonchalance also reflects the establishment of drug testing as an enduring fact of American life. What was once the "immolation of privacy and human dignity" is now business as usual.

While the government has led the way, the normalization of drug testing has occurred mainly in the private sector, where there are no constitutional barriers to the practice. Today about half of all U.S. employers require applicants, workers, or both to demonstrate the purity of their bodily fluids by peeing into a cup on demand. For defenders of liberty, this situation arouses mixed feelings.

On the one hand, freedom of contract means that businesses should be allowed to set whatever conditions they like for employment. People who don't want to let Home Depot or Wal-Mart sample their urine can take their labor elsewhere. The fact that drug testing is widespread suggests either that applicants and employees do not mind it much or that it enhances profits enough to justify the extra cost of finding and keeping workers, along with the direct expense of conducting the tests.

On the other hand, the profit motive is clearly not the only factor driving the use of drug testing. Through mandates and exhortation, the government has conscripted and enlisted employers to enforce the drug laws, just as it has compelled them to enforce the immigration laws. In 1989 William Bennett, then director of the Office of National Drug Control Policy, cited drug testing by employers as an important element of the government's crackdown on rec- reational users. "Because anyone using drugs stands a very good chance of being discovered, with disqualification from employment as a possible consequence," he said, "many will decide that the price of using drugs is just too high." The Institute for a Drug-Free Workplace, a coalition that includes companies that supply drug testing services as well as their customers, echoes this line. "Employers and employees have a large stake and legitimate role to play in the 'war on drugs,'" the institute argues. "A high level of user accountability . . . is the key to winning the 'war on drugs.'"

Why Test?

Federal policies requiring or encouraging drug testing by private employers include transportation regulations, conditions attached to government con- tracts, and propaganda aimed at convincing companies that good corporate citizens need to take an interest in their workers' urine. From the govern- ment's perspective, it does not matter whether this urological fixation is good for a company's bottom line. And given the meagerness of the evidence that drug testing makes economic sense, it probably would be much less popular with employers if it were purely a business practice rather than a weapon of prohibition. If it weren't for the war on drugs, it seems likely that employers would treat marijuana and other currently illegal intoxicants the way they treat alcohol, which they view as a problem only when it interferes with work.

Civilian drug testing got a big boost in 1986, when President Reagan issued an executive order declaring that "drugs will not be tolerated in the Federal workplace." The order asserted that "the use of illegal drugs, on or off duty," undermines productivity, health, safety, public confidence, and national security. In addition to drug testing based on "reasonable suspicion" and following accidents, Reagan authorized testing applicants for government jobs and federal employees in "sensitive positions." Significantly, the order was based on the premise that "the Federal government, as the largest employer in the Nation, can and should show the way towards achieving drug-free workplaces." Two years later, Congress approved the Drug-Free Workplace Act of 1988, which demanded that all federal grant recipients and many contractors "maintain a drug-free workplace." Although the law did not explicitly require drug testing, in practice this was the surest way to demonstrate compliance.

Private employers, especially big companies with high profiles and lucrative government contracts (or hopes of getting them), soon followed the government's lead. In its surveys of large employers, the American Management Association found that the share with drug testing programs increased from 21 percent in 1987 to 81 percent in 1996. A 1988 survey by the Bureau of Labor Statistics estimated that drug testing was required by 16 percent of work sites nationwide. Four years later, according to a survey by the statistician Tyler Hartwell and his colleagues, the share had increased to nearly half. In the 1997 National Household Survey on Drug Abuse (the source of the most recent nationwide data), 49 percent of respondents said their employers required some kind of drug testing.

As many as 50 million drug tests are performed each year in this country, generating revenue in the neighborhood of $1.5 billion. That's in addition to the money earned by specialists, such as consultants and medical review officers, who provide related services. Drug testing mainly affects pot smokers, because marijuana is much more popular than other illegal drugs and has the longest detection window. Traces of marijuana can be detected in urine for three or more days after a single dose, so someone who smoked a joint on Friday night could test positive on Monday morning. Daily marijuana smokers can test positive for weeks after their last puff. Because traces linger long after the drug's effects have worn off, a positive result does not indicate intoxication or impairment. (See [box].)

The relevance of such test results to job performance is by no means clear. But in the late 1980s and early '90s, government propaganda and alarmist press coverage combined to persuade employers that they could no longer rely on traditional methods for distinguishing between good and bad workers. "When employers read in *Time* and *Newsweek* and *U.S. News & World Report* that there was an epidemic of drug abuse in America, they got scared like everyone else," says Lewis Maltby, president of the National Workrights Institute and a leading critic of drug testing. "They didn't want some pot-head in their company causing a catastrophe and killing someone. Drug testing was the only answer that anyone presented to them, so they took it." Because drug testing was seen as an emergency measure, its costs and benefits were never carefully evaluated. "Most firms are understandably rigorous about making major investment decisions," Maltby says, "but drug testing was treated as an exception."

My interviews with officials of companies that do drug testing—all members of the Institute for a Drug-Free Workplace—tended to confirm this assessment. They all seemed to feel that drug testing was worthwhile, but they offered little evidence to back up that impression.

Link Staffing Services, a Houston-based temp agency, has been testing applicants since the late 1980s. "In the industry that we are in," says Amy Maxwell, Link's marketing manager, "a lot of times we get people with undesirable traits, and drug testing can screen them out real quick." In addition to conducting interviews and looking at references, the company does background checks, gives applicants a variety of aptitude tests, and administers the Link Occupational Pre-employment Evaluation, a screening program that "helps identify an applicant's tendency towards characteristics such as absenteeism, theft and dishonesty, low productivity, poor attitude, hostility, and drug use or violence." Although the drug testing requirement may help impress Link's customers, it seems unlikely that urinalysis adds something useful to the information from these other screening tools. Asked if drug testing has affected accident rates or some other performance indicator, Maxwell says, "We probably don't track that, because we have other things that [applicants] have to pass."

TESTING LIMITS:
ALTERNATIVES TO DRUG SCREENING

In the 1980s, when everyone was talking about the dangers posed by addicts in the workplace, Lewis Maltby was executive vice president and general counsel of Drexelbrook Engineering, a Pennsylvania company that designs and manufactures control systems for toxic chemicals. "This company makes a product that, if it doesn't work properly, could cause a Bhopal [1984 tragedy in India in which toxic chemicals burst from a tank at a Union Carbide plant and injured thousands] in the United States," says Maltby, now president of the National Workrights Institute. "Almost every job in the company is safety-sensitive."

Not surprisingly, Drexelbrook considered drug testing. Maltby, long active with the American Civil Liberties Union, was leery of the idea, but he could not deny that the company needed to make sure that its products were assembled properly. Ultimately, he says, "we decided that drug testing was a red herring. The real issue was building an organization that inherently produces quality and reliability."

That meant paying careful attention to every step of the process, including recruitment, hiring, training, supervision, and quality assurance. "We had a very systematic, company-wide program to make sure that everything we did was right," Maltby says. "If we had drug testing, it just would have been a distraction from the real business of safety."

Maltby's experience at Drexelbrook convinced him that drug testing was not the right answer even for employers with serious safety concerns. As an alternative, he has tried to promote impairment testing. Unlike urinalysis, which detects traces of drugs long after their effects have worn off, impairment testing is aimed at assessing an employee's current fitness for duty. The idea is to identify employees who are not up to snuff, whether the cause is illegal drugs, alcohol, medication, illness, personal troubles, or inadequate sleep.

Several different systems are currently available, including an electronic shape recognition test and a device that measures the eye's response to light. But Maltby was able to identify only 18 employers that have ever used such systems, and he suspects the total is not more than 25.

One reason impairment testing has never caught on is its lack of a track record, which poses something of a Catch-22. Although it seems to address safety concerns more directly than urinalysis does, employers are not inclined to adopt a new technology without solid evidence that it works—unless, like drug testing, it has the government's stamp of approval. That factor is especially important for federally regulated industries such as aviation and trucking, where employers who adopted impairment testing would still have to do drug tests.

Impairment testing also could raise new problems for employers, workers, and unions. "The information that impairment testing provides is the information that employers most need, but employers wouldn't know what to do with it," Maltby argues. "Running any kind of a business, you know 5 percent of your employees are showing up not really on the ball every day: sick kids, colds, divorces, death in the family, drugs, alcohol, hangovers. Figuring out what to do about 5 percent of your employees being unfit to work every day is a monumental challenge."

Michael Walsh, a Maryland-based drug testing consultant, calls impairment testing "sort of a holy grail." It's a sound idea in theory, he says, but "I haven't seen a good one that is usable. . . . I have never seen any data that would convince a general audience of scientists that this is the way to go." But then, the same could be said of drug testing.

Eastman Kodak, which makes photographic supplies and equipment, tests all applicants in the U.S. but tests employees (except for those covered by Department of Transportation regulations) only when there's cause for suspicion of drug-related impairment. Wayne Lednar, Eastman Kodak's corporate medical director, says safety was the company's main concern when it started doing drug testing in the 1980s. "Our safety performance has substantially improved in the last 10 years on a worldwide basis, not just in the United States," Lednar says. "That improvement, however, is not one [for which] the drug testing approach in the U.S. can be the major explanation. A very large worldwide corporation initiative driven by line management is really what I think has made the difference in terms of our safety performance."

David Spratt, vice president for medical services at Crown Cork & Seal, a Philadelphia-based packaging manufacturer, says that when the company started doing drug testing in the early 1990s, "there was a concern that employees who used drugs were more likely to have problems in the workplace, be either the perpetrators or the victims of more accidents or more likely to be less productive." But like Eastman Kodak, Crown Cork & Seal does not randomly test employees; once they're hired, workers can use drugs without getting into trouble, as long as they do their jobs well. "What drives our concern is work performance," Spratt says. "If there is such a thing [as] 'recreational use,' we would probably not find that out."

Asked if the company has any evidence that drug testing has been effective, Spratt says: "That's not typically the way these things start out. They typically start out with, 'We gotta do drug testing, because the guy up the street is doing drug testing, and the people who walk in and see his sign will come down and sign up with us for a job.' We're going to get the skewed. . . . They will be a different group who may be less than desirable."

Margot Brown, senior director of communications and public affairs at Motorola, which makes semiconductors, cell phones, and two-way radios, says that when the company started doing drug testing in 1988, "They were trying to control the quality of their products and the safety of their work force." Asked whether the goals were accomplished, she says: "Our productivity per employee did go up substantially. . . . Who knows if that was coincidental or not? Those were good years for Motorola."

Phantom Figures

As those remarks suggest, drug testing became broadly accepted without any firm evidence that it does what it's supposed to do: improve safety, reduce costs, and boost productivity. "Despite beliefs to the contrary," concluded a comprehensive 1994 review of the scientific literature by the National Academy of Sciences, "the preventive effects of drug-testing programs have never been adequately demonstrated." While allowing for the possibility that drug testing could make sense for a particular employer, the academy's panel of experts cautioned that little was known about the impact of drug use on work performance. "The data obtained in worker population studies," it said, "do not provide clear evidence of the deleterious effects of drugs other than alcohol on safety and other job performance indicators."

It is clear from the concessions occasionally made by supporters of drug testing that their case remains shaky. "Only limited information is available about the actual effects of illicit drug use in the workplace," admits the Drug Free America Foundation on its Web site. "We do not have reliable data on the relative cost-effectiveness of various types of interventions within specific industries, much less across industries. Indeed, only a relatively few studies have attempted true cost/benefit evaluations of actual interventions, and these studies reflect that we are in only the very early stages of learning how to apply econometrics to these evaluations."

Lacking solid data, advocates of drug testing tend to rely on weak studies and bogus numbers. The Office of National Drug Control Policy, for example, claims a 1995 study by Houston's Drug-Free Business Initiative "demonstrated that workplace drug testing reduces injuries and worker's compensation claims." Yet the study's authors noted that the "findings concerning organizational performance indicators are based on numbers of cases too small to be statistically meaningful. While they are informative and provide basis for speculation, they are not in any way definitive or conclusive, and should be regarded as hypotheses for future research."

Sometimes the "studies" cited by promoters of drug testing do not even exist. Quest Diagnostics, a leading drug testing company, asserts on its Web site that "substance abusers" are "3.6 times more likely to be involved in on-the-job accidents" and "5 times more likely to file a worker's compensation claim." As Queens College sociologist Lynn Zimmer has shown, the original source of these numbers, sometimes identified as "the Firestone Study," was a 1972 speech to Firestone Tire executives in which an advocate of employee assistance programs compared workers with "medical-behavioral problems" to other employees. He focused on alcoholism, mentioning illegal drugs only in passing, and he cited no research to support his seemingly precise figures.

Another number from the Firestone speech appears on the Web site of Roche Diagnostics, which claims "substance abusers utilize their medical benefits 300 percent more often than do their non-using co-workers."

Roche also tells employers that "the federal government estimates" that "the percentage of your workforce that has a substance abuse problem" is "about 17 percent." This claim appears to be a distortion of survey data collected by the National Institute of Mental Health (NIMH). As summarized by the American Psychiatric Association, the data indicate that "nearly 17 percent of the U.S. population 18 years old and over will fulfill criteria for alcohol or drug abuse in their lifetimes." By contrast, Roche is telling employers that 17 percent of the population meets the criteria *at any given time.* Furthermore, the vast majority of the drug abusers identified by the NIMH were alcoholics, so the number does not bolster the case for urinalysis aimed at catching illegal drug users.

According to a study published last February [2002] in the *Archives of General Psychiatry,* less than 8 percent of the adult population meets the criteria for "any substance use disorder" in a given year, and 86 percent of those cases involve alcohol. The study, based on data from the National Comorbidity Survey, found that 2.4 percent of respondents had a "substance use disorder" involving a drug other than alcohol in the previous year. So Roche's figure— which is also cited by other companies that profit from drug testing, such as RapidCup and eVeriTest—appears to be off by a factor of at least two and perhaps seven, depending upon whether "substance abuse problem" is understood to include alcohol.

Drinking Problems

This ambiguity seems to be deliberate. To magnify the size of the problem facing employers, the government and the drug testing industry routinely conflate illegal drugs with alcohol. But it's clear that employers are not expected to treat drinkers the way they treat illegal drug users. Although drinking is generally not allowed on company time, few employers do random tests to enforce that policy. In 1995, according to survey data collected by Tyler Hartwell and his colleagues, less than 14 percent of work sites randomly tested employees for alcohol. And while 22 percent tested applicants for alcohol, such tests do not indicate whether someone had a drink, say, the night before. In any case, it's a rare employer who refuses to hire drinkers.

When it comes to illegal drugs, by contrast, the rule is zero tolerance: Any use, light or heavy, on duty or off, renders an applicant or worker unfit for employment. "With alcohol, the question has always been not 'Do you consume?' but 'How much?'" notes Ted Shults, chairman of the American Association of Medical Review Officers, which trains and certifies physicians who specialize in drug testing. "With the illegal drugs, it's always, 'Did you use it?'"

The double standard is especially striking because irresponsible drinking is by far the biggest drug problem affecting the workplace. "Alcohol is the most widely abused drug among working adults," the U.S. Department of

Labor notes. It cites an estimate from the Substance Abuse and Mental Health Services Administration that alcohol accounts for 86 percent of the costs imposed on businesses by drug abuse.

In part, the inconsistency reflects the belief that illegal drug users are more likely than drinkers to become addicted and to be intoxicated on the job. There is no evidence to support either assumption. The vast majority of pot smokers, like the vast majority of drinkers, are occasional or moderate users. About 12 percent of the people who use marijuana in a given year, and about 3 percent of those who have ever tried it, report smoking it on 300 or more days in the previous year. A 1994 study based on data from the National Comorbidity Survey estimated that 9 percent of marijuana users have ever met the American Psychiatric Association's criteria for "substance dependence." The comparable figure for alcohol was 15 percent.

According to the testing industry, however, any use of an illegal drug inevitably leads to abuse. "Can employees who use drugs be good workers?" Roche asks in one of its promotional documents. Its answer: "Perhaps, for a while. Then, with extended use and abuse of drugs and alcohol, their performance begins to deteriorate. They lose their edge. They're late for work more often or they miss work all together. . . . Suddenly, one person's drug problem becomes everyone's problem." This equation of use with abuse is a staple of prohibitionist propaganda. "It is simply not true," says the Drug-Free America Foundation, "that a drug user or alcohol abuser leaves his habit at the factory gate or the office door." The message is that a weekend pot smoker should be as big a worry as an employee who comes to work drunk everyday.

Employers respond to the distinctions drawn by the government. Under the Americans With Disabilities Act, for example, alcoholics cannot be penalized or fired without evidence that their drinking is hurting their job performance. With illegal drugs, however, any evidence of use is sufficient grounds for disciplinary action or dismissal.

A Crude Tool

A more obvious reason government policy shapes employers' practices is that many do not want to hire people who break the law. A positive urinalysis "proves someone has engaged in illegal behavior," observes drug testing consultant Michael Walsh, who headed the task force that developed the federal government's drug testing guidelines. "All companies have rules, and this is a way of screening out people who are not going to play by the rules." He concedes that "you are going to rule out some people who would have made really good employees, and you are going to let in some people who make lousy employees." Still, he says, "in a broad way, it's a fairly decent screening device."

Perhaps the strongest evidence in support of drug testing as a screening device comes from research involving postal workers conducted in the late 1980s. A study reported in *The Journal of the American Medical Association* in 1990 found that postal workers who tested positive for marijuana when they were hired were more prone to accidents, injuries, absences, disciplinary action, and turnover. The differences in these rates were relatively small, however, ranging from 55 percent to 85 percent. By contrast, previous estimates had ranged from 200 percent for accidents to 1,500 percent for sick leave. "The findings of this study suggest that many of the claims cited to justify pre-employment drug screening have been exaggerated," the researchers concluded.

Even these comparatively modest results may be misleading. The study's methodology was criticized on several grounds, including an accident measure that gave extra weight to mishaps that occurred soon after hiring. A larger study of postal workers, reported the same year in the *Journal of Applied Psychology,* confirmed the finding regarding absenteeism but found no association between a positive pre-employment drug test and accidents or injuries. On the other hand, workers who had tested positive were more likely to be fired, although their overall turnover rate was not significantly higher.

It's hard to know what to make of such findings. As the National Academy of Sciences noted, "drug use may be just one among many characteristics of a more deviant lifestyle, and associations between use and degraded performance may be due not to drug-related impairment but to general deviance or other factors." On average, people who use illegal drugs may be less risk-averse or less respectful of authority, for example, although any such tendencies could simply be artifacts of the drug laws.

In any case, pre-employment tests, the most common kind, do not catch most drug users. Since people looking for a job know they may have to undergo a drug test, and since the tests themselves are announced in advance, drug users can simply abstain until after they've passed. For light users of marijuana, the drug whose traces linger the longest, a week or two of abstinence is probably enough. Pot smokers short on time can use a variety of methods to avoid testing positive, such as diluting their urine by drinking a lot of water, substituting someone else's urine, or adulterating their sample with masking agents. "Employers are very concerned that there's always a way to cheat on a drug test," says Bill Current, a Florida-based drug testing consultant. "The various validity testing methods that are available are always one step behind the efforts of the drug test cheaters."

Generally speaking, then, drug users applying for jobs can avoid detection without much difficulty. "The reality is that a pre-employment drug test is an intelligence test," says Walsh. The people who test positive are "either addicted to drugs, and can't stay away for two or three days, or just plain stupid. . . . Employers don't want either of those." Alternatively, applicants who fail a drug screen may be especially reckless or lazy. In short, it's not safe to draw conclusions about drug users in general from the sample identified by pre-employment tests. By the same token, however, such tests may indirectly measure characteristics of concern to employers.

The upshot of all this is something that neither supporters nor opponents of drug testing like to admit: Even if drug use itself has little or no impact on job performance—perhaps because it generally occurs outside the workplace—pre-employment testing still might help improve the quality of new hires. If so, however, it's a crude tool. As an index of undesirable traits, testing positive on a drug test could be likened to having a tattoo. Refusing to hire people with tattoos might, on balance, give a company better employees, but not because tattoos make people less productive or more prone to accidents.

How Much?

Maltby, president of the National Workrights Institute, argues that such benefits are too speculative to justify drug testing, and he believes employers are starting to realize that. "Times are tougher than they were 15 years ago," he says. "Money is tighter, and employers are scrutinizing all of their expenditures to see if they are really necessary. Initially, in the late '80s or early '90s, employers looked at drug testing and said, 'Why not?' Now employers look at drug testing like everything else and say, 'Where's the payoff?' And if nobody sees a payoff, programs get cut—or, more often, cut back."

One example is Motorola, which has seen its profits slide recently and plans to eliminate a third of its work force by the end of the year. When Motorola started doing drug testing, the company's communications director says, "The cost wasn't really a factor because we really felt like it was something we should attend to at the time." But Motorola recently scaled back its urinalysis program, which for a decade included random testing of employees; now it tests only applicants.

Motorola's decision may be part of a trend. The share of companies reporting drug testing programs in the American Management Association's surveys of large employers dropped from a peak of 81 percent in 1996 to 67 percent last year. Some of that drop may reflect a new questionnaire the organization started using in 1997. The new survey is less focused on testing, which could have changed the mix of companies that chose to participate. But the downward trend continued after 1997.

Once drug testing became common, it acquired a certain inertia: Employers who didn't do it worried that they might be at a disadvantage in attracting qualified workers or maintaining a positive public image. Employers who did it worried that stopping would hurt their recruitment or reputations. Yet without abandoning drug testing completely, a company can save money by giving up random tests. Even if it keeps random tests, it can save money by testing less frequently—the sort of change that would not be widely noticed.

Still, one reason drug testing endures is that it does not cost very much, especially from the perspective of a large employer. Eastman Kodak, which has more than 100,000 employees worldwide, pays just $12 to $15 per test. Even considering additional expenses (such as the medical review officer's time), and even with thousands of applicants a year, the total cost is a drop in the bucket. Drug tests cost Cork Crown & Seal, which has nearly 40,000 employees worldwide, $25 to $30 per applicant, for a total of less than $100,000 a year. Motorola, which will have about 100,000 employees after this year's cutbacks, spent something like $1 million a year when it was doing random testing of employees—still not a significant concern to a corporation with billions of dollars in revenue (at least, not until profits took a dive).

Small companies, which have always been less inclined to do drug testing, have to pay more per test and are less able to afford it. They also have lower profiles. "If G.M. were to be on the front page of *The Wall Street Journal,* announcing that they dropped their drug testing program, I wouldn't want to own their stock," Maltby says. He recalls a conversation in which the president of a *Fortune* 500 company told him that a few million dollars a year was a small price to pay for the reassurance that drug testing gives stockholders.

The direct costs of drug testing are not the whole story, however. Wayne Sanders, CEO of the paper products giant Kimberly-Clark, has to keep shareholders in mind, but he also worries about the message that drug testing sends to employees. In 1986, when Sanders was the company's head of human resources, managers pressured him to start doing drug testing, arguing that otherwise Kimberly-Clark would get all the addicts rejected by other employers. According to *The Dallas Morning News,* Sanders, "who wasn't about to pee in a bottle," thought the notion was "utter bunk." He successfully argued that "the idea of urine testing was demeaning and completely alien in a culture based on trust and respect."

There is some evidence that the atmosphere created by drug testing can put employers at a disadvantage. A 1998 *Working USA* study of 63 high-tech companies found that pre-employment and random drug testing were both associated with *lower* productivity. The researchers, economists at LeMoyne College in Syracuse, speculated that drug testing programs may create a "negative work environment" that repels qualified applicants and damages employee morale.

The Familiarity Factor

Yet survey data suggest that most Americans have gotten used to the idea that their urine may be part of the price they pay to get or keep a job. In the National Household Survey on Drug Abuse, the share of employees who said they would be less likely to work for a business that tested applicants fell from 8 percent in 1994 to 5 percent in 1997. Random testing of employees was somewhat less popular, with 8 percent saying it would be a negative factor in 1997, compared to 14 percent in 1994. Even among current users of illegal drugs, only 22 percent said pre-employment testing would make a job less appealing in 1997 (down from 30 percent in 1994), while 29 percent said random testing would (down from 40 percent in 1994)—which suggests how ineffective testing is at identifying drug users.

For those who object to drug testing, the natural tendency is to give in and take the test, on the assumption that a few protests are not likely to change a well-established business practice. But in jobs that require a high level of training or experience, even one person's objection can make a difference. An executive with a global management consulting company says he discussed his use of psychedelics with senior management early on "because I didn't want any negative repercussions later." When the company considered starting a drug testing program, he recalls, "I said, 'I'm not going to subject myself to mandatory testing because I don't have a problem. You know I don't have a problem, so testing me is not going to fly. And I think testing a bunch of people you pay upper five figures to mid to upper six figures is silly.' . . . The idea was dropped. I like to think I had some impact on that."

A former librarian who works in sales for a publisher of reference works says he was offered an appealing job with another publisher but balked at taking a drug test, although he has not used illegal drugs in years. He told the company, "I want to take this job, but I can't take a drug test. I think it's invasive. I think it's insulting." The employer dropped the requirement, telling him he could instead sign a statement saying that he doesn't use illegal drugs. Although he ended up not taking the job, he sees the experience as evidence that applicants can have more impact than they might think. "Every single person I've talked with [about drug testing], they don't like it, but they concede," he says. "Even when they say, 'I don't have anything to hide,' they say, 'I really don't like this, but I want the job.'"

Since it sharply reduces the cost that has to be weighed against the uncertain benefits of drug testing, this willingness to go along may be the most important reason, aside from the drug laws, that the practice endures. When push comes to shove, even those who recognize the political roots of drug testing are not inclined to take a stand. A strategic marketer in her 20s who used a variety of drugs in college and still smokes pot occasionally says her attitude toward drug testing has changed. "I think maybe three years ago I would have said, 'Fuck the man. No way am I taking a drug test. I'm standing up for my principles,'" she says. "But now I have to pay my rent, and I have to figure out what's important to me in life: Do I want a really nice apartment, or do I want to hold onto my principles?"

POSTSCRIPT

Is Workplace Drug Testing a Wise Corporate Policy?

Beyond the right-to-privacy argument, discussed here in Jacob Sullum's article, drug-testing critics have raised a host of concerns. Foremost among these is the accuracy of the tests themselves. Critics point out that the repercussions from inaccurate test scores can be devastating not only to the specific individuals involved, but also to the rest of the workforce. Employee confidence in management's neutrality as well as the appropriateness of testing can be severely eroded if innocent individuals are punished or guilty employees go undetected. Testing also seems to send a message of distrust from management to employees regardless of whether such a perception is accurate. A second concern is the expense of drug testing. There is, of course, a cost/accuracy trade-off: Cheap tests are notoriously undependable; highly accurate tests are extremely expensive. Small firms may have no choice but to use inexpensive tests, while large firms with thousands of employees might find the costs to be excessive. Finally, critics express concern about the information obtained from the tests and the manner in which management uses it. Critics are concerned that employers will use the information to target employees for dismissal on grounds that are completely unrelated to job performance (Gollot, Cohen, & Fillman, 1990).

In their article supportive of drug testing, Ying-Tsu Lu and Brian H. Kleiner acknowledge the central role tests play in the debate. They provide detailed suggestions as to what firms can do to minimize their legal liabilities in this area while increasing the likelihood that positive organizational outcomes such as increased productivity will result. Despite the valid points raised by the opposing side, supporters of drug testing note that, often, those individuals who have a reason to fear drug tests are the ones who are the most vocal against their use. Consider the results of an important research study on this topic: Human resource scholars found that students who had never used drugs were much more likely to support workplace drug-testing programs than were students who had used drugs in the past (Murphy, Thornton, & Reynolds in *Perspectives in Business Ethics,* 2nd ed. McGraw-Hill Irwin, 2002).

Suggested Readings

Jane Easter Bahls, Drugs in the workplace. *HR Magazine,* February 1998.

William F. Current, Improving your drug testing ROI. *Occupational Health & Safety,* April 2004, vol. 73, p. 40.

Michael A. Gips, Industry comment shapes drug testing rule. *Security Management,* March 2001.

George R. Gray and Darrel R. Brown, Issues in drug testing for the private sector, in *Perspectives in Business Ethics,* 2nd ed. Edited by Laura P. Hartman. McGraw-Hill Irwin, 2002.

Robert L. Mathis and John H. Jackson, *Human Resource Management,* 10th ed. Thompson South-Western, 2003.

A. McBay, Legal challenges to testing hair for drugs: A review. *The International Journal of Drug Testing,* no. 1, 2000.

Judith A. Swartley, Testing for drugs. *Plumbing and Mechanical,* October 2002, pp. 63–70.

ISSUE 7

Is Diversity in the Workplace a Worthwhile Goal for Corporations?

YES: Nancy R. Lockwood, from "Workplace Diversity: Leveraging the Power of Difference for Competitive Advantage," *HRMagazine* (June 2005)

NO: Roger Clegg, from "Diversity Nonsense," *National Review Online* (January 21, 2002)

ISSUE SUMMARY

YES: Society for Human Resource Management human resource expert Nancy Lockwood discusses several important benefits that result from workplace diversity. Included among these is the possibility of increased organizational productivity and profitability.

NO: The opposing view is presented by social critic Roger Clegg, who attacks the notion that pursuing diversity for its own sake is a wise strategy regardless of whether it occurs in the workplace or in the educational system.

The composition of the U.S. workforce has changed dramatically over the last few decades. Prior to 1980, for example, the typical employee in corporate America was a married, white male with children and a wife at home who did not work. Consider that now, in the early part of the twenty-first century, such an individual is actually in the minority! Indeed, as management scholar Stephen Robbins notes (*Organizational Behavior,* Prentice Hall, 2003, p. 15) 47 percent of the current U.S. labor force are females, many of whom are childless and/or single, while minorities, at about 25 percent, represent the fastest-growing demographic segment of the workforce. This tremendous increase in workplace diversity—Robbins defines the concept as the recognition that organizations are becoming increasingly heterogeneous in terms of race, gender, ethnicity, and other diverse groups of employees—raises important questions for managers and their organizations as we move further into the twenty-first century. For example, an important concern involves the question of whether or not workplace diversity provides beneficial outcomes for businesses. To the extent that it does, organizations will be much more inclined to accept workplace diversity as a worthwhile part of their overall strategic philosophy.

In the pro article that follows this introduction, Nancy Lockwood discusses several important benefits that result from workplace diversity. For example, wise firms will recognize that talent shortages can be addressed by embracing a willingness to actively recruit, hire, and train minorities and females. Firms that intentionally discriminate are, in effect, reducing the size of the talent pool from which they can recruit. Another similar argument raised by Lockwood is based on the notion that, relative to nondiverse firms, diversity-embracing organizations will likely enjoy larger market share since they will have access to a potentially larger customer base. Finally, she notes that diverse work groups tend to produce more decision alternatives as well as providing a wider range of creative solutions than do homogenous groups. Over the course of time, such beneficial outcomes will presumably translate into increased levels of employee productivity and organizational profitability.

Representing the opposing viewpoint in this debate, Roger Clegg attacks the notion that pursuing diversity for its own sake is a wise strategy regardless of whether it occurs in the workplace or in the educational system. Specifically, Clegg takes to task the findings of the Business-Higher Education Forum's Diversity Initiative Task Force, an organization whose mission is to inform "policy makers and the public regarding strategic national challenges of high priority to both business and higher education, and to help shape sound policy to address these challenges" (The Business-Higher Education Forum Web site: http://www.bhef.com/, 2006). A particularly pointed criticism involves the report's assertion that the widespread presence of workplace diversity initiatives indicates that business leaders recognize that "diversity brings value to their enterprises." Rather, Clegg argues, failure to embrace such initiatives is likely to result in lawsuits, legal harassment, increased governmental intervention and regulations, and social and political pressure. From this perspective, maintaining a diverse workplace is simply corporate self-defense masquerading as positive public relations. Another point Clegg takes issue with is the general belief—advocated by the BHEF task force and central to its report—that diverse college campuses benefit corporate America because exposure to people from different cultures and backgrounds provides a necessary training ground for employment in a diverse workplace. He attacks this belief from several angles pointing out, for instance, that this belief presupposes that blacks and whites are so different in how they think and behave on campus and in the workplace and that "it is . . . important to learn these differences that it justifies deliberate racial and ethnic discrimination in order to ensure this racial and ethnic mix on campus."

As you read these articles, keep in mind that this debate requires you to think from the perspective of the organization. You may be completely for diversity in the workplace or completely against it, but the question here is, based on the arguments of the two sides, do you think diversity is a worthwhile goal for corporations to pursue?

YES

Nancy R. Lockwood

Workplace Diversity:
Leveraging the Power of Difference
for Competitive Advantage

Workplace Diversity—An Evolution

From compliance to inclusion, the concept of workplace diversity is evolving. Coming from an organizational viewpoint, this article explores the changing perception of workplace diversity, elements of an inclusive corporate culture, the business case and HP's leadership role to maximize the benefits of a diverse workforce in a changing marketplace. While a broad range of issues is covered, it should be noted that "one size does not fit all," as organizations are in different stages of development regarding workplace diversity. In addition, workplace diversity is not strictly a U.S. concept: a brief discussion on the drivers of workplace diversity in the European Union is presented.

Diversity Defined Today

As predicted in the landmark study Workforce 2020, rapid technological change, globalization, the demand for skills and education, an aging workforce and greater ethnic diversification in the labor market have forever changed the employment landscape.[1] The definition of diversity extends well beyond the traditional view that once focused primarily on gender and race and reflects the broader perspective of workplace diversity today.

"A broad definition of diversity ranges from personality and work style to all of the visible dimensions such as race, age, ethnicity or gender, to secondary influences such as religion, socioeconomics and education, to work diversities such as management and union, functional level and classification or proximity/distance to headquarters."[2]

Integration and Learning: A New Paradigm
for Managing Diversity

Diversity in the United States has evolved since the 1960s. Diversity was first based on the assimilation approach, with everyone being part of the "melting pot." Compliance (e.g., affirmative action, equal employment opportunity) is important in diversity, and key legislation has been an effective tool for change (e.g., Title VII of the Civil Rights Act of 1964, Age Discrimination in Employment Act of 1967, Americans with Disabilities Act of 1990). Today, however, the impetus behind workplace diversity is that of inclusion and the business case, embracing and leveraging differences for the benefit of the organization. The collaboration of cultures, ideas and different perspectives is now considered an organizational asset—bringing forth greater creativity and innovation—with the result that many companies are increasingly focusing on corporate diversity initiatives to improve organizational performance.[3]

Diversity initiatives do not always meet expectations. The traditional schools of thought behind many diversity interventions are: 1) assimilation, based on the idea that "we're all the same" (promoting equal opportunity); and 2) differentiation, from the philosophy "we celebrate differences." Today, groundbreaking research goes beyond the historical framework of workplace diversity. The emerging paradigm is integration and learning. That is, companies promote equal opportunity and value cultural differences, using the talents of all employees to gain diverse work perspectives. To achieve this level of diversity management, however, organizational leaders must have a clear understanding of how they define diversity as well as what exactly the organization does with the experiences of being a diverse workforce.[4]

An Inclusive Corporate Culture

The concept of inclusion is increasingly important in the discussion of workplace diversity. In many ways, this evolution reflects societal values in the workplace. For example, two beliefs commonly held by Americans are that everyone deserves a chance (equal opportunity, sometimes referred to as the "level playing field") and that all people should be treated with dignity and respect.[5] The values of equality, respect and opportunity for all represent the cornerstone of workplace diversity. Inclusiveness is thus a win-win dynamic: it generates opportunities for growth, flexibility and adaptation in the marketplace for both the employee and the organization.

The Business Case for Workplace Diversity

Increasingly, the case for workplace diversity as a business imperative is gaining recognition by leaders in the business world. At a symposium sponsored by The Conference Board regarding diversity in the workplace, for example, 400 executives agreed that "diversity programs help to ensure the creation, management, valuing and leveraging of a diverse workforce that will lead to organizational effectiveness and sustained competitiveness."[6]

One of the major drivers behind the business case is the demographic changes that directly affect the labor pool and available talent. These changes are significant. In an organization, human capital and workforce relationships are the backbone of success. The flow of information between colleagues, work teams, customers and suppliers, for example, depends on the quality of relationships and talent in the workplace.[7] Consequently, workplace diversity is increasingly viewed as an essential success factor to be competitive in today's marketplace.

Advantages

Six key reasons to tie workplace diversity to organizational strategic goals and objectives are: 1) greater adaptability and flexibility in a rapidly changing marketplace; 2) attracting and retaining the best talent; 3) reducing costs associated with turnover, absenteeism and low productivity; 4) return on investment (ROI) from various initiatives, policies and practices; 5) gaining and keeping greater/new market share (locally and globally) with an expanded diverse customer base; and 6) increased sales and profits.

Workplace diversity can be viewed as having both direct and indirect links to the bottom line. In business, the preferred equation for success is a single action that directly impacts financial performance. Workplace diversity, however, is a complex phenomenon. Consequently, the link of workplace diversity to financial success is not always immediately apparent, nor is it always linear. Two examples below illustrate scenarios with direct and indirect links of workplace diversity to organizational performance.[8]

- Direct link: Organizations that expand their customer base most effectively do sc with a workforce that is reflective of their clients. DuPont, for example, considers diversity a business imperative vital to ongoing renewal and competitiveness in the 21st century. This philosophy was illustrated when the company learned how one small change ccould directly translate into significant profits. At DuPont Merck, the sales of an anticoagulant drug in the Hispanic markets were low. When a Hispanic manager noticed that the drug was only labeled in English and consequently translated the instructions into Spanish. sales improved significantly. Now, educational materials for the drug are translated into 15 languages and bring in millions of dollars in new business.[9]
- Indirect link: Having access to and retaining talent from a worlcfwide diverse iabor pool is key to gaining a competitive edge in the global marketplace. To expand and keep their market share, Nortel views lost revenue due to turnover as a reason to support diversity. With the cost of replacing an employee at $55,000 and turnover at 7% (compared to 17% in the information technology industry), the overall turnover cost is still quite high. For example, 7% attrition for 80,000 employees translates to replacing 5,600 people. Thus, when 5,600 (people) is multipiied by $55,000 (the cost of replacing one employee), turnover cost is $30.8 million! Thus, at Nortel, attracting and keeping talent—a key aspect of workplace diversity—has a significant impact on the bottom line.[10]

Firms are increasingly aware of the impact of diversity initiatives on organizational effectiveness. For example, factors that affect organizational profits are highlighted in a study by the Society for Human Resource Management on the impact of diversity on the bottom line. HR professionals from

Figure 1

Diversity and Competitive Advantage

In what ways does your organization actively leverage the diversity of employees for the purpose of increasir competitive advantage? (Number of Respondents = 310)

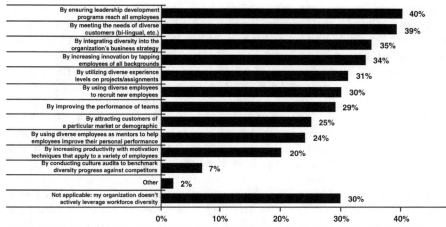

Source: Society for Human Resource Management. (2004, August 3). SHRM/Fortune Diversity Weekly Survey. *Retrieved March 25, 2005, from www.shrm.org.*

companies on Fortune's list of Top 100 Companies to Work For state that diversity initiatives provide organizations with a competitive advantage by positive improvements in corporate culture, employee morale, retention and recruitment (Figure 1). For example, 40% of companies ensure leadership development programs are available to all employees, 34% increase innovation by tapping talent of employees of all backgrounds, and 31% utilize diverse experiences for special projects and assignments.[11]

The importance of positive community relations also illustrates the link between workplace diversity and the business case. When organizations develop external partnerships with minority communities and suppliers, for example, this can lead to good will and a reputation as an "employer of choice."[12] When employees are proud of their organization for its contributions and connections to the community, they are more loyal to their employer and more likely to boast about their company to family and friends. The result is lower turnover and a positive employer brand that better attracts the best talent in the marketplace.[13] A prime example of diversity partnerships is that of Pitney Bowes, the No. 1 company on the 2004 DiversityInc Top 50 Companies for Diversity list, with recruitment initiatives and partnerships developed with organizations such as the National Urban League and the National Society of Hispanic MBAs. Another example is that of Ford Motor Co., the No. 1 company on the 2003 DiversityInc Top 50 list, that made community relations a priority: Ford spent 6% of its total procurement budget ($3.2 billion) with its first-tier diversity suppliers.[14]

Money Talks

The shift in purchasing power in the United States provides further evidence for the business case for workplace diversity. According to the Selig Center for Economic Growth, the purchasing power of minorities in the United States will quickly outpace that of whites in the next five years. In 2009, for example, the combined buying power of African-Americans, Hispanics, Asian-Americans and Native Americans is expected to exceed $1.5 trillion, more than triple the 1990 level by a gain of $1.1 trillion or 242%. In contrast, the buying power of whites will increase by 140%.[15]

Thus, in order to ensure that the company's sales and marketing teams reach the minority groups with funds to purchase its products and services, one of the most effective avenues is to utilize the knowledge of minority employees who can relate to different groups in the marketplace. Verizon Communications, for example, utilizes its African-American spokespeople, such as the actor James Earl Jones, to attract African-American consumers." Fannie Mae, a leading mortgage lending firm, wanted to reach the many minorities who did not yet own homes; in the United States, only 46% of African-Americans and Hispanics own homes, compared with 72% of whites. The company utilized diversity training as a strategic business initiative to reach a segment of the population that could profit from their service.[17]

Finally, the SHRM 2004–2005 Workplace Forecast notes that one of the top economic trends is expansion into the global marketplace.[18] Organizations can better capture, keep and serve their international customer base when their own workforce such as sales, marketing and customer service-understands the needs of other cultural and ethnic groups.

Metrics the ROI of Diversity

As with all business initiatives, measuring the return on investment of diversity makes good business sense. Measurement of diversity management can be considered in a number of areas, such as organizational culture, demographics, accountability, productivity, growth and profitability. For example, measuring diversity leadership commitment may involve many individual factors, such as the development of diversity vision/mission statements by a specific date, the number of times diversity is mentioned as a strategy in executive presentations, the percentage of board representation by group, the percentage of diverse employees who were promoted due to mentorship and the percentage of diversity strategy plans implemented.[19]

To determine the return on investment, hard and soft data must be converted to monetary values. There are five basic steps: 1) identify a unit of measure that represents a unit of improvement; 2) determine the value of each unit; 3) calculate the change in performance data; 4) determine an annual amount for the change; and 5) calculate the total value of the improvement.[20]

The diversity return on investment (DROI) is calculated by using the diversity initiative cost and benefits to get the benefit/cost ratio (BCR). BCR = diversity initiative benefits + diversity initiative costs. This ratio is also referred to as a cost-to-benefit ratio. Specifically, the DROI calculation is the net benefit of the diversity initiative divided by the initiative costs: DROI% = (net diversity initiative benefits + initiative costs) × 100. This formula is the same basic formula used to evaluate other investments in which the ROI is reported as earnings divided by the investment.[21]

For example, the initial cost of a diversity awareness program may be $50,000. The measurable value of the program is determined to be three years. During a three-year period, the program will have a net savings of $30,000 ($10,000 per year). Since the average book value is approximately half the cost, the average investment in this case is $25,000 ($50,000 + −2). The average ROI = annual savings 4 average investment: $10,000 + $25,000 = 40%.

Short- or Long-Term Investment

The business advantage for workplace diversity is clear. Yet companies often expect short-term results. The challenge is to demonstrate measurable impact on financial success as well as realistically manage expectations. Rather than a quick fix, the business case for workplace diversity is a long-term investment and offers sustainability in a competitive marketplace.

Senior Management's Role

Visibility, communication and accountability are key to achieving a competitive diverse workforce. A recent study on what makes and breaks diversity initiatives found three critical points of leadership: 1) accountability; 2) a passion for diversity; and 3) sustained involvement. Visible commitment throughout the organization is important: adding diversity on the agenda at executive meetings and company conferences, appointing diversity candidates to top positions, and assigning clear roles and responsibilities to the senior management team regarding diversity management. Accountability creates sustained involvement-that is, holding managers accountable to deliver diversity results. Participation in diversity councils is recommended as a development path for senior leadership.[22]

However, simply placing women and/or minorities in high-profile positions, for example, is insufficient. Rather, the more effective approach is to hold management accountable for results. Consequently, to get middle management and employee buy-in, top management must establish clear implementation and reporting requirements. At DuPont, for example, senior management ensures accountability for diversity management by integrating diversity into the overall business performance evaluation process, including developing cost and profit objectives as well as how compensation is determined. The company also uses targeted career development initiatives to help diverse people fill key work assignments, thus supporting advancement and addressing glass ceiling issues. The Quaker Oats Company aims to keep diversity management simple by using two key tools: 1) the diversity progress menu; and 2) the diversity accountability guidelines. The company's goal is to supply managers with a best practices list that offers flexibility tied to individual business cultures as well as performance.[23] Nine of the top 50 companies on the 2004 DiversityInc Top 50 Companies for Diversity list tie diversity to managers' compensation. For example, CitiGroup measures its managers' attempts to attract talent and develop a diverse workforce. At Verizon Communications, 5% of bonuses for directors and above are related to diversity.[24] Simple daily actions also communicate commitment to workplace diversity: the CEO greets employees in their native language, and the supervisor takes time to understand direct reports with different cultural values and viewpoints.[25]

Diversity Management and the Board of Directors

Increasingly, the business case for diversity focuses on the board of directors. The impetus to change the board composition is a direct result of the trend toward corporate governance and diversity of the workforce, customer base and other stakeholders. Organizations want a wider range of leadership skills, work styles, perspectives and expertise, as well as increased representation of women and minorities among board directors.[26] There is positive evidence of change. For example, in the Fortune 500 in 2003, women held 14% of board seats (up from 10% in 1995), and 54 companies had 25% or more women on boards of directors (up from 11% in 1995).[27] Finally, change in board composition is also occurring at an international level, as global organizations expand the cultural diversity of their boards with expertise in international business from other countries.[28]

Managing Diversity: HR Challenges and Opportunities

With the changing marketplace and an increasingly diverse labor pool, HR leaders are dealing with a myriad of factors regarding diversity management. Broadly speaking, workplace diversity challenges can be considered within three interrelated categories: attracting and retaining talent, greater diversity among employees and training.

Attracting and Retaining Talent

Competition for talent is growing-from competition abroad, lower education levels of U.S. workers compared with other countries, U.S. immigration challenges and fear of terrorism in the United States.[29] Further, with the retirement of the baby boom generation (those born from 1944 to 1960) in the next 10 years, a key concern is retention of older workers. Organizations are in different stages of preparation regarding this likely loss of talent. As of 2003, 35% were just becoming aware of the issue, 35% did not know if their organizations were ready, 23% were beginning to examine policies, and 4% had proposed specific changes. Many HR leaders are looking for ways to attract and retain older workers. Benefits and workplace programs, such as reward initiatives and flexible work arrangements (e.g., part-time work, phased retirement), are key tools that offer attractive options to older workers.[30]

The skill shortage, however, will hit some industries harder and sooner than others. The nuclear power industry, for example, faces replacing as much as 50% of its workforce. The talent crunch will also strike the expanding service industry: sales positions in the United States, for example, are expected to increase by 25%, yet many in today's sales force are aged 55 or older.[31]

A recent study notes most firms are not paying close attention to retention and promotion strategies. For example, top minority talent is seeking leadership opportunities; yet companies indicate they have difficulty attracting talent for executive leadership (42%) and professional and technical skills (42%).[32] In corporate America, the "revolving door syndrome" is particularly evident for women and minorities. To retain women and minorities, HR professionals should re-evaluate their organization regarding talent, mentoring, career development and succession planning. Strategic initiatives, such as mentoring, on-boarding and "listening" forums, are additional tactics to address minority retention.[33]

Greater Diversity Among Employees

The term "diversity" has typically referred to women and minorities. Today, however, employers are beginning to formally acknowledge other employees as well (e.g., ethnic groups, people with disabilities and self-identified gay, lesbian and bisexual persons). Some firms encourage a welcoming and inclusive environment for all employees by creating diversity network groups. Kraft Foods uses employee councils to build employee development. Through nine employee councils (African-American Council, Hispanic Council, Asian-American Council, Rainbow Council, Women in Sales Council, Black Sales Council, Hispanic/Asian Sales Council, Women in Operations and African-Americans in Operations), Kraft takes an active role in mentoring and supporting its diverse workforce. For example, the company builds relationships with universities to bring in talent through internships and internally sponsors career days focusing on leadership competencies.[34]

Different groups have different needs, and they want their needs recognized and met. Acknowledgment of different needs yields greater employee satisfaction, employer loyalty and, in turn, lower turnover and greater productivity. As a result, more organizations offer programs to address issues such as work/life balance and demands for more flexibility with telecommuting, adoption support, flexible health and dependent care spending accounts, elder care and domestic partner benefits.[35]

Within workplace diversity, one of the least discussed minority groups is people with disabilities. This group is a source of under-represented talent in the workplace. One study reveals that in the majority of companies, individuals with disabilities comprise less than 10% of their total workforce. The study recommends top management lead by example and hire qualified individuals with disabilities on their staff. Through training and focus groups, HR leaders can improve sensitivity toward employees with disabilities.[36]

Training

Within the context of workplace diversity, training plays a key role in retaining talent. The role of training is to promote workplace harmony, learn about others' values, improve cross-cultural communication and develop leadership skills. Awareness training raises understanding of diversity concerns by uncovering hidden assumptions and biases, heightening sensitivity to diversity in the workplace and fostering individual and group sharing. Skill-based diversity training improves morale, productivity and creativity through effective intercultural communication.[37] Leadership development, team building and mentoring programs are also examples of organizational training that promotes growth and collaboration. An overlooked area regarding retention is cross-cultural competence within the organization, often a missed opportunity to address minority retention concerns.[38]

Finally, working in a diverse organization requires diversity competencies for everyone, including HR. Yet not all HR professionals are experts in diversity. A survey notes that only about one-third of companies think their HR staff has the skills to serve a diverse U.S. workforce and only 22% believe HR has the skills to serve a global workforce.[39] HR professionals best qualified to deal with workplace diversity have experience in areas such as team building, change management, conflict resolution and cross-cultural communication.

Aligning the Diversity Process With Strategic Business Goals

The organization that best utilizes the full potential of all employees intentionally and thoughtfully aligns workplace diversity with strategic business goals by following these steps:

Define diversity. Clarify the role of workplace diversity in the organization, including leadership roles and expectations for diversity initiatives. In vision and mission statements, highlight the importance of diversity (for example, is the organization's philosophy on inclusion clearly stated?). Place the vision and mission statements on the company Web site as a public statement of the organization's commitment to workplace diversity. Communicate commitment by allocating the necessary resources-staff, budgets and time-to move the diversity process forward.[40]

Establish accountability. With senior management, HR diversity leaders should develop challenging yet realistic goals for diversity interventions. Demonstrate organizational commitment: 1) appoint senior executives to diversity task forces for succession planning, education and training initiatives: 2) recruit diversity candidates for senior leadership positions; and 3) establish diversity goals and objectives for all leadership levels in the performance management process and reward programs. Demonstrate commitment to workplace diversity by developing solutions when problems are identified through employee attitude surveys, focus groups, etc.[41]

Develop a diversity scorecard. Often overlooked, the scorecard is an important tool to manage diversity. The scorecard includes financial and nonfinancial recognition of diversity ROI initiatives as well as relevant feedback (e.g., change management lessons). When developing the diversity scorecard, include measures aligned with the organization's strategic business goals. When determining measures, keep in mind four themes: 1) key deliverables that leverage the role of diversity in the organization's overall strategy; 2) utilization of diversity in the development of a high-performance work environment; 3) ways in which the corporate culture is aligned with the organization's strategy; and 4) the efficiency of the diversity deliverables.

Studies on Workplace Diversity and the Bottom Line

Several studies link workplace diversity and company performance. The study results run the gamut from identifying critical success factors for diversity initiatives that impact organizational effectiveness to connecting gender and diversity with financial performance.

The "Makes and Breaks" of Diversity Initiatives[42]

This study found that successful initiatives that leverage diversity to enhance organizational effectiveness share certain characteristics and approaches. Specifically, successful workplace diversity initiatives hinge on committed leadership, goals/targets of measures of effectiveness, strong diversity professionals, employee involvement and ties to performance evaluation, as well as data to identify, quantify and communicate progress and challenges.

Diversity Practices That Work[43]

Companies with diversity practices collectively generated 18% greater productivity than the U.S. economy overall. The results of this study suggest that, at a minimum, diversity progress may enhance productivity through effective good leadership and management practices. Key factors that had the greatest impact on overall perceived effectiveness of diversity initiatives were: 1) a track record of recruiting diverse people; 2) management that is accountable for diversity progress and holds others accountable; 3) leaders who demonstrate commitment to diversity; 4) rewarding people who contribute in the area of diversity; and 5) training and education to increase awareness and help employees understand how diversity can impact business results.

The Effects of Diversity on Business Performance[44]

This study looks at the effects of racial and gender diversity on organizational performance. A key finding reveals that racial diversity has a positive effect on overall performance in companies that use diversity as a resource for innovation and learning. Further, the study results suggest that the best performance outcomes occur when diversity is found across entire organizational units.

Connecting Corporate Performance and Gender Diversity[45]

Based on an examination of 353 Fortune 500 companies, this study connects gender diversity and financial performance. (The study does not, however, demonstrate causation.) The key findings show that the group of companies with the highest representation of women on their top management teams experienced better financial performance than the group with the lowest women's representation: that is, 35% higher return on equity and 34% higher total return to shareholders. The study results suggest there is a business case for gender diversity (e.g., recruiting, developing and advancing women)-specifically, organizations that focus on diversity are in a stronger position to tap the educated and skilled talent in the marketplace. This is important because women comprise 47% of the U.S. paid labor force and hold 46% of management positions. In addition, women earn more than half of all bachelor's and master's degrees in the United States (57% and 59%, respectively) and nearly half of all doctorates and law degrees (45% and 47%, respectively).

Notes

1. Judy, R. W., & D'Amico, C. (1997). Workforce 2020: Work and workers in the 21st century. Indianapolis, IN: Hudson Institute.

2. SHRM Glossary of Human Resource Terms, www.shrm.org/hrresources/hrglossary_published/d.asp.

3. Jayne, M. E. A., & Dipboye, R. L. (2004, Winter). Leveraging diversity to improve business performance: Research findings and recommendations for organizations. Human Resource Management, 43, 4, 409–424.

4. Thomas, D. A., & Ely, R. J. (2002). Making differences matter: A new paradigm for managing diversity. Retrieved March 15, 2005, from Harvard Business Online, www.hbsp.harvard.edu.

5. Gardenswartz, L., Rowe, A., Digh, D., & Bennett, M. F. (2003). The global diversity desk reference: Managing an international workforce. San Francisco: John Wiley & Sons, Inc.

6. Hart, M. A. (1997). Managing diversity for sustained competitiveness. New York; The Conference Board.

7. Carr-Ruffino, N. (1999). Diversity success strategies. Boston: Butterworth-Heinemann.

8. Hart, M. A. (1997). Managing diversity for sustained competitiveness. New York: The Conference Board.

9. Ibid.

10. Martino, J. (1999). Diversity: An imperative for business success. New York: The Conference Board.

11. Society for Human Resource Management. (2001). Impact of diversity initiatives on the bottom line. Alexandria, VA: Author.

12. Richard. O. C., & Johnson, N. B. (2001, Summer). Understanding the impact of human resource diversity practices on firm performance. Journal of Managerial Issues, 13, 2, 177–196.

13. Lockwood, N. R. (2004, December). Corporate social responsibility: HR's leadership role. SHRM Research Quarterly, 4.

14. Cole, Y. (2004, June/July). Top 10 companies for diversity. DiversityInc Top, 3, 3, 56–96.

15. Humphreys, J. M. (2004, August). The multicultural economy 2004: America's minority buying power. Georgia Business and Economic Conditions, 63, 3, 1–12.

16. Cole, Y. (2004, June/July). Top 10 companies for diversity. DiversityInc Top, 3, 3, 56–96.

17. Martino, J. (1999). Diversity: An imperative for business success. New York: The Conference Board.

18. Schramm, J. (2004). SHRM 2004–2005 workplace forecast: A strategic: outlook. Alexandria, VA: Society for Human Resource Management.

19. Hubbard, E. E. (2004). The diversity scorecard: Evaluating the impact of diversity on organizational performance. Burlington, MA: Elsevier Butterworth-Heinemann.

20. Ibid.

21. Ibid.

22. Matton, J. N., & Hernandez, C. M. (2004, August). A new study identities the "makes and breaks" of diversity initiatives. Journal of Organizational Excellence, 23, 4, 47–58.

23. Hart, M. A. (1997). Managing diversity for sustained competitiveness. New York: The Conference Board.

24. Cole, Y. (2004, June/July). Top 10 companies for diversity. DiversityInc Top, 3, 3, 56–96.

25. Carr-Ruffino, N. (1999). Diversity success strategies. Boston: Butterworth-Heinemann.

26. Business for Social Responsibility. Board diversity. Retrieved March 4, 2005, from www.bsr.org.

27. Catalyst. (2003). 2003 Catalyst census of women board of directors. Retrieved March 7, 2005, from www.catalystwomen.org/knowledge/titles/files/fact/Snapshot%202004.pdf.

28. The Conference Board. (1999). Board diversity in U.S. corporations. New York: Author.

29. Richard, O. C., & Johnson, N. B. (2001, Summer). Understanding the impact of human resource diversity practices on firm performance. Journal of Managerial Issues, 13, 2, 177–196.

30. Collison, J. (2003, June). SHRM/NOWCC/CED older workers survey. Alexandria, VA: Society for Human Resource Management.

31. Towers Perrin HR Services. (2004, October). The coming talent crisis: Is your organization ready? Retrieved March 21, 2005, from www.towers.com.

32. Hewitt Associates, (n.d.). The workforce is changing: Is your organization? Retrieved March 21, 2005, from www.hewitt.com.

33. Hewitt Associates. (2004, February). Preparing the workforce of tomorrow. Retrieved February 10, 2005, from www.hewitt.com.

34. Cole, Y. (2004, June/July). Top 10 companies for diversity. DiversityInc Top, 3, 3, 56–96.

35. Burke, M. E. (2004, June). SHRM 2004 benefits survey report. Alexandria, VA: Society for Human Resource Management.

36. Lengnick-Hall, M. L. Gaunt, Ph., & Collison, J. (2003, April). Employer incentives for hiring individuals with disabilities. Alexandria, VA: Society for Human Resource Management.

37. Grant, B. Z., & Kleiner, B. H. (1997). Managing diversity in the workplace. Equal Opportunities International, 16, 3, 26–33.

38. Hewitt Associates. (2004, February). Preparing the workforce of tomorrow. Retrieved February 10, 2005, from www.hewitt.com.

39. Ibid.

40.   Hubbard, E. E. (2004). The diversity scorecard: Evaluating the impact of diversity on organizational performance. Burlington, MA: Elsevier Butterworth-Heinemann.

41.   Ibid.

42.   Matton, J. N., & Hernandez, C. M. (2004, August). A new study Identifies the "makes and breaks" of diversity initiatives. Journal of Organizational Excellence, 23, 4, 47–58.

43.   National Urban League. (2004, June). Diversity practices that work: The American worker speaks. New York: Author.

44.   Kochan, T., Bezrukova, K., Ely, R., Jackson, S., Joshi, A., Jen, K., et al. (2002, October). The effects of diversity on business performance: Report of the Diversity Research Network. Building Opportunities for Leadership Development Initiative, Alfred P Sloan Foundation and the Society for Human Resource Management.

45.   Catalyst. (2004). Connecting corporate performance and gender diversity. New York: Author.

 **NO**

Diversity Nonsense

The year is young, but it is not too soon to declare an early frontrunner in the increasingly crowded field of Stupid Pseudo-Scientific Reports in Desperate Defense of Racial and Ethnic Preferences (Subcategory: Corporate-Academic Partnership). Earlier this month, the Business-Higher Education Forum's Diversity Initiative Task Force issued *Investing in People: Developing All of America's Talent on Campus and in the Workplace.*

In a remarkably clumsy and silly attempt to tie the report in with the war on terrorism, task-force member Roberts T. Jones—president and CEO of the National Alliance of Business—declared, "Diversity is another form of national security. As we fight to eradicate terrorism and maintain safety on our shores, we must protect our economic stability by investing in our most valuable resource, our diverse citizenry." But it is unnecessary to consider this statement in awarding Stupid Frontrunner status to the report. It can stand proudly on its own.

The thrust of the report is: (1) American businesses should be racially and ethnically diverse; (2) a disproportionately high number of blacks and Hispanics are not academically prepared to enter the workforce; and so (3) steps must be taken to ensure that these groups are better prepared, including especially racial and ethnic preferences in university admissions.

The BHEF might have written a perfectly plausible report that reasoned, instead: (1) the American workforce should be academically well prepared; (2) too many young people are entering the workforce without adequate academic preparation; and so (3) steps must be taken to ensure that they are better prepared, including especially improving the educational opportunities of children whose parents are less wealthy. But such a report would not have viewed the world through the prism of race and would not have urged the use of racial and ethnic preferences, and so it was not written.

Now, it is undeniable that, the more members of racial and ethnic minority groups America has, the less it can afford for a high proportion of them to be relatively uneducated. This is especially true if the jobs available require more and more, rather than less and less, education. But it is not at all clear that the best way to address this problem is by rewarding underperformance or by pretending that academic disparities don't exist.

The report insists that all children should have access to high-quality education and recommends increased financial aid to students who need it.

Fine, but there is nothing in that proposition that requires race-consciousness. And the reasons that so many African American children reach age 18 with poor educational skills has less to do with the amount of money spent on public schools than on high illegitimacy rates (seven in ten blacks are born out of wedlock, versus two in ten for non-Hispanic whites), the insulation of public schools from competition, and the too-widespread cultural belief that studying hard is "acting white."

The report acknowledges that at many campuses blacks graduate at a much lower rate than whites. Could this be because the black students who are admitted are less academically qualified? This obvious possibility is, predictably, ignored. Finances and unequal quality of elementary and secondary education are raised as possibilities, but the real stress is placed on "find[ing] ways to improve the campus climate and mak[ing] positive efforts to ensure that all students feel a sense of belonging." This can be done, the report suggests, by sensitivity training, offering more courses about "American subgroups," increasing the number of minority faculty and administrators, and "[t]he development of a 'safe harbor' on campus, where groups can meet and interact and share their cultural experiences with students from other groups."

Sorry, but such tripe will be seen as the condescending nonsense it is.

There is, in addition, the problem with defining which groups we will single out for preferential treatment. The report talks about "minorities," but of course it has to concede early on that it isn't really talking about, for instance, Asians. It also has to concede that the numbers for African Americans and Latinos often don't match up; and sometimes it talks about Native Americans and sometimes it doesn't. A rigorous study would also have to distinguish among various subgroups of Latinos (Cubans versus Puerto Ricans, for instance), and among African Americans as well. And even subgroups are not monolithic, so that there is, for instance, no reason to give preferential treatment to middle-class or wealthy African Americans (even though they are the typical beneficiaries of such preferences).

A central argument in the report is that students need to attend campuses that look like the workplace, because otherwise they won't learn how to work with people from other racial and ethnic groups. The immediate problem with this argument is that it is empirically shaky whether there are any educational benefits to diversity in the first place. The report relies heavily on a study prepared by University of Michigan psychology professor Patricia Y. Gurin. It does not mention the devastating critiques of the Gurin study published by Thomas Wood and Malcolm Sherman of the National Academy of Scholars (*Is Campus Racial Diversity Correlated with Educational Benefits?*) or by Robert Lerner and Althea Nagai (*A Critique of the Expert Report of Patricia Gurin in Gratz v. Bollinger*).

But the problems with the argument go deeper than this. It rests on a whole series of very dubious premises: (1) that black people tend to be quite different from white people, and that therefore the way one works with a black person is very different from the way one works with a white person; (2) that these differences cannot be learned on the job quickly; (3) that they also cannot be learned directly, but are instead learned best by going to a campus that happens to have a particular racial and ethnic mix, where they will magically seep into the student's mind, as by a sort of osmosis; and (4) that it is so important to learn these differences that it justifies deliberate racial and ethnic discrimination in order to ensure this racial and ethnic mix on campus. If any of these premises are false, then the argument collapses; in fact, they all are.

Even more improbably, the study suggests that such discrimination can be justified because it produces "better critical thinkers" and people with superior "problem-solving skills" and more "openness to new ideas." Such talents are significantly less likely to exist, we are supposed to believe, among blacks who have not spent enough time with whites on campus, and vice versa. Pity the poor ancient Greeks. What a struggle they must have had to become critical thinkers, to hone their problem-solving skills, to be open to new ideas, when they could talk only with other ancient Greeks (I suspect women were underrepresented at the Lyceum, to boot).

Here is more Stupid Stuff:

- The report asserts that diversity is also essential for businesses "to adapt their services and products, as well as their marketing strategies, to appeal to customers from a wide range of cultural backgrounds." This is why, for instance, Jews have always done so poorly in the retail trades, where most of their customers are non-Jewish. And it is obvious that, in order to understand how to market to foreigners, companies must hire more African Americans, the quintessential Americans. Would the BHEF allow companies that do little business in, say, Asia to limit the number of Asians they hire?
- The report argues that the "proliferation of workplace diversity programs attest[s] that many American business leaders believe that in their world, racial and ethnic diversity brings value to their enterprises." More likely, it makes them less likely to be hounded by the federal government, sued by greedy plaintiffs' lawyers, and mau-mau'ed by Jesse Jackson or Al Sharpton. This, incidentally, also explains why businesses sign on to reports like this one. They don't really believe them—no intelligent person could—but they are useful public-relations insurance.
- The report says that education preferences will make their beneficiaries richer, and this will help the economy. But in the United States those who do not get into one college will still be able to go to college somewhere else, and *recent data* suggest that the correlation between going to a selective school and earning a lot of money is weak or nonexistent. Even if this link did exist, the GNP is not increased by robbing Peter to pay Pablo.
- Another doozy: "There is some evidence suggesting that companies that invest in diversity are rewarded by their investors," because when they received awards from the Department of Labor for exemplary affirmative action programs, their stock prices went up, and when they agreed to settle discrimination cases, their stock prices went down. You see, investors know that diversity is good business, so they reward it when they see it and punish companies that don't have it. But isn't the more plausible explanation—assuming there is anything

more than coincidence at work here—that investors get skittish when they learn a company has run afoul of the law and has to pay out millions of dollars, and are comforted when they learn that a company is in the good graces of the feds?

Ed Blum of the American Civil Rights Institute created a diversity fund out of the companies that signed an amicus brief supporting the University of Michigan's race-based admissions policy, and found that the group was badly underperforming all the major stock-market benchmarks. And, he and I pointed out in an article for *Investor's Business Daily*, that's no surprise. Economics Nobel Laureate Gary Becker pointed out years ago in his seminal 1957 book *The Economics of Discrimination* that those who indulge a "taste for discrimination" and refuse to hire and promote on the basis of merit will have to pay for it.

The report presents survey data that purports to show how pro-diversity America is. But there is all the difference in the world between a general agreement with the proposition that "diversity is nice" and the proposition that, in order to achieve it, it is okay to favor some and disfavor others on the basis of skin color and ancestry. In fact, such preferences are decidedly unpopular, among individuals of all races. A *recent survey*—conducted by the Washington Post, Henry J. Kaiser Family Foundation, and Harvard University, no less—found that 84 percent of Asians, 88 percent of Hispanics, 86 percent of African Americans, and 94 percent of whites thought college admission "Should be based strictly on merit and qualifications other than race/ethnicity," explicitly rejecting the answer "Race or ethnicity should be a factor."

Finally, the report urges schools to stand fast and "intensify efforts" on behalf of "results-oriented approaches to enrolling greater numbers of minority students in higher education," "despite the uncertainty resulting from recent court rulings and referenda." Schools are thus urged to try to find "creative ways" around such legal niceties as a prohibition on racial and ethnic discrimination.

But such laws reflect what the report elsewhere, and hypocritically, declares as a "basic, compelling" principle: that "America needs and promises equality of opportunity." Likewise, William E. Kirwan, president of Ohio State University and co-chair of the BHEF Diversity Initiative, announced: "This report helps move us closer to equality for all American citizens, regardless of their race, creed, or color." The truth is exactly the opposite. The report is an attempt to ensure that Americans are sorted according to skin color and where their ancestors came from, and treated differently depending on which category they fall in.

By all means, improve the education that our children get. But the targeting should be based on substandard schools, not the color of the children attending them. There's nothing wrong with racial diversity, but it has little intrinsic value, and it is certainly not worth the sacrifice of excellence or abandoning the principle of fair treatment.

POSTSCRIPT

Is Diversity in the Workplace a Worthwhile Goal for Corporations?

Is diversity in the workplace a worthwhile goal for corporations? That was the question addressed by the two articles comprising this debate topic. Author Nancy Lockwood answered yes and provided a detailed article that not only defended the sagacity of workplace diversity, but also offered excellent insight as to the numerous ways diversity contributes to the organization's overall strategy. Roger Clegg, vice president and general counsel at the Center for Equal Opportunity, focused his concerns with workplace diversity on the results of a recent report released by the Business-Higher Education Forum's Diversity Initiative Task Force. A particularly important aspect of his critique involves a discussion of the rarely mentioned assumptions underlying the belief that differences in skin color, culture, and background necessarily result in differences in behavior in the workplace.

Before we leave this subject and move on to our next topic, two additional points are in order. First, a comment about Clegg's view that many firms support workplace diversity primarily out of fear. This may be true, but it doesn't follow that doing so is unwise corporate policy. It is true that in today's business environment firms are practically required to diversify their workforce. Legal mandates (i.e., civil rights acts, antidiscrimination legislation) and strong social pressures virtually condemn to failure those organizations that fail to engage in at least some minimal level of diversity-based initiatives. Regardless of intent, firms that maintain a homogenous workforce risk not only legal action, but also being labeled as socially irresponsible. Such a description can be fatal for, once labeled, a firm may not be able to overcome the damage done to its reputation in the marketplace. Thus, opting for a policy supportive of workplace diversity would seem to be a wise business decision given the current business environment.

On the other hand, and despite the assertions of supporters, it *has not been* unequivocally established by research that diversity, in and of itself, results in higher levels of productivity. Although numerous reasons are proffered for why this is the case, paramount among these are the issues of communication and decision making. For example, research on group communications has consistently shown that homogenous groups communicate more effectively and more efficiently than do heterogeneous groups. And, in terms of decision-making processes, although diverse groups provide both greater numbers and more creative solutions to decision situations, achieving group consensus is much more difficult than it is in homogenous groups. In fact, some research suggests that the additional costs—usually in terms of time and money expenditures—incurred by diverse groups trying to reach consensus can far outweigh the benefits provided by their membership diversity.

We hope that, after having read both sides of this debate, you have a greater understanding of the importance and complexity of this controversial business management topic. So, what are your thoughts on this subject now? Do you think that diversity in the workplace is a worthwhile goal for corporations?

Suggested Readings

Forbes Magazine, Building a competitive workforce: Diversity—The bottom line. *Forbes,* April 3, 2000, pp. 181–194.

Fay Hansen, Diversity's business case doesn't add up. *Workforce Management,* April 1, 2003. Crain Communications, Inc.

Demedre R. Heulett, BNA, Inc.: Effectively managing a diverse workforce. *The Metropolitian Corporate Counsel,* Northeast Edition, January, 2004.

R. Koonce, Redefining diversity. *T+D,* December 2001, p. 25.

T. J. Rodgers, In defense of non-diversity. In *Perspectives in Business Ethics,* 2nd ed., p. 469. Edited by Laura P. Hartman. McGraw-Hill, 2002.

Larry Yu, Does diversity drive productivity? *MIT Sloan Management Review,* Winter 2002, p. 17.

ISSUE 8

Is Gender Discrimination the Main Reason Women Are Paid Less Than Men?

YES: Stephen J. Rose and Heidi I. Hartmann, from "Still a Man's Labor Market: The Long-Term Earnings Gap," *Institute for Women's Policy Research* (2004)

NO: Naomi Lopez, from "Free Markets, Free Choices II: Smashing the Wage Gap and Glass Ceiling Myths," *Pacific Research Institute* (1999)

ISSUE SUMMARY

YES: Stephen J. Rose and Heidi I. Hartmann, scholars at the Institute for Women's Policy Research, argue in their 2004 study that discrimination is still the main reason for the persistence in the gender gap.

NO: Naomi Lopez, director of the Center for Enterprise and Opportunity at the Pacific Research Institute in San Francisco, provides evidence that the wage gap is a function of several different variables beyond gender discrimination. She concludes her analysis with the observation that we may never reduce the wage gap entirely and that such an outcome is not necessarily undesirable.

During the 1950s, female workers in the United States earned about 59 cents for every dollar males earned. Not surprisingly, the differential in pay between women and men—the "gender wage gap"—was assumed to be the result of sexual discrimination in the workplace. Critics and social reformers at this time made the issue of wage discrimination—gender, racial, or any other type—an integral part of the overall civil rights movement that was sweeping the country in the first part of the 1960s. As a result, two critically important laws were passed that directly addressed the issue of discrimination and the wage gaps produced by it. The Equal Pay Act of 1963 requires employers to pay equivalent rates for similar work regardless of gender. Similar pay must occur for jobs requiring equal skill, equal effort, equal responsibility, or jobs with similar working conditions (Mathis and Jackson, *Human Resource Management*, Thomson South-Western, 2003, p. 388). In 1964, the Civil Rights Act was passed, which, among other things, further solidified the basis of the Equal Pay Act as a discrimination barrier in the workplace. Over the next three decades, the gender wage gap slowly, but consistently, declined as women gained access to jobs and pay levels typically reserved for men. By the mid-1990s, women, on average, earned 70 cents on the male dollar, a fact generally interpreted as evidence that the legislative actions of the 1960s were having the desired effect on workplace gender discrimination.

Despite the apparent large gains women have made in this area over the last several decades, the question of gender discrimination in wage rates has seen renewed interest in the last few years. The main reason for this is data from the U.S. Census bureau indicating that the trend in female wage gains may be reversing. Women have seen their pay levels decline from 76.5 percent of male pay in 1999 to 75.5 percent in 2003 (U.S. Census Bureau, "Income, Poverty, and Health Insurance Coverage in the United States: 2003," U.S. Department of Commerce, Economics and Statistics Administration). This decline represents the largest move backward in women's wages since 1991 and has caused many social commentators to wonder if discrimination against women is on the upswing as we move into the twenty-first century. The comments of Dr. Barbara Gault, director of research at the Institute for Women's Policy Research (IWPR), are typical: "To address the continuing disparities between women and men, we need to raise the minimum wage, improve enforcement of Equal Employment Opportunity laws, help women succeed in higher-paying, traditionally male occupations, and create more flexible, family friendly workplace policies" (IWPR, "Women's Earning Fall: U.S. Census Bureau Finds Rising Gender Wage Gap," *IWPR News*, August 27, 2004).

Although there is no dispute about the existence of the gender wage gap, there is definitely a difference of opinion as to its cause. On one side are those who believe the answer is straightforward—the persistence of the wage gap is due to gender discrimination. The above comments of the IWPR director of research exemplify this position nicely. On the other side are those who argue that other factors play a more important role in the gender wage gap. According to Howard J. Wall, senior economist at the Federal Reserve Bank of St. Louis, "The weight of evidence suggests that little of the wage gap is related to wage discrimination at all. Instead, wage discrimination accounts for, at most, about one-fourth of the gap, with the remainder due to differences between men and women in important determinants of earnings such as the number of hours worked, experience, training and occupation. Moreover, even this one-fourth of the gap may have less to do with wage discrimination than with the accumulated effects of shorter hours and interrupted careers on women's earnings and promotion prospects" (Wall, "The Gender Wage Gap and Wage Discrimination: Illusion or Reality," *The Regional Economist*, October 2000).

In the following selections, Stephen J. Rose and Heidi I. Hartmann, scholars at the IWPR, argue that discrimination is still the main reason for the persistence in the gender gap. Naomi Lopez, director of the Center for Enterprise and Opportunity at the Pacific Research Institute in San Francisco, provides evidence that the wage gap is a function of several different variables beyond gender discrimination.

YES

**Stephen J. Rose and
Heidi I. Hartmann**

Still a Man's Labor Market:
The Long-Term Earnings Gap

Many argue that women's prospects in the labor market have steadily increased and that any small remaining gap in earnings between women and men is not significant. They see the remaining differences as resulting from women's own choices. Others believe that with women now graduating from college at a higher rate than men and with the economy continuing its shift toward services, work and earnings differences between women and men may disappear entirely.

Although the wage gap, measured by conventional methods, *has* narrowed in the last several decades, with women who work full-time full-year now earning 77 percent of what men earn (compared with 59 cents on the male dollar 40 years ago), its sweeping effects are largely unacknowledged because its measurement is limited to a single year and restricted to only a portion of the workforce. *When accumulated over many years for all men and women workers, the losses to women and their families due to the wage gap are large and can be devastating.*

For many families, the quality of children's care and education suffers from women's low earnings throughout their child rearing years. Even with increased time in the labor market after their children are grown, women cannot make up the loss in lifetime earnings. Moreover, most women enter retirement without pensions, either from their own or their husband's employment, and thus lack security in old age.

A New Measure Highlights Wage Gap Understatement

The conventional way of measuring the differences in earnings and labor force experience between women and men is misleading because it fails to capture the difference in men's and women's total lifetime earnings. The more commonly cited wage ratio is based on comparing the annual earnings of women and men who work full-time, full-year in a given year. Using a more inclusive 15-year time frame (1983–1998), and taking into account women's lower work hours and their years with zero earnings due to family care, this study finds that women workers, in their prime earning years, make only 38 percent of what men earn. *Across the 15 years of the study, the average prime age working woman earned only $273,592 while the average working man earned $722,693 (in 1999 dollars).* This gap of 62 percent is more than twice as large as the 23 percent gap commonly reported.

This new measure of the long-term earnings gap is based on comparing the average annual earnings, across 15 years, of prime-age workers between the ages of 26 and 59 years, regardless of how many hours they worked or how many years they had earnings. The data used are from the Panel Study of Income Dynamics, a longitudinal data set that tracks the same groups of women and men over many years. *Compared with men, women are more likely to work part-time, less likely to work year-round, and more likely to have entire years out of the labor force.* Thus, the conventional 77 cent comparison under-plays all of these factors by focusing only on the earnings of the approxi-mately half of women and the 85 percent of men who work full-time for at least 50 weeks in a given year. To measure the access women and men have to economic resources through working, earnings for all prime-age women and men is a more relevant statistic.

Across 15 years, the majority (52 percent) of women but just 16 percent of men have at least one complete calendar year without any earnings. A career interruption like this has a large effect on the earnings of both men and women independent of their education and previous experience, and such interruptions partially account for women's lower life-time earnings. But even among men and women who have earnings in all 15 years, men's average annual earnings are $49,068 while women's are $29,507, or 57 cents on the dollar. Again, this figure is considerably below the commonly cited 77-cent comparison.

Women Are More Likely to Be Long-Term Low Earners

Women's lower average earnings mean that women are much more likely than men to be low earners overall. Even among those who have earnings every year in the 15-year study, 17 percent of women but only 1 percent of men average less than $15,000 per year in earnings—just above the poverty line for a family of three. Women are less likely than men to move up and out of low-wage work. In fact, more than 90 percent of long-term low earners among prime-age adults are women. Furthermore, in the new economy, one's educational background plays more of a role than ever before. Yet, women with a bachelor's degree earn less than men with only a high school diploma or less (even when the compari-son is restricted to those with earnings in all 15 study years).

Again when only committed workers, those with earnings in all 15 years, are considered, the earnings range of $25,000–$49,999 annually is the most common earnings range for both men and women with nearly half of both sexes earning in that range. But for men, that range is effectively the bottom, since 42 percent of men earn more than $50,000 annually, while for women it is effectively the top, since only 9 percent of women average above that amount.

Gender Segregation in the Labor Market Results in Lower Pay for Women

One major reason for the gender gap in earnings is that women work in 'women's jobs'—jobs that are predominantly done by women, while men work in 'men's jobs'—those predominantly done by men. This phenomenon is known as the gender segregation of the labor market.

In this report, we develop a three-tier schema of elite, good, and less-skilled jobs; within each tier, there is a set of occupations that are predominantly male and a set that are predominantly female. In the elite tier, women are concentrated in teaching and nursing while men are business executives, scientists, doctors, and lawyers; in middle tier jobs, women are secretaries while men are skilled blue collar workers, police, and fire fighters; and in the lowest tier, women are sales clerks and personal service workers while men work in factory jobs. Among prime-age workers who are continuously employed (have earnings every year in the 15-year study period), nearly 60 percent are employed consistently at least 12 of 15 years in one of these six occupational clusters.

Within each of the six gender-tier categories, at least 75 percent of the workers are of one gender. In each tier, women's jobs pay significantly less than those of their male counterparts even though both sets of occupations tend to require the same level of educational preparation.

Perhaps largely because of the generally low pay scales in the female career occupations, only 8 percent of men work in them. In contrast, 15 percent of continuously employed women, apparently more eager to seek higher-paying male jobs, work consistently in male occupations. These women, however, earn one-third less than their male counterparts in male elite and less-skilled jobs. Among the few women who make it into the middle tier of good male jobs (the skilled, blue collar jobs), the more formal wage structures (due to unions and civil service regulations) mean that their pay lags men's by only one-fifth. Increasing women's entry into this tier of male good jobs would thus increase their earnings substantially.

For the preponderance of women who remain in the female sector of each tier, earnings are strikingly low. In general, even restricting the comparison to women who work full-time, women in women's jobs earn less than men in men's jobs one tier below: women in female elite jobs earn less than men in male good jobs, and women in female good jobs earn less than men in male less-skilled jobs.

Time Spent in Family Care Limits Women's Own Earnings

Women's working experience is conditioned on their experience in families, where they often do most of the child and elder care and family and household maintenance. Because the United States lags behind many other countries in providing subsidized childcare and paid family leave, families are left to their own resources to meet the challenges of combining family care and paid work.

Most women spend the majority of their prime-age years married. As a result, women's average standard of living (as measured by average household income over 15 years, assuming that all family members share equally in this income) lags men's by only 10 percent (despite women's much lower earnings). For married women, it is still their connection to men that insulates them at least partially from their own low earnings. For women with few years of marriage, however, their family income lags men's with similar marital histories by more than 25 percent.

Women's lack of own earning power limits their options (in the worst case, they may feel forced to stay in an abusive relationship) and exposes them to great risk of poverty and near poverty when they divorce or if they never marry (especially if there are children present). Women who never experienced a year as a single parent during the 15-year study period had an average annual income of $70,200, compared with women who experienced single parenthood in at least 5 of 15 years, who had an average annual income of less than $35,800. Moreover, after the prime earnings years observed in this study, approximately half of women enter the retirement years alone, no longer married even if they once were. Women's low earnings come home to roost in old age, when widowed, divorced, and never married women all share high poverty rates of approximately 20 percent.

The Gendered Division of Labor Is Self-Reinforcing But Increasingly Unstable

Another major reason for the gender gap in cumulative earnings is the self-reinforcing gendered division of labor in the family and its implications for women's labor market time. First, families need childcare and other activities to be performed. Second, since the husband usually earns more than his wife, less income is lost if the lower earner cuts back on her labor force participation. Third, employers, fearing that women will leave their jobs for family responsibilities, are reluctant to train or promote them and may take advantage of women's limited opportunities by paying them less than they would comparable men. Fourth, a set of jobs evolves with little wage growth or promotion opportunities but part-time hours and these jobs are mainly held by women. Fifth, an ideology develops that proclaims this the natural order, resulting in many more men in men's jobs with higher pay and long work hours and many more women working in women's jobs with lower pay and spending considerable time on family care. Women without men particularly suffer from this ideology since they often support themselves and their families on jobs that pay women's wages.

This self-reinforcing arrangement, while long lasting, is also increasingly unstable. Women are demanding more independence and greater economic security throughout the life cycle, whether single or married. Many women and men believe that women's talents are being underutilized and undercompensated.

In the United States, the flipside of women typically being the caregivers and men typically the breadwinners has led to very high working hours, especially for men. Compared with other advanced countries, the United States has developed a set of institutions that leads to significantly longer labor market hours and considerably less leisure.

Policy Changes Can Bring Improvement

Several policy recommendations are offered to help move U.S. institutions toward supporting greater equity between women and men. Among them are: strengthening enforcement of existing equal opportunity laws, increasing access to education and training in high paying fields in which women are currently underrepresented, developing new legal remedies for the comparable worth problem (the tendency of 'women's jobs' to pay less at least partly because women do them), making work places more 'family friendly' through more flexible hours, providing more job-guaranteed and paid leaves of absence for sickness and family care, encouraging men to use family leave more, increasing subsidies for childcare and early education, encouraging the development of more part-time jobs that pay well and also have good benefits, and improving outcomes for mothers and children after divorce. Certainly, the United States should be able to develop a better way to share responsibility for family care and work, resulting in increased gender equity in earnings, family work, and leisure and greater long-term economic security for both women and men.

ᘛᗜᘚ

Policy Implications

While experts disagree about the significance that should be attributed to the remaining differences found in women's and men's work experiences in and out of the labor market, we argue in this report that they are significant for many reasons.

- First, the gender gap in earnings has a major influence on families' life choices and poverty rates, on older women's retirement security, and on single mothers' ability to provide for their children's care and education. More and more women, both single mothers and married women, are contributing to their family's income through their paid work. Nearly all families with women earners or would-be earners would have a higher standard of living if women's wages and lifetime earnings were higher.
- Second, there is ample evidence that women's low earnings are not primarily the result of their preferences for low-wage work. Rather women face discrimination in the labor market and in pre-labor market preparation as well. The degree of sex segregation in the labor market is striking and women's jobs at all educational levels pay less than men's jobs at the same level. Women's access to the better paying jobs and occupations is still constrained. Women deserve equal opportunity in the labor market.

- Third, while many women spend more time on family care than many men, the choices women and men make in allocating their time between work and family are heavily constrained. The lack of societal provisions for family care such as subsidized child and elder care means that most families have to fend for themselves. Women's lower earnings, of course, make it more practical for the family to sacrifice the woman's rather than the man's earnings and, given the loss of the woman's earnings, the man often works even more hours.

- Thus, a kind of perverse internal logic perpetuates a system with a rigid division of labor both in the workplace and in the home. Employers may feel justified in discriminating against women workers if they think they will be less devoted to their jobs because of family responsibilities. They may structure jobs as part-time and dead-end for this reason and many women may accept them because they cannot find better-paying jobs. Labor market discrimination means lower earnings for women; women's low earnings mean women spend more time in family care; women's commitments to family care contribute to discrimination against them. Single mothers especially suffer as they must attempt to support their families on women's lower wage levels.

- Finally, such a system surely fails to use human talent productively. How much total output is lost to society because the skills of women are not developed and put to work in the most productive way? To what extent are economic resources misallocated because of the constraints noted above? To what extent are both men and women denied the opportunity to allocate their time between home and work as they would most prefer? . . .

As this study demonstrates, the pay gap remains quite large and is bigger than many people think. Women still retain primary responsibility for family care in many families, making it difficult for women workers to compete equally with their male counterparts. Ideological attacks on women's equality also seem to be growing (or in any case not abating). Every few years, the media reassert that working moms may be hurting their children and wearing themselves out under the strain of the double burden.[1] In late 2002, Allison Pearson's *I Don't Know How She Does It: The Life of Kate Reddy, Working Mother* (Anchor Books) provided an example of this trend. And in late 2003 Lisa Belkin in "The Opt-Out Revolution" (*New York Times Magazine,* October 26) argued that highly educated and high earning women (with high earning husbands) are increasingly stepping off the fast track voluntarily, without presenting much evidence to support an actual increase. Her article also seemed to down play the evidence she had collected in her interviews of this small, select group, showing that several of the women dropped out only because their employers would not offer more family friendly work schedules. The cultural war over the demands of childrearing and work represents a real dilemma that society must face. The critics of working mothers and the champions of at-home mothers, however, tacitly assume that it is primarily the responsibility of women alone to solve the problem.

The genie is out of the bottle. Women, even those with young children, are working for significant portions of their lives. And, despite the economic slowdown and the continuing critique of women's increased employment, women continue to devote more and more hours to work and fewer to family care. They don't appear to be changing their minds and going back home.[2] While many married women are partially insulated from the effects of their own lower earnings by living with higher earning men, overall women are acting to reduce their economic dependence on husbands and to protect themselves from the vulnerabilities of divorce. Women are choosing the path to greater independence, arranging childcare, balancing their work and care giving tasks as best they can, and trying to get their partners to put in their fair share of housework and care giving.[3] Women are spending less of their adult lives in marriage, marrying later, and having fewer children. One third of prime age working women have at least one year as a single parent. Women's needs for equal earnings are increasing as they spend less time living with men.

The current system also places a burden on American men, who have the longest work hours in the advanced industrialized world, and the least leisure. The relative lack of infrastructure to support working parents in the United States (subsidized childcare, paid family leave) means that families are left to cope on their own. Most do so by increasing male work hours, enabling women to work less and spend more time on family care in the short run, but increasing women's economic vulnerability in the long run.

And to the extent that women's unequal pay contributes to poverty, it places a strain on our social safety net. The cumulative effect of years of lower earnings for women raises the cost to our welfare system, and reduces tax revenues.

Can the system change to become more conducive to women's equality? Certainly nothing is fixed in the long run, but many barriers remain in the United States. If Women in the United States hope to improve their economic standing and achieve greater economic parity with male workers, there must be a systematic change in both practices and policies with regard to work and family life. Among the policy strategies that are needed are the following:

- Strengthening equal employment opportunity (EEO) enforcement, by increasing federal support for government oversight agencies, both the Equal Employment Opportunity Commission (EEOC) and the Office for Federal Contract Compliance Programs (OFCCP). Complaints could be resolved more quickly with more resources, and, if more cases were resolved in the plaintiffs' favor, due to stronger and more timely enforcement efforts, employers would have larger incentives to improve their employment practices. The OFCCP could target federal contractors in egregious industries (e.g. construction) to encourage them to adhere to their affirmative action plans, much like mining and banking were targeted in the 1970s. One promising approach might be to audit many large employers regularly for discrimination, much the way large federal contractors have their financial transactions continually monitored by on-site auditors. Women's greater entry into predominately male jobs in the middle tier—in fire fighting, police work, or skilled trades—would be especially important in raising women's wages since women's jobs in this tier are particularly underpaid relative to men's jobs.

- Opening up educational and job training opportunities. Unfortunately there are still too many women who have been discouraged from pursuing higher education and/or job training for occupations that are not traditionally held by women. Jobs in the skilled trades and in the computer industry, for example, frequently require pre-job preparation that women are less likely to have access to. Programs that help women get to the starting gate with equal skills will benefit women tremendously.

- Developing new EEO remedies to address unequal pay for jobs of comparable worth (the tendency for jobs done disproportionately by women to pay less than jobs that require similar skill, effort, and responsibility but are traditionally held by men). Employers could be required to show that comparable jobs are paid fairly, using tools such as job evaluation systems that measure job content on many dimensions. Both men and women in jobs that are underpaid because they are done predominantly by women would stand to gain from comparable worth implementation.

- Improving workers' bargaining power in the workplace, such as through encouraging increased unionization in unorganized sectors and raising the minimum wage, especially since women are over-represented among the non-unionized and low-wage work force. Living wage campaigns and efforts to tie the federal or state minimum wages to cost of living increases all raise public awareness about the importance of setting a reasonable wage floor. A reasonable wage floor disproportionately benefits women workers and the children they support.

- Creating more good part-time jobs that provide decent pay, benefits, and promotion opportunities. A less than optimal equilibrium may have formed in the labor market where many good jobs require more than 40 hours of work per week. This prevents workers from entering such jobs if they want to work fewer hours, and employers miss the opportunity to learn whether part-time workers in these jobs can contribute equally (on a per hour basis). Career part-time jobs could be fostered by public sector employers and, if successful, private sector employers could be encouraged to follow suit. Single parents would also be especially helped by the greater availability of part-time jobs with good hourly pay and benefits since their family care responsibilities generally limit their hours to less than full-time.

- Making work places 'family friendly'—including flexible hours, parental and other family care leave (including paid leave), and paid sick leave. Too often it is the lowest-paid workers who have the least access to these benefits since they are not legally required of most employers. Yet if such leaves were made more available and if they were used equally by both sexes, new workplace norms would be developed that recognize that all workers, male or female, have responsibilities to others that sometimes take them away from their jobs. Such paid leave programs could be provided through social insurance schemes, such as the recent expansion of the Temporary Disability Insurance system in California to include paid leave for family care. More wide spread use of leaves should, over time, reduce the earnings penalties observed for time out of the labor market.

- Providing more high quality, affordable childcare, through subsidized childcare centers at workplaces and in the community, and more public subsidies for higher education as well. Since well-reared and well-educated children are an asset to the whole society it makes no economic sense that most parents shoulder the financial responsibility for children's care and education alone. This arrangement disadvantages single mothers particularly since they have only one wage, and a lower one at that, with which to provide for their children.

- Encouraging men to be full participants in family care. Such sharing can be encouraged by government requirements for both parents to share available parental leave (as is done in the Nordic countries) and by utilizing the bully pulpit to educate employers and the public about the positive benefits of encouraging men to exercise options for flexible work arrangements when available and spend more time with children and less time working. A full-scale public education campaign against the double-standard in parenting, in which mothers seem to be expected to meet a higher standard of care than fathers, is needed.

- Reducing income tax rates on secondary earners, most often women, and reducing the 'marriage penalty' for dual earner couples. Higher tax rates for married couples are found up and down the income scale and they generally depress the work effort of the lower earning member of the couple.

- Improving access to non-custodial fathers' incomes or otherwise raising incomes in single mother families. Since single mothers and their children suffer disproportunately from poverty and near-poverty, even when the mother works (as the mothers in this study do), additional measures are needed to improve their income and support their work effort. In addition to paid leave and other family-friendly benefits, benefits such as subsidized housing or child care should be extended further up the income scale. Child support should be increased and income and property settlements at divorce should be more generous to the custodial parent. A strong safety net and work supports are necessary for low-income parents to maintain their employment and enable them to gain from long-term, steady employment.

- Democratizing the 'old boy' network. Since many positions in the economy depend on strong social interactions, these seemingly non-work relationships have economic consequences. The refusal of the Augusta National Golf Club to admit women in the spring of 2003 is one example of a principal location where the 'old boy' network remains intact. More surprising, perhaps, is the failure of male corporate leaders to resign from the club quickly once its exclusive membership policies became generally known. Federal EEO regulations and tax laws could be strengthened to clarify that employer support of such networks is discriminatory and not allowable as a business related tax deduction.

- Reducing working time norms. As long work hours increasingly become the standard, women can be more easily excluded because they are less likely to be able to meet this requirement. Most European countries manage to both provide more public support for parenting and have lower working hours on average. Reducing work hour norms, perhaps through eliminating or setting a cap on mandatory overtime, increasing the required premium paid for overtime work, or reducing the standard work week to 35 hours could spread the work and jobs more equitably across all members of society, increase gender equality in family care time, and increase the time available for leisure and civic engagement.

Achieving equality in the work place will likely require several more decades. The important thing is to keep the momentum going and prevent backsliding toward the reestablishment of the feminine mystique or 1950s family values. Instead, we must continue the progress our society has been making toward equal opportunity and fair compensation for women in the labor market and the more equitable sharing of family care between women and men.

Notes

1. Interestingly, research shows that mothers today, despite spending much more time working for pay, spend about as much time directly interacting with their children as mothers a generation ago (Bianchi 2000).

2. While data show a small drop from 1998–2002 in the labor force participation of mothers with infants (children less than one year of age), at approximately the same time the economic recession and slow recovery reduced labor force participation generally. The long-run trend in the labor force participation of mothers has been one of considerable increase. For mothers of infants, for example, the proportion in the labor force increased from 31 percent in 1976 to 55 percent in 1995, roughly the same as the 2002 figure of 54.6 percent (U.S. Census Bureau 2003b: Figure 2).

3. In an overview of changes in women's well-being, Blau (1998) shows that housework time decreased for almost everyone between 1978 and 1988. Married men were the only group to increase their housework time, indicating that married women were having some success in getting household tasks reallocated.

Naomi Lopez  **NO**

Free Markets, Free Choices II: Smashing the Wage Gap and Glass Ceiling Myths

Executive Summary

Despite women's rapid gains in the working world, gender preference advocates and the media often portray working women as victims of rampant discrimination. This discrimination, such advocates argue, results in a wage gap and renders women powerless in the face of an impenetrable glass ceiling. While discrimination does exist in the workplace, levels of education attainment, field of education, and time spent in the workforce play a far greater role in determining women's pay and promotion.

Today, the average American woman earns about 74 cents for every dollar the average man earns. Women compose about 11 percent of corporate officers in the Fortune 500 companies. While such statistics are routinely used as evidence of gender discrimination, they ignore the many variables that affect position and earnings. More important, these claims serve to devalue women's choices—such as family, volunteer work, and self-employment—when they are not geared towards the corporate boardroom.

The reality is that, when considering men and women with similar fields of study, educational attainment, and continuous time spent in the workforce, the wage gap disappears. This is true for some women in high-paying "male" fields such as engineering, chemistry, and computer science.

Women make up 60 million of the nation's 138 million workers and have more than doubled their salaries, in real terms, over the past 50 years. These trends are only expected to continue as more women pursue higher education and seek professional career tracks.

Today, many women's groups have abandoned equal opportunity and are now calling for government action to create gender preferences that aim to guarantee women equal outcomes in earnings and representation in management. These advocates presume that unequal outcomes are due to discrimination, ignoring individual differences, preferences, and decisions.

When gender discrimination does occur, a formal, legal process exists to compensate alleged victims and protect them from retaliation from employers. The process also punishes alleged perpetrators and protects them from false claims.

Women's most dramatic employment gains occurred well before equal-pay legislation, civil-rights legislation, and affirmative-action programs. Furthermore, women's greatest gains in earnings occurred during the early 1980s—without hiring quotas and comparable-worth pay.

Women's continued success in the workplace will be secured by promotion of the original intent of the Civil Right's Act—equal opportunity, not special preferences. Enforcement of anti-discrimination laws also has a role to play, along with free-market economic policies, such as reducing the tax and regulatory burdens for small business. In these ways, the United States can create and maintain equal opportunity for women and all Americans.

Introduction

Women's dramatic gains in academia, the workplace, and the political world are well documented and cause for celebration. But as feminist leaders continue to use the wage gap and glass ceiling as rallying cries for further government action, some have come to believe that, absent gender preferences, women would not have achieved dramatic gains in these areas. There is no doubt that technological advances, attitudinal changes towards women's roles, and the women's movement profoundly contributed to these gains. The role of government in attempting to eliminate gender discrimination, however, deserves careful attention.

Women's labor force participation has dramatically increased since the turn of the century. Economist and Nobel laureate Gary Becker points out that market forces play a powerful role in determining women's labor force participation and earnings. Becker notes that:

> . . . the growth in employment and earnings of women over time is explained mostly by market forces rather than by civil rights legislation, affirmative-action programs, or the women's movement. Such programs can hardly explain the steady growth in the employment of women prior to 1950, or its accelerated growth during the 1950s and 1960s, since neither civil rights programs nor women's movements were yet widespread. Nor can equal-pay-for-equal-work legislation alone explain the narrowing earnings gap between men and women in the past 15 years. For one thing, the gap also narrowed in countries, such as Italy and Japan, that did not introduce such legislation.

By failing to examine historic trends in women's labor force participation—including participation in white collar jobs, such as managers—and educational attainment, one can mistakenly over-credit civil rights and equal-pay legislation for many of the opportunities women now enjoy. That is not to say that women have not benefited from equal protection under the law, but it is important to realize there is a significant distinction between opportunity and preference. Opportunity, however unequal, is responsible for many of the gains and successes that women now enjoy.

Whether at the turn of the century or today, the single necessary condition of women's success is affirmative action in its original sense—equality of opportunity. This should be the guiding principle of today's women's movement. According women anything beyond the same rights and opportunities as men, without special preferences, assumes that women will not continue to succeed.

The Wage Gap

The wage gap is the alleged difference between female and male earnings. In 1959, women earned about 59 cents for every dollar a man earned. Today, the wage gap has narrowed to about 74 cents for every dollar a man earns. When we compare educational attainment, we still find a significant gap even as education rises. Based on these disturbing numbers, it is easy to see why there is so much interest in this issue. But this is only part of the story.

Women do earn less than men, even at the highest educational levels. Upon further examination, however, we find that field of study has a major role in determining earnings. A 1970 U.S. Census Bureau study revealed that, among men with four-year degrees or higher who had earnings in 1966, fields of study accounted for wide disparities in subsequent earnings. Men specializing in law, health professions, and engineering garnered the highest earnings, while men specializing in religion, the humanities, education, and the biological sciences earned lower. While we know that women made significant strides in educational attainment earlier in the century; we do not have detailed information on their field of study until the mid-1960s.

A 1976 Census Bureau study examined field of study for two- and four-year college students between 1966 and 1974. While this study did not provide information on matriculation, level of degree earned, or highest degree earned, it indicated the rapid entrance of women into higher education; the dramatic increases of women in most non-humanities fields of study; and, with the notable exception of the health profession, a concentration of women in lower-yield fields of study.

Decades later, whether between men and men or men and women, field of study is still an important factor in subsequent earnings. In fact, many of the high-yield fields in the mid-1960s continue to be among the most lucrative today. Women are continuing their pursuit of these fields as evidenced by a continuous gravitation towards these high-yield fields and attainment of graduate degrees in these fields.

What is particularly striking is that, for women between the ages of 25 and 34 with bachelor's degrees, there does not appear to be a wage gap with their male counterparts in some of the same fields of study that require "men's" quantitative and scientific aptitudes. Architecture and environmental design are male-dominated fields but women's earnings in this area are a full 95 percent of men's. Engineering, another male-dominated field, yielded women 99 percent of men's earnings. Women earned 97 percent of men's earnings in chemistry and 94 percent in computer and information sciences.

Women between the ages of 35 and 44 with bachelor's degrees leaped ahead of men in architecture and environmental design, at a rate of 109 percent. Economics, another male-dominated field, saw women break even at 100 percent of men's earnings. One must question how these women managed to fare this well in some of the most competitive, highest-paying, and male-dominated fields in the face of rampant gender discrimination, which some claim begins in the earliest years of one's education.

Love and Marriage

The remaining piece of the wage gap puzzle lies in continuous time spent in the workforce. This factor is critical because it is not readily apparent at first glance. For example, knowing that six out of every ten women were in the workforce in 1997 does not reveal whether they were the same six still in the workforce in 1999.

According to U.S. Bureau of the Census and Bureau of Labor Statistics data, men consistently log more work activity than women, regardless of educational level. In the aggregate, however, women are actually earning more per hour than men. In these ways, time spent away from the workforce adversely affects earnings and seniority.

As women's roles have changed from homemaker to breadwinner, women still assume a disproportionate share of housework. Economists Joni Hersch and Leslie S. Stratton found that wives' domestic responsibilities adversely affect income and that time spent on housework is responsible for eight or more percent of the wage gap. While this may not come as a surprise to mature wives, there are indications that Generation X couples are likely to more equally divide domestic responsibilities which should mitigate this housework/income trade-off for wives.

Since the early 1970s, never-married women in their thirties with continuous labor force participation earn slightly higher incomes than their male counterparts with the same background. Furthermore, women without children have earnings approaching 98 percent of men's.

In addition to changing the composition of the American workforce, married women are also "bringing home the bacon." Today, about one out of five married women is earning more than her husband. This trend will likely continue in the future, especially as men assume more domestic responsibilities and as women have fewer children and bear them later in life. Some households are now relocating to new cities to accommodate the wife's job, a trend almost unheard of in the 1960s.

Personal decision making—choices such as level of education attainment, field of study, time spent in the workforce, and, yes, time spent in the kitchen—plays a far greater role in determining women's pay and promotion than gender discrimination.

The Glass Ceiling

Good For Business: Making Full Use of the Nation's Human Capital, the report of the 1995 Federal Glass Ceiling Commission, claimed that only five percent of senior managers at Fortune 1000 companies are women. This finding has since become a rallying cry for advocates of gender-based preference policies. The "glass ceiling" refers to the idea that discrimination against women in the workplace remains a formidable barrier to their upward mobility in the corporate world.

While disturbing, this figure both fails to reveal the dramatic gains women have made in management over the past few decades and the future trend of women in these positions. This figure overlooks the fact that, of the qualified labor pool, women are accurately reflected in these senior management positions. Furthermore, this five percent figure is a minuscule portion of managers in a small, select group of companies, not reflecting the wide array of management positions in the broader workforce.

U.S. Department of Labor statistics reveal that, though they represent only 46 percent of the U.S. labor force, women hold about half of all management jobs, and in the aggregate, hold fewer bachelor's and higher degrees than their male counterparts. Since the Glass Ceiling Commission report was released, the number of women in Fortune 500 senior management positions has tripled.

What about the future prospects of women in the Fortune 500? The typical qualifications for senior corporate management positions are a MBA and 25 years in the labor force. Looking back 25 years, fewer than 7 percent of MBA graduates were women. Assuming that no women left the workforce over the 25-year period between 1974 and 1999, one would only expect to find around 7 percent of women holding these jobs—far less than the current 11 percent. And with women representing more than one third of MBA graduates, women are now in the "pipeline" for these positions.

Rather than choosing to climb the ladder in corporate America, many women are instead seeking success in their own firms and are fulfilling their desire for more flexibility and independence.

Today, women-owned businesses account for one third of all firms in the United States. According to the National Foundation of Women Business Owners (NFWBO), there were almost 8 million women-owned businesses in the United States in 1996. Estimates also reveal that the number of women-owned firms grew by 78 percent between 1987 and 1996 and that employment in those firms grew by 183 percent.

Women are also engaging in job-sharing arrangements and telecommuting in greater numbers, reflecting both the individual's desire for a more flexible lifestyle and employers' desire to allow greater freedom.

The End of Discrimination? Not Likely

There is no doubt that women face gender discrimination in the workplace, but a statistical disparity or the mere appearance of discrimination does not make it so. For example, the parents of a child that receives several injuries over the course of a year—far more than the average child—are not automatically guilty of child abuse or neglect. Accompanied by additional evidence, however, such a case might be proven true. Attempting to use statistical disparities, which are often the rule rather than the exception in America, as the sole arbitrator of discriminatory practices sets a dangerous precedent.

According to the U.S. Equal Employment Opportunity Commission (EEOC), fewer than one in five sexual harassment charges results in a meritorious outcome and fewer than one in twenty is found to have reasonable cause. Of sex-based charges, about one in eight charges result in a meritorious outcome. Only one in 25 is found to have reasonable cause. A formal, legal process, based on evidence not conjecture, exists to compensate alleged victims and protect them from retaliation. The process also punishes alleged perpetrators and protects them from false claims. Equating seeming disparities in pay to discrimination, without carefully scrutinizing the facts, undermines the important legal protections and processes that have been carefully established.

Many women's groups are abandoning these legal protections that ensure equal opportunity in pursuit of government action to create gender preferences that aim to guarantee women equal outcomes in earnings and representation in management. These advocates presume that unequal outcomes are due to discrimination, ignoring individual choices, preferences, and personal decisions. This, in turn, undermines opportunity, however unequal, which has been the cornerstone of women's achievements throughout this century.

Conclusion

Women may never achieve parity with men in the workplace, but that is not bad news for women. Some will choose not to work, while others will set their sights to lead the top corporations in America. The majority of women will fall somewhere in between.

Women's dramatic gains in academia, the workplace, and the political world are cause for celebration. The record confirms that these dramatic gains were achieved without government gender preferences. Whether at the turn of the century or today, the single necessary condition of women's success in affirmative action in its original sense—equality of opportunity. This should be the guiding principle of today's women's movement. According women anything beyond the same rights and opportunities as men, without special preferences, assumes that women will not continue to succeed.

The record shows otherwise, and refutes the notion that women need special preferences and government programs. No rehashing of shopworn grievances can change the facts. Given equal opportunity, women achieve at the highest levels and their record of achievement will continue to grow.

POSTSCRIPT

Is Gender Discrimination the Main Reason Women Are Paid Less Than Men?

Another way of viewing the wage gap debate is understanding it as an "equality of outcome" versus "equality of opportunity" issue. The goal of the former approach is equality in the sense that people are economically, socially, and legally equal. Regardless of where they start, this view holds that equity exists only when everyone enjoys the same results. Persistent differences in outcomes are indicative of discriminatory forces and can only be remedied through social initiatives designed to provide redress to victims. At the workplace, this approach argues that, within reason, all groups should be equally represented at each level of the organization. There should also be no persistent differences in pay between males and females. To the extent that there is, gender discrimination is presumed to be the cause. And, as researchers Stephen J. Rose and Heidi I. Hartmann note in their article here, women's access to high-paying career paths is constricted, thus indicating that "women face discrimination in the labor market and in the pre-labor market preparation as well."

Those who believe our societal obligations extend no further than providing everyone with a level playing field argue from a perspective of equal opportunity. Advocates of this view recognize that what accounts for the differences in women and men's pay and other indicators of corporate success has little to do with discrimination and much more to do with factors such as motivation levels, skill differences, and willingness to work hard. In the article you just read, Naomi Lopez has strong words for those who disagree with her viewpoint: "These advocates [equality of outcome supporters] presume that unequal outcomes are due to discrimination, ignoring individual choices, preferences, and personal decisions. This, in turn, undermines opportunity, however unequal, which has been the cornerstone of women's achievements throughout this century."

Suggested Readings

Samuel Cohn, Why are women paid less than men? *Race and Gender Discrimination at Work*. Westview Press, 2000.

Government Accountabililty Office (GAO), Women's Earnings: Work Patterns Partially Explain Difference between Men's and Woman's Earnings. *Reports and Testimony, GAO-04-35*, October 31, 2003.

Sally J. Haymann, The widening gap: Why America's working families are in jeopardy and what can be done about it. Basic Books, 2000.

Wendy McElroy, Wage gap reflects women's priorities. Foxnews.com, September 22, 2004. http://www.foxnews.com/story/0,2933,133088,00.html

Staffs of Representatives John D. Dingell and Carolyn B. Maloney, A new look through the glass ceiling: Where are the women? *U.S. General Accounting Office,* January 2002.

Howard J. Wall, The gender wage gap and wage discrimination: Illusion or reality. *The Regional Economist,* October 2000. http://stlouisfed.org/publications/re/2000/d/pages/economic-backgnd.html

ISSUE 9

Would Reforming Social Security Be Good for American Business?

YES: James Morrison, from "Social Security Reform Helps Small Business," *The Heritage Foundation Backgrounder* (October 17, 2001)

NO: Greg Anrig, Jr. and Bernard Wasow, from "Twelve Reasons Why Privatizing Social Security Is a Bad Idea," *TCF Issue Brief,* The Century Foundation (December 14, 2004)

ISSUE SUMMARY

YES: Political consultant and Social Security expert Dr. James Morrison presents an argument supporting Social Security reform and shows how it would be extremely beneficial to American business, particularly small business.

NO: The con side of this debate is provided by two important members of The Century Foundation: vice president Greg Anrig, Jr. and senior fellow Bernard Wasow. Their article consists of 12 reasons why privatizing Social Security is bad for business and bad for the country.

T he Great Depression represents the most prolonged and intense economic downturn in the history of the United States. Most historians believe that it was the social and economic policies of President Roosevelt's New Deal programs that were responsible for ending the Depression and restoring the economy to its previous health. The New Deal agenda consisted of a myriad of legislative actions designed to address specific economic and social ills. The centerpiece of the New Deal framework was the Social Security Act (SSA), passed by Congress in 1935. The purpose of this act was to address the rise in poverty, particularly among those at or near retirement age. Indeed, some accounts put the poverty rate for seniors at the time at nearly 50 percent (en.wikipedia.org: see *Social Security Act*). The act provides for benefits to be paid to retirees, those unemployed, and to survivors of eligible workers upon their death. The SSA program was developed as a transfer program, as described here by Cato Institute Social Security expert Michael Tanner: "The payroll taxes from each generation of workers are not saved or invested for that generation's retirement, but are used to pay benefits for those already retired. The current generation of workers must then hope that when their retirement comes, the next generation of workers will pay the taxes to support their benefits, and so on." (*Follow the Math*, The Cato Institute, January 14, 2005).

In the seven decades since the SSA became law, demographic changes in America have strained the Social Security system to the point where experts believe it will become bankrupt sometime in the middle of this century unless drastic changes are made. Basically, the problem is that there are not enough workers currently paying in to finance the payments future retirees are entitled to receive. Consider that currently, there are three workers paying in to every one retiree receiving benefits; in 1950, there were *16* workers paying in for every one retiree taking out. And it gets worse: when the baby boomer generation retires, the ratio drops to two paying for every one receiving! (Tanner, 2005). What this means, of course, is that current workers must pay more in taxes to support the system. As Tanner notes, "The original Social Security tax was just 2 percent on the first $3,000 that a worker earned, a maximum tax of $60 per year. By 1960, payroll taxes had risen to 6 percent. Today's workers pay a payroll tax of 12.4 percent. It is going to get much worse. In order to continue funding retiree benefits, the payroll tax will have to be raised to more than 18 percent. That's nearly a 50 percent increase." Obviously, something needs to be done, otherwise millions of current workers paying into the system may very well receive nothing for their efforts when they retire.

Not surprisingly, addressing this "Social Security crisis" is a top priority for President Bush in his second term. Indeed, he tried to promote his idea for Social Security reform early in his second term, but met with severe resistance from both sides of the political aisle. Although his initial efforts failed, Bush's advocacy of Social Security reform has substantially increased public awareness of the problem and has opened the topic up to lively debate. Chief among those likely to be affected by reform are American businesses.

We believe that as someone interested in issues important to managers, you should be provided with the opportunity to learn more about this extremely important topic and its impact on business in the United States. To that end, we present you with two articles comprising our next debate: Would reforming Social Security be good for American business?

Arguing that reforming Social Security is desirable is James Morrison, Ph.D, a veteran of three presidential administrations and the head of Morrison and Associates, a Washington-based business consulting firm. Dr. Morrison focuses his attention specifically on the numerous benefits that would accrue to small businesses, pointing out that reform would lead to more capital for small businesses and allow entrepreneurs and other small business owners to determine the manner in which their taxes are being spent. The no response is provided by Greg Anrig, Jr., a vice president at The Century Foundation, and Bernard Wasow, an economist and senior fellow at TCF. These scholars attack the idea that Social Security should be privatized and offer twelve reasons why doing so is bad for business and society. As you read the two articles, keep in mind that this is a topic that affects you and every dollar you earn!

YES

James Morrison

Social Security Reform
Helps Small Business

Small business has much to gain and very little to lose if Congress establishes Social Security personal retirement accounts. These accounts, which would allow taxpayers to invest a portion of their Social Security retirement taxes, would make capital more available to small businesses without adding any appreciable administrative burden. In addition, since Social Security benefits are more likely to fund a larger share of the retirements of small-business owners, reducing the program's impending financial problems is even more important to their financial security.

Why Focus on Small Business?

Small business exercises an immense influence on the American economy. More than 99 percent of all U.S. employers are small, and they employ just over 50 percent of the private-sector work force. Such firms provide 75 percent of the nation's net new jobs and 50 percent of its private-sector economic output.[1]

But current statistics alone tell only part of the story. While larger businesses tend to create *process* innovations that strengthen economic efficiency, smaller businesses and entrepreneurs are responsible for the lion's share of *product* innovations that create new businesses and industries.[2] Technological developments that are likely to play a central role in future U.S. economic growth—such as biotechnology, lasers, and computer software—have been closely linked to smaller technology enterprises. This is an unusual feature of the American economy.[3] And it is not a new feature: A recent study of *Fortune* 200 companies has shown that 197 of them could be traced back to entrepreneurial founders.[4]

Small firms also are blazing trails in the rapidly globalizing economy. Between 1987 and 1997, the number of U.S. small business exporters tripled to over 200,000, and these companies were 20 percent more productive—with 20 percent faster job growth and 15 percent higher wages—than the rest of America's businesses.[5]

At the same time, small business traditionally has provided a portal into the economic mainstream for younger and lesser skilled workers, the economically displaced, immigrants, and people leaving public assistance.

From *The Heritage Foundation Backgrounder,* no. 1494, October 17, 2001, pp. 1–9. Copyright © 2001 by The Heritage Foundation. Reprinted by permission.

Consequently, Americans hold small business in very high regard. A 1997 Gallup poll found large majorities agreeing that small business represents "one of the best ways to get ahead in America" and saying that they admired small-business owners. Indeed, 92 percent of respondents said they would be pleased if a son or daughter started a small business.[6] These survey findings are essentially constant across age, ethnicity, gender, socioeconomic status, political philosophy, and partisan identification, and they are significantly more positive than the results of comparable surveys taken abroad.

Factors like these have led to an unusual degree of political and partisan comity on many national small-business issues. The substantial impact of small businesses in a broad range of arenas strongly suggests that it is economically, socially, and politically vital that small business be helped—or at least not harmed—by decisions that are made regarding the future of Social Security.

Reform should be crafted with a recognition of the particular needs and vulnerabilities of small businesses and entrepreneurs. These can be explored in terms of two categories—concerns that affect the small business community as a whole and those related to the operation of specific businesses.

Concerns Affecting the Entire Business Community

The debate over resolving Social Security's coming financial problems involves considerations that affect all small businesses. In addition to concerns that would affect the day-to-day operations of individual small businesses, some factors would affect the entire small business community. These include:

- Greater Dependence on Social Security for Retirement Income. Employees of small businesses and entrepreneurs almost certainly will be more dependent on Social Security benefits than those entering retirement from larger enterprises. Most people in small businesses do not have pensions. While 79 percent of mid- to large-size businesses offer employer-supported retirement benefits, far fewer smaller businesses do so. Among businesses with 25–99 employees, the figure is 46 percent; for businesses with 10–24 employees, it is 34 percent; and for those with one–nine employees, it drops to 22 percent.[7]

  Despite efforts to encourage Americans to save adequate funds for retirement, most workers have not done so. Only 15 percent have saved more than $100,000, and only 30 percent have saved more than $25,000.[8] While some of those with higher savings may be younger workers, this still is very little money for periods of retirement that are likely to span 10–20 years. Figures on personal savings for retirement are not generally available by business size. However, a study by the National Association for the Self-Employed found that more than three-quarters (78 percent) of the entrepreneurs it represents had saved less than $100,000 for retirement even though virtually none of them had private-sector pensions and their median age was 46.[9]

  With generally inadequate pensions and personal savings, entrepreneurs would be seriously and disproportionately affected by Social Security benefit cuts—unless these cuts are offset by an increase in personal accounts or other reforms. At the same time, such benefit cuts would make retirement planning an even more daunting challenge for small business. Many would surely turn away from entrepreneurship in favor of "safer" choices—with damaging consequences for the nation's economic openness, growth, and innovation.

• The Impact of Marginal Taxes. Entrepreneurs (who already face high taxes) are probably more sensitive to changes in tax rates and tax structure than wage-and-salary workers are. Entrepreneurship entails risks, and those risks will not be taken without prospects for rewards that the entrepreneur regards as adequate.[10] Policymakers in Washington seem to grasp the importance of this "knife-edge" risk–reward calculus with regard to capital gains taxes but seem to ignore it when other taxes are being considered. Yet it is *marginal* tax rates—the taxes on that "next dollar" of income—that the entrepreneur must weigh regarding any and all revenue that cannot be treated as capital gains.

This entrepreneurial calculus is apparent in a recent analysis of Internal Revenue Service data on sole proprietorships. Recent research indicates that a 5 percent increase in marginal tax rates leads to a 10.4 percent decrease in the probability of investment by those sole proprietors[11] and that marginal tax rates that are high and progressive strongly discourage entry into self-employment and business ownership.[12] Even the current level of Social Security taxes substantially distorts occupational choice and effort, as noted economist Martin Feldstein has demonstrated.[13]

Social Security taxes already drive marginal rates above 40 percent for many taxpayers. A taxpayer in the 28 percent federal income tax bracket, for example, typically pays 5 percent in state income taxes and 15.3 percent in Social Security and Medicare taxes.

For entrepreneurs, Social Security taxes are even more threatening than income taxes. The entrepreneur must directly pay both the employer's and the employee's share of the taxes and must do so whether it has been a good year or bad year—regardless of what the cash flows and accounts receivable may be, and regardless of whether or not the business makes a profit.[14]

Absent reform, the Social Security-driven marginal rates for small-business owners could well exceed 50 percent. Payroll taxes left on "automatic pilot" would rise eventually by more than 33 percent, increasing the annual taxes on a couple earning $50,000 by more than $2,000.[15] It would be hard to overestimate the damage this would wreak on entrepreneurship and small-business ownership. Marginal tax rates that are well above 50 percent for even the smallest entrepreneur almost certainly would lead to a precipitous decline in new business formations.

Like other countries with punitive taxes on starting and running a small business, the United States could expect to see the growth of a large "informal" sector of entrepreneurial activity. As in those countries, such "gray market" businesses would not be able to enter into binding contracts, obtain loans or venture capital, advertise, hire more than a few employees, offer those employees any legal protections or mandated benefits, grow, or provide the government with the kind of data it needs to make rational economic decisions.

- Access to Capital. Small businesses need better access to capital than they historically have received. That is the resounding conclusion of three separate White House Conferences on Small Business over the past two decades. Hundreds of delegates to these conferences, elected by small-business owners themselves, indicated that "access to capital" was the number one small-business concern.

Later, in the later 1990s, when this country's pace of business and technological innovation became the envy of the world, it was the agility and liquidity of American capital markets—exemplified by venture capital companies—that were widely identified as a linchpin for business development. While a large majority of small businesses are started with private savings or personal loans, most small business expansions depend upon banks and investors. For the whole system to work, small businesses must represent comparatively good risks for lending and investing, and sufficient capital to do so must be available.

The decisions that Congress makes on Social Security will have far-reaching implications for capital access. A decision to do little or nothing in the immediate future means that Social Security will not become an even partially "prefunded" retirement program. Instead, it will remain a 100 percent "pay-as-you-go" system. Its multitrillion-dollar unfunded liability will remain unfunded.

Given the country's likely demographic changes, additional debt and debt servicing costs would be almost inevitable. Government borrowing will compete with private borrowing and will almost certainly crowd out some of it. Interest rates are likely to rise higher, given the government's significant new demands on the capital markets, and this in turn will raise small businesses' costs of borrowing. If the political decision were made to use public debt to finance most or all of the coming Social Security shortfall, that additional debt would rise by approximately $47 trillion by 2075.[16]

Moreover, unlike borrowing to finance a transition to a prefunded system, borrowing to maintain the current system could never be repaid from Social Security tax receipts. The existing debt load exceeds $10 trillion, and the system's "pay-go" structure would continue making it larger, given the demographic shifts underway in the U.S. population.

Such an open-ended borrowing approach also would risk substantial inflation, in addition to which the sheer scale of the fiscal irresponsibility inherent in that approach could jeopardize the dollar's international standing in denominating debt and also as a "reserve" currency.

Financing Social Security debt out of general tax receipts (largely income tax receipts) most likely would lead to significantly higher income tax rates. As noted above, higher marginal tax rates are a serious hindrance to entrepreneurship and business ownership. Higher taxes, like reduced Social Security benefits, would take money from the pockets of individuals and companies, thereby shrinking personal savings and retained earnings as sources of capital.

But the United States need not pursue this ominous scenario of fiscal dead-ends.

A "Virtuous Cycle"

Allowing Social Security recipients to place a portion of their taxes in personal accounts that they own and control would initiate a "virtuous cycle" for capital markets.

For one thing, it would begin reducing trillions of dollars in unfunded liabilities,[17] which would create a favorable climate for balanced budgets or surpluses. If the experience of the past few years is any indication, federal budgets that have surpluses instead of massive deficits are good for small-business capital needs. Since 1998, small business has enjoyed the best access to capital on record, according to economic data tracked by the National Federation of Independent Business.[18]

For another thing, creating personal accounts would have an effect not unlike creating employer-provided pensions. Capital would build up and would be put to productive use. Small business would benefit—directly, through investments from the funds themselves and, indirectly, through transactions with financial service intermediaries with access to the funds. This process is succinctly summarized in a World Bank survey of global pension reform:

> [P]ension funds are critical players in "symbiotic" finance, the simultaneous and mutually reinforcing presence of many important elements of modern financial systems. They can support the development of factoring, leasing, and venture capital companies, all of which specialize in the financing of new and expanding small firms.[19]

The experience of Chile is instructive in this regard. Chile's Social Security personal account system is the world's oldest, dating back 20 years. Since then, the country has sustained robust economic growth averaging 7 percent a year, and both its capital markets and small businesses have flourished.[20] Among the more than 30 nations that have adopted personal accounts since then, none has reported a contradictory economic experience.

Perhaps most important, personal accounts would dramatically improve the rate of return that entrepreneurs could expect on their payroll tax payments and thereby enhance their retirement income. Some of the most persuasive evidence of this dynamic is found in an analysis of the University of Michigan's long-running *Panel Study of Income Dynamics*. The analysis carefully tracked more than 200 independent business owners over a 35-year period. It showed that they could expect rates of return averaging about 3 percent to 3.5 percent within the Social Security system (in contrast to a 7 percent historical rate of return on equities). Over a working lifetime, 92 percent of the business owners would lose between $300,000 and $700,000 if they were to pay Social Security taxes rather than invest the same amount in a conservative portfolio of 50 percent blue chip stocks and 50 percent long-term government bonds.[21] Brighter retirement income prospects for small businesses and entrepreneurs would allow more people to take the many other risks that small-business ownership and entrepreneurship entail.

In sum, personal accounts offer two fundamental-macroeconomic advantages for small business: what the government would *not* do (unnecessarily raise taxes, cut Social Security benefits, or borrow) and what the private sector *would* do (build up and deploy capital and improve retirement incomes).

The foregoing discussion has touched on four of the five basic options that the government could utilize to address Social Security's future financing needs. A fifth option would be to reduce other government spending sufficiently to cover Social Security's expected funding shortfalls.

Normally, this option might interest many small businesses, but the scale of the spending reductions required—perhaps $30 trillion to $50 trillion over time—renders it completely unrealistic. Funding for entire functions of government—for example, veterans programs, the administration of justice, transportation, space exploration, environmental protection—would have to be redirected. In 1994, in spite of the powerful mandate for belt-tightening evidenced by the Republican landslide, Congress barely summoned the political will to extinguish the Pennsylvania Avenue Development Commission. It would be utter fantasy to assume that Congress would opt to abolish entire departments on the scale of Transportation, Environmental Protection, or Veterans Affairs rather than borrowing, raising taxes, or cutting Social Security benefits.

Even if this were possible, moreover, it would send the wrong message: that every function of government should be subordinated to the imperative of providing retirement benefits. That is not a message that small-business owners (or, for that matter, any group of Americans) should want to be sent. As a prominent Democratic Party journal put it:

> [Democrats opposed to Social Security reform] should drop the motto "Social Security First" and start using "Social Security Only"—it more accurately reflects their position's logical endpoint. Democrats must ask themselves whether every other issue they care about—inner-city poverty, public schools, the environment, job training, universal access to health care—should be sacrificed or starved to maintain [today's] Social Security. If raising payroll taxes is part of the solution, exactly how much of a burden in regressive taxes on low-to-middle income Americans are Democrats willing to tolerate?[22]

Concerns Regarding Operations of Individual Businesses

The debate about Social Security reform also entails concerns regarding day-to-day business operations, one of which is the purported administrative burden that personal retirement accounts would place on small businesses.[23] Before examining the substance of this assumption, it should be noted that major small business associations in the United States—associations that presumably have had ample time to study the issue—have been strongly urging Congress to enact personal accounts for years.[24]

While the "small business administrative burden" avenue of criticism has helped to identify various practical issues relating to the implementation of personal accounts, these critiques often overlook or misinterpret the approach entailed by the most widely accepted current proposals for personal accounts, which minimizes the administrative burden on employers.[25] Most of the current proposals for personal savings accounts do *not* require employers to:

- Select investment funds or fund managers for their employees;
- Set aside or independently deposit any funds;
- Transmit any funds to workers;
- Separately transmit any funds to the federal government;
- Frequently submit information relating to personal accounts;
- Choose annuities for workers; or
- Bear legal or fiduciary responsibility for the performance of any of their employees' investments.

In fact, the proposals generally follow the example of the Thrift Savings Plan that is currently available to federal government workers. Under this scheme, a portion of the employees' Social Security taxes would automatically be reserved by the Treasury Department for Social Security. This money would be deposited by that agency or the Social Security Administration into a "default" fund, indexing a large number of stocks, or purchasing low-risk Treasury securities, or both. As these accounts reached a specified size, workers would be given the option to choose from a group of carefully selected and regulated investment options. They, and not employers, would most likely do so by checking a box on a form at the time of employment or subsequently.[26]

As for the employer's "administrative burden," the most that any of the current proposals entail is an annual reconfirmation of the "box" that employees have checked. Employers who want to do more may do so. For example, under recently enacted law, employers may, if they choose, offer free investment advice to employees, and this advice is not treated as a taxable benefit.[27]

Indeed, it is significant that opponents' claims that private investments would bring excessive administrative burdens to employers (a potentially explosive criticism) have done little to reduce the strong support that small-business owners and entrepreneurs have registered for personal accounts. In one survey, the respondents were asked how they felt about being "required to help administer a Social Security account system" and whether they would be willing, at the extreme, to spend up to $1,000 per employee per year to implement a personal account system.[28] In another survey, respondents were told that employers would have to "separately deduct" the amounts for personal accounts and "deposit" these deductions "in a different place" from the taxes that are normally withheld for the federal government.[29]

Yet, despite these misleading or false assumptions regarding likely administrative burdens for employers, the majority of respondents to both surveys still favored personal accounts. Indeed, only 20 percent were less enthusiastic after having been told, in the first survey, that they would shoulder a significant administrative responsibility for the system. Only 16 percent found the " separate deposit" procedure described in the second survey to be a "very serious new burden"; 41 percent said it was "not very serious."

To anyone familiar with small businesses' typically strident reaction against government-mandated paperwork, these survey findings are nothing short of astonishing. They suggest not an ambivalence toward Social Security reform, but a powerful depth of conviction favoring it.

Although the survey questions described above may have been the result of genuine uncertainties about how personal accounts modeled on the federal Thrift Savings Plan (TSP) would work, descriptions of employer responsibilities given by opponents of Social Security reform have often been intentionally exaggerated and distorted. The truth is that the administrative "burden" on small businesses would be very minor under such a TSP approach and that small businesses stand to benefit substantially from Social Security reform that includes personal accounts.

Conclusion

The energy invested in attempts to *mis*lead small-business owners regarding Social Security reform should be countered with efforts to provide leadership on this issue. That is the task of those who favor personal accounts. They may find inspiration in the words of President Franklin D. Roosevelt:

> Social Security is a "development towards [a] goal, rather than a finished product. [W]e should be constantly seeking to perfect and strengthen it in the light of our accumulating experience and growing appreciation of social needs."[30]

Notes

1. U.S. Small Business Administration, Office of Advocacy, *Small Business—Frequently Asked Questions*, August 2001.
2. Zoltan Arcs and David Audretsch, *Innovation and Small Firms* (Cambridge, Mass.: MIT Press, 1996).
3. Richard Nelson, *National Innovation Systems* (Oxford, UK: Oxford University Press, 1993).
4. Courtney Purrington and Kin Bettcher, *From the Garage to the Boardroom: The Entrepreneurial Roots of America's Largest Corporations*, National Commission on Entrepreneurship, August 2001.
5. Exporter Data Base, U.S. Department of Commerce, Office of Trade and Economic Analysis.
6. William J. Dennis, Jr., *The Public Reviews Small Business*, NFIB Education Foundation, 1998. Based on a 1997 Gallup poll of 1,108 American adults.
7. Employee Benefit Research Institute, *EBRI Notes*, Vol. 22, No. 1 (January 2001). Data compiled from U.S. Department of Commerce, Bureau of the Census, *Current Population Surveys*, March 1995–March 2000. The figures are for 1999.
8. American Savings Education Council and Employee Benefit Research Institute, *Retirement Confidence Survey*, 2001.
9. National Association for the Self-Employed, *Social Security and the Self-Employed*, testimony, National Commission on Retirement Policy, Center for Strategic and International Studies, May 1997.

10.   Douglas Holtz-Eakin *et al.*, "Horatio Alger Meets the Mobility Tables," *Small Business Economics*, Vol. 14, No. 4 (2000).

11.   Robert Carroll *et al.*, "Personal Income Taxes and the Growth of Small Firms," in James Poterba, ed., *Tax Policy and the Economy* (Cambridge, Mass.: MIT Press, 2001).

12.   William M. Gentry and R. Glenn Hubbard, "Tax Policy and Entry Into Entrepreneurship," Columbia University, Graduate School of Business, August 20, 2001, at *www.columbia.edu/~wmg6*. Using the 1979–1993 Panel Study of Income Dynamics, the research found, among other things, that the 1993 increase in the marginal tax rate lowered the probability for entry into self-employment by upper-middle-income households by as much as 20 percent.

13.   Martin Feldstein, Richard T. Ely Lecture to the American Economic Association, *American Economic Review*, Vol. 86, No. 2 (1996).

14.   Entrepreneurs believe that they pay higher payroll taxes than wage-and-salary workers, and beliefs can affect economic behavior, but are their taxes *really* higher? Is there really a "payroll tax penalty on entrepreneurship"? Most economists say no. The prevailing view is that employers simply reduce the wages and benefits of employees enough to cover the employer's share of payroll taxes. Thus, wage-and-salary workers are said to shoulder payroll taxes equal to those of the self-employed. But do employers actually follow this formula? That seems to depend on two fairly shaky assumptions: that all employer costs are constant and that employers weigh all costs equally. One wonders how the theory would apply, for example, to the business environment of the late 1990s, which included robust economic growth, rising productivity, commodity deflation, and labor shortages. Why would a business "pass through" all employer payroll taxes to scarce and/or valued employees in such an environment when so many more amicable and less visible alternatives for cost recovery were available? A recent Gallup Organization poll of business owners casts additional doubt on the "employee pass through" view. The survey found that, even under the more difficult economic conditions and higher unemployment of mid-2001, fewer than one employer out of eight would freeze or cut employee wages and benefits as a response to increased payroll costs. In fact, the "pass through" option ranked a distant fourth to (a) absorbing the increased payroll costs through lower profitability, (b) laying off employees, and (c) raising prices. See William J. Dennis, Jr., ed., "Adjusting to Cost Increases," *National Small Business Poll*, Vol. 1, No. 4, National Federation of Independent Business, forthcoming 2001. By contrast, self-employed workers would tend to have much less flexibility in cost shifting. "Absorbing" a cost, when one is self-employed, usually means paying for it personally. And there is no one else to "lay off." Even "raising prices" is probably a less viable option, so the entrepreneur most likely pays the taxes. Thus, the "belief" of the self-employed that they are paying higher taxes than wage-and-salary workers—a "payroll tax penalty on entrepreneurship"—may well be more empirically true than is currently acknowledged.

15.   President's Commission to Strengthen Social Security, *Interim Report*, August 2001. Congress and President Bush recently enacted a schedule of personal income tax rate reductions, in Public Law 107–16, that could partially offset these increases. However, most of those cuts are several years away, they could be changed by economic conditions or the outcome of elections during the intervening years, and they are scheduled to end in 2009.

16.   President's Commission to Strengthen Social Security, *Interim Report*. Data derived from *2001 Annual Report of the Board of Trustees of the Federal Old-Age and Survivors Insurance and Disability Insurance Trust Funds*, Social Security Administration, March 19, 2001.

17. It is worth noting that the "transition costs" to a prefunded Social Security system are not "costs," strictly speaking, but rather the explicit recognition of these unfunded liabilities.

18. William C. Dunkelberg, ed., *Small Business Economic Trends*, monthly publication, National Federation of Independent Business, 1973 to date; see especially issues for 1998–2000.

19. Dimitri Vittas, *Pension Reform and Capital Market Development: "Feasibility" and "Impact" Preconditions*, World Bank *Policy Research Working Paper* No. 2414, August 2000, at *http://econ.worldbank.org/search.php*. Note, however, that this "virtuous cycle" would be disrupted if the federal government itself were to do the investing and own the equities. The government's investments presumably would include only the largest and safest companies, and the capital buildup would remain inside its treasury. Under such conditions, there would be no obvious point of access to the accumulated capital for entrepreneurs and small businesses. Even if there were, it would be problematic. The perils of political meddling in the selection of investments, worrisome enough with large and highly visible investments, would be magnified for smaller, more obscure investments. An equally profound danger would be federal government bias toward the larger companies in which the government held equity. That could adversely affect small businesses across a wide swath of issues—such as taxes, competition policy, intellectual property rights, and government procurement—where there is friction between large and small business interests.

20. "Chilean Social Security Reform as a Prototype for Other Nations," *EBRI Notes*, Vol. 18, No. 8 (August 1997), and Barry Bosworth *et al.*, eds., *The Chilean Economy: Policy Lessons and Challenges* (Washington, D.C.: Brookings Institution, 1994).

21. *The Impact of Social Security's Old Age and Survivors Insurance Program on Owners of Independent Businesses*, A Report of the Heritage Foundation Center for Data Analysis, October 25, 1999. It is important to note that this study was not based on a specific legislative proposal. Rather, it calculated Social Security's *historical* rate of return for a group of independent business owners from 1968–1993 and then compared that to a notional portfolio over the same period. Current legislative proposals for personal accounts would yield different results, because their investment parameters are different and because Social Security's *future* rate of return is expected to be well *below* the 3 percent to 3.5 percent found in the study. The study's underlying message—that personal accounts would yield better retirement incomes than an unreformed Social Security system—has been corroborated by additional nonpartisan studies by the Congressional Budget Office, the Social Security Administration's own actuaries, and others.

22. Editorial, "Now for the Hard Part," *The New Democrat*, Democratic Leadership Council, Vol. 10, No. 6 (November 1998).

23. Kelly Olsen and Dallas Salisbury, "Individual Social Security Accounts: Issues in Administrative Feasibility and Costs," *EBRI Special Report and Issue Brief* No. 203, November 1998. This report also makes a number of other criticisms about the administrative efficiency of personal accounts that are beyond the scope of this paper but have been analyzed elsewhere. See, for example, Robert Genetski, *Administrative Costs and the Efficiency of Public and Private Social Security Systems, SSP* No. 15, Cato Institute, March 9, 1999.

24. For example, the membership of the ardently pro-personal account Alliance for Worker Retirement Security includes the National Association for the Self-Employed, the National Federation of Independent Business, and the U.S.

Chamber of Commerce—three of the nation's largest small business associations—as well as small-business-dominated industry associations like the National Restaurant Association and the Printing Industries of America. It is equally striking that there have been no "eruptions" of small business discontent about administrative burdens in any of the more than 30 countries that currently offer some form of personal account.

25. See, for example, H.R. 2771 of the 107th Congress, introduced by Representatives Jim Kolbe (R–AZ), Charles Stenholm (D–TX), *et al.*, especially Part B, Subpart 1, Sections 251–253, 261–262, and 273, and Subpart H, Section 532. See also S. 2774 of the 106th Congress, introduced by Senators Judd Gregg (R–NH), John Breaux (D–LA), *et al.*, especially Section 2, Subpart B, Sections 251–254.

26. According to a recent account of the Clinton Administration's planning for personal accounts, Treasury Department and Social Security Administration officials favored placing the "check-off" box on the face of the individual income tax forms (Form 1040). See Douglas Emendorf *et al.*, *Fiscal Policy and Social Security Policy During the 1990's,* paper presented at conference on "American Economic Policy in the 1990's," Harvard University, June 2001, p. 43.

27. Public Law 107–16, Title VI, Part 2, Subtitle F, Section 645.

28. Employee Benefit Research Institute, "The Small Business Community and Individual Social Security Accounts," *EBRI News Release*, April 16, 1999. Based on a survey of 500 small business owners in September–October 1998 by Matthew Greenwald & Associates, Washington, D.C. The survey presented three employer options for personal accounts, including an option similar to a TSP-style plan, but it strongly implied that all three options would be costly and intrusive for small businesses.

29. National Federation of Independent Business, *Small Business Assesses Social Security*, Washington, 1998.

30. Quoted in Senator John Breaux, "Rising to the Challenge," *The New Democrat,* Vol. 10, No. 6 (November 1998).

Greg Anrig, Jr., and
Bernard Wasow

 **NO**

Twelve Reasons Why Privatizing Social Security Is a Bad Idea

Introduction

President George W. Bush repeatedly has emphasized that one of his foremost second-term priorities will be to transform Social Security fundamentally. Enacted in 1935 and amended many times since-including major changes in 1983-Social Security provides benefits to workers and their family members upon retirement, disability, or death. Since the program's inception, the size of those benefits always has depended on the earnings of workers over the course of their careers. President Bush wants to change the system so that the amount that each worker collects from Social Security upon retirement instead would hinge on the size of investments in his or her own personal account.

Although the President has not yet endorsed a specific plan, the President's Commission to Strengthen Social Security put forward three proposals in 2002 that likely will form the basis for his plan to create private accounts. An analysis of those proposals showed that paying for new personal accounts while continuing to provide benefits to Social Security's current beneficiaries would require some combination of federal borrowing, tax increases, and benefit cuts **amounting to between $2 trillion and $3 trillion** over the coming decades.

President Bush and others who support private accounts argue that such dramatic changes are necessary because Social Security faces a financing shortfall, according to projections of the system's trustees. The trustees' latest estimates, based on economic and population assumptions they call neither optimistic nor pessimistic, show that Social Security will continue to be able to pay benefits in full until its trust funds are exhausted in the year 2042. After that, funding would be sufficient to provide about 70 percent of currently promised benefits. (The Congressional Budget Office, perhaps more realistically, recently projected that the reserves would last until 2052 and would be able to pay about 80 percent of current benefits thereafter.) Private account advocates also emphasize that while today's retirees generally receive far more from Social Security than they contributed in taxes, the so-called "rate of return" for tomorrow's retirees is projected to be substantially less generous.

Much is at stake in this debate. More than 96 percent of workers pay Social Security taxes and thereby are entitled to collect benefits from the program. More than 47 million Americans today receive checks from the Social Security

From *TCF Issue Brief*, February 14, 2005. Copyright © 2005 by The Century Foundation. Reprinted by permission.

system. Although the average monthly payment to those individuals is a modest $895, Social Security constitutes more than half of the incomes of nearly two-thirds of retired Americans. For one in five, it is their only income. Like past generations of Americans, today's workers of all ages will need Social Security to protect them against forces beyond their control-economic ups and downs, inflation, fluctuating investment markets, and possible disability or premature death of a family member. That insurance has been essential in even the best of times, and will be all the more important in an increasingly global economy with large and growing federal budget and trade deficits.

Addressing Social Security's potential long-term financing challenges by taking the dramatic step of diverting its payroll taxes to create new personal accounts would represent a radical departure; it also would be a bad idea. Here are twelve reasons why less costly, less risky, and less painful changes should be considered instead:

Reason #1: Today's Insurance to Protect Workers and Their Families Against Death and Disability Would Be Threatened

"Rate of return" calculations neglect the value of Social Security's insurance protections. Of the 45 million Americans who collect payments from the Social Security program, over one-third (almost 17 million) are not retired workers. Among those currently receiving Social Security payments are 5 million spouses and children of retired and disabled workers, 7 million spouses and dependent children of deceased workers, and 5 million disabled workers. Proposals to privatize Social Security involve shifting some of the money financing the current insurance program into investment accounts assigned to each worker. But the payroll taxes carved out to pay for personal accounts are resources that are needed to support today's payments to recipients of Social Security's survivors and disability insurance as well as retirement benefits. Simple arithmetic suggests that every dollar shifted from Social Security programs to personal accounts is a dollar less to provide guaranteed income to the 37 percent of beneficiaries who are not retired workers.

The three alternatives put forward by the President's Commission to Strengthen Social Security would, in the absence of individual accounts, restore long-term Social Security solvency either largely or entirely through benefit reductions that would apply to all beneficiaries-including the disabled. In the principal proposals put forward by the Commission, **the reduction in disability benefits was draconian**, with cuts ranging from 19 percent to 47.5 percent after the year 2030. The commission itself somewhat disavowed this aspect of its proposals, suggesting that a subsequent commission or other body that specializes in disability policy might revise how its plans apply to the disabled.

Economists Peter A. Diamond (MIT) and Peter R. Orszag (Brookings) have noted that the disabled would have limited ability to mitigate the effects of these benefit reductions by securing income from individual accounts. One reason is that their individual accounts often would be meager, since those who become disabled before retirement age may have relatively few years of work during which they could make contributions to their accounts. Second, under the commission proposals, disabled beneficiaries (like all other beneficiaries) would not be allowed access to their individual accounts until they reached retirement age.

As the Bush commission itself acknowledged, preserving existing disability and survivor's insurance greatly escalates the cost of financing private accounts. It is difficult to imagine how any Social Security privatization plan can avoid significant cuts in those essential protections.

Reason #2: Creating Private Accounts Would Make Social Security's Financing Problem Worse, not Better

Social Security is funded by a flat tax of 12.4 percent of each worker's wage income, up to $90,000 in 2005, split evenly between employers and employees. About four out of five of those tax dollars go immediately to current beneficiaries, and the remaining dollar is used to purchase U.S. Treasury securities held in the system's trust funds. Beginning in 2018, well after the huge generation of baby boomers born between 1946 and 1964 begins to retire, a portion of general income tax revenues will be needed to pay interest and eventually principal on those bonds to fully finance benefits. A "crisis" is not forecast to arise until the program becomes entirely "pay as you go" again (as it was throughout its history before 1983) in either 2042 according to the trustees' forecast or 2052 according to the Congressional Budget Office. (By way of perspective, in 2052 the oldest surviving baby boomers will be 106 years old and the youngest will be 88.)

Diverting 2 or 4 percent of payroll to create private accounts as proposed by the President's Commission to Strengthen Social Security doesn't sound very radical, but it would shorten significantly the time until current benefit levels could only be sustained by raising taxes. In part, this is because funds now being set aside to build up the trust funds to provide for retiring baby boomers would be used instead to pay for the privatization accounts. The government would have to start borrowing from the private sector almost immediately to be able to meet commitments to retirees and near-retirees. In such a short time frame, the investments in the personal accounts will not be nearly large enough to provide an adequate cushion. The upshot: a much larger share of today's workers would confront large benefit cuts, or tax increases, than if no changes were implemented.

Reason #3: Creating Private Accounts Could Dampen Economic Growth, Which Would Further Weaken Social Security's Future Finances

Privatizing Social Security will escalate federal deficits and debt significantly while increasing the likelihood that national savings will decline-all of which could reduce long-term economic growth and the size of the economic pie available to pay for the retirement of the baby boom generation. The **2004 Economic Report of the President** included an analysis of the fiscal impact over time of the most commonly discussed privatization proposal by the president's commission. It found that the federal budget deficit would be more than 1 percent of gross domestic product (GDP) higher every year for roughly two decades, with the highest increase being 1.6 percent of GDP in 2022. The national debt levels would be increased by an amount equal to 23.6 percent of GDP in 2036. *That means that, thirty-two years from now, the debt burden for every man, woman, and child would be $32,000 higher because of privatization.*

One impact of those seemingly abstract numbers after privatization is that interest rates are likely to be substantially higher, raising the cost to the average household of mortgages, car loans, student loans, credit cards and so on. As a result, the economy would be likely to grow more slowly than it would otherwise.

Creating private accounts with increased federal borrowing at first blush would seem unlikely to affect national savings, because additional savings in the new accounts would offset exactly any new government borrowing to pay for those accounts. Economists believe that increased national savings, especially in a country with savings levels as low as they are in the United States, can increase growth by keeping interest rates low and financing investments in productive activities.

But privatization is actually more likely to reduce than increase national savings. **Diamond and Orszag point out** that evaluating the overall effect on national savings requires taking into account the likely responses of government, employers, and households. Historically, neither the government nor businesses have changed their spending levels consistently in response to large changes in deficit levels. But households that consider the new accounts to constitute meaningful increases in their retirement wealth might well reduce their other saving. Diamond and Orszag argue, "If anything, our impression is that diverting a portion of the current Social Security surplus into individual accounts could reduce national saving." That, in turn, would further weaken economic growth and our capacity to pay for the retirement of the baby boomers.

Reason #4: Privatization Has Been a Disappointment Elsewhere

Advocates of privatization often cite other countries such as Chile and the United Kingdom, where the governments pushed workers into personal investment accounts to reduce the long-term obligations of their Social Security systems, as models for the United States to emulate. But the sobering experiences in those countries actually provide strong arguments against privatization.

A report this year from the World Bank, once an enthusiastic privatization proponent, expressed disappointment that in Chile, and in most other Latin

American countries that followed in its footsteps, "more than half of all workers [are excluded] from even a semblance of a safety net during their old age."

Other cautionary points made in the World Bank report and other studies about the experience in Chile:

- Investment accounts of retirees are much smaller than originally predicted-so low that 41 percent of those eligible to collect pensions continue to work.
- Voracious commissions and other administrative costs have swallowed up large shares of those accounts. The brokerage firm CB **Capitales calculated** (see english language discussion by Stephen Kay here) that when commission charges are taken into consideration in Chile, the total average return on worker contributions between 1982 and 1999 was 5.1 percent-not 11 percent as calculated by the superintendent of pension funds. That report found that the average worker would have done better simply by placing their pension fund contributions in a passbook savings account.
- **The transition costs** of shifting to a privatized system in Chile averaged 6.1 percent of GDP in the 1980s, 4.8 percent in the 1990s, and are expected to average 4.3 percent from 1999 to 2037. Those costs are far higher than originally projected, in part because the government is obligated to provide subsidies for workers failing to accumulate enough money in their accounts to earn a minimum pension.

In the United Kingdom, which began encouraging workers to divert payroll taxes to personal investment accounts in 1978, many citizens were victimized by poor investment choices as well as unscrupulous brokers. The national government was left with substantial new administrative expenses, lost tax revenues, and responsibilities to bail out some failed private pension plans. Indeed, the problems were so wide-ranging that even the most enthusiastic supporters of private accounts now say that the United Kingdom simply did not do it right.

A British government commission headed by Adair Turner reported in October 2004 that Britain had been living in "a fool's paradise" by thinking it had solved its pension problems. According to pension experts at the Organization for Economic Cooperation and Development (OECD), the Adair Turner report has sounded alarm bells. "What looked like a very good idea from a financial perspective in cutting costs has put pensioner poverty, which had been all but eradicated, back on the agenda."

Reason #5: The Odds Are Against Individuals Investing Successfully

Privatization advocates like to stress the appeal of "individual choice" and "personal control," while assuming in their forecasts that everyone's accounts will match the overall performance of the stock market. But studies by Yale economist Robert J. Shiller and others have demonstrated that individual investors are far more likely to do worse than the market generally, even excluding the cost of commissions and administrative expenses. Indeed, research by Princeton University economist Burton Malkiel found that even professional money managers over time significantly underperformed indexes of the entire market.

Moreover, a number of surveys show that most people lack the knowledge to make even basic decisions about investing. For example, a Securities and Exchange Commission report synthesizing surveys of investors found that only 14 percent knew the difference between a growth stock and an income stock, and just 38 percent understood that when interest rates rise, bond prices go down. Almost half of all investors believed incorrectly that diversification guarantees that their portfolio won't suffer if the market drops and 40 percent thought that a mutual fund's operating costs have no impact on the returns they receive.

While predictions vary significantly about how investment markets will perform in the decades ahead, it's safe to say that any growth in individual accounts under privatization will be significantly lower than what the overall markets achieve.

Reason #6: What You Get Will Depend on Whether You Retire When the Market Is Up or Down

In the twentieth century, when stocks generally grew significantly, there were three twenty-year periods over which the market either declined or did not rise. The volatility of investment markets means that it matters a great deal whether you retire during an upswing or downturn. For example, a worker who invested his or her retirement fund in a stock portfolio that matched the Standard & Poor's 500 index and cashed out upon retirement in March 2000 would have a nest egg almost a third larger than someone who retired just a year later using exactly the same investment strategy. Of course, that is because the stock market plunged over those twelve months.

Reason #7: Wall Street Would Reap Windfalls from Your Taxes

Brokerage houses, banks, and mutual funds have been very active in the campaign to privatize Social Security. Small wonder, since they stand to gain enormous fees if billions of dollars are shifted each year from Social Security payments into accounts under Wall Street management. Of course, those fees must come from somewhere, namely from the balances in individual accounts.

Among the one hundred best stock mutual funds, management fees range from 0.2 percent per year to 1.4 percent of the asset value of an account. The average is near the high end of that range, however, and many mutual funds charge substantially more. Smaller accounts require proportionately larger management fees because many costs such as gathering and mailing out information do not depend on account size. Indeed, most mutual funds actively discourage small accounts by setting a minimum opening deposit of $1,000 to $3,000.

Experience in the United Kingdom offers a warning about what the future could bring regarding management costs. Workers there have been allowed to open private accounts starting in 1988, since which time management fees and marketing costs among financial intermediaries have eaten up an average of 43 percent of the return on investment.

Reason #8: Private Accounts Would Require a New Government Bureaucracy

From the standpoint of the system as a whole, privatization would add enormous administrative burdens. Instead of the current trust fund accounts, the government would need to establish and track many small accounts, perhaps as many accounts as there are taxpaying workers-147 million in 1997.

Many workers' accounts would be so small that they would be of no interest to profit-making firms. The average taxable earnings of a worker are roughly $25,000 (in 1997, the last year with complete data, the average taxable earnings of the workers who paid into the system were $22,400). Two percent of $25,000 comes to $500 per year. Francis X. Cavanaugh, who has supervised the thrift savings program for federal employees, a program that privatization advocates often point to as a model, **has argued** that the costs of administering so many small accounts would overwhelm any benefits to be gained from the stock market. For example, he estimates that the government would need to hire 10,000 highly trained workers just to oversee the accounts and answer questions from workers. In contrast, today's Social Security has minimal administrative costs amounting to less than 1 percent of annual revenues.

Reason #9: Young People Would Be Worse Off

Social Security privatization is often sold to young adults as a much better deal for them than the current system. But two recent studies show that if Social Security is converted to a system of private accounts, younger generations will be the ones who bear the costs of transforming the program. The added costs arise from the huge increases in federal borrowing needed to finance the new accounts while continuing to direct payroll taxes toward existing benefits for current retirees. According to the **Congressional Budget Office**, "to raise the rate of return for future generations by moving to a funded system, some generations must receive rates of return even lower than they would have gotten under the pay-as-you-go system."

A July 2004 **Congressional Budget Office** analysis of a private account proposal by the President's Commission to Strengthen Social Security compares it with the existing system. It looked at two scenarios for the traditional Social Security system, one with payments continuing in full indefinitely and the other with the trust funds becoming depleted in a few decades and payments shrinking to three-fourths their current level. In both scenarios, nearly all birth cohorts at all income levels born from the 1940s through the first decade of the 21st century on average do worse under the proposed system of private accounts. Only individuals in the lowest earning quintiles from the 1950s and the 1990s do slightly better, on average. Even assuming a worst case scenario where the trust funds evaporate and benefits are cut substantially, cohorts from the 1960s to 2000s would see reductions with private accounts between 1 percent and 17.5 percent on average, depending on their income and birth year.

An earlier analysis by economists Henry Aaron, Alan Blinder, Alicia Munnell, and Peter Orszag used the broad outlines of then-Governor Bush's Social Security privatization proposals to compare retirement benefits under current law to those if private accounts were introduced. They found that benefits for an average earning worker who retired in 2037 at age 67 (someone aged 34 today) would be 20 percent lower than they are now given historical rates of return over a fifty-year period.

Reason #10: Women Stand to Lose the Most

The Social Security system is gender-blind. None of its provisions treat women differently from men. But that does not mean that the results are gender-neutral. Various cultural and biological differences add up to the fact that **Social Security is much more essential, and a much better deal, for women than for men**. Of all groups, none has more to lose from the privatization of Social Security than women. Compared to the average man, the average woman

- works fewer years outside the home,
- earns less per year, and
- lives longer after retiring.

Together, these differences mean that women depend more than men do on spousal and survivors' benefits, they collect benefits for more years than men do, and a greater proportion of their total retirement income comes from Social Security.

Since women on average work fewer years at lower pay, they contribute less in payroll taxes over their lifetimes than do men. But in their various roles as retirees, spouses, and widows, women collect Social Security benefits for more years than men. The result is that women get more net benefits over their lifetimes than do men.

There are fourteen women for every ten men aged 62 or older. Above age 85, this ratio reaches twenty-four women per ten men. Consequently, 60 percent of all Social Security beneficiaries are women. Among those receiving survivor and disability benefits, women and children constitute 85 percent. Women also depend more on Social Security. Older women who are not part of a couple (either widows, divorcees, separated, or never married) get 51 percent of their income from Social Security, and 25 percent of them have no income but Social Security. For men in the same situation (a far smaller proportion of the total), the figures are 39 and 20 percent, respectively.

The poverty rate for older women is almost twice that of older men (in 1997, 13.1 percent versus 7.0 percent). For older women who are not in a couple, the rate gets much higher: more than one in four lives below the poverty line. Fewer than half of them had incomes in 1997 above $1,000 per month. Without Social Security's guaranteed benefits, the already marginal income security for older women would be much worse.

In spite of the improvement in employment opportunities for women, the role of homemaker and primary parent still falls unequally on wives and mothers. Private accounts would jeopardize income that wives, widows, and divorcees now receive under Social Security. The more individual control that passes to workers, the fewer rights their dependents will retain to secure retirement income. If the guarantees and redistributive features of Social Security are replaced with a system that provides benefits according only to how much a worker earns over that worker's lifetime and how fortunate that worker is in financial markets, the average woman, especially the average widow, will lose security and income from already low levels.

Reason #11: African Americans and Latin Americans Also Would Become More Vulnerable Under Privatization

Privatization advocates often claim that converting Social Security to a system of private accounts would disproportionately help African Americans and Latin Americans because those groups are purportedly shortchanged by the current system. But in fact there is almost no difference in Social Security's payback by race. And because both of those groups on average earn lower lifetime earnings than whites, those minorities would be at greater risk of facing poverty in their retirement under privatization.

African Americans on average have two characteristics that are disadvantageous under Social Security: shorter life expectancy and a lower marriage rate. But **they also have traits that lead to greater benefits under Social Security**: a higher disability rate, more survivors receiving benefits, and lower average wages. Latinos also have relatively low incomes on average, but **a longer life expectancy and fewer average years in the workforce**.

But because African-Americans and Latinos on average have substantially less wealth upon retirement than whites, they are far more dependent on Social Security. Converting the program into a system where their retirement income would be more dependent on investment markets would make those groups even more vulnerable to poverty.

Reason #12: Retirees Will not Be Protected Against Inflation

Social Security privatization plans, including all three recommended by the President's Commission to Strengthen Social Security, require retirees to convert the lump sums in their personal accounts into annuities that provide them with monthly payments until their death. The reason for that is that otherwise retirees could outlive their nest eggs, or even squander them, requiring taxpayers to bail them out.

The market for annuities, which are financial contracts sold by insurance companies, is very thin now, with relatively few bought and sold. Such a market would probably develop under privatization, but **it is unlikely that those annuity payments would increase in line with inflation, as today's Social Security benefits do**. Without inflation protection, the purchasing power of retirees' pensions would fall precipitously during times when prices are rising rapidly. Because insurance companies would bear significant new risks for offering inflation protection, they would be likely to charge very substantial fees over and above the already steep 10 percent that they now charge.

Conclusion

Current Social Security insurance protections have served the country well for decades. Diluting those protections in exchange for new accounts poses all kinds of new risks while making the relatively manageable long-term challenges confronting Social Security far more immediate and severe.

Notes

Introduction

". . . amounting to be between $2 trillion and $3 trillion . . ." Peter A. Diamond and Peter R. Orszag, **"Reducing Benefits and Subsidizing Individual Accounts: An Analysis of the Plans Proposed by the President's Commission to Strengthen Social Security,"** Center on Budget and Policy Priorities and The Century Foundation, June 2002, p. 7.

Reason #1

Diamond and Orszag, pp. 10–11.

See also Greg Anrig and Bernard Wasow, **"What Would Really Happen under Social Security Privatization? Part IV: Insecurity for the Disabled and Dependents of Workers and Retirees who Die,"** The Century Foundation, New York City, December 10, 2001.

Reason #3

Economic Report of the President (Washington, D.C.: Government Printing Office, February 2004), p. 144.

"If anything, our impression . . ." Peter A. Diamond and Peter R. Orszag, **Saving Social Security: A Balanced Approach** (Washington, D.C.: Brookings Institution Press, 2004), p. 161.

Reason #4

"more than half of all workers . . ." Indermit S. Gil, Truman Packard, and Juan Yermo, **Keeping the Promise of Old Age Income**

Security in Latin America (Washington, D.C.: The World Bank, 2004), p. 10.

"Investment accounts of retirees are much smaller . . ." Stephen J. Kay and Milko Matijascic, Social Security at the Crossroads: Toward Effective Pension Reform in Latin America, Unpublished paper prepared for the XXVI Conference of the Latin America Studies Association-LASA, Las Vegas, Oct. 6–8, 2004, p. 6.

"The World Bank found that . . ." **Gil et al**, p. 8.

"The brokerage firm CB Capitales . . ." **Tema Especial: ¿Cuál ha sido la verdadera Rentabilidad del Sistema de AFP?** CB Capitales, Departamento de Estudios, April 8, 1999; also see Stephen J. Kay, **State Capacities and Pensions**, Unpublished paper prepared for the Latin American Studies Association XXIV International Conference in Dallas, March 27–29, 2003, p.12.

"The transition costs of shifting . . ." José E. Devesa-Carpio and Carlos Vidal-Meliá, **The Reformed Pension Systems in Latin America**, Social Protection Discussion Paper Series, No. 0209.

"A British government commission . . ." Andrew Balls and Chris Giles, "Dubious Special Relationship Links Two Pension Reform Schemes," Financial Times, November 18, 2004, p. 2.

Reason #5

"Indeed, research by Princeton economist Burton G. Malkiel . . ." Burton G. Malkiel, "Returns from Investing in Equity Mutual Funds 1971 to 1991," The Journal of Finance 50, no. 2 (June 1995): 572.

"For example, a Securities and Exchange Commission report . . ." **"The Facts on Saving and Investing: Excerpts from Recent Polls and Studies Highlighting the Need for Financial Education,"** The Securities and Exchange Commission, Washington, D.C., April, 1999.

Reason #6

"Gary Burtless of the Brookings Institution demonstrated . . ." Gary Burtless, personal communication, see also **"Risk and Returns of Stock Market Investments Held in Individual Retirement Accounts,"** Testimony before Task Force on Social Security Reform, House Budget Committee, May 11, 1999.

Reason #7

"Among the one hundred best mutual funds . . ." Consumer Reports, March 2001.

Reason #8

"Francis X. Cavanaugh . . . has argued . . ." **Statement of Francis X. Cavanaugh before the Senate Budget Committee**, July 21, 1998.

Reason #9

"According to the Congressional Budget Office . . ." **"How Pension Financing Affects Returns to Different Generations,"** Congressional Budget Office, Washington, D.C., September 22, 2004.

"A June 2004 Congressional Budget Office analysis . . ." **"Long-Term Analysis of Plan 2 of the President's Commission to Strengthen Social Security,"** Congressional Budget Office, Letter to Senatior Larry E. Craig, July 21, 2004 (updated September 30, 2004).

"An earlier analysis . . ." Henry J. Aaron, Alan S. Blinder, Alicia H. Munnell, and Peter R. Orszag, **"Governor Bush's Individual Account Proposal: Implications for Retirement Benefits,"** Issue Brief 11, The Century Foundation, New York, 2000.

Reason #10

Bernard Wasow, **"Setting the Record Straight: Women and Social Security,"** The Century Foundation, New York City, April 1, 2002.

Reason # 11

Bernard Wasow, **"Setting the Record Straight: Two False Claims about African Americans and Social Security,"** The Century Foundation, New York City, March 1, 2002.

Bernard Wasow, **"Social Security Works for Latinos,"** The Century Foundation, New York City, May 1, 2002.

Reason #12

Greg Anrig and Bernard Wasow, **"What Would Really Happen Under Social Security Privatization? Part II: Millionaires One and All?"** The Century Foundation, New York City, December 10, 2001.

POSTSCRIPT

Would Reforming Social Security Be Good for American Business?

As evidenced by the two articles you have just read, much of the debate on Social Security reform centers on practical concerns. For example, Dr. Morrison argues of the financial benefits accruing to small businesses if reform happens, while Anrig and Wasow argue that reform would make Social Security's financial problems worse, not better. And though the practical aspects of reform are obviously important and carry considerable weight, there is another, deeper level at which this debate can be viewed. A growing number of social commentators and scholars have observed that there are different philosophical viewpoints underlying the two positions.

Fundamental to the position that Social Security should not be privatized is the philosophical belief that government is, and should be, responsible in some measure for the welfare of its citizens. Indeed, President Roosevelt's entire reaction to the Great Depression was predicated on the assumption that the U.S. government had both the right and the responsibility to help its citizens; in this instance, through massive government spending and legislative activity such as the Social Security Act. From this view, privatizing Social Security represents a conscious, intentional move away from the philosophical position that has dominated American culture since the time of Roosevelt's New Deal programs in the 1930s.

Those who want to privatize Social Security argue that it would be the first important step towards reestablishing the primacy of individual rights and private property as envisioned by the Founding Fathers. They contend that not allowing individuals a say in how their retirement monies are spent is a direct violation of their individual rights and, therefore, patently unconstitutional. Interestingly, this very argument against Social Security is not new—like many of Roosevelt's New Deal pieces of legislation, the Social Security Act was attacked as being unconstitutional. Not surprisingly, the SSA was very controversial.

So, if you are still not certain as to where you stand on this topic, perhaps a more detailed historical and philosophical account will help. To that end, we recommend the following additional articles on Social Security reform.

Suggested Readings

Andrew Biggs, A wealth of benefits. The Cato Institute, July 16, 2002. www.socialsecurity.org/pubs/articles/art-biggs020716.html.

Jason Burrell, Counterpoint: The case against social security reform. *International Social Science Review,* vol. 80, no. 1 & 2, 2005.

Francis X. Cavanaugh, *Feasibility of Social Security Individual Accounts.* The Public Policy Institute, September 2002.

Alex Epstein, End social security. The Ayn Rand Institute, January 18, 2005. http://www.aynrand.org/site/News2?news_iv_ctrl=-1&page=NewsArticle&id= 10797.

John Kempel, Administrative constraints on individual social security accounts. In *Beyond Ideology: Are Individual Social Security Accounts Feasible?* Employee Benefits Research Institute, 1999.

Derrick A. Max, Social security reform: The case for business/employer involvement. *The Alliance for Worker Retirement Security,* February 23, 2005.

Michael Tanner, The 6.2 percent solution. The Cato Project on Social Security Choice, February 17, 2004.

On the Internet . . .

The Cato Institute

The Cato Institute is a nonprofit public policy think tank based on the traditional American "principles of limited government, individual liberty, free markets and peace." Cato has published policy commentary on a wide array of important business topics including outsourcing.

http://www.cato.org/

The Sarbanes-Oxley Act Community Forum

This site is an interactive portal designed to assist organizations who are attempting to comply with the massive requirements and regulations of Sarbanes-Oxley. Additional tips, resources, and links are also provided.

http://www.sarbanes-oxley-forum.com/

The International Corporate Governance Network

ICGN is a leading international authority on corporate governance. The organization provides research and policy recommendations to governments and organizations across the globe in order to elevate the quality of corporate governance.

http://www.icgn.org/

The Strategic Management Society

SMS is composed of academics, business practitioners, and consultants, and focuses its attention on the development and dissemination of insights on the strategic management process, as well as on fostering contacts and interchange among members from around the world.

http://www.smsweb.org/

PART 3

Strategic Management

*M*ost investors and executives do their utmost to help their firms grow and to increase profits. It seems obvious: Successful firms are growing firms. So why would highly knowledgeable and respected business scholars and observers argue that growth is not necessary for a firm to be successful? For answers to this question and other emotionally charged issues, dive into the five topics comprising the third section of this text.

- Is Outsourcing a Wise Corporate Strategy?

- Are U.S. CEOs Overpaid?

- Corporate Governance Reform: Is Sarbanes-Oxley the Answer?

- Is First-to-Market a Successful Strategy?

- Must Firms Constantly Grow to Be Considered Successful?

ISSUE 10

Is Outsourcing a Wise Corporate Strategy?

YES: Sarah Anderson and John Cavanagh, from "Outsourcing: A Policy Agenda," *Foreign Policy in Focus* (April 2004)

NO: Daniel W. Drezner, from "The Outsourcing Bogeyman," *Foreign Affairs* (May/June 2004)

ISSUE SUMMARY

YES: Sarah Anderson and John Cavanagh argue that outsourcing is a real threat to the economic health of the United States and provide several suggestions as to the types of governmental actions necessary to keep American jobs from moving overseas. Included in their discussion is an analysis of the views of the two 2004 presidential candidates, John Kerry and George W. Bush.

NO: Dr. Daniel Drezner argues that the controversy surrounding outsourcing is not new and that its current form is more hype than substance. He shows how outsourcing is actually economically beneficial to America, despite the warnings of critics. Dr. Drezner also asserts that the concept of outsourcing is consistent with a solid understanding of free-market capitalism and an appreciation of traditional American principles and values.

As his Democratic party foes constantly pointed out during the 2004 election year, President George W. Bush's early years in the White House were characterized by, among other things, a steady increase in the number of jobs lost as a result of the recession, which started almost immediately upon his taking office in 2001. An interesting residual effect of this situation was the increased attention both economists and politicians gave to outsourcing. Indeed, if one were to believe the media, offshore outsourcing—the transferring of work previously done by Americans to foreign countries as a strategic response to pressures to keep costs low—occurred at epic rates and was partly responsible for the economic downturn of the early part of the decade. Democratic presidential nominee John Kerry campaigned on a platform built, in part, on the promise that he would keep American jobs in America. The implication, of course, is that outsourcing is unpatriotic. On the surface, such corporate behavior would indeed appear to be unpatriotic—after all, what could be more anti-American than moving American jobs to foreign countries? But is this indeed the case?

Those who argue that outsourcing is bad business and anti-American maintain this is so simply because it moves jobs out of America. Sarah Anderson and John Cavanagh note that this is no small trend: Millions of jobs have left American shores in recent years, and many millions more are vulnerable. Critics also point to the alarming growth of outsourcing in the service sector. The historical justification for outsourcing was built on the belief that jobs lost in manufacturing would be replaced by jobs in the service sector as the United States shifted from an industrial to a service-based economy. Since the current outsourcing wave is primarily service-based, the concern is that outsourcing will accelerate further as we move toward a service-oriented society. Finally, many charge that outsourcing is nothing more than American firms exploiting cheaper labor in other countries in order to increase profits (see Issue 17 regarding sweatshops for further insight into this contentious topic). Do you agree with this point and, if so, how patriotic is this type of corporate behavior?

Proponents of outsourcing have strong points on their side of the issue as well. The call to end outsourcing is, in their view, merely protectionism in disguise, a concept entirely at odds with traditional American political and economic principles. American capitalism and prosperity were built on free trade; forcing American firms to forego cheap overseas labor in the name of patriotism will ultimately cause U.S. firms, and society, to suffer. In terms of the exploitation of foreign labor argument, supporters respond that it is not exploitation at all. Consider these comments by Edwin Locke, Dean's Professor of Leadership and Motivation at the University of Maryland, and Ayn Rand, Institute contributing author:

> . . . the claim that multinational companies [e.g., American firms] exploit workers in poor countries by paying lower wages than they would pay in their home countries. Well, what is the alternative? It is: no wages! The comparative advantage of poorer countries is precisely that their wages are low, thus reducing the costs of production. If multinational corporations had to pay the same wages as in their home countries, they would not bother to invest in poorer countries at all and millions of people would lose their livelihoods.

In the following selections, you will be exposed to both sides of this controversial topic. Sarah Anderson and John Cavanagh defend an anti-outsourcing perspective. During the course of their discussion, the authors present an analysis of the viewpoints on outsourcing held by Democratic nominee John Kerry and Republican President George W. Bush just prior to the 2004 presidential election. Daniel Drezner, professor of political science at the University of Chicago, provides a pro-outsourcing perspective in his article. Among other things, Professor Drezner invites his readers to consider the following question: In today's increasingly competitive global marketplace, wouldn't domestic political actions designed to curb outsourcing ultimately make American firms less competitive?

YES

Sarah Anderson and
John Cavanagh

Outsourcing: A Policy Agenda

Don't worry; they'll get better jobs in the service sector." During the last three decades of the 20th century, this was the mantra of most government and business leaders when corporations transferred auto or apparel jobs to Mexico or China. That line doesn't work anymore, since U.S. companies have started shifting a wide range of service jobs as well—from high-skill computer programming to entry-level call center jobs—to India and other lower-wage nations. This breaching of the final frontier of American jobs has caused understandable anxiety and has become a hot-button issue in the presidential election campaign.

The trend toward foreign "outsourcing" of service jobs is an extension of a longstanding practice of cutting costs by subcontracting parts of business operations to nonunion shops within the United States. The practice has gone global, in part because of technological changes. Massive amounts of information can now be transmitted across the world at low cost, making geographic distances less important. International financial institutions and trade agreements have also facilitated the trend by promoting investment liberalization and privatization of public services, creating new opportunities for U.S. corporations in overseas markets.

Forrester Research estimates that about 40 percent of Fortune 1,000 firms have already outsourced some work and that at least another 3 million service jobs will leave the United States by 2015, led by information technology work. A study by the University of California, Berkeley estimates that 14 million U.S. jobs (11 percent of the total work force) are vulnerable to being outsourced.

Although the number of jobs lost so far is small relative to the total work force, these layoffs have a huge impact on the affected communities, and the potential for white-collar jobs to be offshored is deeply unsettling for many American workers. In addition to job cuts, service workers must now also contend with the enhanced power of highly mobile, increasingly unregulated global corporations to bargain down U.S. wages and working conditions by threatening to move jobs elsewhere.

According to McKinsey and Company, a consulting firm that helps businesses develop offshore operations, U.S. companies make up about 70 percent of the global outsourcing market. Their top destination in the developing world is currently India, where domestic subcontractors perform a range of

From *Foreign Policy In Focus Brief*, Volume 9, No. 2, April 2004, pp. 1–3. Copyright © 2004 by Foreign Policy In Focus. Reprinted by permission.

services for the U.S. market. At the low-skill end, Indian workers earn $1 or less per hour to handle customer service calls for firms like Earthlink and Travelocity. Among the higher-skill workers are Indian computer programmers, who earn about one-tenth the pay of their U.S. counterparts to write code for multinational corporations like Citigroup. Given a lack of other economic opportunities, Indian workers are often eager to secure new jobs catering to the U.S. market. However, there is also a nagging fear that these jobs may evaporate as soon as companies can find lower costs elsewhere.

China, of course, looms on the horizon. It is already the second-biggest developing-country draw for service work, offering rock-bottom wages and an official ban on basic union rights. Though it lacks India's English-speaking advantage, this may not be the case forever, as Beijing is heavily promoting English-language education. Mexico's experience in competing with China over manufacturing jobs could foreshadow events to come. Although employment in Mexico's border export zone more than doubled after the implementation of the North American Free Trade Agreement (NAFTA) in 1994, the country has in recent years lost several hundred thousand of these jobs, partly in economic flight to lower-wage China. India has even lost some foreign manufacturing jobs to China.

Public pressure has galvanized U.S. state and federal legislators to introduce a flurry of bills to curb outsourcing, primarily by requiring that government contract work not be performed overseas. However, there is stiff resistance from the corporate lobby, such as the new Coalition for Economic Growth and American Jobs, which represents some 200 trade groups, including the U.S. Chamber of Commerce and the Information Technology Association of America. These and other pro-outsourcing groups argue that the practice is good for U.S. workers, because it lowers the cost of services for U.S. consumers and enhances the overall competitiveness of U.S. companies. Another common claim is that recent job losses are due to productivity gains, not outsourcing. However, because workers are facing a "jobless" recovery and see few personal benefits from enhanced productivity, these arguments convince very few.

One reflection of public opinion is that concerns about U.S. trade policy have spread up the income ladder. Lower- and middle-class workers have been consistently skeptical of U.S. trade policies, but a February 2004 University of Maryland poll showed that even among Americans earning over $100,000 a year, support for actively promoting more "free trade" has dropped from 57 percent in 1999 to 28 percent in 2004.

Problems with Current U.S. Policy

As they vie for votes in layoff-ridden swing states, both presidential candidates are offering solutions to the prevailing American angst about trade and outsourcing. Railing against "Benedict Arnold" companies, Sen. John Kerry has vowed to eliminate government incentives for outsourcing. For example, he would place conditions on most government contracts to require that the work be performed in the United States. He would also eliminate a tax break that currently allows U.S. businesses to defer tax payments on income earned abroad, and he proposes to use the resulting revenue to lower the overall corporate tax rate from 35 to 33.25 percent. Similarly, Kerry would offer incentives to encourage transnational corporations to repatriate earnings and would then channel these revenues into an employer tax credit for new hires. Regarding trade, Kerry has vowed to include stronger labor and environmental protections in future trade pacts and to review all existing agreements.

The Bush administration has delivered mixed messages regarding outsourcing. Two prominent officials have publicly endorsed the practice—Treasury Secretary John Snow and Gregory Mankiw, chairman of the Council of Economic Advisers. Both have argued that foreign outsourcing of service jobs is good for the American economy, because it helps companies become more efficient. Meanwhile, President Bush has sought to distance himself from such statements and instead to focus public attention on his administration's new "21st Century" jobs plan. Bush argues that the real driving forces behind outsourcing are "frivolous" lawsuits, excessive regulation, and high taxes. He also claims that NAFTA and other trade agreements have been good for U.S. workers, and he promises that by breaking down even more trade barriers his policies will boost export-related jobs. "The best product on any shelf anywhere in the world says, 'Made in the USA,'" Bush told an audience of women entrepreneurs in Cleveland.

But the Bush administration's jobs plan ignores the historical record and thus misdiagnoses the problem. Government figures show that U.S. employment for American multinational corporations grew only 25 percent between 1982 and 2001, while employment at their overseas affiliates increased 47 percent. (These figures likely underestimate foreign expansion, because they do not include information on employment through subcontractors, data the U.S. government does not require businesses to report). This period of rapid overseas expansion has coincided with increased trade and investment liberalization and a declining corporate tax burden. U.S. employers are leaders in outsourcing, even though their share of the national tax bill is considerably lower than the average for employers in other industrial nations.

Bush's claim that companies are fleeing "Big Government" is also dubious. McKinsey and Company claims that U.S. corporations have led the outsourcing trend not to escape burdensome regulations, but because the relatively unregulated U.S. labor market facilitates sending jobs abroad. McKinsey, a pro-outsourcing consulting firm, points out that compared to most European counterparts, the United States has "liberal employment and labor laws that allow companies greater flexibility in reassigning tasks and eliminating jobs."

Kerry's early jobs plan is encouraging, but it addresses only one side of the issue. His proposal to end taxpayer subsidies for outsourcing, whether through government contracting or tax breaks, is long overdue. Citizens should not have to pay higher taxes to subsidize the evaporation of their jobs. To ensure effectiveness, any reforms must be carefully crafted to prevent potential loopholes. More effort will also be needed to address the threat posed by existing international agreements to domestic legislation that requires public contract work to be performed in the United States. For example, under World Trade Organization rules, the Government Procurement Agreement bans governments from favoring domestic firms in procurement contracts. Although only 25 countries have signed the agreement thus far, plans are under way to expand its scope and incorporate similar rules in other trade pacts.

Kerry's primary focus on domestic measures will have only a modest impact on the jobs issue, because these policies cannot make up for the extreme gap in labor costs, which is the primary driving force behind outsourcing. McKinsey estimates that global pay gaps result in a net cost savings for outsourcers of at least 45–55 percent (after accounting for higher infrastructure and other costs). If this is true, figures in a 2003 University of California, Berkeley study suggest that companies could save around $300 billion a year if they outsourced all of the estimated 14 million U.S. service jobs considered feasible to transfer overseas.

Kerry's promises to change U.S. trade policy are also a step in the right direction. If there were effective international mechanisms to strengthen labor rights enforcement, developing-country workers would have a better chance of obtaining fair wages. Research commissioned by the AFL-CIO indicates that labor rights violations in China artificially depress wages by 47–86 percent and that if the country were to respect basic internationally recognized labor rights, wages would likely increase 90 to 95 percent. However, the goal of strengthening labor rights protections should be pursued as part of a broader strategy to uplift conditions generally in poorer countries. Without overall economic improvements, developing-country governments will continue to face strong pressure to attract foreign investment by offering lax labor rights enforcement, thereby undermining efforts to maintain high standards in the richer countries.

Toward a New Foreign Policy

The overall goal of U.S. policy on outsourcing should be to attack the factors that make workers—in the U.S. as well as around the world—vulnerable to exploitation by increasingly mobile and unregulated global corporations. The approach needs to recognize that raising standards overseas is vital to retaining stable and substantial jobs at home. This requires a multifaceted response encompassing changes in domestic tax, procurement and labor laws as well as in multilateral trade, finance and aid policies.

On the domestic side, a first step should be to reform tax and procurement policies at all levels of government to ensure that they support good jobs in the United States. Additional subsidies that enhance the incentives for corporations to shift jobs overseas should also be eliminated. These include risk insurance and loan guarantees provided by the Overseas Private Investment Corporation as well as technical assistance and other supports offered by the U.S. Trade and Development Agency. Moreover, the U.S. government should ensure that U.S. authorities, as well as their counterparts around the world, have the right to use tax and procurement policies as instruments to support social goals without being undermined by international trade agreements.

The domestic policy response should also involve labor law reforms that reduce current obstacles to union organizing and that beef up rules related to laying off workers. Most European countries require that corporations guarantee higher severance pay based on years of service, which substantially raises the cost of moving jobs. Many European countries also oblige companies that are planning to close an operation to consult with unions and sometimes to negotiate over the decision. By contrast, under U.S. law, unions may only bargain over the effects of a closure. Thus, although European countries also experience outsourcing-related job loss, the practice is not as advanced as in the United States.

However, domestic measures, while significant, do not address the biggest incentive for outsourcing—extreme wage gaps. Tackling this problem will require a long-term commitment to supporting sustainable economic activity in poor countries and should focus on the factors that make workers around the world vulnerable to exploitation by global companies.

One of these factors is lax enforcement of internationally recognized labor rights, which artificially depresses wages. U.S. policymakers must learn from the failure of NAFTA's weak labor rights mechanism and should develop a better model. The Hemispheric Social Alliance has proposed involving the International Labor Organization in monitoring compliance and investigating complaints related to rights violations. If necessary, assistance would be provided to help countries achieve compliance. Only if this approach was unsuccessful would sanctions be applied, and if the perpetrator was a specific company, the punishments would be targeted at the company rather than at the host government.

Any labor rights initiative, however, should be integrated within a broader strategy toward poorer nations. Other factors that make workers vulnerable are high unemployment and poverty. Although national governments are not without responsibility for these problems, international financial institutions and trade agreements have played an exacerbating role. For example, the World Bank, the International Monetary Fund and the World Trade Organization all threaten the livelihoods of tens of millions of farmers by pressuring poor-country governments to eliminate tariffs and agricultural subsidies. Likewise, privatization supported by these international financial institutions has often resulted in mass layoffs and weakened social services. These multilateral agencies should instead join governments in promoting "global green deal" policies that stimulate stable and substantial employment while protecting the environment.

Regarding trade, Washington should withdraw its support for rules—such as in Chapter 11 of NAFTA—that grant excessive protection to U.S. investors against public interest laws and other host government actions that diminish profits. Such trade rules undermine democracy and encourage U.S. firms to shift jobs overseas.

To enhance this new and broader strategy toward poorer nations, the U.S. government should advocate for stronger international mechanisms to transfer resources from richer to poorer countries. Where appropriate, this would include debt reduction or cancellation. Washington could also promote the adoption of international taxes on both foreign exchange transactions and arms sales to generate revenues for development purposes. The U.S. must also revamp its development aid policies to emphasize anti-poverty measures, healthy communities and a clean environment rather than handouts to U.S. corporations like Halliburton and Bechtel.

In short, a comprehensive response to corporate outsourcing requires a sea change in the outlook of both the U.S. public and its politicians toward America's role in the world. Just as Americans are less secure when much of the world is plagued by extreme poverty, inequality and instability, worker exploitation overseas translates into exploited workers and less secure jobs at home. The electoral debate over outsourcing offers an opportunity to create a new policy approach that combines solidarity with self-interest in a whole-scale effort to benefit the entire world.

Sources for More Information

Organizations

Economic Policy Institute
1660 L St. N.W., Suite 1200
Washington, DC 20036
Voice: (202) 775-8810
Fax: (202) 775-0819
Email: epi@epinet.org
Web site: http://www.epinet.org/

WashTech
2900 Eastlake Avenue East, Suite 200
Seattle, WA 98102
Voice: (206) 726-8580
Fax: (206) 323-6966
Email: contact@washtech.org
Web site: http://www.washtech.org/

Publications

Ashok Deo Bardhan and Cynthia A. Kroll, "The New Wave of Outsourcing," Fisher Center for Real Estate and Urban Economics, University of California, Berkeley, available at: <http:// www.haas.berkeley.edu/news/Research_Report_Fall_2003.pdf>.

Hemispheric Social Alliance, "Alternatives for the Americas," available at <http://www.art-us.org/docs/alternatives%20dec%202002.pdf>.

McKinsey Global Institute, "Offshoring: Is It a Win-Win Game?" available at: <http://www.mckinsey.com/knowledge/mgi/offshore/>.

North American Alliance for Fair Employment, "Outsource This? American Workers, the Jobs Deficit and the Fair Globalization Solutions," available at: <http://www.fairjobs.org/docs/OutsourceThis!.pdf>.

Web sites

Communications Workers of America
http://www.cwa-union.org/outsourcing/

India Resource Center
http://www.corpwatchindia.org/

Daniel W. Drezner  **NO**

The Outsourcing Bogeyman

The Truth Is Offshore

When a presidential election year coincides with an uncertain economy, campaigning politicians invariably invoke an international economic issue as a dire threat to the well-being of Americans. Speechwriters denounce the chosen scapegoat, the media provides blanket coverage of the alleged threat, and legislators scurry to introduce supposed remedies.

The cause of this year's commotion is offshore outsourcing—the alleged migration of American jobs overseas. The depth of alarm was strikingly illustrated by the firestorm of reaction to recent testimony by N. Gregory Mankiw, the head of President George W. Bush's Council of Economic Advisers. No economist really disputed Mankiw's observation that "outsourcing is just a new way of doing international trade," which makes it "a good thing." But in the political arena, Mankiw's comments sparked a furor on both sides of the aisle. Democratic presidential candidate John Kerry accused the Bush administration of wanting "to export more of our jobs overseas," and Senate Minority Leader Tom Daschle quipped, "If this is the administration's position, I think they owe an apology to every worker in America." Speaker of the House Dennis Hastert, meanwhile, warned that "outsourcing can be a problem for American workers and the American economy."

Critics charge that the information revolution (especially the Internet) has accelerated the decimation of U.S. manufacturing and facilitated the outsourcing of service-sector jobs once considered safe, from backroom call centers to high-level software programming. (This concern feeds into the suspicion that U.S. corporations are exploiting globalization to fatten profits at the expense of workers.) They are right that offshore outsourcing deserves attention and that some measures to assist affected workers are called for. But if their exaggerated alarmism succeeds in provoking protectionist responses from lawmakers, it will do far more harm than good, to the U.S. economy and to American workers.

Should Americans be concerned about the economic effects of outsourcing? Not particularly. Most of the numbers thrown around are vague, overhyped estimates. What hard data exist suggest that gross job losses due to offshore outsourcing have been minimal when compared to the size of the entire U.S. economy. The outsourcing phenomenon has shown that globalization can affect white-collar professions, heretofore immune to foreign competition, in the same way that it has affected manufacturing jobs for years. But Mankiw's statements on outsourcing are absolutely correct; the law of comparative advantage does not stop working just because 401(k) plans are involved. The creation of new jobs overseas will eventually lead to more jobs and higher incomes in the United States. Because the economy—and especially job growth—is sluggish at the moment, commentators are attempting to draw a connection between offshore outsourcing and high unemployment. But believing that offshore outsourcing causes unemployment is the economic equivalent of believing that the sun revolves around the earth: intuitively compelling but clearly wrong.

Should Americans be concerned about the political backlash to outsourcing? Absolutely. Anecdotes of workers affected by outsourcing are politically powerful, and demands for government protection always increase during economic slowdowns. The short-term political appeal of protectionism is undeniable. Scapegoating foreigners for domestic business cycles is smart politics, and protecting domestic markets gives leaders the appearance of taking direct, decisive action on the economy.

Protectionism would not solve the U.S. economy's employment problems, although it would succeed in providing massive subsidies to well-organized interest groups. In open markets, greater competition spurs the reallocation of labor and capital to more profitable sectors of the economy. The benefits of such free trade—to both consumers and producers—are significant. Cushioning this process for displaced workers makes sense. Resorting to protectionism to halt the process, however, is a recipe for decline. An open economy leads to concentrated costs (and diffuse benefits) in the short term and significant benefits in the long term. Protectionism generates pain in both the short term and the long term.

The Sky Is Falling

Outsourcing occurs when a firm subcontracts a business function to an outside supplier. This practice has been common within the U.S. economy for some time. (Witness the rise of large call centers in the rural Midwest.) The reduction of communication costs and the standardization of software packages have now made it possible to outsource business functions such as customer service, telemarketing, and document management. Other affected professions include medical transcription, tax preparation, and financial services.

The numbers that are bandied about on offshore outsourcing sound ominous. The McKinsey Global Institute estimates that the volume of offshore outsourcing will increase by 30 to 40 percent a year for the next five years. Forrester Research estimates that 3.3 million white-collar jobs will move overseas by 2015. According to projections, the hardest hit sectors will be financial services and information technology (IT). In one May 2003 survey of chief information officers, 68 percent of IT executives said that their offshore contracts would grow in the subsequent year. The Gartner research firm has estimated that by the end of this year, 1 out of every 10 IT jobs will be outsourced overseas. Deloitte Research predicts the outsourcing of 2 million financial-sector jobs by 2009.

At first glance, current macroeconomic indicators seem to support the suspicion that outsourcing is destroying jobs in the United States. The past two years have witnessed moderate growth and astonishing productivity gains, but overall job growth has been anemic. The total number of manufacturing jobs has declined for 43 consecutive months. Surely, many observers insist, this must be because the jobs created by the U.S. recovery are going to other countries. Morgan Stanley analyst Stephen Roach, for example, has pointed out that "this is the first business cycle since the advent of the Internet—the enabler of a new real-time connectivity to low-cost offshore labor pools." He adds, "I don't think it's a coincidence that this jobless recovery has occurred in such an environment." Those who agree draw on anecdotal evidence to support this assertion. CNN's Lou Dobbs routinely harangues U.S. companies engaged in offshore outsourcing in his "Exporting America" series.

Many IT executives have themselves contributed to this perception. When IBM announced plans to outsource 3,000 jobs overseas this year, one of its executives said, "[Globalization] means shifting a lot of jobs, opening a lot of locations in places we had never dreamt of before, going where there's low-cost labor, low-cost competition, shifting jobs offshore." Nandan Nilekani, the chief executive of the India-based Infosys Technologies, said at this year's World Economic Forum, "Everything you can send down a wire is up for grabs." In January testimony before Congress, Hewlett-Packard chief Carly Fiorina warned that "there is no job that is America's God-given right anymore."

That last statement chills the blood of most Americans. Few support the cause of free trade for its own sake, out of pure principle. The logic underlying an open economy is that if the economy sheds jobs in uncompetitive sectors, employment in competitive sectors will grow. If hi-tech industries are no longer competitive, where will new jobs be created?

Inside the Numbers

Before answering that question, Americans need to separate fact from fiction. The predictions of job losses in the millions are driving the current outsourcing hysteria. But it is crucial to note that these predictions are of gross, not net, losses. During the 1990s, offshore outsourcing was not uncommon. (American Express, for one, set up back-office operations in India more than a decade ago.) But no one much cared because the number of jobs leaving U.S. shores was far lower than the number of jobs created in the U.S. economy.

Similarly, most current predictions are not as ominous as they first sound once the numbers are unpacked. Most jobs will remain unaffected altogether: close to 90 percent of jobs in the United States require geographic proximity. Such jobs include everything from retail and restaurants to marketing and personal care—services that have to be produced and consumed locally, so outsourcing them overseas is not an option. There is also no evidence that jobs in the high-value-added sector are migrating overseas. One thing that has made offshore outsourcing possible is the standardization of such business tasks as data entry, accounting, and IT support. The parts of production that are more complex, inter-active, or innovative—including, but not limited to, marketing, research, and development—are much more difficult to shift abroad. As an International Data Corporation analysis on trends in IT services concluded, "the activities that will migrate offshore are predominantly those that can be viewed as requiring low skill since process and repeatability are key underpinnings of the work. Innovation and deep business expertise will continue to be delivered predominantly onshore." Not coincidentally, these are also the tasks that generate high wages and large profits and drive the U.S. economy.

As for the jobs that can be sent offshore, even if the most dire-sounding forecasts come true, the impact on the economy will be negligible. The Forrester prediction of 3.3 million lost jobs, for example, is spread across 15 years. That would mean 220,000 jobs displaced per year by offshore outsourcing—a number that sounds impressive until one considers that total employment in the United States is roughly 130 million, and that about 22 million new jobs are expected to be added between now and 2010. Annually, outsourcing would affect less than .2 percent of employed Americans.

There is also reason to believe that the unemployment caused by out-sourcing will be lower than expected. Gartner assumed that more than 60 percent of financial-sector employees directly affected by outsourcing would be let go by their employers. But Boston University Professor Nitin Joglekar has exam-ined the effect of outsourcing on large financial firms and found that less than 20 percent of workers affected by outsourcing lose their jobs; the rest are repositioned within the firm. Even if the most negative projections prove to be correct, then, gross job loss would be relatively small.

Moreover, it is debatable whether actual levels of outsourcing will ever match current predictions. Despite claims that the pace of onshore and offshore outsourcing would quicken over time, there was no increase in 2003. In fact, TPI Inc., an outsourcing advisory firm, even reports that the total value of business process outsourcing deals in the United States fell by 32 percent in 2003.

There is no denying that the number of manufacturing jobs has fallen dramatically in recent years, but this has very little do with outsourcing and almost everything to do with technological innovation. As with agriculture a century ago, productivity gains have outstripped demand, so fewer and fewer workers are needed for manufacturing. If outsourcing were in fact the chief cause of manufacturing losses, one would expect corresponding increases in manufacturing employment in developing countries. An Alliance Capital Management study of global manufacturing trends from 1995 to 2002, how-ever, shows that this was not the case: the United States saw an 11 percent decrease in manufacturing employment over the course of those seven years; meanwhile, China saw a 15 percent decrease and Brazil a 20 percent decrease. Globally, the figure for manufacturing jobs lost was identical to the U.S. figure—11 percent. The fact that global manufacturing output increased by 30 percent in that same period confirms that technology, not trade, is the pri-mary cause for the decrease in factory jobs. A recent analysis of employment data from U.S. multinational corporations by the U.S. Department of Commerce reached the same conclusion.

What about the service sector? Again, the data contradict the popular belief that U.S. jobs are being lost to foreign countries without anything to replace them. In the case of many low-level technology jobs, the phenomenon has been somewhat exaggerated. For example, a Datamonitor study found that global call-center operations are being outsourced at a slower rate than previously thought—only five percent are expected to be located offshore by 2007. Dell and Lehman Brothers recently moved some of their call centers back to the United States from India because of customer complaints. And done properly, the offshore outsourcing of call centers creates new jobs at home. Delta Airlines outsourced 1,000 call-center jobs to India in 2003, but the $25 million in savings allowed the firm to add 1,200 reservation and sales positions in the United States.

Offshore outsourcing is similarly counterbalanced by job creation in the high-end service sector. An Institute for International Economics analysis of Bureau of Labor Statistics employment data revealed that the number of jobs in service sectors where outsourcing is likely actually increased, even though total employment decreased by 1.7 percent. According to the Bureau of Labor Statistics "Occupation Outlook Handbook," the number of IT-related jobs is expected to grow 43 percent by 2010. The case of IBM reinforces this lesson: although critics highlight the offshore outsourcing of 3,000 IT jobs, they fail to mention the company's plans to add 4,500 positions to its U.S. payroll. Large software companies such as Microsoft and Oracle have simultaneously increased outsourcing and domestic payrolls.

How can these figures fit with the widespread perception that IT jobs have left the United States? Too often, comparisons are made to 2000, an unusual year for the technology sector because Y2K fears and the height of the dot-com bubble had pushed employment figures to an artificially high level. When 1999 is used as the starting point, it becomes clear that offshore outsourcing has not caused a collapse in IT hiring. Between 1999 and 2003, the number of jobs in business and financial operations increased by 14 percent. Employment in computer and mathematical positions increased by 6 percent.

It is also worth remembering that many predictions come from management consultants who are eager to push the latest business fad. Many of these consulting firms are themselves reaping commissions from outsourcing contracts. Much of the perceived boom in outsourcing stems from companies' eagerness to latch onto the latest management trends; like Dell and Lehman, many will partially reverse course once the hidden costs of offshore outsourcing become apparent.

If offshore outsourcing is not the cause of sluggish job growth, what is? A study by the Federal Reserve Bank of New York suggests that the economy is undergoing a structural transformation: jobs are disappearing from old sectors (such as manufacturing) and being created in new ones (such as mortgage brokering). In all such transformations, the creation of new jobs lags behind the destruction of old ones. In other words, the recent recession and current recovery are a more extreme version of the downturn and "jobless recovery" of the early 1990s—which eventually produced the longest economic expansion of the post-World War II era. Once the structural adjustments of the current period are complete, job growth is expected to be robust. (And indeed, current indicators are encouraging: there has been a net increase in payroll jobs and in small business employment since 2003 and a spike in IT entrepreneurial activity.)

Offshore outsourcing is undoubtedly taking place, and it will likely increase over the next decade. However, it is not the tsunami that many claim. Its effect on the U.S. economy has been exaggerated, and its effect on the U.S. employment situation has been grossly exaggerated.

The Upside of Outsourcing

To date, the media's coverage of outsourcing has focused on its perceived costs. This leaves out more than half of the story. The benefits of offshore outsourcing should not be dismissed.

The standard case for free trade holds that countries are best off when they focus on sectors in which they have a comparative advantage—that is, sectors that have the lowest opportunity costs of production. Allowing countries to specialize accordingly increases productivity across all countries. This specialization translates into cheaper goods, and a greater variety of them, for all consumers.

The current trend of outsourcing business processes overseas is comparative advantage at work. The main driver of productivity gains over the past decade has been the spread of information technology across the economy. The commodification of simple business services allows those benefits to spread further, making growth even greater.

The data affirm this benefit. Catherine Mann of the Institute for International Economics conservatively estimates that the globalization of IT production has boosted U.S. GDP by $230 billion over the past seven years; the globalization of IT services should lead to a similar increase. As the price of IT services declines, sectors that have yet to exploit them to their fullest—such as construction and health care—will begin to do so, thus lowering their cost of production and improving the quality of their output. (For example, cheaper IT could one day save lives by reducing the number of "adverse drug events." Mann estimates that adding bar codes to prescription drugs and instituting an electronic medical record system could reduce the annual number of such events by more than 80,000 in the United States alone.)

McKinsey Global Institute has estimated that for every dollar spent on outsourcing to India, the United States reaps between $1.12 and $1.14 in benefits. Thanks to outsourcing, U.S. firms save money and become more profitable, benefiting shareholders and increasing returns on investment. Foreign facilities boost demand for U.S. products, such as computers and telecommunications equipment, necessary for their outsourced function. And U.S. labor can be reallocated to more competitive, better-paying jobs; for example, although 70,000 computer programmers lost their jobs between 1999 and 2003, more than 115,000 computer software engineers found higher-paying jobs during that same period. Outsourcing thus enhances the competitiveness of the U.S. service sector (which accounts for 30 percent of the total value of U.S. exports). Contrary to the belief that the United States is importing massive amounts of services from low-wage countries, in 2002 it ran a $64.8 billion surplus in services.

Outsourcing also has considerable noneconomic benefits. It is clearly in the interest of the United States to reward other countries for reducing their barriers to trade and investment. Some of the countries where U.S. firms have set up outsourcing operations—including India, Poland, and the Philippines—are vital allies in the war on terrorism. Just as the North American Free Trade Agreement (NAFTA) helped Mexico deepen its democratic transition and strengthen its rule of law, the United States gains considerably from the political reorientation spurred by economic growth and interdependence.

Finally, the benefits of "insourcing" should not be overlooked. Just as U.S. firms outsource positions to developing countries, firms in other countries outsource positions to the United States. According to the Bureau of Labor Statistics, the number of outsourced jobs increased from 6.5 million in 1983 to 10 million in 2000. The number of insourced jobs increased even more in the same period, from 2.5 million to 6.5 million.

Political Economy

When it comes to trade policy, there are two iron laws of politics. The first is that the benefits of trade diffuse across the economy, but the costs of trade are concentrated. Thus, those made worse off by open borders will form the more motivated interest group. The second is that public hostility toward trade increases during economic downturns. When forced to choose between statistical evidence showing that trade is good for the economy and anecdotal evidence of job losses due to import competition, Americans go with the anecdotes.

Offshore outsourcing adds two additional political pressures. The first stems from the fact that technological innovation has converted what were thought to be nontradeable sectors into tradeable ones. Manufacturing workers have long been subject to the rigors of global competition. White-collar service-sector workers are being introduced to these pressures for the first time—and they are not happy about it. As Raghuram Rajan and Luigi Zingales point out in "Saving Capitalism From the Capitalists," globalization and technological innovation affect professions such as law and medicine that have not changed all that much for centuries. Their political reaction to the threat of foreign competition will be fierce.

The second pressure is that the Internet has greatly facilitated political organization, making it much easier for those who blame outsourcing for their troubles to rally together. In recent years, countless organizations—with names such as Rescue American Jobs, Save U.S. Jobs, and the Coalition for National Sovereignty and Economic Patriotism—have sprouted up. Such groups have disproportionately focused on white-collar tech workers, even though the manufacturing sector has been much harder hit by the recent economic slowdown.

It should come as no surprise, then, that politicians are scrambling to get ahead of the curve. During the Democratic primary in South Carolina—a state hit hard by the loss of textile jobs—billboards asked voters, "Lost your job to free trade or offshore outsourcing yet?" Last Labor Day, President Bush pledged to appoint a manufacturing czar to get to the bottom of the outflow of manufacturing positions. In his stump speech, John Kerry bashes "Benedict Arnold CEOs [who] send American jobs overseas."

Where presidential candidates lead, legislators are sure to follow. Senator Charles Schumer (D-N.Y.) claimed in a January "New York Times" op-ed authored with Paul Craig Roberts that because of increased capital mobility, the law of comparative advantage is now null and void. Senator Tom Daschle (D-S.D.) has observed, "George Bush says the economy is creating jobs. But let me tell you, China is one long commute. And let me tell you, I'm tired of watching jobs shift overseas." Senator Christopher Dodd (D-Conn.) and Representative Nancy Johnson (R-Conn.) are sponsoring the USA Jobs Protection Act to prevent U.S. companies from hiring foreign workers for positions when American workers are available. In February, Senate Democrats announced their intentions to introduce the Jobs for America Act, requiring companies to give public notice three months in advance of any plan to outsource 15 or more jobs. In March, the Senate overwhelmingly approved a measure banning firms from federal contracts if they outsource any of the work overseas. In the past two years, more than 20 state legislatures have introduced bills designed to make various forms of offshore outsourcing illegal.

Splendid Isolation?

There are clear examples of jobs being sent across U.S. borders because of U.S. trade policy—but not for the reasons that critics of outsourcing believe. Consider the example of candy-cane manufacturers: despite the fact that 90 percent of the world's candy canes are consumed in the United States, manufacturers have sent much of their production south of the border in the past five years. The attraction of moving abroad, however, has little to do with low wages and much to do with protectionism. U.S. quotas on sugar imports have, in recent years, caused the domestic price of sugar to become 350 percent higher than world market prices. As candy makers have relocated production to countries where sugar is cheaper, between 7,500 and 10,000 workers in the Midwest have lost their jobs—victims not of outsourcing but of the kind of protectionism called for by outsourcing's critics.

A similar story can be told of the steel tariffs that the Bush administration foolishly imposed from March 2002 until December 2003 (when a ruling by the World Trade Organization prompted their cancellation). The tariffs were allegedly meant to protect steelworkers. But in the United States, steel users employ roughly 40 times more people than do steel producers. Thus, according to estimates by the Institute for International Economics, between 45,000 and 75,000 jobs were lost because higher steel prices made U.S. steel-using industries less competitive.

These examples illustrate the problem with relying on anecdotes when debating the effects of offshore outsourcing. Anecdotes are incomplete narratives that fail to capture opportunity costs. In the cases of steel and sugar, the opportunity cost of using protectionism to save jobs was the much larger number of jobs lost in sectors rendered less productive by higher input prices. Trade protectionism amounts to an inefficient subsidy for uncompetitive sectors of the economy, which leads to higher prices for consumers and a lower rate of return for investors. It preserves jobs in less competitive sectors while destroying current and future jobs in sectors that have a comparative advantage. Thus, if barriers are erected to prevent offshore outsourcing, the overall effect will not be to create jobs but to destroy them.

So if protectionism is not the answer, what is the correct response? The best piece of advice is also the most difficult for elected officials to follow: do no harm. Politicians never get credit for inaction, even when inaction is the best policy. President George H.W. Bush, for example, was pilloried for refusing to follow Japan's lead by protecting domestic markets—even though his refusal helped pave the way for the 1990s boom by letting market forces allocate resources to industries at the technological frontier. Restraint is anathema to the political class, but it is still the most important response to the furor over offshore outsourcing. As Robert McTeer, president of the Federal Reserve Bank of Dallas, said when asked about policy responses to outsourcing, "If we are lucky, we can get through the year without doing something really, really stupid."

The problem of offshore outsourcing is less one of economics than of psychology—people feel that their jobs are threatened. The best way to help those actually affected, and to calm the nerves of those who fear that they will be, is to expand the criteria under which the Trade Adjustment Assistance (TAA) program applies to displaced workers. Currently, workers cannot apply for TAA unless overall sales or production in their sector declines. In the case of offshore outsourcing, however, productivity increases allow for increased production and sales—making TAA out of reach for those affected by it. It makes sense to rework TAA rules to take into account workers displaced by offshore outsourcing even when their former industries or firms maintain robust levels of production.

Another option would be to help firms purchase targeted insurance policies to offset the transition costs to workers directly affected by offshore outsourcing. Because the perception of possible unemployment is considerably greater than the actual likelihood of losing a job, insurance programs would impose a very small cost on firms while relieving a great deal of employee anxiety. McKinsey Global Institute estimates that such a scheme could be created for as little as four or five cents per dollar saved from offshore outsourcing. IBM recently announced the creation of a two-year, $25 million retraining fund for its employees who fear job losses from outsourcing. Having the private sector handle the problem without extensive government intervention would be an added bonus.

The Best Defense

Until robust job growth returns, the debate over outsourcing will not go away—the political temptation to scapegoat foreigners is simply too great.

The refrain of "this time, it's different" is not new in the debate over free trade. In the 1980s, the Japanese variety of capitalism—with its omniscient industrial policy and high nontariff barriers—was supposed to supplant the U.S. system. Fifteen years later, that prediction sounds absurd. During the 1990s, the passage of NAFTA and the Uruguay Round of trade talks were supposed to create a "giant sucking sound" as jobs left the United States. Contrary to such fears, tens of millions of new jobs were created. Once the economy improves, the political hysteria over outsourcing will also disappear.

It is easy to praise economic globalization during boom times; the challenge, however, is to defend it during the lean years of a business cycle. Offshore outsourcing is not the bogeyman that critics say it is. Their arguments, however, must be persistently refuted. Otherwise, the results will be disastrous: less growth, lower incomes—and fewer jobs for American workers.

POSTSCRIPT

Is Outsourcing a Wise Corporate Strategy?

The controversy surrounding foreign outsourcing not only incites strong passions, but cuts across party lines. Consider the following comments from Democrats John Kerry, "Unlike the Bush Administration, I want to repeal every tax break and loophole that rewards any Benedict Arnold CEO or corporation for shipping American jobs overseas" and Hillary Rodham Clinton, "I don't think losing American jobs is a good thing. The folks at the other end of Pennsylvania Avenue apparently do." Republican House Speaker Dennis Hastert said of a Bush economist's support for outsourcing, "[His] theory fails a basic test of real economics. An economy suffers when jobs disappear." (Quotes taken from Daniel T. Griswold, 2004.)

The war on American outsourcing has moved beyond the talking stage: In March 2004, the Senate passed an amendment that denies certain federal contracts from being awarded to organizations that outsource work overseas. This action has been echoed at the state level as well. Indiana, for example, cancelled a contract with an Indiana-based firm to upgrade the state's computer systems when it was discovered that the company employed workers in India. Instead, they spent $8 million more of taxpayer's money and awarded the contract to another firm. Clearly, the alarmist tone of the above quotes is manifesting itself in the concrete actions of federal and state legislation designed to penalize firms that choose to send work overseas. Is this a wise response to the current wave of corporate outsourcing? Is outsourcing unpatriotic and bad for American business? Where do you stand on this important management topic?

Both of the articles presented here raised important points and presented strong evidence in support of their views. Sarah Anderson and John Cavanagh argue that outsourcing is a real threat to the economic health of the United States and provide several suggestions as to the types of government actions necessary to keep American jobs from moving overseas. Dr. Daniel Drezner argues that the controversy surrounding outsourcing is more hype than substance, is actually economically beneficial to America, and is consistent with American principles and values.

Suggested Readings

For anti-outsourcing articles, see the last page of the Anderson and Cavanagh article.

Radley Balko, Outsourcing debate tainted by myths, misconceptions. Foxnews.com, April 22, 2004.

Daniel T. Griswold Outsource, outsource, and outsource some more. *Center for Trade Policy Studies,* The Cato Institute, May 3, 2004. http://www.freetrade.org/pubs/articles/dg-05-03-04.html.

Edwin A. Locke, On May Day celebrate capitalism. *The Ayn Rand Institute.* April 24, 2003. http://www.aynrand.org/site/News2?page=NewsArticle&id=7449.

McKinsey Global Institute, "Offshoring: Is It a Win-Win Game?" San Francisco, CA, August 2003.

ISSUE 11

Are U.S. CEOs Overpaid?

YES: Lisa H. Newton, from "The Care and Feeding of the Truly Greedy: CEO Salaries in World Perspective," *Taking Sides: Business Ethics and Society* (McGraw-Hill Dushkin, 2000)

NO: Ira T. Kay and Steven E. Rushbrook, from "The U.S. Executive Pay Model: Smart Business or Senseless Greed?" *WorldatWork Journal* (First Quarter, 2001)

ISSUE SUMMARY

YES: Lisa Newton believes that the typical U.S. CEO should not receive ten or more times the annual pay of CEOs in other industrial countries. She also points out, in no uncertain terms, that CEOs are only partly responsible for the ultimate success of their organization and the accompanying increase in shareholder wealth.

NO: Ira Kay and Steven Rushbrook believe that U.S. CEOs are entitled to whatever levels of pay they receive. They argue from a free-market perspective where labor, like every other business input, is subject to free-market forces. They also provide a discussion on the incredible amount of wealth U.S. CEOs have created for their shareholders.

Over the last 15 years or so, it has become a spring ritual as nearly anticipated in some circles as the first pitch of the new baseball season. Business magazines and newspapers across the country, in blazing titles written to arouse reader antipathy, report on the incredible pay received by chief executive officers (CEOs) in the previous year at some of the nation's largest corporations. Often, the articles include photos with a prominently displayed figure—the number of employees laid off the previous year by these apparently shameless and greedy CEOs! The intent of such prejudicial headlines is, obviously, to sell copy by painting CEOs as gluttonous fat cats and thereby appealing to the consumer's sense of fairness. But beyond the legitimate economic objective of generating revenues, articles of this sort raise an important question for corporate America: On the whole, are U.S. CEOs overpaid? For many individuals whose sole exposure to this topic comes through popular media publications and news outlets, the answer is obviously "yes." But, like most things in life, there are two sides to this story. In academic circles and corporate boardrooms across the country, there is much passionate debate on CEO pay with plenty of advocates on both sides. So, by way of introduction, let us consider a few points on each side of the question.

Those who argue that U.S. CEOs are overpaid raise several interesting points in support of their position. One of their most powerful arguments appeals to the apparent unfairness of paying a CEO tens of millions of dollars while the corporation is simultaneously laying off hundreds or even thousands of employees. Why should a CEO be rewarded for cutting the workforce? Related to this is the fact that some boards of directors have shown a willingness to award large bonuses not just to high-performing CEOs but also to CEOs whose organizations were clear underperformers the previous year. Such actions suggest that a CEO's pay may not be tied to how well he or she performs, a situation that most would agree is not fair. Perhaps the strongest argument put forth by those who think U.S. CEOs are overpaid is based on a comparison of the CEO pay-to-worker pay ratio in America to that of other industrialized countries. Critics frequently point out that U.S. executives typically make several hundred times more in annual income than the lowest paid employees in their firms. In other countries, however, the ratio is considerably smaller. In Japan, for example, the typical CEO makes only about 15 times the lowest worker, and many member countries of the European Union restrict top executive pay to around 20 times the lowest worker's pay.

On the other side of the debate, defenders of current U.S. CEO pay point out that CEO pay is, like most jobs in America, subject to labor market influences. Currently, the market for quality CEOs is very tight, and wage-increasing bidding wars are the norm. Thus, CEO pay is clearly subject to labor market conditions. In response to the layoff issue, proponents of existing CEO pay levels argue that CEOs are paid to make and execute difficult decisions. They point out that often the alternative to downsizing and staying in business is laying off no one and going out of business entirely. Another reason that U.S. CEOs deserve their pay is because of the incredible amount of wealth created by their organizations over the last two decades. When compared to how much wealth CEOs have made for their shareholders, their pay levels look very reasonable.

The two articles that follow address the issue of whether or not U.S. CEOs, as a group, are overpaid. Lisa H. Newton argues that they are overpaid. In so doing, she raises and addresses several of the points made above. As you read her article, ask yourself whether you find her position convincing, particularly the last section where she argues that high CEO pay is against the public interest. The "no" article was written by Ira T. Kay and Steven E. Rushbrook. Their article covers all the points typically espoused by CEO pay advocates and throws in a few more for good measure. Particularly noteworthy is their discussion on the amount of wealth created by American CEOs over the last 20 years. Do you find this point to be particularly influential in the debate?

YES

Lisa H. Newton

The Care and Feeding of the Truly Greedy: CEO Salaries in World Perspective

In 1996, Jack Welch, CEO of General Electric, received $21.4 million in salary and performance bonuses (and about $18 million in stock options); Lawrence Coss of the Green Tree Financial Corporation received $102.4 million in salary and bonus (plus stock options worth at least $38 million). Michael Eisner of Disney added $196 million in stock to his previous holding, somewhere around a third of a billion. The list goes on: Intel's Andrew Grove took home $97.6 million, Traveler's Group Sanford Weill made $94.2 million, and Citicorp's John Reed got $43.6 million. (These figures from John Cassidy's piece, aptly titled "Gimme," in *The New Yorker* of April 21, 1997; See also "The Top Ten List" in *The Nation,* December 8, 1997.) According to a preliminary study of 60 companies by Pearl Meyer & Partners, the CEO of a multibillion-dollar company received an average of $4.37 million in compensation in 1995. That was a 23% increase from 1994. (That number from an anonymous squib, "Checking in on the CEO's Pay," in *HR Focus,* May 1996, p. 15.) As Cassidy points out, we're not supposed to think those figures excessive:

> But, according to *Business Week,* when you add together salary, bonuses, and options packages the typical C.E.O. at a large company saw his pay envelope grow by just fifty-four per cent—barely eighteen times the increase necessary to keep pace with the cost of living. (All told, his pay-check was only two hundred and nine times as big as the average factory employee's.)

Meanwhile, World Resource Institute figures from a few years earlier show that average annual compensation for a citizen (or Gross Domestic Product per capita, which is as close to the same thing as we can get in largely non-cash economies), in U.S. dollars, was less than $100 in Mozambique and Tanzania, less than $200 in seven other African countries (Burundi, Chad, Malawi, Rwanda, Sierra Leone, Somalia, Uganda), plus Nepal and Vietnam, under $300 in another 15 countries worldwide. (That list from *World Resources 1996–1997,* published by the World Resources Institute, p. 166.) We are not living in a rich world. But some CEO's are rich, very rich.

How, the untaught observer might ask, is this kind of disparity justified? How can it be that one of the world's inhabitants has a yearly compensation equal to the combined resources of 43,700 other of the world's inhabitants? We can understand that some people are lucky (born with perfect pitch) and others are not (born without arms). But the agreement to compensate an executive to the tune of tens of millions is not a matter of luck. It's a human decision if ever there was one. What on earth could make it the right human decision?

Justifications abound. Justifications are products, and like all products, are for sale for a fair market price. They are not always necessary or desirable, but become so very quickly if something not quite right—something that just doesn't *smell* very good—is happening. Having an annual compensation 209 times that of your employees, and 43,700 times that of fellow humans across the world, is one of those conditions that assaults the nostrils, so CEO's need justifications; and with that much money to spend, there's bound to be some left after the mortgage and the groceries to splurge on a justification or two. It's a perfect free market situation: a willing buyer (the CEO and his loyal staff) meets a willing seller (a well-educated and articulate wordsmith who really needs money), and a justification changes hands. A rudimentary knowledge of human psychology tells you that the wordsmith will instantly convince himself (or herself: this is an equal opportunity sellout) that CEO's really are worth the enormous amount of money they're getting, and that the CEO will instantly convince himself (never herself: equal opportunity has not yet reached this level) that the justification is sound. But it isn't. As we might expect of products turned out at such speed in such an uncritical market, the quality isn't the best. It might be worthwhile to count some of the errors.

It won't do, for instance, to claim that the CEO contributes 43,700 times as much value to the world as the shepherd in Tanzania or the farmer in Chad. Even if the movies, or software, or candy bars produced by the CEO's company are really worth that many times the wool or corn produced by the Africans, they are not made by the CEO, who never goes near the production floor, but by the minions of the company, making 1/209 their CEO's annual pay. Whatever value the company produces, in short, could equally well be produced with a CEO making half that annual compensation, or, most likely, no CEO at all. (That suggestion might be worth examining.)

Nor will it do to claim that a company simply *has* to pay that much for such rare talent, that you really *can't* get a good CEO these days for under that price, given all the competition. The reason why that rings somehow false is that these decisions are made by the Board of Directors of the company, being a very small club of similarly compensated executives (on whose Boards of Directors the CEO will also sit), and the whole decision stays within that little overpaid group. One wonders if, given another Search Committee, someone could not have been found to do the job for, say, $2,000,000 per annum. Or maybe $650,000, which will pay most of the bills that a CEO might run up in the course of a year.

Comparisons with other high-paid talent also ring false. Entertainers, to be sure, make big bucks, singing or acting or shooting baskets. But here we have direct value for money, paid by those who are entertained. The entertainers make a lot of money: but their careers come to an end as soon as *our* tastes change or attention wanders, and for the time being, they are at least fun to watch. Careers can also end in a minute with a car accident or even a badly twisted knee. But the CEO is not at all fun to watch, and he seems to be immune to the changing of consumer tastes or accidental assaults on the body; he can write his memos from a wheelchair.

Now we come to the crux of the value! He writes memos. What is he *writing,* in those memos, that makes him so valuable? For an answer to that question, a review of the incentive structures of the publicly held corporation is needed:

The Corporation From Cradle to Grave

How does the corporation get started? An investor, or a group of investors, decide that there is a good market for a good or service (i.e. a high demand coupled with the money to buy that which will fill the demand), and that the revenue from sales will exceed the cost of making the good or service available by a healthy margin (i.e. they're going to make a lot of money), so they buy the machinery and supplies and office space and talent required for the production of this good or service, and the production and marketing and advertising begin. In a magic metaphysical moment the articles of incorporation are signed, and a bouncing baby company is launched. Pretty soon the money's rolling in and the investors are very happy.

Now, it's always possible for one of these investors to decide he wants his money back, possibly to invest in some other enterprise; he can try to sell out his share in the enterprise, to one of the other investors or to a stranger. He may have problems doing that if the enterprise is not doing well or if he owns a very large share. To make a long story very short, that problem and myriads of others were solved by a common Stock Market where all such shares can be bought and sold. In the present day, if an investor decides he no longer wants to be a shareholder, an investor, in Acme Corporation, he can sell his shares on the open market and invest instead in Beter Corporation. His choice.

Why would a shareholder want to sell out? The reason he bought in was to make money, and the company he set up is doing fine. If he wants continuing income, he'll do better to hang on to the stock and continue collecting dividends. But suppose he just wants lots of cash right now: fine, he sells his shares, "liquidates" his share of the assets of the company, and he gets the cash. Now of course, if all the original investors early in the company's history decided to do that at once, the whole company would be liquidated. But that's not likely to happen. (In the contemporary stock market, it's almost impossible, just because of the huge volume of stock traded; some mutual funds turn over their entire portfolio in the course of the year, and stray stocks are likely to be picked up.)

Why is it not likely to happen, at least in the original model of shareholdership? Because a funny thing happens when you put your money into a company as an investor. You begin to think of the company as "yours," which is appropriate, because it is, in part. You become anxious for its fortunes, not only for the monetary value of your initial investment, but for its own sake, as you would be anxious for the fortunes of a nephew. You watch its coverage in the press, cheering when it is favorable, grousing when it is not. You get attached to the company. You don't call your broker and have him sell it if it goes down a few points. For one thing, by the time you got hold of your broker and he got the stock offered for sale, the whole situation would have changed; for another, his fee would wipe out any gains; but for a third, your sense of ownership has become tinged with loyalty: you don't "sell out" until something really big, college or retirement or a new house, comes along. Besides, the individual shareholder is important in the company. If you are the owner of the company, even a part owner, you are the "principal," and all the company's employees are your "agents"—they act for you and for your interests. The CEO has to please you or (in theory: it almost never happened) you can wage a proxy fight at the annual meeting, bring about the election of your own Board of Directors, and have them hire a new CEO who will represent your interests more perfectly. So the CEO wants to keep you happy. But what does the CEO of your company have to do to please you? Not much: keep the company on an even keel, no scandals, distribute profits regularly, but remember to keep some of those profits to reinvest for the long term, because the long term is what you're in for.

That was the American shareholder up into the 1960's. There were mutual funds, of course, that owned stock, effectively pooling the investment funds of small shareholders to give them a diversified portfolio. Mutual funds did not operate like individual shareholders, for their managers, under the same fiduciary obligation to *their* shareholders, were not permitted to get attached to the companies they held—their job was to increase the total amount of stock value in the fund, and they didn't care what companies they had to hold shares in, in order to do that. But the funds were not really big players at the time.

They could become big players if they were joined by the vast money salted away in huge trust funds—pension funds and the like, and the endowments of not-for-profit institutions of all kinds. But these funds always invested in bonds, for the sake of safety; they didn't buy stocks. Until the 1960's, that is. Then these huge funds decided that 1929 was a long time ago, that stocks were quite as safe as bonds, and that it was time to trade in creditorship for ownership. Slowly they moved into the market, and took it over.

Again: what a fund manager wants from the investments he makes is rapid growth, the swift increase in the total amount of money in the fund. If it is a pension fund, that money is what the workers are going to retire on, and he (or she) works for the workers. If the fund is an investment pool, the manager works for the investors; if it is the endowment fund of a University, the manager works for the University. He will keep his huge funds invested in a company for the long term only if it is pouring money into his fund at a rate unmatched anywhere else in the market, or if he really has no choice. For a long time, the customs of the market and the available technology kept the funds' money moving slowly through the market, as well-weighted decisions moved the cash from blue chip to blue chip. But in the 1980's, the established ways of the market broke down, the white-shod country clubbers were shoved aside by the new breed of traders and arbitragers, and computer technology advanced to the point of allowing program trading (programming your computer to make trades automatically, in a split second, in response to certain changes in the market) and otherwise very rapid shifts of money from one stock to another.

Then it all came together. The new breed of trader talked the managers of the huge slowmoving funds into becoming players in a new rapid-fire market, and their money funded the leveraged buyouts, the mergers and acquisitions, and the infamous hostile takeovers for which the 1980's became famous. In the process a new breed of fund manager was born, one who is acutely aware, first, that his fund (for instance, my favorite pension fund), CREF, owns very large chucks of (say) Acme Company, second, that the Acme Board of Directors had therefore better take CREF's interests seriously or he'll have them replaced (he may even demand, and get, his own Director on the Board), third, that his obligation is to increase the amount of money in CREF as rapidly as possible, fourth, that therefore the Acme Board of Directors must instruct the Acme CEO to run the company in such a way that CREF's stock position appreciates, and fifth, that if the CEO is unresponsive to that instruction, the Board must fire him and get a more responsive one. This is what we call an "active" investor: no longer does the fund manager simply sell Acme and buy Beter when Acme is not running the way he wants it to run. He gets in there and makes it do what he wants. (Oh, but doesn't CREF offer a "social responsibility" track, in which only stocks in socially responsible corporations are purchased, for conscientious investors? Yes indeed; and CREF's fund manager manages those funds just as aggressively as all the others.)

Once a CEO is on board who promises to extract money from the company's workings and move it into shareholder hands faster than ever, the Board kind of makes *sure* he doesn't forget what to do by structuring incentives to help his memory: the more the dividends flow and the price per share of the stock goes up, the greater his bonus.

That, of course, is the link between the new way of doing business and the CEO's compensation.

Now, what was on that memo? How does the CEO suddenly put lots more money into shareholder hands? We know that the size profit to be divided among the shareholders is based in part on the ratio of corporate revenue to corporate costs—best understood as a fraction with revenue as a numerator and costs as the denominator—so the CEO has to increase the numerator, the revenue stream, or cut costs, the denominator, or, preferably, both. Let me count the ways he might do that: (1) He can discover that the company's operations were rife with waste, inefficiency, theft, whatever; tighten it up, get things working the way they should, and the company saves oodles of money, squeezing down the denominator, without changing operations at all. He'll always say that's what he's doing, but it's unlikely that much savings will be got that way. (2) He can try to raise the numerator, the revenue, by raising price. In some markets he can get away with that for awhile, but in a highly competitive market that's just likely to reduce sales, theoretically to zero. (3) He can try to raise revenue by developing new products, new markets, or both. That's a good idea, but it requires more investment, therefore lower distributions of profits right now. CREF is not interested in waiting. It wants money now. (4) There aren't any other ways to raise revenue, so he has to cut costs. He can cut the paper clip budget and pick up cheaper raw materials for his manufacturing, and he'll do that, but it's not enough. The big item in any company is payroll, not only for the meager salaries and wages the workers make, but also for those infinitely expensive medical and other insurance plans the company signed on for and now can't back out of. Fire a worker, and you save all that money. Fire (lay off) lots of workers, and you save lots of money. The denominator goes way down, raising profits, and the stock price goes way up. And that was the object of the expedition.

So that's what the memo was about. The CEO was setting the ball in motion to lay off thousands of workers. CREF will see the stock price go way up, and will be happy when the Board of Directors presents the CEO with a wonderful year-end bonus. That's why CEO compensation is so high, millions of dollars for successfully pink-slipping the company.

What does CREF do next? Sells the stock, obviously. After all, the prospects for the company are not good. They've cut way back on the quality of their materials, refused to reinvest in better plant or equipment, and laid off the folks who were doing the work, all to cut costs and send the price of the stock way up. In effect, they sold off some fraction of the value of the company, "liquidated" it, for quick cash, and distributed the cash. Now the company is worth a lot less, and CREF has no intention of holding on to worthless goods. Seeing the stock go up, investors who do not know why it went up will buy into Acme now on the expectation that it will go higher. CREF will take their cash and invest in the stock of (say) Beter, and promptly insist that Beter go through the same round of liquidation—cost-cutting, laying off, and neglecting reinvestment. Then Beter's stock will go up, CREF will sell it, and repeat the process. And all other funds are doing the same thing. In theory, the process could lead to the liquidation of the entirety of American industry. The grave of the productive corporation is already prepared; we await the death rattle. However long it takes, the CEO's will be well paid throughout.

In the Public Interest

What's wrong with very high CEO compensation? Two things: First, it is bad stewardship for people to take more than they can use, and unjust that some people should be making 43,700 times what other people make, especially when at least some of those other people are starving. John Locke, high priest of private property, put the case for the morality of private property very simply: each man may take from the commons (the world resources available to all) only as much as he can use, and only as long as enough and as good is left for others. The CEO fails on both counts.

Second, this compensation system is destroying American industry. It is commonplace by now that our cost-saving schemes have cost us the economy: our products made obsolete by foreign companies that invested in R & D [research and development] when we did not, and invested in new plants when we did not, our industrial jobs lost as our obsolete plants have to be shuttered, as pink slips flutter from the corner offices in the most recent "downsizings" and "rightsizings," as the actual work is assigned to East Asian and Mexican factories and American workers are handed over to unemployment. We are moving, we are told, from an era of manufacturing to an era of information-driven service industries. These are precisely the industries for which the vast majority of the population is not prepared and from which they cannot profit. We are condemning a majority of working-age adults to temporary, underpaid, service jobs, while the tiny minority feeds off the global wealth generated by the exploitation of the rest of the world. The entire system is unjust, and cries out to heaven, and to an informed citizenry, for remedy. The compensation of the truly greedy might be a good place to start.

**Ira T. Kay and
Steven E. Rushbrook**

 **NO**

The U.S. Executive Pay Model

CEO pay has been under media scrutiny for more than 20 years, but the nature of that scrutiny has shifted recently. During the mid- to late-1980s, critics argued that compensation for CEOs and other executives was largely unrelated to the financial or stock market performance of their companies. These critics included the media, government, government agencies (e.g., Securities and Exchange Commission, Internal Revenue Service, Financial Accounting Standards Board), and institutional investors, including public employee pension funds.

During the mid-1990s, while some criticism was exaggerated, there was a marked move to strengthen the relationship between CEO pay and the stock price of their companies, primarily through increases in stock option grants and executive stock ownership. This pay/stock price linkage, combined with improved proxy disclosure and better governance by compensation committees, has played a role in motivating the increase in the value of the U.S. stock market.

Today the criticism continues, but the focus has again shifted. Executive pay has continued to rise dramatically along with the stock market. E-commerce, the Internet and technology sectors have created enormous wealth among founders and key employees. This new wealth has put significant pressure on boards to increase pay for their own CEOs, including those in the traditional economy. Critics contend that:

- CEOs are not worth their pay.
- CEO pay is too high in general.
- CEO pay is unrelated to performance.
- CEO pay went up because the stock market went up; the U.S. stock market would have performed just as well without stock options.
- CEO pay will not go down if the stock market goes down.
- CEO pay is part of a "winner-take-all" society.

This article will examine:

- Some of the reasons for record CEO pay levels
- The reasons that CEO performance is so vital to our economy
- The arguments for and against CEO worth
- When to measure CEO performance against pay
- The academic and author research relevant to this analysis
- A prognosis for the future.

Why CEO Pay Is So High

There is little doubt that executive pay has risen faster (10 to 15 percent annually) than average employee earnings (3 to 4 percent annually) and the rate of inflation (less than 3 percent annually).

However, increases in CEO compensation packages should be kept in perspective. Arguably, three primary factors account for the rapid escalation of CEO pay packages:

1. **A scarcity of CEO talent creates "bidding wars."** Despite occasional performance failures, boards are willing to pay breathtaking sums to CEOs who can generate record financial performance. Clearly, the escalation of CEO packages is due in large part to the scarcity of proven CEO talent. Boards now are turning to outside candidates more frequently in search of talent to help them compete in an increasingly competitive global business community. The notion of promoting from within is being balanced by boards that need to globalize their operations and find proven talent quickly. Research has shown that the percentage of CEOs hired from the outside has risen dramatically in the past 10 years (nearly one in five). The high technology sector has exploded in the last two years, and the executive talent drain is apparent. Even with the NASDAQ market correction starting in early 2000, old-line companies continue to compete with high tech companies in search of scarce CEO talent. Subsequently, the equity packages offered by the high tech firms are escalating CEO packages at all companies even further.
2. **The "winner take all" mentality is pervasive.** The CEO and the senior executive team work under significant pressure and public scrutiny, and the most successful CEO candidates are often those who are able to assume extraordinarily high levels of risk and still win. In contrast to Japan and Germany, where senior executives function more often as a risk-sharing team, the typical U.S. model requires the CEO to assume the greatest risk and responsibility. It is certainly true that this model has worked successfully in the United States for at least the past 10 years. CEO pay packages often provide the counterbalance to the risk inherent in these positions, and boards are willing to pay such packages to a limited pool of candidates.
3. **CEOs are compensated for making unpopular decisions.** As CEOs become celebrities, unpopular decisions such as downsizing, mergers and divestitures rest squarely on their shoulders. Increased media attention on the business community exacerbates this effect. In addition, large institutional shareholders often are quite vocal about CEO pay packages and company performance, and their actions exert significant control over a company's stock price. As a result, high CEO packages, in part, compensate for the stigma associated with the position.

Is CEO Performance Important?

The obvious answer is yes. High-performing CEOs are essential to the success of most companies. But the real answer is less obvious and has far-reaching social consequences beyond the executive suite.

Stronger Job Security and Better Career Opportunities for All Employees

CEOs who perform well are more likely to create and sustain successful companies and, in turn, employees are more likely to enjoy greater job security and better career opportunities. In the late 1980s and early 1990s, when downsizing was prevalent, employees who survived these waves of change were better positioned for the long term.

Today, while downsizing is less common, the pace of mergers and acquisitions has increased, and the U.S. economy has created a record number of jobs in the past decade. Successful CEOs, driven in large part by stock-based incentives, have created larger, more international companies serving a global customer base.

Stronger Retirement Security for Employees and Their Dependents

One aspect of higher CEO performance is an increase in the value of pension plan assets, thereby increasing the security of all pension plans. It is a great irony that public employee pension funds sometimes breed the most vocal opponents of pay-for-performance CEO plans because they, as well as state and local government employees, benefit so directly from the superior stock performance of Corporate America.

Over-funded pension plans, the result of higher stock values, allow companies to increase earnings per share (EPS). Increases in stock prices also contribute to portable retirement plans, such as the 401(k), allowing individual investment alternatives and mobility.

Are CEOs Worth It?

Spectacular headline CEO pay packages, especially in the e-commerce sector, have caused a flurry of media coverage. Obviously, that influences the general labor market for CEOs and executives, but it is not limited to them.

A study completed in the April 2000 issue of Forbes found 12 CEOs recruited within the prior 12 months from the traditional sector to the dot-com sector with packages valued at more than $100 million. Examples include Richard Braddock of Priceline and Margaret Whitman of eBay at more than $1 billion each. Are they worth it? Is this labor market "efficient"?

Because CEOs have alternatives, the labor market appears efficient. They could become consultants or venture capitalists or entrepreneurs, or go to another dot-com. Thus, the real question becomes, 'What do you have to pay them to buy them out of their risk to go?'

For example, a well-known executive changes companies from one telecommunications company to another and he gets reimbursed first class airfare for his mother. Another high technology executive is given a $40 million jet with a tax gross-up to cover the jet's value.

On the other hand, the Wilshire 5000, one of the broadest market indices available, recorded total market capitalization at $15.8 trillion dollars for 2000, up

24 percent from 1999, and a 300-plus percent increase from 1995. In addition, according to the Crystal Report, aggregate total CEO pay went up 43 percent from 1995 to 1999, but the figure represented only a fraction of a percent (.3 percent) of the market capitalization for those companies. While the stock market has corrected in the last half of 2000, the crucial point remains: While CEOs are well paid, they have created enormous economic value.

During 1999, the Standard & Poor's (S&P) 500 Index yielded a 21 percent return, and the bull market span has extended nearly 20 years. Annually, the S&P 500 Index has earned 19.9 percent (or 20 times) the original investment since August 1982. In addition, the Internet boom has pushed U.S. economic growth to record levels. Internet market capitalization represented well above 10 percent of the entire U.S. equity market at its peak. Internet companies also were responsible for more than 50 percent of stock market gains in 1999, as a result of 140 percent return and significant market weighting. In 1999, 257 Internet companies went public with a combined market capitalization of $242 billion. Even factoring in the correction of 2000, the returns remain quite remarkable.

Depending on how it is analyzed, the average large company CEO pay package is currently valued between $10 million and $20 million. The average increase was between 10 and 40 percent. But in sum, it still adds up to just 30 basis points—again, .3 percent of market capitalization for those companies.

Is mankind in the midst of a modern industrial revolution with all of the productivity and benefits to humanity? Or is it a decade of greed with people being paid what they're really not worth? There is a sense of paradox. The question is, can theory or hypothesis explain it? In short, yes.

In economic terms, the fundamental question is "Are the best resources being allocated to their optimal use?" In effect, the labor market is saying that Margaret Whitman will add more to eBay, and to society, under Adam Smith's invisible hand, than she would at her former employer. Are the resources (executives, in this case) being put to optimal use?

The theory behind executive pay rests on the principle that CEOs are the agents of shareholders; they are separate from owners. Occasionally, this agent/owner gap creates a conflict of interest. Executive pay programs, especially stock ownership and stock options, are explicitly designed to close the gap and create alignment between CEOs and shareholders. This "agency theory" clearly states that CEO pay opportunity could help create an increase in performance.

When Do You Measure CEO Performance?

The most fundamental question is whether pay causes performance. To examine whether causation exists, an appropriate methodology and performance period should be chosen. Frequently, an inappropriate time period is chosen and hence, an erroneous conclusion is drawn.

The following two perspectives yield the most valid results:

- **Pay Opportunity vs. Subsequent Performance.** Current pay opportunity should be correlated with future performance. A high pay opportunity today (e.g., annual cash bonus opportunity or stock option grants) should cause a CEO to create future high performance for the organization. For example, examine the cash bonus opportunity three years ago and then consider performance in subsequent years.

- **Actual Pay vs. Prior Performance.** Current actual pay, such as cash bonuses or stock option profits, should be correlated with prior performance in the past several years. Often, in journal articles and media clips, attempts to correlate past pay-outs with subsequent performance, or current pay opportunities (e.g., stock option grants) with past performance (e.g., three-year total returns to shareholders) result in wholly inappropriate perspectives that mislead the audience.

To measure and assess pay for performance, two criteria should be considered: pay and stock ownership. Consider today's pay, plus "in-the-money" options, compared to total shareholder return (TSR) in the past five years. As for stock ownership, take the opposite perspective and consider past stock ownership with performance in the subsequent five years.

For example, consider Company A and Company B, each of which granted 1 million options to their CEOs at $20 each in 1998.

- Company A had a $15 stock price in 1996, a $20 stock price in 1998 and a $20 stock price in 2000. Its Black-Scholes present value was approximately 50 percent, or $10 million in 1998, and there were no other stock option grants.
- Company B had a stock price that went from $25 to $20 to $40. The Black-Scholes value also is $10 million. But in-the-money value is $20 million in 2000.

One method would be to consider the 1998 Black-Scholes value compared with the 1996 to 1998 TSR, which includes the increase in stock price plus dividends.

- Company A had $10 million in pay, and 33 percent TSR from 1996 to 1998; the stock price increased from $15 to $20.
- Company B had $10 million in Black-Scholes value, but the stock price fell $5 from $25 to $20, down 20 percent.

At first glance, it is assumed that no pay for performance exists because both companies had CEO pay of $10 million under this methodology, one with TSR of positive 33 percent and the other with a negative 20 percent TSR.

The alternative methodology is more appropriate because it considers the correct time period—actual pay in the year 2000 vs. TSR for the prior three years. For Company A, there is zero pay and zero TSR. For Company B, there is $20 million pay and 100 percent TSR. With this alternative, the conclusion is that there is pay for performance.

The answer depends completely on the methodology. A case could be made that the large option grant motivated Company B's CEO to succeed, and while Company A did not succeed, there was no pay for that low performance.

Academic Research

The following six points categorize questions that most researchers seek to answer in relation to CEO pay:

1. Is there pay for performance? Is a CEO's pay sensitive to company performance? Is there a correlation?
2. Does stock ownership matter? In other words, can companies ignore CEO stock ownership and grant stock options? If stock ownership is important, do stock ownership guidelines work? Do stock ownership guidelines create CEO ownership, which improves company performance?
3. Are there motivational differences between stock ownership and stock options? Are executives afraid to buy stock if the price is volatile? Do large stock option grants motivate expensive company stock repurchase programs?
4. Do stock options create ownership?
5. Are poor performing CEOs terminated?
6. Is the U.S. model being exported?

According to Research Findings

Is There Pay for Performance?

CEO pay, including stock, is highly sensitive to company performance. CEO compensation in Year 1 is positively correlated with corporate performance in Year 2, the appropriate measurement period.

This demonstration of the pay/performance link is particularly important in light of the criticism that CEOs receive high pay for superior performance, and receive high severance packages when poor performance leads to termination.

Does CEO Stock Ownership Matter?

CEO stock ownership has increased dramatically, and company performance is positively correlated with the percentage of stock held by managers. In addition, executive stock ownership guidelines improve company performance.

Are There Motivational Differences Between Stock Ownership and Stock Options?

Large stock option grants are correlated with increased stock price volatility, suggesting that CEOs who receive large stock option grants may subsequently cause stock price volatility. Companies with volatile stock prices have executives with less stock ownership, confirming that executives are reluctant to purchase highly volatile stock. Stock option grants, without stock ownership guidelines, may increase stock price volatility and reduce executive stock ownership levels. In addition, stock options are correlated with lower stock dividends and increased stock repurchase levels.

Stock Dividends

Because the current stock price is inversely related to the expected future stream of dividends, lower dividend payments to shareholders will likely result in higher future stock prices and therefore greater potential stock option gains.

Company Stock Repurchases

Companies are repurchasing shares at an unprecedented rate to fuel their stock option programs. To fund these repurchases, companies are either using cash or borrowing funds, increasing both their debt/equity ratios and their risk significantly, and reducing the risk adjusted value of their stock.

Do Stock Options Create Ownership?

Stock options do not create stock ownership but tend to serve as an imperfect proxy for stock ownership. Stock options can help, but they must be combined with executive stock ownership guidelines and vehicles to assist executives achieve the required ownership levels. Stock option gains, even those for e-billionaires, can evaporate quickly during an economic downturn.

One way to promote stock ownership is a management stock purchase plan, which allows executives to purchase discounted company stock with a portion of their cash bonus and/or salary. This plan has significant tax, accounting and financial planning advantages.

Are Poor Performing CEOs Terminated?

Several sources of academic literature indicate that poor performing CEOs are, in fact, terminated.

Is the U.S. CEO Pay Model Being Exported?

Yes, the U.S. CEO pay model is being exported, but with significantly less performance sensitivity than the U.S. models. For example, Germany, Japan, France and other nations are incorporating pay-for-performance plans, but on a more limited basis.

Comparisons of U.S. and overseas CEO pay packages are difficult given the vastly different size of the countries and companies. Because CEO pay tracks with company size, given the complexity and risk involved, the U.S. CEO pay packages are likely to be larger than those found overseas. In addition, international studies often do not account for differences in culture, local welfare benefits and tax rates.

CEO Pay Study 2000–2001

U.S. executive pay, especially CEO pay, continues to generate controversy, with some in the media believing that it has gone beyond appropriate limits. Others, including most institutional investors, believe that the way U.S. CEOs are paid is a source of significant competitive advantage.

Can America's Economic Success Be Attributed to CEO Pay-for-Performance?

While there are outliers—such as high paying companies with low performance, and low paying companies with high performance—on the average, there is a strong correlation between CEO pay and company performance. Having shown this correlation, causation is difficult to prove. Still, the greater the CEO's financial stake in a company, the more likely he/she is to act in the best interests of shareholders.

Is CEO Cash Compensation Sensitive to Market Performance?

Yes, in terms of total shareholder return (TSR), a CEO's total cash compensation is sensitive to a company's stock market performance. In a Watson Wyatt survey sample, CEOs with above-median change in total cash compensation (TCC, or base salary plus cash bonus) correlated with an 18.8-percent five-year annualized TSR, vs. 9.8 percent annualized TSR for CEOs with below-median change in TCC. . . .

Does CEO Stock Ownership Correlate With Market Value?

An effective way to examine this issue is to first calculate Tobin's Q, the ratio of stock market valuation plus long-term debt divided by the replacement cost of the company's assets. This measure, developed by James Tobin of Yale University, also is known as intellectual capital, or the premium that the market is willing to pay for how well the company manages its assets (including human capital). Values above 1.0 imply that the market views the company as more valuable than the sum of its assets. Then, after examining CEO stock and the ratio of CEO ownership to CEO base salary, the Tobin's Q of companies with high CEO stock ownership proved to be 40 percent greater than that of companies with low CEO stock ownership.

Evidently, the market is willing to pay a premium for companies with leaders who have aligned their interests with the shareholders'.

The New Millennium

Given the dramatic change in the past decade, predicting even the near future seems a daunting task. Based on client work and continuing research, the following should hold true in the next 10 years:

- Pay-for-performance plans will continue at the CEO and executive levels, and will spread deeper into organizations. Companies with broad-based stock plans will continue to significantly outperform those with narrow stock plan coverage.
- CEO total pay increases will level off as salary increases have done in the recent past. Many incentive plans may have already reached optimal leverage levels. Continued outcry by the media and public are likely to check pay excesses for the executive team in most cases.

- Individual investors and large institutional shareholders will resist further stock option overhang and the expensive share repurchase programs that have fueled record stock option grant levels.
- Stock option overhang will level off in the 10 to 15 percent range for most industries, and at 20 to 25 percent for the high technology sector, including e-commerce. Push-back from investors, combined with sufficient incentive pay plan opportunities, has already started to level off overhang levels.
- Stock ownership levels, particularly for the CEO and the senior executive team, will continue to rise.
- European and Pacific Rim companies will emulate the U.S. executive pay model, including pay-for-performance and stock ownership. While overseas compensation professionals may view this as executive greed, most companies probably will tailor plans to suit their own cultures.
- Actual year-to-year CEO pay levels will fluctuate with stock market and economic performance indicators. While compensation opportunities, including stock options, will grow modestly, actual payouts are likely to decline if the stock market corrects further. Any future stock market correction will be smaller because of significant CEO stock ownership levels, which have provided the U.S. economy with a "cushion" of high performance.
- Pay programs at traditional companies and new economy companies will converge, with proven best practices being adopted by the majority.
- And finally, CEO pay will, of course, remain controversial.

Undoubtedly, U.S. companies are on the right track given the record financial performance of the past decade. Performance-based pay for CEOs, combined with programs that encourage stock ownership, should fuel steady job creation and financial success in the future.

The answer to the question of whether U.S. CEOs are overpaid depends on who answers. Clearly shareholders, including private investors and large institutional shareholders, would respond with a resounding "no." The record performance-based CEO pay packages are a small price to pay for unprecedented productivity and growth.

On the contrary, some would argue that the average worker should share in the success to a greater extent. As research indicates, including all employees in pay-for-performance and stock-based incentives should result in even higher levels of performance.

POSTSCRIPT

Are U.S. CEOs Overpaid?

So, how high are U.S. CEO salaries? In 2001, the *average* U.S. CEO annual income was $13 million (*Business Week*, April 16, 2001, pp. 77–108). While this figure may seem large, consider that it includes the extremely few—though highly publicized—cases of exorbitant CEO pay such as the $293 million, $164 million, and $157 million recently paid to the heads of Citigroup, AOL/Time Warner, and Cisco Systems, respectively. A few extreme cases such as these can easily skew the numbers, suggesting that there are many CEOs in America making considerably less than the $13 million average. Nevertheless, figures such as these beg the question: Are American CEOs overpaid?

You have just read two different answers to this question. Lisa Newton believes that the typical U.S. CEO should not receive ten or more times the annual pay of CEOs in other industrial countries. She also points out, in no uncertain terms, that CEOs are only partly responsible for the ultimate success of their organization and the concomitant increase in shareholder wealth. Further, she argues, no matter how much responsibility a CEO actually does carry, it isn't enough to justify the levels of compensation currently being paid to top executives in America. She concludes her argument with an appeal to the reader's emotions by declaring that it is immoral, in effect, for a CEO to "take" more than he/she can use, particularly "when people in the world are starving." Despite its emotional appeal, one must be careful to embrace this last line of attack without considerable thought: After all, it has more than a little in common with the basic tenets and principles of communism.

Ira Kay and Steven Rushbrook believe that U.S. CEOs typically earn every nickel they make and are, therefore, entitled to whatever levels of pay they receive. Theirs is a free-market view—that labor, like every other business input, is subject to free-market forces. For the typical CEO, annual compensation accurately reflects his or her worth in the market. According to these authors, in this sense, U.S. CEO pay is both fair and equitable.

Suggested Readings

Louis Aguilar, Exec-worker pay gap widens to gulf. *The Denver Post,* July 8, 2001, p. 16a.

Kerry A. Dolan, The age of the $100 million CEO. *Forbes,* April 3, 2000, vol. 165, issue 8.

Jack Dolmat, Executive pay for performance. *WorldatWork Journal,* First Quarter 2001, pp. 19–27.

Elan Journo, Why are CEOs paid so much? *The Ayn Rand Institute,* April 12, 2004. http://www.aynrand.org/site/News2?page=NewsArticle&id=8404

Louis Lavelle, Executive pay. *Business Week,* April 16, 2001, pp. 77–108.

Louis Lavelle, CEO pay: The more things change. . . . *Business Week,* October 6, 2000, pp. 106–108.

Kevin J. Murphy, Top executives are worth every nickel they get. *Harvard Business Review,* March/April 1986.

Alan Reynolds, CEO pay parade. *The Cato Institute,* April 18, 2004. http://www.cato.org/dailys/04-18-04.html

ISSUE 12

Corporate Governance Reform: Is Sarbanes-Oxley the Answer?

YES: Federal News Service, from "Conference Report on Corporate Responsibility Legislation," Capital Hill Hearing, *Federal News Service* (July 24, 2002)

NO: Alan Reynolds, from "Sarbanes-Oxley in Retrospect," *The State of Corporate Governance: A Retrospective on Sarbanes-Oxley* (Hill Briefing, December 12, 2003)

ISSUE SUMMARY

YES: Actual testimony taken from a congressional hearing just prior to the vote on the act itself is presented in this article. Included are comments from the authors of the act, Paul Sarbanes (D-MD) and Michael Oxley (R-OH).

NO: Cato Institute senior fellow Alan Reynolds provides his audience with a scathing indictment of the mind-set and philosophy beyond the creation of the act in his argument that Sarbanes-Oxley was not a positive reaction to the call for corporate governance change.

On July 30, 2002, President George W. Bush signed into law the Sarbanes-Oxley Act, an enormous piece of legislation spawned in the wake of the massive WorldCom and Enron scandals that rocked Wall Street and corporate America just a few years beforehand. This act is routinely considered to be the most comprehensive and significant legislative action directed at corporate governance activities since the Securities Act of 1933 and the Securities Exchange Act of 1934 (Mondaq Business Briefing, Mondaq Ltd., August 9, 2004). Interestingly, at the time of these scandals, there were numerous pieces of independent corporate governance legislation that, for various reasons, were floundering in Congress and had not been enacted. The Enron and WorldCom scandals enraged the public to the point that political action was considered necessary, the result of which is the Sarbanes-Oxley Act of 2002.

Sarbanes-Oxley was designed to address the numerous violations of corporate governance rules and procedures executives committed during the wave of scandals that affected corporate America over the last five years.

Sarbanes-Oxley expert Jorge E. Guerra provides the following list of the most common transgressions (Guerra, "The Sarbanes-Oxley Act and Evolution of Corporate Governance," *The CPA Journal*, March 2004, p. 14): (1) executive compensation grossly disproportionate to corporate results, (2) misuse of corporate funds, (3) trading on insider information, particularly managers exercising stock options that have rewarded short-term thinking, (4) misrepresentation of true earnings and financial condition by too many companies, and (5) obstruction of justice by concealing activities or destroying evidence.

The net result of these wrongdoings is a crisis of investor confidence in corporations, their executives, and corporate governance policies and procedures. So, who is to blame? Guerra again provides us with a list: (1) passive, nonindependent, and rubber-stamping boards of directors, (2) nonaccountable CEOs and senior management involved in serious conflicts of interest, (3) transaction-driven investment bankers and market-makers, and biased and nonindependent investment analysts, (4) nonindependent public accounting firms, and (5) regulators paying more attention to the manifestations of the problem than to the systemic conflicts of interest at the core of poor governance practices (Guerra, 2004).

The Sarbanes-Oxley Act was the government's reaction to the public's growing skepticism about the ability of existing corporate governance laws and regulations to control and discourage immoral and illegal business activities. Guerra notes that "Corporate governance reengineering should begin with a clear definition of the authority, duties, and accountability of the board of directors and management. Special emphasis must be placed on the accountability (duty to account) of the board of directors to the shareholders, and on its independence from management" (Guerra, 2004). The Sarbanes-Oxley Act has numerous provisions and requirements addressing virtually all aspects of corporate governance. Some of the principal areas of emphasis of the act include: (1) increased regulation and oversight of the accounting profession, (2) more stringent auditor and audit committee independence requirements, (3) greater corporate responsibility and accountability, (4) increased issuer disclosure, (5) increased regulation of securities analysts, (6) increased criminal penalties, and (7) new professional responsibility standards for attorneys (Mondaq Business Briefing, Mondaq Ltd., August 9, 2004).

Given the tremendous increase in governmental oversight of corporate behavior that this act entails, it is not at all surprising that there are many who are vehemently against it. In the two articles that follow, you will be exposed to both sides of the question of whether or not this act is good for American business. The first article is actual testimony taken from a congressional hearing just prior to the vote on the act itself. Included are comments from the authors of the act, Paul Sarbanes (D-MD) and Michael Oxley (R-OH), as well as other members of the senate. Not surprisingly, their comments about the legislation are extremely positive in nature. The second article is a speech given by Cato Institute Senior Fellow Alan Reynolds at a Hill Briefing on the act. Reynolds provides his audience with a scathing indictment of the mind-set and philosophy beyond the creation of the act and condemns it as "more rules and regulations piled on top of others rules and regulations that had clearly failed."

YES

Conference Report on Corporate Responsibility Legislation

July 24, 2002 Wednesday
Capitol Hill Hearing
Rayburn House Office Building,
Washington, D.C.

REP. OXLEY: (Strikes gavel.) The committee will come to order.

The committee is meeting today to consider the conference report on H.R. 3763, the only business in order at this meeting. All members will given three minutes to make opening remarks. The chair now recognizes himself for a briefing opening statement.

This has been a difficult period for those who love and cherish the free enterprise system. Our capital markets, the most respected in the world, have suffered a series of blows, mostly self-inflicted, which have led to the loss of literally trillions of investor dollars. "Investor confidence" is almost an oxymoron these days. Good, honest companies have been caught in this indiscriminate crossfire and thoroughly punished by angry and disillusioned investors.

It is important to remember that the market decline is not the result of any fundamental change in the ability of American companies to compete and excel. The fundamentals are strong. Rather, the market drop is tied to a series of high-profile scandals involving corporate officials misleading investors in order to line their own pockets and some accountants looking the other way.

The free market system relies primarily on trust and full and accurate disclosures. These tenets have been violated. It is not a systemic problem, but sadly, it is more than just a few bad apples.

Today offers a great deal of encouraging news. In addition to this bipartisan agreement, the Dow has increased nearly 500 points in just one day—perhaps the beginning of a restoration of confidence in the markets, although we're never sure. Additionally, the U.S. attorney and the Securities and Exchange Commission are to be commended for the strong action they have taken against the shocking fraud at Adelphia Communications. And that was just today.

In April, the House acted first in response to this crisis of confidence. Legislation was passed by the House on a bipartisan basis which would

From Capital Hill Hearing at the Ryburn House, July 24, 2002.

236

require the creation of a regulatory body for auditors, an unprecedented regulatory body with real teeth, possessing the power to sanction accountants for violating standards of ethics, competence and independence. The bill also increased disclosure to Investors and required greater corporate responsibility.

Earlier this month, Senator Sarbanes built on these ideas to produce legislation aimed towards the same goals. Today we meet to consider a conference committee report that will implement the reforms we all agree are needed to make market participants more accountable to America's 85 million investors.

When we began this process last Friday, I announced it was the House's intention to build on both bodies' efforts by incorporating four key ideas into the final product. These were the adoption of Richard Baker's FAIR proposal to ensure investors receive the proceeds of sanctions levied on malfeasant corporate executives, the adoption of real-time disclosure provisions as passed by the House, the adoption of tougher criminal penalties also as adopted by the House, and increased SEC oversight of the Auditor Oversight Board.

I'm happy to report that the agreement we consider today includes all these ideas as well as other improvements which will make this legislation stronger and more responsive to the needs of investors. I am pleased, and I know Senator Sarbanes shares this view, that we now have a bill that is superior to legislation passed by either body. The language we consider today will make the capital markets more accountable to investors, increase the transparency that serves as a foundation of our markets, and make corporate executives who break the law and abuse the public trust pay severely.

Jail time for corporate executives who commit crimes is clearly in order.

Having said all that, all of us know, however, that there is no law that can make all corporate officials act responsibly. After all, we have laws against bank robberies, and they occur every day. The fact that the vast majority of American businessmen and women are enterprising, honest and hard-working is what has made American in its brief 200-plus years the most prosperous civilization the world has ever known.

There is no law Congress can pass which would match the entrepreneurial talents of the American people. Indeed, it is quite often the case that we can run the risk of restraining those talents when we rush to legislate in times of crisis. In this area Congress must proceed with extreme caution, because there is a direct correlation between the amount of freedom in a society and its ultimate success of failure.

I want to take this time to commend the senior senator from Maryland, Senator Sarbanes, for the wisdom, professionalism and bipartisanship that he has brought to this process. As I stated on Friday, it was our intention to work in good faith, and we expected the other body to do the same. Senator Sarbanes has returned our good faith, and then some. His willingness to move constructively has allowed us within a very short period of time to produce a document which reflects the best intentions of all of us.

Senator Sarbanes, thank you for your good work. I know that American investors will benefit from your efforts.

I now recognize the senator from Maryland for an opening statement. . . .

❧❦❧

SEN. SARBANES: . . . This week, we will send to the president legislation to ensure accounting and auditor integrity, to set high standards for corporate governance, higher penalties for failure of corporate governance, address stock analyst conflict of interest and provide adequate funding resources for the Securities and Exchange Commission. This legislation reflects our determination to see that the confidence of investors in our capital markets is restored. For when trust is lost, the markets falter, with serious consequences for our economy. Indeed, with serious consequences for the world economy.

It has been our great and urgent challenge to come to agreement on the reform measures that will accomplish our objective. This has obviously not been an easy task. The problems we confront are both numerous and complex, and they are not amenable to easy solutions. From time to time, we obviously have disagreed amongst ourselves about the most effective means to resolve them, but I think we've been steady in our approach. We've worked through each problem in a careful and determined way, seeking out the best advice from experts in the field and consulting across party lines.

Traditionally, our markets have been the fairest, the most efficient and the most transparent in the world. We intend to see that they merit that reputation.

It's obviously time to act decisively, and I'm pleased that we will shortly send to the president a strong bill and that we now can look forward to this legislation becoming law. I think it's important for the Congress to set in place a statutory framework to address the challenges with which we are confronted, within which framework the regulatory agencies and the private sector can then go to work to do the many things that they have to do in order to address this situation. I have said repeatedly that unless we can bring this situation under control, I'm concerned that the economy, in the end, will suffer in a major way, with all of the implications of such a development. . . .

We hope that the SEC and other responsible agencies will be able to move swiftly to implement the provisions of this legislation, lay a strong and credible foundation for the restoration of investor confidence in our marketplace, which is critical to our economic well-being. . . .

❧❦❧

REP. JOHN LAFALCE (D-NY): Thank you very much, Mr. Chairman.

The agreement that we will reach today on corporate accountability legislation is an enormous victory. It's a victory for workers, it's a victory for investors. By moving quickly in conference on a strong bipartisan basis to essentially embrace the Sarbanes bill, which in so many key respects parallels legislation that we had introduced much earlier this year when this process began, we are prescribing exactly the strong medicine necessary to restore market integrity and confidence and help move our economy forward.

This conference report will include many major reforms which will fundamentally reshape the way our financial markets operate, which will toughen regulatory oversight and offer new protections to investors. Our conference report will end accounting industry self-regulation, which has proved to be a considerable failure, through the establishment of a strong, independent, legislatively created public accounting oversight board with legislatively defined powers.

The board will have full investigatory, disciplinary and standard-setting powers and full authority to enforce the securities laws that apply to the public accounting firms that the board will regulate.

The bill will also set high standards for auditor independence. Our conference report retains the strong auditor independence standards that are necessary to prohibit the conflicts that auditors currently face. Auditors will essentially be prohibited from providing consulting services that create conflicts. Audit committees will be given full authority over the hiring, the firing, the compensation of auditors and will be required to pre-approve any services provided by auditors.

The conference report retains the Senate provisions that give the new board full authority to implement the statutory standards of independence and auditor conduct through regulations. Foreign accounting firms will not be exempted from the act, and the SEC will not have authority to create exemptions.

Our conference report will ensure punishment of corporate wrongdoers. The final bill takes the increased penalties provided in Mr. Sensenbrenner's bill, but it retains the stronger provisions of Senator Leahy's amendment to the Senate legislation, including providing a private right of action for whistle-blowers, restoring the statute of limitations on private rights of actions under the securities laws, and stronger document-shredding prohibitions.

The final conference report will maintain reliable and independent funding for the new board and for FASB. The final conference report will reject the proposal to give the SEC complete control over the setting of fees that are to fund the new board and FASB, and permits issuers to join the two boards as auxiliary members.

The final bill will also maintain the provision that permits the new board and FASB to play a central role in the setting of fees that support them.

The final conference report will also hold corporate executives legally accountable for the accuracy of their companies' financial statements. It includes my proposal, which requires CEO's to conduct a detailed inquiry into the preparation of the company's financial statements so that they cannot claim ignorance of deceptive and misleading practices, requires CEO's to certify to the accuracy of those statements and imposes substantial penalties for the filing of false statements. . . .

⸰⸛◉⸛⸰

SEN. PHIL GRAMM (R-TX): I want to thank you. I want to congratulate you and Senator Sarbanes.

I believe that you have put together a bill that will do more good than harm, but I do not believe that the bill does as much good as it could do. I think it does more harm than it should do because it doesn't address the practical problems of making this new law work, not just for the Dow Jones industrial average companies, not just for the S&P 500, but for the 16,254 companies that will be governed by this law. I am afraid that we have written a one-size-fits all prescription when that one size clearly does not fit all.

We have the ability of the board to grant waivers on an individual basis, but the way the law is structured, it is almost destined to mean that thousands of small incorporated businesses that have their stocks traded publicly will be forced to hire lawyers and to hire lobbyists and to come to Washington and to ask for individual waivers. And yet once the board has granted 2,000 waivers under exactly the same conditions, it can't grant a blanket waiver to everybody else who would potentially benefit from that waiver. I am concerned that companies that have resources will hire—be able to hire the people to get the waiver; those that are often in need will not be able to do that. I am very concerned about the avenues of new litigation that will occur under this bill. I am concerned about what I see as an unnecessary change in a law passed earlier that was aimed at preventing strike lawsuits.

So I'm not saying that this bill is not an improvement over the status quo, I'm expressing disappointment that in conference, when you normally try to deal with practical problems and you try to address how is this law going to work, and can we make it practical in applying to all the circumstances in all of the companies it will apply to, in the environment that we're in today, that has been impossible. And so, I hope that this does the maximum amount of good it can do. I hope the harm it does is minimal. But I am concerned about it. I am convinced that we will be back here next year or the year after, correcting problems in the bill I think that could have been avoided, and I am disappointed by that. . . .

And so, while I'm not happy with the final product today, while I think it could have easily been much better, as tough as you want it to be, but reasonable and practical—and I think people have gotten confused between the two—it certainly could have been worse. If I were investing billions of dollars on Wall Street, I would look at this bill and conclude what I've concluded; that is, A, it's going to be very unworkable, it's going to create endless paperwork, there are going to be too may lawsuits. But in the end, we'll come back after the fact and fix it, and the American economy can continue to prosper under this bill.

I'm not going to vote for this bill because it could have and should have been better. These things should have been dealt with. But I'm not here saying the world's coming to and end because of its adoption. . . .

⋘⊙⋙

SEN. CHRISTOPHER DODD (D-CT): . . . This is an historic piece of legislation. It's not one size fits all. I appreciate the comments of my friend from Texas, but we went out of our way, as a result of the efforts of Senator Enzi and others to make sure that we did not reach too far to create the cascading effects that you could produce if we did not try to limit this to public companies, where the public is invested, where the public makes judgments based on the claims or assertions by the accounting industry and others that the condition of public companies are such that you have enough confidence in them to invest hard-earned dollars.

And certainly, there are larger and smaller public companies, but it's not too much to ask to see to it that when the certified public accountants make assertions about companies, that that information ought to be basically correct. And too often, it has not been so. And as a result, it was needed to pass this legislation.

In fact, this legislation was needed before the events of last October, but it took the events of last October and subsequent events to provoke this institution to begin to respond to them. So, I am pleased that we have put this bill together. . . .

The purpose of the original securities laws, passed more than 70 years ago, was to increase the public trust in America's public companies and financial markets, and the reliability of disclosed corporate information, financial information. These laws, which are part of the economic foundation of our country, were designed to promote market efficiency and inspire investor confidence. The resulting market confidence and the statements of financial health of publicly owned companies has paved the way for America's economic expansion over these decades. . . .

·◦◦·

SEN. PATRICK LEAHY (D-VT): Thank you. . . . The criminal-law parts that I was involved with are nearly identical to the Corporate and Criminal Fraud Accountability Act, which we introduced in February and the Senate Judiciary Committee voted in April. We've—today's report will have a tough new crime and securities fraud (sic). It will cover any scheme or artifice to defraud investors—worked (sic) with the House counterparts. This provision is ample, with a 25-year maximum term.

Now there are three central provisions in here from the Senate bill that I think are extremely important: We extend the statute of limitations in security-fraud cases—something that would've helped so many people who were defrauded by Enron and others. We include meaningful protections for corporate whistle-blowers. We learned from Sharon Watkins of Enron that Enron lawyers said that Texas law would allow them to just ignore her and would not have her protected. We've taken care of that. And we include new anti-shredding crimes. We want to make sure that key documents don't get shredded in the first place. It only takes a few minutes to shred something; it might take years to put together a case. This makes sure the cases will be there.

Lastly, I would say that while we can't stop greed, we can stop greed from succeeding. And nothing is going to focus someone's moral compass more than knowing that if they don't do what is right and moral, they're going to be a guest of the state behind iron bars for a long, long time. . . .

·◦◦·

SEN. ROBERT BENNETT (R-UT): Thank you, Mr. Chairman, . . . I will once again part company with my leader on the committee, Senator Gramm, in that I will vote for the conference report and I will vote—I will sign the conference report and I will vote for the bill.

I do find it easy, however, to restrain my overwhelming enthusiasm for everything in the bill, and that makes me something of a dissenting voice here for the chorus that I'm hearing.

I believe that adjustments will be made in the accounting profession to the new reality of this bill. And accountants, be they the CFOs or the auditing firms, once they get acquainted with the new rules and the new circumstances, will go forward with their business in as professional a fashion as they have in the past. I think we will probably see a net improvement, but the net improvement will come from their desire to see to it that they attract investors to the stock and that they attract customers to their accounting firms every bit as much as it will be that they will try to comply with the law.

I think while adjustments will be made and the accounting profession will survive just fine under this law, costs will go up as they make those adjustments, and those costs will be passed on to the consumer as they always are.

And unfortunately, stupidity will not disappear. The folks at Enron believed that their schemes would pay off. They didn't go into those partnerships expecting disaster, they went into those partnerships expecting glorious profits. And they were in an area they didn't understand. They were being stupid, and they got caught by the realities of the marketplace, and they have paid the price the marketplace always demands when somebody makes a stupid business decision.

The market is the fastest, quickest punisher of stupidity. And that's what happened.

Now, maybe as a result of this law we will know a little sooner than we would have known before that the stupidity had taken place. But we cannot tell ourselves that by virtue of passing this law stupidity will disappear. I'm reminded that Alan Greenspan warned against irrational exuberance in terms of where the stock market was, and it was approaching the stratospheric level of 6,000 on the Dow, which is more than 2,000 below where we are now. A large part of the problem that we have had is not because we didn't pass the proper laws, it was because there was a culture that existed in the mid- to late '90s that everything you touched turned to gold, every decision you made would have a multiple attached to it of 10, 20, 50, a hundred times, and markets have always told us those kinds of multiples don't exist over time and we have to come back to earth.

So I think this bill is a positive step forward. I think the Congress had to act to demonstrate that we were aware of the problem. But I think all of us should take a somewhat sobering dose of humility and recognize that the markets don't pay as much attention to us as we pay to ourselves. . . .

<hr/>

REP. CHRISTOPHER COX (R-CA): Thank you very much, Mr. Chairman. . . . Fraud and unfair dealing are the enemies of the free enterprise system.

And as we can see from the turmoil in our markets, our country is paying a very high price because those in power have broken faith with their employees and their investors.

We have tough laws on the books to deal with all manner of crime, including corporate crime. But just as bacteria mutate to defeat antibiotics, those who cook the books practice a devious art and constantly change their recipes, and we must keep our laws and our remedies up to date.

The legislation we're adopting today is carefully tailored to the abuses that were uncovered in House and Senate hearings and investigations. Enron and Global Crossing and WorldCom and other cases in which investors have been defrauded, all have centered around accounting. Abuses of accounting rules were central to each of these scandals. And so, using the regulatory thicket of detailed accounting rules as cover, the malefactors in these cases intentionally structured sham transactions in order to hide their true financial position. That is why the central reform in both the House-passed legislation and the Senate-passed legislation that we are reconciling here today has been the creation of an Accounting Oversight Board that will delve deeply into the ways that accounting and accountants have become accomplices to deceit. Its mission is to see to it that accounting standards once again make financial reports truthful, honest and clear.

Using existing laws, our government will, undoubtedly, soon put those most culpable into prison, I have no doubt. But today we are enacting good, tough, strong, new rules.

I should add, in conclusion, that no amount of new rules, no amount of government enforcement can eliminate the importance of honesty and character and ethics in our capital markets and in our places of work. (Brief audio break)—problems of ethics. And in this, the leadership of President Bush has been essential.

He has asked every American to meet a higher standard. And as we raise the legal standard here today, we should bear in mind our obligation to do still more to ensure that the best and the brightest will still want to join the accounting profession, to make sure that our most experienced citizens, possessed of good judgment and good reputation, will be willing to perform the crucial oversight functions of the board of directors, and that entrepreneurs will still take the risks and dream boldly, without fear of being second-guessed if the race is not won. . . .

Alan Reynolds  **NO**

Sarbanes-Oxley in Retrospect

Sarbanes-Oxley was based on a dubious analysis of the nature of the problem to be solved, and of the goals to be achieved. The problem was thought to be merely a matter of accounting, as though better bookkeeping could have somehow kept Enron and WorldCom solvent. And the stated objective was "to restore investor confidence" in the short term rather than preventing future Enron-like crises by making lasting improvements in institutional constraints and incentives.

The key congressional assumption appeared to be that any problems in business or accounting must be the fault of businessmen and accountants, not the fault of any governmental institutions (such as the IRS, SEC or FASB), or any laws (such as the 1968 Williams Act to protect spendthrift managers against hostile takeovers). So the solution, as usual, was more rules and regulations piled on top of other rules and regulations that had clearly failed.

I believe Sarbanes Oxley was unnecessary, harmful and inadequate.

It was *unnecessary* because the SEC had ample authority to oversee, investigate and enforce honest accounting and auditing. It is already proving to be *harmful* in ways I'll explain later, mainly because it greatly increases the costs and risks of doing business as a publicly traded U.S. corporation and increases the risks of serving as a director or officer. Finally, it is *inadequate* because it failed to encourage the development of institutions and incentives (including an excessive incentive to retain earnings before the individual tax on dividends was reduced) to improve corporate governance over the long haul.

I am first going to highlight a few prominent showpieces of the law, and then cite a few studies and news reports suggesting things are not working out as expected—that the law is already creating many "unintended consequences" but no apparent benefits (except to a growing industry of corporate governance consultants).

Perhaps the most visible symbolic change is that Sarbanes-Oxley required the CEO and CFO to certify that their financial statements "fairly" represent "financial conditions and results," and face prison sentences if they are wrong. The SEC always had the power to require such a certification ceremony, and in fact did so before Sarbanes-Oxley was enacted. But Section 302(a) is more extreme. It threatens prison sentences of up to 20 years for executives who "*willfully*" certify incorrectly that reports have "*fairly*" presented "financial conditions and results," or 10 years for doing so "knowingly." Executives can be banned from serving as an officer or director because of undefined "misconduct." They can be required to forfeit one year of back pay if earnings have to be restated due to "material noncompliance." Nobody can know in advance what "willfully" or "fairly" or "misconduct" or "material noncompliance" means, so all these potentially capricious punitive measures fail to live up to the rule of law. Certification puts the CEO in the position of a nervous auditor—a job few CEOs are qualified to do—rather than a general manager who properly delegates such specialized chores to experts.

Another significant changes it that Sarbanes-Oxley required that each Board's audit committee be comprised entirely of independent directors with no company experience, plus one financial expert who claims to understand all 4500 pages of generally accepted accounting principles. The pretentious effort to redesign corporate boards in Washington D.C. certainly did not follow from any analysis of what went wrong at Enron. The Enron board was 86 percent independent, with a dozen non-employee outsiders including five CEOs and four academics. It was chaired by an accounting professor from the Stanford business school.

In 2000, *Chief Executive* magazine rated Enron's board among the five best. By contrast, the check-the-box formulas being peddled by corporate governance consultants invariably give Berkshire Hathaway a terrible rating because Warren Buffet has too many people on the Board who know him and his business very well. Yet Berkshire Hathaway's stock beat the S&P 500 for all but four years since 1965. Stockholders know more than legislators about who should be directors and officers of the companies they invest in.

A particularly grandiose gesture in Sarbanes-Oxley was the creation of a new Public Company Accounting Oversight Board, financed by what is essentially a tax on stockholders. That taxing authority—as well as the power to put some accounting firms out of business and favor others—raises serious questions about the Constitutionality of the new Board. The Board evades the rules governing federal agencies, such as the rules for appointments and salaries ($452,000), by pretending to be a private nonprofit—a dot-org, not a dot-gov. But no genuinely private organization can force us to both pay and obey.

Sarbanes-Oxley requires that non-accountants be a majority of the Board overseeing accounting, which is like having non-physicians oversee the practice of medicine. They will obviously need to rely on accountants, and Board is expected to hire about a hundred of them to do what the SEC and FASB were supposed to do. Having held a job with the Board will look terrific on any accountant's resume, of course, so the Board came up with a code of ethics in the hope of throwing a little sand in the revolving door. That is it's only accomplishment to date.

Let's outline a few of Sarbanes-Oxley's most obvious problems—those that [have] even been noticed by the press:

First, Sarbanes-Oxley makes it harder to attract and retain qualified directors, particularly the required financial expert. "Many companies are having trouble filling this slot," reports *The Wall Street Journal* (July 29, 2002), "because candidates fear they will be held responsible for auditing problems." Compensation of outside directors has increased to compensate for increased responsibilities and risks. A study of the Fortune 1000 firms, by Axentis LLC found that compensation of outside directors rose from $40,000 to $100,000.

Second, Sarbanes-Oxley reduces the availability of liability insurance for directors and officers, and greatly increases the cost of such insurance for those who can get it. The Axentis study found the premiums for D&O insurance quadrupled. "Directors' Insurance Fees Get Fatter" was the headline of a *Wall Street Journal* report (July 12, 2002) that found premiums up by as much as 100–300 percent despite reductions in coverage. This is partly due to Sarbanes-Oxley mandates, such as extending the statue of limitations for securities litigation to five years, and to the risk that the law will dramatically expand the potential liability of directors and officers.

A survey of 32 mid-sized companies by the law firm Foley & Lardner found the average price of being a public firm nearly doubled after Sarbanes-Oxley, from $1.3 million to almost $2.5 million. The cost of D&O insurance rose from $329,000 to $639,000. Directors' fees doubled, as did accounting, audit and legal fees.

Third, Sarbanes-Oxley makes it harder (particularly for smaller firms) to attract and retain qualified CEOs and CFOs. A new survey by Burson-Marsteller found that 73 percent of chief executive officers said they have thought about quitting, a record high. And 35 percent of other senior executives said they'd turn down the job of CEO if it were offered, up from 27 percent in 2001. When the talent pool shrinks, either the pay of American CEO's will rise (which was certainly an unintended consequence) or the quality of American CEOs will fall. The best executive talent may be lured to private or foreign firms.

Fourth, the punitive approach of Sarbanes-Oxley appears likely to make executives overly timid, afraid to take make bold investments in risky new technologies or products. Jeffrey Garten, Dean of Yale's School of Management, predicts, "CEOs are going to become more risk-averse and big investments on risky projects are going to be held back." This makes sense, and it is consistent with the unusually slow recovery of business investment since the 2001 recession. *Washington Post* columnist David Ignatius, in his column "Risk-Takers, Look Out" (June 26, 2002), also worried that, "The new rules and regulations will apply Washington's 'zero-defect culture"—its tendency to criminalize failure—to corporate America. . . . In a zero defect culture, the engine of economic growth begins to freeze up. For this is a barren landscape where only lawyers can survive for long."

Fifth, Sarbanes-Oxley is a "Boon for Slew of Consultants," to quote a recent headline from *The Wall Street Journal* story (August 19, 2003). The article went on to describe "a corporate governance gold rush." The reason is the Sarbanes-Oxley contains so many ambiguities and contradictions that companies faced with draconian punishments for vaguely defined offenses have no choice but to hire expensive consulting services. What is income to the consultants, however, is just like another tax on corporate stockholders—like the fees used to finance the well-paid Accounting Oversight Board.

Sixth, Sarbanes-Oxley makes it much less attractive to be a publicly traded U.S. firm. An article on "Why Companies Harbor Doubts on Doing IPOs" in The *Wall Street Journal* (March 24, 2003) noted that "it costs 60% to 100% more for an audit" because of the increased risk to auditing firms, and "insurance coverage for directors and officers' liability has risen drastically as well." The number of companies going public, though initial public offerings, dropped from 352 in 2000 to 27 in the first nine months of 2003. Fewer public companies means fewer investment opportunities for smaller investors and less public information about U.S. business (because private firms can keep their information private).

In "The Case for going private" (January 25, 2003) *The Economist* notes that an unusually large number of publicly traded U.S. firms have been taken private since Sarbanes-Oxley became law (26 percent more by one calculation). *The Economist* adds that taking public firms private "will seem even more tempting as the latest round of corporate governance reforms take effect in public firms." Foreign companies such as Porsche have also said they will not list on the New York stock exchange because doing so would subject them to Sarbanes-Oxley rules, some of which are offensive or illegal in their home countries. The EU complains of this effort to impose U.S. regulations beyond our borders. Concessions to foreign firms are inevitable, but such concessions will then leave foreign firms with the advantage of lower regulatory costs and litigation risks.

Seventh, Sarbanes-Oxley is drastically shrinking the number of accounting firms willing and able to do audits. A *Washington Post* report, "Small Accounting Firms Exit Auditing" (August 27, 2003) noted that many small accounting firms are planning to abandoning auditing of public companies, partly because of difficulty and expense of insuring themselves if something goes wrong. The GAO recently noted with some alarm that the Big Four accounting firms, down from the Big Eight in 1980, now audit 78 percent of the publicly traded companies in the U.S. Small companies report difficulty finding anyone willing to do their auditing, even at the inflated fees prevalent since this law was passed.

In short, the most concrete consequences of Sarbanes-Oxley are reduced profitability and competitiveness of U.S. public corporations due to higher costs of regulatory compliance, greater exposure to the legal expenses of class action suits, and greater expenses for insurance and directors' compensation to compensate for added personal risks of civil and criminal penalties.

What was *done* in Sarbanes-Oxley clearly created many more costs than benefits (if there are any benefits). Yet what was left *undone* may well be more important. Sarbanes-Oxley suffers from delusions of adequacy.

POSTSCRIPT

Corporate Governance Reform: Is Sarbanes-Oxley the Answer?

One of the major goals of the Sarbanes-Oxley Act of 2002 was to restore investor and public faith in the ability of corporations to govern themselves in an ethical, forthright manner. Two years after the act was signed into law, public opinion appears to be supportive, although not to levels that might be expected: A Harris poll taken in early 2004 found that 59 percent feel the act will help protect their stock investments, while 57 percent indicate that they would be very unlikely to invest in a company that did not comply with the provisions of the act.

But what of businesses? How do they feel about the law two years into its existence? *The Wall Street Journal* (*WSJ*) set out to get answers to this question and reported its findings in a June 2004 article by Judith Burns entitled, "Corporate Governance: Is Sarbanes-Oxley Working?" (June 21, 2004, pg. R8). Below are some typical responses from the experts queried by *WSJ*:

Janet Dolan, president and CEO of Tennant Co., a Minneapolis maker of industrial cleaning products "complains that the law is especially burdensome for smaller-cap firms such as Tennant. . . . 'We're all having to do about the same thing, but it's less of a burden for General Electric than for us. . . .' Ms. Dolan says that outside audit fees may double over 2003 as a result of complying with all the Sarbanes-Oxley requirements.

Logan Robinson, vice president and general counsel, Delphi Corp., an auto-parts supplier in Troy, Michigan "believes there's a 'lot more right than wrong' with Sarbanes-Oxley. The law 'was an appropriate response to a real crisis . . . the core of the law is a good law that has defended our capital markets.' But 'reporting out is more of a problem . . . if you turn all the lawyers in the world into enforcement agents who are compelled to run to the SEC, there's going to be a huge problem in getting people to tell their lawyers anything.

Nell Minow, editor of the Corporate Library, a Portland, Maine, research firm specializing in corporate governance: "Ms. Minow says she wouldn't make any 'substantive changes' to Sarbanes-Oxley, although she does believe it can use some 'fine-tuning' . . . she says, mandating that the role of chairman being separate from the chief executive is 'meaningless.' She says a better approach might be to let shareholders vote on who should chair the company's board.

Suggested Readings

Yaron Brook and Alex Epstein, The cost of the 'ethical' assault on honest-businessmen. Media release, *The Ayn Rand Institute*, July 8, 2003. http://www.aynrand.org/site/News2?page=NewsArticle&id=7307.

Del Jones, Sarbanes-Oxley: Dragon or White Knight? *The USA Today*, October 20, 2003, p. 1B.

Floyd Norris, Too much regulation? Corporate bosses sing the Sarbanes-Oxley blues. *The New York Times*, January 23, 2004, p. C1.

Paul Volcker and Arthur Levitt, Jr., In defense of Sarbanes-Oxley. *The Wall Street Journal*, June 14, 2004, p. A16.

ISSUE 13

Is First-to-Market a Successful Strategy?

YES: William T. Robinson and Sungwook Min, from "Is the First to Market the First to Fail? Empirical Evidence for Industrial Goods Businesses," *Journal of Marketing Research* (February 2002)

NO: William Boulding and Markus Christen, from "Sustainable Pioneering Advantage? Profit Implications of Market Entry Order," *Marketing Science* (Summer 2003)

ISSUE SUMMARY

YES: Scholars William T. Robinson and Sungwook Min provide results of a study indicating that the advantages from being first outweigh the risks of implementing the strategy.

NO: William Boulding and Markus Christen take a contrary position and argue that first moving is not necessarily a wise strategy, presenting evidence from their own research that, in the long-run, first-movers actually experience performance disadvantages.

T he idea of being the first-to-market with a new product or service has strong intuitive appeal. Certainly it seems that being first would be an advantageous position for a firm to occupy. Two companies that are often cited as excellent examples of successful first movers are Amazon.com and Ebay. These tremendously successful and well-known companies apparently owe much of their success to first-mover advantages. On the other hand, the dot-com bust represented a situation where numerous first movers struggled or failed miserably. That debacle left a bad taste in investor's mouths for the idea of first moving as a corporate strategy. In light of the first move, dot-com fiasco, one might reasonably ask whether Amazon.com and Ebay really did secure advantages from being first or if they just got lucky. Or, perhaps, they were excellent firms that would have succeeded whether they were first, second, or ninety-eighth to market. The debate presented here specifically addresses the issue of market entry timing by asking, "Is first-to-market a successful strategy?"

Not surprisingly, persuasive arguments exist for both sides of this important question. Advocates of the first-to-market strategy often point to advantages that can be gained by first moving firms. In an important, time-tested paper management scholars Marvin Lieberman and David Montgomery discuss three advantages accruing to first movers: (1) the ability to influence consumers; (2) the ability to develop an advantage through the use of technology, and (3) securing important strategic assets before competitors do (*Strategic Management Journal*, 1988 vol. 9, 41–58). Consider the first advantage: first-to-market means that a company will be the first on the radar screen of consumers thus increasing the likelihood it can influence its customers. It may, for instance, try to convince consumers that its product is not only unique, but also the best. Since consumers have nothing against which to compare this new product, they are likely to accept the view that the new product sets and defines the market for all subsequent products introduced by firms acting in a follower capacity. Concerning the second advantage, the first mover may have an advantage since following companies will need time to understand the technology, thus forcing them to play catch up in the marketplace. While followers work to produce a competitive product, the first mover is working to ingrain its product in the market. An example of the final type of advantage occurs when a first mover preempts inputs from its competitors. The first mover may contract with suppliers to lock-in supply of a component for their new product before competitors realize that the component is necessary. With limited access to this component the later movers will find it harder to respond, thus giving an advantage to the first mover.

Despite the potential advantages of being first-to-market, there are many examples of first-to-market firms that have failed. Clearly this suggests that first moves are very risky, and come with no guarantees of success. Not surprisingly, as compared to first movers, it is easy—perhaps easier—to name successful later movers. In fact, successful later movers have dominated many large, important markets. Two examples are Microsoft Windows and its graphical user interfaces and Apple's MP3 player, iPod. Given all the evidence against first moving, it is certainly reasonable to question whether this is a successful strategy or not.

The two readings that follow present different viewpoints of about the viability of first moving as a business strategy. The article supporting the "yes" side is by management scholar William T. Robinson and marketing scholar Sungwook Min. They provide an analysis of the survival of first moving firms as compared to the survival of firms that enter later. Their results indicate the advantages from being first outweigh the risks of implementing the strategy. In the second article, also a scholarly research project, authors William Boulding and Markus Christen adopt a contrary position and argue that first moving is not necessarily a wise strategy. Indeed, they provide research evidence suggesting that, in the long-run at least, moving first leads to performance disadvantages! In any event, regardless of your perspective on this topic before you picked up this text, we are confident that your perspective will be affected by the persuasive points and arguments comprising this *Taking Sides* debate topic.

YES

William T. Robinson and Sungwook Min

Is the First to Market the First to Fail? Empirical Evidence for Industrial Goods Businesses

When entering a new market, the first entrant typically faces the greatest market and technological uncertainties. Memorable phrases reflect the associated survival risk, such as "the first to market is the first to fail" and "the pioneer is the one with the arrows in its back." Although research estimates the market pioneer's survival rate, the typical pioneer survival rate has not been compared with that of early followers. The authors' study compares survival rates for 167 first-entrant market pioneers versus 267 early followers. For these industrial goods businesses, 66% of the pioneers versus 48% of the early followers survived at least ten years. The main conclusion is that the pioneer's temporary monopoly over the early followers plus its first-mover advantages typically offset the survival risks associated with market and technological uncertainties. These results are consistent with previous research in the sense that first-mover advantages that increase a pioneer's market share also help protect the pioneer from outright failure.

Do market pioneers have unusually low survival rates? Unusually low survival rates can offset the pioneer's market share reward that often arises for surviving businesses (Robinson and Fornell 1985) and surviving brands (Urban et al. 1986). Unusually low survival rates can also deter investing in the costly and risky attempt to pioneer a new market.

In a recent *Management Science* article, Shepherd (1999, p. 623) says, "Common wisdom from the strategy literature suggests that . . . pioneers have higher returns if they are successful, . . . but [they] bear a higher risk of failure." Common or conventional wisdom in marketing seems to reach a similar conclusion. Research by both Lambkin and Day (1989, p. 15) and Golder and Tellis (1993) predicts a relatively high market pioneer attrition rate. Golder and Tellis (1993), for example, report a lifetime market pioneer survival rate of only 53%. Tellis and Golder (1996) provide many valid reasons why the first to market can be the first to fail.

Although conventional wisdom highlights survival risks, it does not highlight two key market pioneer benefits. Because a market pioneer is typically defined as the first entrant, a short-term benefit arises when the first entrant has a

From *Journal of Marketing Research,* vol. 39, no. 1, February 2002, pp. 120–122, 126–128. Copyright © 2002 by American Marketing Association. Reprinted by permission.

monopoly before the second entrant's arrival. If a market pioneer does not face any competitors, its survival should be easier. After one or more competitors enter the market, a long-term benefit arises from first-mover advantages. First-mover advantages include brand loyalty, switching costs, broad product lines that preempt competition, and scale economies (see Kerin, Varadarajan, and Peterson 1992; Lieberman and Montgomery 1998). Given these conflicting forces, the impact of order of market entry on survival is an empirical issue.

In Kalyanaram, Robinson, and Urban's (1995) survey, industry studies cover 7 cigarette markets (Whitten 1979), 18 Iowa newspaper markets (Glazer 1985), 39 chemical product markets (Lieberman 1989), 11 consumer nondurable markets (Sullivan 1992), and 5 medical diagnostic imaging subfields (Mitchell 1991). Because these industry studies yield mixed results, the authors conclude that order of market entry does not appear to be related to long-term survival rates (see Emerging Empirical Generalization #4).

More recent research by Agarwal and Gort (1996) and Agarwal (1996, 1997) uses *Thomas Register of American Manufacturers* data to examine survival rates in 33 markets. Long time-series data yield a negative relationship between entry by product life cycle stage and survival rates, which supports the importance of first-mover advantages.

In contrast to Agarwal's research, our study relates survival rates to order of market entry. Robinson and Fornell (1985), Robinson (1988), and Lambkin and Day (1989) classify an entrant as a market pioneer, an early follower, or a late entrant. Because Agarwal's research combines market pioneers and early followers in the product life cycle's introductory stage, it is silent in terms of their respective survival rates.

Our study compares survival rates for market pioneers versus early followers but does not examine late entrants. Agarwal's research indicates that late entrants have relatively low survival rates than earlier life cycle stage entrants do. This may arise because late entrants tend to have a relatively low market share (Kalyanaram, Robinson, and Urban 1995), and low market share businesses appear to be more vulnerable to market exit (Caves 1998).[1]

We use the *Thomas Register of American Manufacturers* to develop a broad cross-section of 167 first-entrant market pioneers and 267 early followers. Our random sample covers new markets for manufactured industrial goods.

In contrast to previous research in marketing, our primary conclusion is that market pioneers have significantly higher survival rates than early followers do. This indicates that the pioneer's temporary monopoly and its first-mover advantages tend to offset the survival risks of market pioneering. Therefore, at least for industrial goods, the first to market does not appear to be the first to fail.

A second and less important research contribution examines the impact of pioneer lead time on survival. Brown and Lattin (1994) and Huff and Robinson (1994) show that firstmover advantages are also influenced by pioneer lead time. Consistent with prior research, increasing pioneer lead time tends to increase pioneer survival rates. A new result from our study is that a short delay tends to increase an early follower's survival chance. This can arise when a short delay helps resolve important market and technological uncertainties. However, any further delay tends to decrease early follower survival rates.

Hypotheses

The hypotheses compare market pioneers with early followers in the early years of a market's evolution. Because many forces influence survival, the hypotheses do not directly test a single theoretical mechanism. Instead, they compare the strength of the pioneer's first-mover advantages and pioneer lead time with the combined impact of market and technological uncertainty.

First-Mover Advantages and Survival

Market pioneers typically face the greatest market and technological uncertainties. Market uncertainty arises because it is unusually difficult to forecast sales for a pioneering product. In many cases, market entry is similar to "an archer shooting at a target shrouded by a veil of fog" (Hamel and Prahalad 1994, p. 238). Because an early follower has more time to learn about customer needs and wants, reduced uncertainty should increase its survival chance.

Yip (1982) describes how technological change provides a gateway for entry. Technological change is especially likely to arise during the market's early years. When an early follower has time to obsolete the pioneer's technology, a gateway for entry arises. Again, delayed entry reduces uncertainty, which enhances an early follower's chance of survival.

In summary, conventional discussions of market pioneer survival in the early years of a market's evolution typically emphasize market and technological uncertainties. Memorable phrases reflect the notion that pioneers face the greatest risk. The phrases include "the first to market is the first to fail" and "the market pioneer is the one with the arrows in its back." Because of market and technological uncertainties, conventional wisdom yields the following:

H_1: When pioneer lead time is held constant, market pioneers have a lesser chance than early followers of surviving.

An alternative hypothesis is that first-mover advantages increase the pioneer's survival chance (see Kerin, Varadarajan, and Peterson 1992; Lieberman and Montgomery 1998). Although several first-mover advantages can arise, this literature is typically downplayed in discussions of market pioneer survival.

Some empirical evidence supports the importance of firstmover advantages. In Table 1, Agarwal's (1997) sample covers 33 categories of consumer, industrial, and military products. For entry into various stages of the product life cycle, her introductory stage entrants (Stage 1) have the highest 12-year survival rates. Introductory-stage entrants include both market pioneers and early followers. Assuming that late entry occurs after the early growth stage (Stage 2), late-entrant survival rates are relatively low. Shepherd's (1999) survey of Australian venture capitalists also supports relatively low late entrant survival rates. Therefore, if firstmover advantages more than offset market and technological uncertainties, we have the following:

$H_{1\ alt}$: When pioneer lead time is held constant, market pioneers have a greater chance than early followers of surviving.

Table 1

12-Year Survival Rates by Product Life Cycle Stage
for 33 Product Categories

Product life cycle stage and name	12-year survival rates (%)	Number of entrants
Stage 1: introduction	55.9	238
Stage 2: early growth	48.5	1911
Stage 3: growth	38.4	229
Stage 4: transition to maturity	37.5	431
Stage 5: maturity	45.3	626

Notes: The data are from Agarwal (1997, Table 1). The five life cycle stages are from Gort and Klepper's (1982) model. To link this material to the marketing literature, we have added product life cycle names, such as introduction, early growth, and so forth.

Pioneer Lead Time and Survival

Increasing pioneer lead time should increase the pioneer's chance of survival. A short-term benefit arises from the pioneer's monopoly before the second entrant's arrival. If the market pioneer does not face any competitors, its survival should be easier. A long-term benefit arises because increasing lead time tends to strengthen first-mover advantages (see Brown and Lattin 1994; Huff and Robinson 1994). By lengthening the pioneer's temporary monopoly and strengthening its first-mover advantages, we have the following:

H_2: Increasing pioneer lead time increases the market pioneer's chance of surviving.

Because increasing pioneer lead time makes the pioneer stronger, to the extent that the pioneer and early followers are competing for scarce resources, an early follower's chance of surviving should decrease. By strengthening the pioneer's first-mover advantages, even a short delay hurts an early follower. This yields the following:

H_3: Delayed market entry decreases an early follower's chance of surviving.

An alternative hypothesis for H_3 points to an inverted-U relationship. In the first year or two of the market's evolution, decreased market and technology uncertainties yield substantial benefits for an early follower. If so, a short delay can help an early follower's chance of survival. As time goes by, an early follower's learning yields diminishing marginal returns. With diminished learning and a pioneer that is developing stronger first-mover advantages, a long delay should hurt an early follower's survival chance. This yields the following:

$H_{3\ alt}$: Delayed market entry initially increases an early follower's chance of survival. Any additional delay decreases an early follower's chance of surviving.

Data

The *Thomas Register of American Manufacturers* is a national buying guide that "is a comprehensive, detailed guide to the full range of products manufactured in the United States" (Lavin 1992, p. 129). The *Thomas Register* attempts to achieve comprehensive coverage by subscribing to a broad range of industry newsletters, searching for startup ventures in university incubators, and, last but not least, providing a free listing in each annual issue.[2]

The 1999 *Thomas Register* includes approximately 157,000 firms and roughly 63,700 product categories, so many products have numerous and highly specialized categories. The 1999 *Thomas Register,* for example, lists 128 different types of lights. They range from aircraft lights, airport lights, and aisle lights all the way down to water lights, waterproof lights, and work lights.

Market Boundaries

Thomas Register market boundaries are established by grouping together close product substitutes. The *Thomas Register*'s professional staff does the grouping. Having a professional staff identify new markets helps an academic researcher avoid many subjective decisions—for example, when a new market starts and what competitors should be included in each market. A professional staff also helps gather a large and diverse group of new markets.

One potential danger with the *Thomas Register*'s highly specialized product categories is that the first entrant in a highly specialized category is not a market pioneer. Instead, the first entrant is a late entrant in a broader market, such as lights. Even so, *Thomas Register* market boundaries attempt to reflect how industrial buyers shop for products. Industrial buyers do not just shop for a light, they shop for aircraft lights, airport lights, and aisle lights. Because specialized categories reflect specialized buyer demands, market boundaries are driven by industrial buyers' behavior. In contrast, in the *United States Census of Manufacturers* data, similar production processes often drive the Standard Industrial Classification (SIC) code market boundaries (Scherer and Ross 1990, p. 75).

Some new categories in the *Thomas Register* data are complementary products. Mechanical credit card imprinters, for example, were pioneered in 1962. With only three credit card manufacturers listed in 1960, the credit card market appears to have been in its infancy in the early 1960s. Other new categories represent a new technology, such as distance-measuring instruments, which are electronic devices that were pioneered in 1972. This is the same time period when other electronic devices were first introduced, such as the Bowmar pocket calculator (Schnaars 1994, p. 150).

A *Thomas Register* product category also needs to maintain meaningful product uniqueness over time. Animal access doors, for example, were first listed in 1972. In 1988, 14 firms were listed as manufacturing animal access doors. In 1989, this category was merged into the access doors category, which suggests that general purpose access doors had evolved to the point at which they could also be used for animal access.

Thomas Register Sample

As a national buying guide, the *Thomas Register* typically omits firms with exclusively local sales. (In the past five to ten years, local markets have received more coverage, especially in the *Thomas Regional* directories.) By excluding local markets, our sample emphasizes regional and national markets.

The *Thomas Register* includes international firms if they have a manufacturing facility, office, or distribution channel in the United States. Even so, because the *Thomas Register* highlights U.S. manufacturers, imported manufactured goods are often excluded. Therefore, our sample deletes product categories with a relatively high share of imports.[3]

Food and food-related products are covered in a separate issue, the *Thomas Food Industry Register*. By excluding food and food-related products, our random sample was too small to make accurate inferences about consumer goods. Therefore, our sample covers only industrial goods.

Overall, the *Thomas Register* provides detailed coverage of domestic manufacturing for nonfood products in regional and national markets. Given these strengths and the use of the *Thomas Register* in several survival studies in the economics literature (Agarwal 1996, 1997, 1998; Agarwal and Gort 1996; Gort and Klepper 1982), the data should provide meaningful insights into market pioneer versus early follower survival rates. . . .

Summary

Market pioneers typically face more market and technological uncertainty than early followers and late entrants do. Market uncertainty arises because it is difficult to forecast customer response to a pioneering innovation. Technological uncertainty arises because a pioneer's first-generation technology may not work very well. When an early follower learns from the pioneer's mistakes, its risks are reduced.

However, survival rates for market pioneers are typically enhanced by their temporary monopoly. After their monopoly disappears, market pioneers often benefit from firstmover advantages, such as retaining customer loyalty, setting the industry standard, having superior distribution, and having a broad product line. Although first-mover advantages are discussed in several contexts, conventional survival discussions typically emphasize market and technological uncertainties.

Because market and technological uncertainties are most prominent in the market's early years, survival rates are compared for 167 first entrant market pioneers versus 267 early followers. Across this sample of industrial goods businesses, market pioneers have significantly higher five- and ten-year survival rates than early followers do. Results from a logit regression analysis suggest that pioneers' first-mover advantages more than offset the market and technological uncertainties. Market pioneers' survival also tends to increase as their lead time over the first early follower increases. Increasing lead time gives the pioneers a longer temporary monopoly, which makes survival easier and should help strengthen their first-mover advantages.

In the early years of a market's evolution, an early follower's learning from a short delay can help its chance of survival. The data support this point in the sense that delayed entry initially increases but eventually decreases an early follower's chance of survival. This suggests that an early follower's learning from a short delay resolves a material amount of uncertainty. A longer delay, though, can hurt an early follower when additional learning is modest and the pioneer is getting stronger and stronger over time.

Limitations and Further Research

Because the *Thomas Register* has relatively narrow market boundaries, market and technological uncertainty should be lower than in broadly defined markets. This is because new markets with relatively narrow boundaries often extend existing knowledge on markets and technologies. Even so, first-mover advantages should also be weaker in markets with narrow boundaries. Therefore, research should examine the extent to which survival rates are influenced by market boundary breadth.

Our sample covers only industrial goods. Would similar results arise in markets for consumer goods? Services? High-technology products? Because market uncertainties, technological uncertainties, and first-mover advantages can vary dramatically across different types of markets, further research should examine the robustness of higher pioneer survival rates across various industry settings.

Risks of Market Pioneering

Absolute survival rates are strongly influenced by the scale of commercialization. A *Thomas Register* entrant only needs to sell its product in a regional market. In Golder and Tellis's (1993) study, a pioneer only needs to sell its product in a local market.[4] In Urban and colleagues' (1986) study, an entrant must sell its product nationally. By excluding small entrants that failed to achieve a national scope, Urban and colleagues' sample yields higher pioneer survival rates. This helps explain why Urban and colleagues (1986, p. 655) did not locate any market pioneer exits, whereas our study and Golder and Tellis's (1993) report market pioneer survival rates in the 53% to 87% range.

From this perspective, three key steps arise in the market entry process: (1) investing in the attempt to enter a new market, (2) entering the market on a local or regional scale, and (3) expanding to a national scale. Our results, along with those of Urban and colleagues (1986), suggest that when a regional or national scale of operations is achieved, survival rates tend to be higher for market pioneers than for early followers.

In the market entry process, empirical research has not yet linked order of market entry to the survival rate for firms that are attempting to pioneer a new market. We speculate that this is where the greatest risk arises for market pioneer hopefuls, because it is difficult to generate and commercialize an idea that will pioneer a new market.

To address these problems, Hamel and Prahalad (1994, Ch. 11) recommend experimenting with multiple options that are both fast and inexpensive. Although experimentation leads to many small failures, perhaps nine of every ten attempts, these small losses are easily offset by the large gains from pioneering new markets of the future. Thus, a market pioneering strategy has both high risks and high returns, and the greatest risk of failure arises before product launch.

Conclusion

Conventional wisdom on market pioneer survival highlights market and technological uncertainties. Although market pioneers face the greatest uncertainties, they also benefit from first-mover advantages and from the temporary monopoly that arises before they face the first early follower. For our sample of 167 industrial goods markets, market pioneer first-mover advantages plus their temporary monopoly more than offset these market and technological uncertainties. In showing that pioneers often survive past the early and turbulent years of a market's evolution, our results are consistent with Shepherd's (1999) recent survey of Australian venture capitalists. Both studies indicate that the first to market is typically not the first to fail.

Notes

1. Also, in the *Thomas Register* data, it is not always clear when an entrant shifts from being an early follower to being a late entrant, so it is often difficult to identify a late entrant objectively.
2. Many of the data insights are based on telephone conversations and e-mail communications with Glenn H. Moore, Associate Publisher/Editor of the *Thomas Register.*
3. To estimate the market share of imported goods, data from the *United States Census of Manufacturers* at the four-digit SIC code level estimate the ratio of imports divided by domestic shipments less exports plus imports. Because a natural break in our sample arises between 33% and 40%, our sample excludes the 13 import-oriented markets that exceed 33%.
4. Golder and Tellis's (1993) data include local markets, such as the Brooklyn, N.Y., market for Trommer's Red-Letter light beer. As mentioned previously, the *Thomas Register* excludes most but not all local markets.

References

Agarwal, Rajshree (1996), "Technological Activity and Survival of Firms," *Economics Letters,* 52 (July), 101–108.

⸻ (1997), "Survival of Firms over the Product Life Cycle," *Southern Economic Journal,* 63 (3), 571–84.

⸻ (1998), "Evolutionary Trends of Industry Variables," *International Journal of Industrial Organization,* 16 (July), 511–25.

—— and Michael Gort (1996), "The Evolution of Markets and Entry, Exit, and survival of Firms," *Review of Economics and Statistics,* 78 (November), 489–98.

Brown, Christina and James M. Lattin (1994), "Investigating the Relationship Between Time in Market and Pioneering Advantage," *Management Science,* 40 (October), 1361–69.

Caves, Richard E. (1998), "Industrial Organization and New Findings on the Turnover and Mobility of Firms," *Journal of Economic Literature,* 36 (December), 1947–82.

Dunne, Timothy, Mark J. Roberts, and Larry Samuelson (1989), "Patterns of Firm Entry and Exit in U.S. Manufacturing Industries," *RAND Journal of Economics,* 19 (Winter), 495–515.

Glazer, A. (1985), "The Advantages of Being First," *American Economic Review,* 75 (June), 473–80.

Golder, Peter N. and Gerard J. Tellis (1993), "Pioneer Advantage: Marketing Logic or Marketing Legend?" *Journal of Marketing Research,* 30 (May), 158–70.

Gort, Michael and Steven Klepper (1982), "Time Paths in the Diffusion of Product Innovations," *Economic Journal,* 92 (September), 630–53.

Griffin, Abbie (1997), "PDMA Research on New Product Development Practices: Updating Trends and Benchmarking Best Practices," *Journal of Product Innovation Management,* 6 (November), 429–58.

Hadlock, Paul, Daniel Hecker, and Joseph Gannon (1991), "High Technology Employment: Another View," *Monthly Labor Review,* 114 (July), 26–30.

Hamel, Gary and C.K. Prahalad (1994), *Competing for the Future.* Boston, MA: Harvard Business School Press.

Huff, Lenard C. and William T. Robinson (1994), "The Impact of Leadtime and Years of Competitive Rivalry on Pioneer Market Share Advantages," *Management Science,* 40 (October), 1370–77.

Kalyanaram, Gurumurthy, William T. Robinson, and Glen L. Urban (1995), "Order of Market Entry: Established Empirical Generalizations, Emerging Generalizations, and Future Research," *Marketing Science,* 14 (2), G212–G221.

—— and Glen L. Urban (1992), "Dynamic Effects of Order of Entry on Market Share, Trial Penetration, and Repeat Purchases for Frequently Purchased Goods," *Marketing Science,* 11 (Summer), 235–50.

Kerin, Roger A., P. Rajan Varadarajan, and Robert A. Peterson (1992), "First-Mover Advantage: A Synthesis, Conceptual Framework, and Research Propositions," *Journal of Marketing,* 56 (October), 33–52.

Lambkin, Mary and George S. Day (1989), "Evolutionary Processes in Competitive Markets: Beyond the Product Life Cycle," *Journal of Marketing,* 3 (July), 4–20.

Lavin, Michael R. (1992), *Business Information: How to Find It, How to Use It.* Phoenix: Oryx Press.

Lieberman, Marvin B. (1989), "The Learning Curve, Technological Barriers to Entry, and Competitive Survival in the Chemical Processing Industries," *Strategic Management Journal,* 9 (Summer), 431–47.

—— and David B. Montgomery (1998), "First-Mover (Dis)Advantages: Retrospective and Link with the Resource-Based View," *Strategic Management Journal,* 19 (December), 1111–25.

Mitchell. W. (1991), "Dual Clocks: Entry Order Influences on Incumbent and New-comer Market Share and Survival When Specialized Assets Retain Their Value," *Strategic Management Journal,* 12 (January/February), 85–100.

Robinson, William T. (1988), "Sources of Market Pioneer Advantage: The Case of Industrial Goods Industries," *Journal of Marketing Research,* 25 (February), 87–94.

—— and Claes Fornell (1985), "Sources of Market Pioneer Advantage in Con-sumer Goods Industries," *Journal of Marketing Research,* 22 (August), 305–17.

Scherer, F. M. and David Ross (1990), *Industrial Market Structure and Economic Performance,* 3d ed. Boston: Houghton Mifflin.

Schmalensee, Richard (1982), "Product Differentiation Advantages of Pioneering Brands," *American Economic Review,* 27 (June), 349–65.

Schnaars, Steven P. (1994), *Managing Imitation Strategies.* New York: The Free Press.

Shepherd, Dean A. (1999), "Venture Capitalists' Assessment of New Venture Survival," *Management Science,* 45 (May), 621–32.

Sullivan, Mary W. (1992), "The Effect of Brand Extension and Other Entry Decisions on Survival Time," working paper, Graduate School of Business, University of Chicago (June).

Tellis, Gerard J. and Peter N. Golder (1996), "First to Market, First to Fail? Real Causes of Enduring Market Leadership," *Sloan Management Review,* 37 (Winter), 65–75.

Urban, Glen L., Theresa Carter, Steven Gaskin, and Zofia Mucha (1986), "Market Share Rewards to Pioneering Brands: An Empirical Analysis and Strategic Implications," *Management Science,* 32 (June), 645–59.

Whitten, Ira T. (1979), *Brand Performance in the Cigarette Industry and the Advan-tages of Early Entry, 1913–73.* Washington, DC: Federal Trade Commission.

Yip, George S. (1982), *Barriers to Entry: A Corporate-Strategy Perspective.* Lexington, MA: Lexington Books.

**William Boulding and
Markus Christen**

Sustainable Pioneering Advantage? Profit Implications of Market Entry Order

There is strong theoretical and empirical evidence supporting the idea that "first-to-market" leads to an enduring market share advantage. In sharp contrast to these findings, we find that at the business unit level being first-to-market leads, on average, to a long-term *profit disadvantage*. This result holds for a sample of consumer goods as well as a sample of industrial goods and leads to questions about the validity of first mover advantage, in and of itself, as a strategy to achieve superior performance. . . .

Introduction

"First mover advantage" is an oft-cited strategic principle for achieving superior performance. This principle is often high on managers' list of arguments to justify strategic moves such as, for example, the entry into emerging markets such as China, or the recent rush into e-business. Moreover, an impressive body of research in marketing, strategy and economics supports the validity of this principle. For example, at both the business unit level and the brand level, a strong inverse relationship between order of market entry and long-run market share has been found (e.g., Robinson and Fornell 1985, Urban et al. 1986). Empirical evidence is so extensive that this relationship exists as an "empirical generalization" in the marketing literature (Kalyanaram et al. 1995). At the consumer level, experiments have shown that the order of entry can have a significant impact on customer preferences, memory, learning, and judgment (Carpenter and Nakamoto 1989, Kardes and Kalyanaram 1992, Zhang and Markman 1998).

Surprisingly, there exists virtually no empirical research about the effect of entry order on business profit, even though reviews of the entry order literature have repeatedly pointed to profit implications as one of the key unanswered questions in this area of research (Lieberman and Montgomery 1988, 1998; Kerin et al. 1992; Robinson et al. 1994).[1] Whether a market share advantage is sufficient to support the existence of a sustainable profit advantage is questionable given the uncertainties in both the market share-profit relationship

From *Marketing Science,* vol. 22, no. 3, Summer 2003, pp. 371–386. Copyright © 2003 by Institute for Operations Research and the Management Sciences. Reprinted by permission.

(e.g., Jacobson 1988, Boulding and Staelin 1993) and the entry order-cost relationship (Lieberman and Montgomery 1988).

The main objective of this paper is to address this gap in the literature and empirically examine the long-term profit implications of the order of market entry for a *business unit*. Consistent with the existing literature, we focus on the long-term consequences to identify whether profit differences persist even after competitive entry. A significant difference would suggest, for example, that part of today's profit difference in cola beverages between the Coca-Cola Company and PepsiCo could be attributed to the fact that the former created the cola market about 10 years before the latter entered. Our analysis, therefore, provides insights about the profit implications of entry order strategies.

To be precise, our interest is in looking at profit differences between pioneers and followers solely attributable to the timing of market entry, and not differences due to other characteristics (e.g., resources) of pioneers and followers. In all likelihood, these differences exist because, as first noted by Lieberman and Montgomery (1988), firms' resources and capabilities affect their choice of entry timing. That is, entry timing is an endogenous choice variable. For example, Sony generally tries to create new markets, while Matsushita pursues a strategy of following Sony into these markets. Therefore, Sony and Matsushita likely differ in ways that reflect the difference in their market entry strategies. More formally, the resource-based-view literature (e.g., Wernerfelt 1984, Barney 1986) suggests that an enduring competitive advantage must be due to differences in underlying resources. This literature is explicit in stating that there can be *no* pioneering advantage without heterogeneity in resources across firms (Barney 1991), and empirical research supports the presence of systematic firm differences associated with entry strategies (Robinson et al. 1992, Murthi et al. 1996). . . .

We start our analysis by determining the effect of entry order on profit for an average business unit. For two samples of business units derived from the PIMS database—a sample of consumer goods and a sample of industrial goods—we find a *long-term profit disadvantage of pioneering* for the average business unit. This result holds for both net income and ROI when used as measures of business unit profit. Given the strong evidence in the literature for the existence of a long-term demand-side advantage, this profit result implies that first-to-market must lead to a long-term average cost disadvantage. Thus, for both samples and with the same estimation methodology, we estimate the effect of entry order on demand and average cost, i.e., the economic components of profit, and find strong support for this conjecture. Pioneering leads to a long-term demand advantage and an even larger long-term cost disadvantage. We test the robustness of these results by varying the model specification and the instruments used to obtain consistent estimates. This sensitivity analysis strongly confirms the long-term profit disadvantage due to an average cost disadvantage.

We then examine conditions for which a pioneering profit advantage can exist. First, given the long-term profit disadvantage, it appears that pioneering a new market makes sense for the average business only if an early profit advantage exists (assuming rational decision making). We therefore examine the time path of profits for pioneers and find, for both samples and profit measures, an initial profit advantage, which decreases over time and turns into a disadvantage after 12 to 14 years. Second, we examine the moderating effect on the long-term profit difference for three factors: the likelihood of customer learning, the market share position of a business unit, and the presence of patent protection. Based on the existing literature, we hypothesize that these factors enable pioneering firms to avert the long-term profit disadvantage or even sustain a profit advantage.

In sum, this paper provides the first detailed empirical analysis of the profit implications of the order of market entry at the business unit level. . . .

Pioneering Advantages and Disadvantages

An extensive theoretical and empirical literature investigates the effects of the market entry order. This literature has been well summarized in various review articles (Lieberman and Montgomery 1988, Kerin et al. 1992, Robinson et al 1994, Kalyanaram et al. 1995). Rather than repeat these findings, we very briefly point to two findings of relevance to the research herein.

First, as noted, there is an extensive list of theoretical arguments in favor of a pioneering demand advantage. These theoretical arguments are supported by strong empirical evidence, including findings based on experiments that are not subject to methodological problems raised in the literature (see Golder and Tellis 1993). Second, there is no unambiguous theoretical prediction about the effect of entry order on cost. The literature points to possible advantages due to patents, accumulation of experience, and preemption of scarce resources. At the same time, the literature also points to possible disadvantages due to followers' ability to free ride on information and market building efforts and incumbent inertia. Further, in contrast to the empirical generalization of a pioneering market share (demand) advantage (Kalyanaram et al. 1995), there is no systematic empirical evidence with respect to the effect of entry order on cost. Because of this ambiguity in the effects of entry order on cost, the effect of entry order on overall profit is also uncertain, and we next consider two possible profit scenarios.

Entry Order Profit Scenarios

We propose two possible profit scenarios capture the current state of knowledge about pioneering effects, i.e., a demand advantage and an ambiguous cost effect.[2] Under the first scenario, we assume that motivation to enter first is driven by the likelihood of obtaining the "known" demand-side advantage, an advantage shown in both theoretical and empirical work. As argued in the strategy literature (e.g., Wensley 1982, Erickson and Jacobson 1992), if knowledge about a strategic relationship exists, (e.g., first entrants are more profitable), then without what Wensley refers to as "isolating mechanisms," firms will compete away the returns implied by this relationship. Thus, knowledge about a demand-side pioneering advantage could lead to a race to entry that competes away this advantage through cost disadvantages. In sum, this scenario argues for a demand advantage, a cost disadvantage, and no significant long-term profit differences due to the order of market entry.

This same profit prediction emerges from the resource-based view of the firm. Given this view strategic actions like the decision to create a new market are contingent on business unit resources. Thus, there can be no sustainable advantage to the entry strategy, per se, unless firms have inimitable resources, because the entry strategy itself is perfectly imitable (Barney 1991). Consequently, after controlling for resource differences across firms (as we do in our empirical analysis), there should be no effect of entry order on profit. Importantly, if entry choices are driven by differences in firm resources, the market entry order must be an endogenous decision.

In addition to a sustainable demand advantage, the first entrant can also benefit from a period of monopoly profits that are eroded over time as later entrants make inroads. However, if in fact competition dissipates differences in lifetime profits due to entry order, this leads to an interesting prediction. Specifically, we should observe an initial profit advantage for the pioneering firm that is offset by a profit disadvantage in later years. While profit differences can exist at any given point in time, dissipation of economic rents should occur over time and there should be no lifetime profit differences due to entry order. . . .

Discussion

. . . Contrary to common expectations, our results show that, on average, *first-to-market leads to a long-term profit disadvantage relative to later entrants*. We replicate, in an economic framework, the well-established consumerbased *long-term demand advantage*, and show that first-to-market leads to an *even larger long-term average cost disadvantage*. These results hold for a sample of business units selling consumer goods as well as for a sample of business units selling industrial goods. . . .

In the extended analysis we provide evidence of two kinds of pioneering profit advantage. First, we show that for both data samples pioneering leads to an *initial profit advantage that erodes over time*. The advantage lasts for about 12 to 14 years. Second, we show that the likelihood of customer learning, the market share position of a business, and patent protection—product patents for consumer goods and process patents for industrial goods—moderate the long-term profit effect of entry order. The moderating effects tend to be stronger for the consumer goods sample, where *limited customer learning, a strong market share position, or patent protection can eliminate the long-term profit disadvantage and even lead to a sustainable pioneering profit advantage*. Future research should focus on identifying other conditions and specific firm resources that moderate the effect of market entry order. . . .

What are the managerial implications of our findings? First, the presence of a long-term profit disadvantage does not mean that a pioneering strategy is strictly unprofitable. It means that in the long run, entering a market later is, on average, more profitable than pioneering. Thus, it would be incorrect to predicate an entry strategy on the sustainability of profits by being first to market. In this regard, it would be interesting to know what exactly managers expect when they pursue a strategy of being first-to-market.

Second, the worries of firms like Procter & Gamble that have not created new markets in a long time and instead rely on the profits from existing "pioneering" brands in well-established markets could be justified (Jarvis 2000). The initial profit advantage that appears to last little over a decade suggests that firms may be better off pursuing a strategy that continuously creates new markets.

Third, pioneering firms may be able to benefit by paying closer attention to later entrants and in particular to their organization and processes, which yield lower average costs. In this regard, more theoretical and empirical work is needed to understand the relationship between entry order and costs beyond average cost. . . .

In sum then, while we believe our empirical findings provide new insights, many unanswered questions remain for future research. Still, we believe our empirical findings cast doubt on the basic strategic principle of "first mover advantage." When managers articulate and evaluate an entry timing strategy, we urge that consideration be given to precisely why and how the strategy will provide a sustainable advantage. . . .

Notes

1. Unpublished work (Boulding and Moore 1987, Srinivasan 1988) suggests that pioneering does not provide a profit advantage.

2. To be complete, one could posit a pioneering profit disadvantage, which could be explained by two different effects. First, an ex-ante overvaluation of the demand advantage could lead to overspending to obtain this advantage (i.e., the winner's curse). Second, loss aversion could lead to an ex-post overvaluation of the demand advantage and overspending to defend market share in the face of competitive entry. This could happen if the pioneer's initial market share provides the reference point and changes in market share after competitive entry fall in the loss domain.

References

Barney, Jay B. 1986. Strategic factor markets: Expectations, luck, and business strategy. *Management Sci.* **32** 1231–1241.

———. 1991. Firm resources and competitive advantage. *J. Management* **17**(1) 99–120.

Boulding, William. 1990. Unobservable effects and business performance: Do fixed effects matter? *Marketing Sci.* **9**(Winter) 88–91.

———, Michael J. Moore. 1987. Pioneering and profit: Structural estimates from a nonlinear simultaneous equations model with endogenous pioneering. Working paper, Fuqua School of Business, Duke University, Durham, NC.

———, Richard Staelin. 1993. A look on the cost side: Market share and the competitive environment. *Marketing Sci.* **12**(Spring) 144–166.

Carpenter, Gregory S., Kent Nakamoto. 1989. Consumer preference formation and pioneering advantage. *J. Marketing Res.* **26**(August) 285–298.

Erickson, Gary, Robert Jacobson. 1992. Gaining comparative advantage through discretionary expenditures: The returns to R&D and advertising. *Management Sci.* **38**(September) 1264–1279.

Golder, Peter N., Gerard J. Tellis. 1993. Pioneering advantage: Marketing logic or marketing legend? *J. Marketing Res.* **30**(May) 158–170.

Jacobson, Robert. 1988. Distinguishing among competing theories of the market share effect. *J. Marketing* 9(October) 68–80.

Jarvis, Steve. 2000. P&G's challenge. *Marketing News.* August 28. 1 13.

Kalyanaram, Gurumurthy, William T. Robinson, Glen L. Urban. 1995. Order of market entry: Established empirical generalizations, emerging empirical generalizations, and future research. *Marketing Sci.* 14(2) G212–G221.

Kardes, Frank R., Gurumurthy Kalyanaram. 1992. Order-of-entry effects on consumer memory and judgment: An information integration perspective. *J. Marketing Res.* 29(August) 343–357.

Kerin, Roger A., P. Rajan Varadarajan, Robert A. Peterson. 1992. First-mover advantage: A synthesis, conceptual framework, and research propositions. *J. Marketing* 56(October) 33–52.

Lieberman, Marvin B., David B. Montgomery. 1988. First-mover advantages. *Strategic Management J.* 9(Summer) 41–58.

Murthi, B. P. S., Kannan Srinivasan, Gurumurthy Kalyanaram. 1996. Controlling for observed and unobserved managerial skills in determining first-mover market share advantages. *J. Marketing Res.* 33(August) 329–336.

Robinson, William T. 1988. Sources of market pioneer advantages: The case of industrial goods industries. *J. Marketing Res.* 25(February) 87–94.

———, Claes Fornell. 1985. Sources of market pioneer advantages in consumer goods industries. *J. Marketing Res.* 22(August) 305–317.

———, ———, Mary W. Sullivan. 1992. Are market pioneers intrinsically stronger than later entrants? *Strategic Management J.* 13(November) 609–624.

———, Gurumurthy Kalyanaram, Glen L. Urban. 1994. First-mover advantages from pioneering new markets: A survey of empirical evidence. *Rev. Indust. Organ.* 9(February) 1–23.

Srinivasan, Kannan. 1988. Pioneering versus early following in new product markets. Unpublished Ph.D. dissertation, University of California, Los Angeles, CA.

Urban, Glen L., Theresa Carter, Steven P. Gaskin, Zo.a Mucha. 1986. Market share rewards to pioneering brands: An empirical analysis and strategic implications. *Management Sci.* 32(June) 645–659.

Wernerfelt, Birger. 1984. A resource-based view of the firm. *Strategic Management J.* 5 171–180.

Wensley, Robin. 1982. PIMS and BCG: New horizons or false dawn. *Strategic Management J.* 3(April–June) 147–158.

Zhang, Shi, Arthur B. Markman. 1998. Overcoming the early entrant advantage: The role of alignable and nonalignable differences. *J. Marketing Res.* 35(November) 413–426.

POSTSCRIPT

Is First-to-Market a Successful Strategy?

Determining when to enter a market is a critical decision faced by virtually all corporations at some point in their existence. This is particularly true in today's fast-paced business environment where innovation and technological advancement are virtually mandatory. But when to enter? Should a firm strive to be first with a new product or service or should it avoid the accompanying risks and act as a follower? The two articles comprising the debate presented here offer opposing views on these questions.

In a study that supports the first-to-market strategy, William Robinson and Sunwook Min questioned whether there might too much focus on the risk of failure and not enough on the advantages that come from first moving. Their work examined the strategic moves of 167 companies that were first-to-market and 267 companies that were early-to-follow in industrial goods businesses. They concluded that advantages of being first-to-market are greater than the risks and uncertainties faced by the firm. Did you find their arguments and research findings persuasive enough to convince you that first-to-market is a successful strategy?

However, before you commit yourself, ponder the findings of the research discussed in the "Con" side article by William Boulding and Markus Christen. There is no doubt that their findings cast serious doubt on the effectiveness of moving first in securing performance gains, at least in the long-run. In a study of both consumer and industrial goods corporations, the two marketing researchers asked the question of whether or not the order of market entry affects firm performance. They provide evidence that being first actually results in "long-term profit disadvantage," a result that flies directly in the face of the conventional belief that first-moving is a wise and desirable corporate strategy.

Both articles presented here provided insightful analysis concerning the first-to-market strategy. So, given what you have just read, do you think that being first-to market is a successful strategy?

Suggested Readings

William T. Robinson and Jeongwen Chiang (2002), "Product Development Strategies for Established Market Pioneers, Early Followers, and Late Entrants," *Strategic Management Journal*, 23, 855–866.

Fernando Suarez and Gianvito Lanzolla (2005). The half-truth to first-mover advantage. *Havard Business Review*, April 2005, p. 121.

Gary Hamel (2001). Inside the revolution: Smart mover, dumb mover. *Fortune,* September 3, 2001.

William Boulding and Markus Christen (2001). First-mover disadvantage. *Harvard Business Review,* October 2001, p. 20.

Marvin Lieberman and David Montgomery (1998). First-mover (dis)advantages: Retrospective and link with the resource-based view. *Strategic Management Journal,* 19, 1111–1125.

David Ketchen, Charles Snow, and Vera Street (2004). Improving firm performance by matching strategic decision-making processes to competitive dynamics. *Academy of Management Executive,* 18, 29–43.

ISSUE 14

Must Firms Constantly Grow to Be Considered Successful?

YES: Clayton M. Christensen and Michael E. Raynor, from *The Innovator's Solution* (Harvard Business School Press, 2005)

NO: Jim Mackey and Liisa Välikangas, from "The Myth of Unbounded Growth," *MIT Sloan Management Review* (Winter 2004)

ISSUE SUMMARY

YES: Clayton M. Christensen and Michael E. Raynor argue that firms are subject to pressures to continually grow from sources both inside and outside of the organization.

NO: Business scholars Jim Mackey and Liisa Välikangas cite many interesting statistics to support the view that lasting growth is elusive and unrealistic and, thus, not necessary to define a firm as successful.

Open any business periodical nowadays and you might expect to see headlines like these from recent editions of the *Wall Street Journal:*

> "Caterpillar Gets Bugs Out of Old Equipment; Growing Remanufacturing Division Is Central to Earnings-Stabilization Plan" (July 5, 2006, pg. A.16)
>
> "Changing the Light Bulb; No Joke: LED Technology Fuels Fast Growth in the Once-Staid Industry" (June 8, 2006, pg. B.1)
>
> "Churchill Downs Searches for Growth" (May 24, 2006, pg. B.3A)

What do these headlines have in common? If you noticed each assumes that corporate growth is a good and necessary strategy, kudos to you. Without a doubt growth can be beneficial for both corporations and society at large. Indeed, Caterpillar found that growth in remanufacturing was beneficial even when the economy was down, and the lighting industry is brightening up because of growth in the light-emitting diodes market.

On the other hand, it is also true that sustained growth is a difficult and elusive goal. For instance, consider these recent *Wall Street Journal* headlines:

"Cadbury Schwepps PLC: Margin-Growth Target Stifled by Rising Energy Costs" (June 8, 2006, pg. n/a)

"Telenor's Messy Excursion in Russia Shows Pitfalls of Hunting for Growth" (July 7, 2006, pg. C.1)

Both of these articles detail problems resulting from strategic decisions driven by the need for growth. In fact, many business observers suggest that such predicaments seem to be the rule rather than the exception for companies attempting a growth strategy. This leaves us with the current debate where we ask—Must firms constantly grow to be considered successful?

Clayton M. Christensen and Michael E. Raynor argue that pressures to meet this "growth imperative" come from both inside and outside of the organization. Externally, the perpetuation of this imperative is largely fueled by shareholders who expect to see value created through growth. These expectations for growth are built in to the stock market's valuation of a company's stock. Indeed, if a firm fails to meet its expectations for growth—typically reflected in lower than anticipated earnings—the company will take a beating in the stock market. Moreover, if a company does meet its expectations for growth, it is often rewarded with even higher growth expectations for the future. And, although a company's main demand for growth may be from its shareholders, this is certainly not the only source of pressure the company needs to recognize. Typically, in a growing company, employees will expect that they will have opportunities to move up and gain better positions for themselves. In this manner, employees also demand growth. Thus, it is not surprising that most top-level executives consider growth as the dominant, underlying goal of the organization.

But what about the other side of the debate? Isn't it possible that the continuous, unbounded growth companies and investors hope for is really just a "myth" for most firms? This is the claim of the article by Jim Mackey and Liisa Välikangas. They cite many interesting statistics to support the view that lasting growth is elusive and unrealistic. Further, they argue, such growth is not only elusive, but can be very costly, particularly if the firm is currently not in a growth phase. To illustrate their point, Mackey and Välikangas state, "When stalled companies make massive investments in an attempt to return to double-digit growth, it seems analogous to spending life savings on a lottery ticket" (p. 90). Furthermore, although the company may experience resistance from investors and other stakeholders interested in corporate growth, there are other nongrowth options available that firms should consider as legitimate, realistic alternative business behaviors. Nevertheless, Mackey and Välikangas concede that the attitude in today's environment is toward propagating growth and warn investors, CEOs, and employees alike to be wary of potential pitfalls that may accompany a growth strategy. Their advice is wise, and we recommend it to you next time you pick up a business journal, read a headline about a company failing to meet its growth expectations, and conclude that the firm is failing.

271

YES

Clayton M. Christensen and
Michael E. Raynor

The Growth Imperative

Growth is important because companies create shareholder value through profitable growth. Yet there is powerful evidence that once a company's core business has matured, the pursuit of new platforms for growth entails daunting risk. Roughly one company in ten is able to sustain the kind of growth that translates into an above-average increase in shareholder returns over more than a few years.[1] Too often the very attempt to grow causes the entire corporation to crash. Consequently, most executives are in a no-win situation: equity markets demand that they grow, but it's hard to know *how* to grow. Pursuing growth the wrong way can be worse than no growth at all.

Consider AT&T. In the wake of the government-mandated divestiture of its local telephony services in 1984, AT&T became primarily a long distance telecommunications services provider. The break-up agreement freed the company to invest in new businesses, so management almost immediately began seeking avenues for growth and the shareholder value that growth creates.

The first such attempt arose from a widely shared view that computer systems and telephone networks were going to converge. AT&T first tried to build its own computer division in order to position itself at that intersection, but was able to do no better than annual losses of $200 million. Rather than retreat from a business that had proved to be unassailable from the outside, the company decided in 1991 to bet bigger still, acquiring NCR, at the time the world's fifth-largest computer maker, for $7.4 billion. That proved only to be a down payment: AT&T lost another $2 billion trying to make the acquisition work. AT&T finally abandoned this growth vision in 1996, selling NCR for $3.4 billion, about a third of what it had invested in the opportunity.

But the company *had* to grow. So even as the NCR acquisition was failing, AT&T was seeking growth opportunities in technologies closer to its core. In light of the success of the wireless services that several of its spun-off local telephone companies had achieved, in 1994 the company bought McCaw Cellular, at the time the largest national wireless carrier in the United States, for $11.6 billion, eventually spending $15 billion in total on its own wireless business. When Wall Street analysts subsequently complained that they were unable to properly value the combined higher-growth wireless business within the lower-growth wireline company, AT&T decided to create a separately traded stock for the wireless business in 2000. This valued the business at $10.6 billion, about two-thirds of the investment AT&T had made in the venture.

But that move left the AT&T wireline stock right where it had started, and the company *had* to grow. So in 1998 it embarked upon a strategy to enter and reinvent the local telephony business with broadband technology. Acquiring TCI and MediaOne for a combined price of $112 billion made AT&T Broadband the largest cable operator in the United States. Then, more quickly than anyone could have foreseen, the difficulties in implementation and integration proved insurmountable. In 2000, AT&T agreed, to sell its cable assets to Comcast for $72 billion.[2]

In the space of a little over ten years, AT&T had wasted about $50 billion and destroyed even more in shareholder value—all in the hope of *creating* shareholder value through growth.

The bad news is that AT&T is not a special case. Consider Cabot Corporation, the world's major producer of carbon black, a compound that imparts to products such as tires many of their most important properties. This business has long been very strong, but the e markets haven't grown rapidly. To create the growth that builds shareholder value, Cabot's executives in the early 1980s launched several aggressive growth initiatives in advanced materials, acquiring a set of promising specialty metals and high-tech ceramics businesses. These constituted operating platforms into which the company would infuse new process and materials technology that was emerging from own research laboratories and work it had sponsored at MIT.

Wall Street greeted these investments to accelerate Cabot's growth trajectory with enthusiasm and drove the company's share price to triple the level at which it had languished prior to these initiatives. But as the losses created by Cabot's investments in these businesses began to drag the entire corporation's earnings down, Wall Street hammered the stock. While the overall market appreciated at a robust rate between 1988 and 1991, Cabot's shares dropped by more than half. In the early 1990s, feeling pressure to boost earnings, Cabot's board brought in new management whose mandate was to shut down the new businesses and refocus on the core. As Cabot's profitability rebounded, Wall Street enthusiastically doubled the company's share price. The problem, of course, was that this turnaround left the new management team no better off than their predecessors: desperately seeking growth opportunities for mature businesses with limited prospects.[3]

We could cite many cases of companies' similar attempts to create new-growth platforms after the core business had matured. They follow an all-too-similar pattern. When the core business approaches maturity and investors demand new growth, executives develop seemingly sensible strategies to generate it. Although they invest aggressively, their plans fail to create the needed growth fast enough; investors hammer the stock; management is sacked; and Wall Street rewards the new executive team for simply restoring the *status quo ante:* a profitable but low-growth core business.[4]

Even expanding firms face a variant of the growth imperative. No matter how fast the growth treadmill is going, it is not fast enough. The reason: Investors have a pesky tendency to discount into the *present* value of a company's stock price whatever rate of growth they *foresee* the company achieving. Thus, even if a company's core business is growing vigorously, the only way its managers can deliver a rate of return to shareholders in the future that exceeds the risk-adjusted market average is to grow *faster* than shareholders expect. Changes in stock prices are driven not by simply the *direction* of growth, but largely by *unexpected* changes in the *rate of change* in a company's earnings and cash flows. Hence, one company that is projected to grow at 5 percent and in fact keeps growing at 5 percent and another company that is projected to grow at 25 percent and delivers 25 percent growth will both produce for future investors a market-average risk-adjusted rate of return in the future.[5] A company must deliver the rate of growth that the market is projecting just to keep its stock price from falling. It must *exceed* the consensus forecast rate of growth in order to boost its share price. This is a heavy, omnipresent burden on every executive who is sensitive to enhancing shareholder value.[6]

It's actually even harder than this. That canny horde of investors not only discounts the expected rate of growth of a company's *existing* businesses into the present value of its stock price, but also discounts the growth from new, yet-to-be-established lines of business that they expect the management team to be able to create in the future. The magnitude of the market's bet on growth from unknown sources is, in general, based on the company's track record. If the market has been impressed with a company's historical ability to leverage its strengths to generate new lines of business, then the component of its stock price based on growth from unknown sources will be large. If a company's past efforts to create new-growth businesses have not borne fruit, then its market valuation will be dominated by the projected cash flow from known, established businesses.

Table 1-1 presents one consulting firm's analysis of the share prices of a select number of *Fortune 500* companies, showing the proportion of each firm's share price or. August 21, 2002, that was attributable to cash generated by existing assets, versus cash that investors expected to be generated by new investments.[7] Of this sample, the company that was on the hook at that time to generate the largest percentage of its total growth from future investments was Dell Computer. Only 22 percent of its share price of $28.05 was justified by cash thrown off by the company's present assets, whereas 78 percent of Dell's valuation reflected investors' confidence that the company would be able to invest in new assets that would generate whopping amounts of cash. Sixty-six percent of Johnson & Johnson's market valuation and 37 percent of Home Depot's valuation were grounded in expectations of growth from yet-to-be-made investments. These companies were on the hook for *big* numbers. On the other hand, only 5 percent of General Motors's stock price on that date was predicated on future investments. Although that's a chilling reflection of the track record of GM's former management in creating new-growth businesses, it means that if the present management team does a better job, the company's share price could respond handsomely.

Probably the most daunting challenge in delivering growth is that if you fail once to deliver it, the odds that you ever will be able to deliver in the future are very low. This is the conclusion of a remarkable study, *Stall Points* that the

Table 1-1

Portion of Selected Firms' Market Value That Was Based on Expected Returns from New Investments on August 21, 2002

Fortune 500 rank	Company name	Share price	Percent of Valuation That Was Based on:	
			New investments	Existing assets
53	Dell Computer	$28.05	78%	22%
47	Johnson & Johnson	$56.20	66%	34%
35	Procter & Gamble	$90.76	62%	38%
6	Genaral Electric	$32.80	60%	40%
77	Lockheed Martin	$62.16	59%	41%
−1	Wal-Mart Stores	$53.88	50%	50%
65	Intel	$19.15	49%	51%
49	Pfizer	$34.92	48%	52%
9	IBM	$81.93	46%	54%
24	Merck	$53.80	44%	56%
92	Cisco Systems	$15.00	42%	58%
18	Home Depot	$33.86	37%	63%
16	Boeing	$28.36	30%	70%
11	Verizon	$31.80	21%	79%
22	Kroger	$22.20	13%	87%
32	Sears Roebuck	$36.94	8%	92%
37	AOL Time Warner	$35.00	8%	92%
3	General Motors	$49.40	5%	95%
81	Phillips Petroleum	$35.00	3%	97%

Source: CSFB/HOLT; Deloitte Consulting analysis.

Corporate Strategy Board published in 1998.[8] It examined the 172 companies that had spent time on *Fortune*'s list of the 50 largest companies between 1955 and 1995. Only 5 percent of these companies were able to sustain a real, inflation-adjusted growth rate of more than 6 percent across their entire tenure in this group. The other 95 percent reached a point at which their growth simply stalled, to rates at or below the rate of growth of the gross national product (GNP). Stalling is understandable, given our expectations that all growth markets become saturated and mature. What is scary is that of all these companies whose growth had stalled, only 4 percent were able to successfully reignite their growth even to a rate of 1 percent above GNP growth. Once growth had stalled, in other words, it proved nearly impossible to restart it.

The equity markets brutally punished those companies that allowed their growth to stall. Twenty-eight percent of them lost more than 75 percent of their market capitalization. Forty-one percent of the companies saw their market value drop by between 50 and 75 percent when they stalled, and 26 percent of the firms lost between 25 and 50 percent of their value. The remaining 5 percent lost less than 25 percent of their market capitalization. This, of course, increased pressure on management to regenerate growth, and to do so quickly—which made it all the more difficult to succeed. Managers cannot escape the mandate to grow.[9] Yet the odds of success, if history is any guide, are frighteningly low.

Is Innovation a Black Box?

Why is achieving and sustaining growth so hard? One popular answer is to blame managers for failing to generate new grow—implying that more capable and prescient people could have succeeded. The solve-the-problem-by-finding-a-better-manager approach might have credence if failures to restart growth were isolated events. Study after study, however, concludes that about 90 percent of all publicly traded companies have proved themselves unable to sustain for more than a few years a growth trajectory that creates above-average share-holder returns.[10] Unless we believe that the pool of management talent in established firms is like some perverse Lake Wobegon, where 90 percent of managers are below average, there has to be a more fundamental explanation for why the vast majority of good managers has not been able to crack the problem of sustaining growth.

A second common explanation for once-thriving companies' inability to sustain growth is that their managers become risk averse. But the facts refute this explanation, too. Corporate executives often bet the future of billion-dollar enterprises on an innovation. IBM bet its farm on the System 360 mainframe computer, and won. DuPont spent $400 million on a plant to make Kevlar tire cord, and lost. Corning put billions on the line to build its optical fiber business, and won big. More recently it sold off many of its other businesses in order to invest more in optical telecommunications, and has been bludgeoned. *Many* of the executives who have been unable to create sustained corporate growth have evidenced a strong stomach for risk.

There is a third, widely accepted explanation for why growth seems so hard to achieve repeatedly and well, which we also believe does not hold water: Creating new-growth businesses is simply unpredictable. Many believe that the odds of success are just that—odds—and that they are low. Many of the most insightful management thinkers have accepted the assumption that creating growth is risky and unpredictable, and have therefore used their talents to help executives manage this unpredictability. Recommendations about letting a thousand flowers bloom, bringing Silicon Valley inside, failing fast, and accelerating selection pressures are all ways to deal with the allegedly irreducible unpredictability of successful innovation.[11] The structure of the venture capital industry is in fact a testament to the pervasive belief that we cannot predict which new-growth businesses will succeed. The industry maxim says that for every ten investment—all made in the belief they would succeed—two will fail outright, six will survive as the walking wounded, and two will hit the home runs on which the success of the entire portfolio turns. Because of this belief that the process of business creation is unfathomable, few have sought to pry open the black box to study the *process* by which new-growth businesses are created.

We do not accept that most companies' growth stalls because the odds of success for the next growth business they launch are impossibly low. The historical results may indeed seem random, but we believe it is because the process for creating new-growth businesses has not yet been well understood. In this book we intend to pry open the black box and study the processes that lead to success or failure in new-growth businesses.

To illustrate why it is important to understand the processes that create those results, consider these strings of numbers:

1, 2, 3, 4, 5, 6
75, 28, 41, 26, 38, 64

Which of these would you say is random, and which is predictable? The first string looks predictable: The next two numbers should be 7 and 8. But what if we told you that it was actually the winning numbers for a lottery, drawn from a drum of tumbling balls, whereas the second is the sequence of state and county roads one would follow on a scenic tour of the northern rim of Michigan's Upper Peninsula on the way from Sault Ste. Marie, Ontario to Saxon, Wisconsin? Given the route implied by the first six roads, you can reliably predict the next two numbers—2 and 122—from a map. The lesson: You cannot say, just by looking at the result of the process, whether the process that created those results is capable of generating predictable output. You must understand the process itself. . . .

How to Manage the Dilemma of Investing for Growth

The dilemma of investing for growth is that the character of a firm's money is good for growth only when the firm is growing healthily. Core businesses that are still growing provide cover for new-growth businesses. Senior executives who are bolstered by a sense that the pipeline of new sustaining innovations in established businesses will meet or exceed investors' expectations can allow new businesses the time to follow emergent strategy processes while they compete against nonconsumption. It is when growth slows—when senior executives see that the sustaining-innovation pipeline is inadequate to meet investor expectations—that investing to grow becomes hard. The character of the firm's money changes when new things must get very big very fast, and it won't allow innovators to do what is needed to grow. When you're a corporate entrepreneur and you sense this shift in the corporate context occurring, you had better watch out.

This dilemma traps nearly every company and is the causal mechanism behind the findings in *Stall Points,* the Corporate Strategy Board's study that we cited in chapter 1. This study showed that of the 172 companies that had spent time on *Fortune*'s list of the 50 largest companies between 1955 and 1995, 95 percent saw their growth stall to rates at or below the rate of GNP growth. Of the companies whose growth stalled, only 4 percent were able to successfully reignite their growth even to a rate of 1 percent above GNP growth. Once growth had stalled, the corporations' money turned impatient for growth, which rendered it impossible to do the things required to launch successful growth businesses.

In recent years, the dilemma has become even more complex. If companies whose growth has stalled somehow find a way to launch a successful new-growth business, Wall Street analysts often complain that they cannot value the new opportunity appropriately because it is buried within a larger, slower-growing corporation. In the name of shareholder value, they demand that the corporation spin off the new-growth business to shareholders so that the full value of its exciting growth potential can be reflected in its own share price. If executives respond and spin it off, they may indeed "unlock" shareholder value. But after it has been unlocked they are left locked again in a low-growth business, facing the mandate to increase shareholder value.

In the face of this sobering evidence, chief executives—whose task it is to create shareholder value—*must* preserve the ability of their capital to nourish growth businesses in the ways that they need to be nourished. When executives allow the growth of core businesses to sag to lackluster levels, new-growth ventures must shoulder the whole burden of changing the growth rate of the entire corporation's top and bottom lines. This forces the corporation to demand that the new businesses become very big very fast. Their capital as a consequence becomes poison for growth ventures. The only way to keep investment capital from. spoiling is to use it when it is still good—to invest it from a context that is still healthy enough that the money can be patient for growth.

In many ways, companies whose shares are publicly held are in a self-reinforcing vise. Their dominant shareholders are pension funds. Corporations pressure the managers of their pension fund investments to deliver strong and consistent returns—because strong investment performance reduces the amount of profits that must be diverted to fund pension obligations. Investment managers therefore turn around and pressure the corporations whose shares they own to deliver consistent earnings growth that is unexpectedly accelerating. Privately held companies are not subject to many of these pressures. The expectations that accompany their capital therefore can often be more appropriate for the building of new-growth businesses.

Notes

1.   Although we have not performed a true meta-analysis, there are four recently published studies that seem to converge on this estimate that roughly one company in ten succeeds at sustaining growth. Chris Zook and James Allen found in their 2001 study *Profit from the Core* (Boston: Harvard Business School Press)

that only 13 percent of their sample of 1,854 companies were able to grow consistently over a ten-year period. Richard Foster and Sarah Kaplan published a study that same year, *Creative Destruction* (New York: Currency/Doubleday), in which they followed 1,008 companies from 1962 to 1998. They learned that only 160, or about 16 percent of these firms, were able merely to survive this time frame, and concluded that the perennially outperforming company is a chimera, something that has never existed at all. Jim Collins also published his *Good to Great* (New York: HarperBusiness) in 2001, in which he examined a universe of 1,435 companies over thirty years (1965–1995). Collins found only 126, or about 9 percent, that had managed to outperform equity market averages for a decade or more. The Corporate Strategy Board's findings in *Stall Points* (Washington, DC: Corporate Strategy Board, 1988), which are summarized in detail in the text, show that 5 percent of companies in the *Fortune* 50 successfully maintained their growth, and another 4 percent were able to reignite some degree of growth after they had stalled. The studies all support our assertion that a 10 percent probability of succeeding in a quest for sustained growth is, if anything, a generous estimate.

2. Because all of these transactions included stock, "true" measures of the value of the different deals are ambiguous. Although when a deal actually closes, a definitive value can be fixed, the implied value of the transaction at the time a deal is announced can be useful: It signals what the relevant parties were willing to pay and accept at a point in time. Stock price changes subsequent to the deal's announcement are often a function of other, exogenous events having little to do with the deal itself. Where possible, we have used the value of the deals at announcement, rather than upon closing. Sources of data on these various transactions include the following:

NCR

"Fatal Attraction (AT&T's Failed Merger with NCR)," *The Economist,* 23 March 1996.

"NCR Spinoff Completes AT&T Restructure Plan," *Bloomberg Business News,* 1 January 1997.

McCaw and AT&T Wireless Sale

The Wall Street Journal, 21 September 1994.

"AT&T Splits Off AT&T Wireless," AT&T news release, 9 July 2001.

AT&I; TCI, and MediaOne

"AT&T Plans Mailing to Sell TCI Customers Phone, Web Services, *The Wall Street Journal,* 10 March 1999.

"The AT&T-Mediaone Deal: What the FCC Missed," *Business Week,* 19 June 2000.

"AT&T Broadband to Merge with Comcast Corporation in $72 Billion Transaction," AT&T news release, 19 December 2001.

"Consumer Groups Still Questioning Comcast-AT&T Cable Merger," Associated Press Newswires, 21 October 2002.

3. Cabot's stock price outperformed the market between 1991 and 1995 as it refocused on its core business, for two reasons. On one side of the equation, demand for carbon black increased in Asia and North America as car sales surged, thereby increasing the demand for tires. On the supply side, two other American-based producers of carbon black exited the industry because they were unwilling to make the requisite investment in environmental controls, thereby increasing Cabot's pricing power. Increased demand and reduced

supply translated into a tremendous increase in the profitability of Cabot's traditional carbon black operations, which was reflected in the company's stock price. Between 1996 and 2000, however, its stock price deteriorated again, reflecting the dearth of growth prospects.

4.   An important study of companies' tendency to make investments that fail to create growth was done by Professor Michael C. Jensen: "The Modern Industrial Revolution, Exit, and the Failure of Internal Control Systems," *Journal of Finance* (July 1993): 831–880. Professor Jensen also delivered this paper as his presidential address to the American Finance Association. Interestingly, many of the firms that Jensen cites as having productively reaped growth from their investments were disruptive innovators—a key concept in this book.

Our unit of analysis in this book, as in Jensen's work, is the individual firm, not the larger system of growth creation made manifest in a free market, capitalist economy. Works such as Joseph Schumpeter's *Theory of Economic Development* (Cambridge, MA: Harvard University Press, 1934) and *Capitalism, Socialism, and Democracy* (New York: London, Harper & Brothers, 1942) are seminal, landmark works that address the environment in which firms function. Our assertion here is that whatever the track record of free market economies in generating growth at the macro level, the track record of individual firms is quite poor. It is the performance of firms within a competitive market to which we hope to contribute.

5.   This simple story is complicated somewhat by the market's apparent incorporation of an expected "fade" in any company's growth rate. Empirical analysis suggests that the market does not expect any company to grow, or even survive, forever. It therefore seems to incorporate into current prices a foreseen decline in growth rates from current levels and the eventual dissolution of the firm. This is the reason for the importance of terminal values in most valuation models. This fade period is estimated using regression analysis, and estimates vary widely. So, strictly speaking, if a company is expected to grow at 5 percent with a fade period of forty years, and five years into that forty-year period it is still growing at 5 percent, the stock price would rise at rates that generated economic returns for shareholders, because the forty-year fade period would start over. However, because this qualification applies to companies growing at 5 percent as well as those growing at 25 percent, it does not change the point we wish to make; that is, that the market is a harsh taskmaster, and merely meeting expectations does not generate meaningful reward.

6.   On average over their long histories, of course, faster-growing firms yield higher returns. However, the faster-growing firm will have produced higher returns than the slower-growing firm only for investors in the past. If markets discount efficiently, then the investors who reap above-average returns are those who were fortunate enough to have bought shares in the past when the future growth rate had not been fully discounted into the price of the stock. Those who bought when the future growth potential already had been discounted into the share price would not receive an above-market return. An excellent reference for this argument can be found in Alfred Rappaport and Michael J. Mauboussin, *Expectations Investing: Reading Stock Prices for Better Returns* (Boston: Harvard Business School Press, 2001). Rappaport and Mauboussin guide investors in methods to detect when a market's expectations for a company's growth might be incorrect.

7.   These were the closing market prices for these companies' common shares on August 21, 2002. There is no significance to that particular date: It is simply the time when the analysis was done. HOLT Associates, a unit of Credit Suisse First Boston (CSFB), performed these calculations using proprietary methodology applied to publicly available financial data. The percent future is a

measure of how much a company's current stock price can be attributed to current cash flows and how much is due to investors' expectations of future growth and performance. As CSFB/HOLT defines it,

> *The percent future is the percentage of the total market value that the market assigns to the company's expected future investment. Percent future begins with the total market value (debt plus equity) less that portion attributed to the present value of existing assets and investments and divides this by the total market value of debt and equity.*

CSFB/Holt calculates the present value of existing assets as the present value of the cash flows associated with the assets' wind down and the release of the associated nondepreciating working capital. The HOLT CFROI valuation methodology includes a forty-year fade of returns equal to the total market's average returns.

Percent Future = [Total Debt and Equity (market) − Present Value Existing Assets]/[Total Debt and Equity (market)]

The companies listed in table 1-1 are not a sequential ranking of *Fortune* 500 companies, because some of the data required to perform these calculations were not available for some companies. The companies listed in this table were chosen only for illustrative purposes, and were not chosen in any way to suggest that any company's share price is likely to increase or decline. For more information on the methodology that HOLT used, see <http://www.holtvalue.com>.

8. See *Stall Points* (Washington, DC: Corporate Strategy Board, 1998).

9. In the text we have focused only on the pressure that equity markets impose on companies to grow, but there are many other sources of intense pressure. We'll mention just a couple here. First, when a company is growing, there are increased opportunities for employees to be promoted into new management positions that are opening up above them. Hence, the potential for growth in managerial responsibility and capability is much greater in a growing firm than in a stagnant one. When growth slows, managers sense that their possibilities for advancement will be constrained not by their personal talent and performance, but rather by how many years must pass before the more senior managers above them will retire. When this happens, many of the most capable employees tend to leave the company, affecting the company's abilities to regenerate growth.

    Investment in new technologies also becomes difficult. When a growing firm runs out of capacity and must build a new plant or store, it is easy to employ the latest technology. When a company has stopped growing and has excess manufacturing capacity, proposals to invest in new technology typically do not fare well, since the full capital cost and the average manufacturing cost of producing with the new technology are compared against the marginal cost of producing in a fully depreciated plant. As a result, growing firms typically have a technology edge over slow-growth competitors. But that advantage is not rooted so much in the visionary wisdom of the managers as it is in the difference in the circumstances of growth versus no growth.

10. Detailed support for this estimate is provided in note 1.

11. For example; see James Brian Quinn, *Strategies for Change: Logical Incrementalism* (Homewood, IL: R.D. Irwin, 1980). Quinn suggests that the first step that corporate executives need to take in building new businesses is to "let a thousand flowers bloom," then tend the most promising and let the rest wither. In

this view, the key to successful innovation lies in choosing the right flowers to tend—and that decision must rely on complex intuitive feelings, calibrated by experience.

More recent work by Tom Peters (*Thriving on Chaos: Handbook for a Management Revolution* [New York: Knopf/Random House, 1987]) urges innovating managers to "fail fast"—to pursue new business ideas on a small scale and in a way that generates quick feedback about whether an idea is viable. Advocates of this approach urge corporate executives not to punish failures because it is only through repeated attempts that successful new businesses will emerge.

Others draw on analogies with biological evolution, where mutations arise in what appear to be random ways. Evolutionary theory posits that whether a mutant organism thrives or dies depends on its fit with the "selection environment"—the conditions within which it must compete against other organisms for the resources required to thrive. Hence, believing that good and bad innovations pop up randomly, these researchers advise corporate executives to focus on creating a "selection environment" in which viable new business ideas are culled from the bad as quickly as possible. Gary Hamel, for example, advocates creating "Silicon Valley inside"—an environment in which existing structures are constantly dismantled, recombined in novel ways, and tested, in order to stumble over something that actually works. (See Gary Hamel, *Leading the Revolution* [Boston: Harvard Business School Press, 2001].)

We are not critical of these books. They can be very helpful, given the present state of understanding, because if the processes that create innovations were indeed random, then a context within which managers could accelerate the creation and testing of ideas would indeed help. But if the process is *not* intrinsically random, as we assert, then addressing only the context is treating the symptom, not the source of the problem.

To see why, consider the studies of 3M's celebrated ability to create a stream of growth-generating innovations. A persistent highlight of these studies is 3M's "15 percent rule": At 3M, many employees are given 15 percent of their time to devote to developing their own ideas for new-growth businesses. This "slack" in how people spend their time is supported by a broadly dispersed capital budget that employees can tap in order to fund. their would-be growth engines on a trial basis.

But what guidance does this policy give to a bench engineer at 3M? She is given 15 percent "slack" time to dedicate to creating new-growth businesses. She is also told that whatever she comes up with will be subject first to internal market selection pressures, then external market selection pressures. All this is helpful information. But none of it helps that engineer create a new idea, or decide which of the several ideas she might create are worth pursuing further. This plight generalizes to managers and executives at all levels in an organization. From bench engineer to middle manager to business unit head to CEO, it is not enough to occupy oneself only with creating a context for innovation that sorts the fruits of that context. Ultimately, every manager must create something of substance, and the success of that creation lies in the decisions managers must make.

All of these approaches create an "infinite regress." By bringing the market "inside," we have simply backed up the problem: How can managers decide which ideas will be developed to the point at which they can be subjected to the selection pressures of their internal market? Bringing the market still deeper inside simply creates the same conundrum. Ultimately, innovators must judge what they will work on and how they will do it—and what they should consider when making those decisions is what is in the black box. The acceptance of randomness in innovation, then, is not a stepping-stone on the way to greater understanding; it is a barrier.

Dr. Gary Hamel was one of the first scholars of this problem to raise with Professor Christensen the possibility that the management of innovation actually has the potential to yield predictable results. We express our thanks to him for his helpful thoughts.

Jim Mackey and
Liisa Välikangas

 **NO**

The Myth of Unbounded Growth

Growth is not perpetual and its continued pursuit can be a death knell, especially for large, mature companies.

Imagine the CEO of a growth company telling its shareholders, "Henceforth we will be pursuing no risky new research, acquisitions or new business ventures. We will concentrate on being stewards of our existing business and will simply pay all profits as dividends." This is an unlikely scenario, to say the least. The reality is that markets expect growth. There is a deeply held assumption that neither a company nor its management is viable unless it is able to grow. Growth gives investors a feeling that management is doing its job. Growth is typically perceived as a proactive (rather than a defensive) strategy. Or maybe, as the Red Queen says in Lewis Carroll's *Through the Looking Glass,* "Here it takes all the running you can do to keep in the same place. If you want to get somewhere else, you must run at least twice as fast as that!"

"The only way managers can deliver a return to shareholders that exceeds the market average," Clayton Christensen and Michael Raynor wrote in *The Innovator's Solution,* "is to grow *faster* than shareholders expect," however irrational that may be.[1] Indeed, a recent CSFB HOLT study found that 50% of the valuation of the 20 most valuable companies was based on expected cash flows from future investments.[2] Nevertheless, it has become almost a national sport to suggest that there is a set of visionary, great or otherwise noteworthy companies that can grow indefinitely—only to have those companies, almost invariably, fall from grace shortly thereafter. "The golden company that continually performs better than the markets has never existed. It is a myth," wrote Richard Foster and Sarah Kaplan in *Creative Destruction.*[3] Indeed, of the companies on the original *Forbes* 100 list in 1917, only 18 remained in the top 100 by 1987 and 61 had ceased to exist. Of these highly respected survivors, Foster and Kaplan point to only two companies— General Electric Co. and Eastman Kodak Co.—which outperformed the 7.5% average return on the S&P 500 during this 70-year period, and they beat the average by only 0.3%.

The truth is, companies are successful until they are not.[4] The consistent pattern of stalled or halted growth among the largest U.S. corporations over the last 50 years is eye-opening. Research by the Corporate Strategy Board (CSB) in 1998[5] suggested that there is a "cloud layer" at which growth starts to stall, beginning in the $30 billion range (CPI-adjusted 1996 dollars).[6] Of the 172 companies that have made it to the *Fortune* 50 from 1954 to 1995,[7] only 5%

From *MIT Sloan Management Review,* Winter 2004. Copyright © 2004 by Sloan Management Review (MIT). Reprinted by permission.

were able to sustain a growth rate above the GDP (and half of those have stalled since the study).[8] In addition, once stalled, no U.S. company larger than $15 billion has been able to restart growth that exceeded that of the GDP. In *How To Grow When the Markets Don't*,[9] Adrian Slywotzky, Richard Wise and Karl Weber call this "the Great Divide, moving from a past of strong growth . . . into a future of low or no growth." The authors say that many companies did so without fully recognizing the change, thereby exacerbating the problem, sometimes fatally. Companies often see a stall as a temporary blip, soon to be overcome with investment and execution of their growth strategy, but in their book *Permanently Failing Organizations*,[10] Marshall Meyer and Lynn Zucker write that many of these companies are merely lingering in a state of decay before they ultimately fail.

As companies increase in size, the variability in growth rate decreases (that is, growth slows down).[11] The classical model of growth—assuming a log-normal distribution of company sizes in a population of companies[12]—fails to explain this phenomenon.[13] Strictly from a numerical perspective, sustaining rapid growth is a massive challenge for a *Fortune* 50 company. For example, to sustain its current 17% growth rate, Merck & Co. Inc. (the 17th largest with revenue of $52 billion) must add $9 billion in revenue this year, $11 billion next year and so on. In five years, Merck's revenues would need to be $114 billion—more than double its current number.

The Cost of the Growth Chase

For a large company, not only are the odds of consistently achieving this kind of growth quite long, but the pursuit of that growth can also be very costly. To pursue billion dollar growth targets quickly, executives feel they must invest billions in the quest.[14] The result is falling profitability often accompanied by huge restructuring charges. Whereas the market cap decline may begin before or after the stall, the eventual fall is dramatic. The CSB study found that 28% of stalled firms lost over 75% of market cap relative to the Dow Jones Industrial Average (DJIA), and 69% lost at least 50%; the average valuation fell by 61%.[15] When this happens, a once great company begins to search for its lost formula, often until the very viability of the company is eventually questioned, as was the case for Sears, Roebuck and Co., IBM Corp., Digital Equipment Corp., Xerox Corp., Motorola Inc., Lucent Technologies and many others. Employees suffer as well. In 53% of the stalls, head count was reduced by over 20%, and morale declined noticeably.

Kodak, as noted, outperformed the S&P 500 for 70 years—from 1917 to 1987—but today it is the poster child for stalled companies. Its revenue stopped growing faster than the GDP in 1980 when it was No. 29 on the *Fortune* 50 list. Its recent *nominal* market cap is 41% below its 1980 level. When benchmarked against the 10-fold increase in the DJIA since 1980, Kodak's relative market cap has fallen a whopping 94%. Cutting more than 70% of its semiannual dividend, Kodak now seeks to migrate from film[16] and plans to invest $3 billion in digital photography, in which it has been investing since 1972. Kodak also recently announced its $250 million acquisition of Scitex Corp.'s Digital Printing to bolster its entry into the inkjet printer market. Yet film still accounts for about 50% of Kodak's profits.[17] Thus the odds that Kodak can reignite growth are not judged to be good. Kodak's long-term debt is rated triple-B-minus, one notch above speculative, by Standard & Poor's. In an unprecedented revolt, "investors have lost confidence" in Kodak's growth investments and now seek "radically different strategies to maximize shareholder value."[18]

Given the dismal track record that stalled growth companies have when attempting to return to double-digit internal growth, the massive (and often belated) investments they make in that regard seem analogous to spending the company's life savings on a lottery ticket. The reality for many shareholders is that unless the company is sold while still healthy, the promised payoff never comes, due to low valuation in the sale of nonperforming assets, restructuring charge write-offs, goodwill depreciation and pension- or product-related liabilities. The hard-earned equity evaporates, and assets are sold at near book value in fire sales or in bankruptcy to creditors. *Fortune* 50 bankruptcies are relatively rare,[19] but Enron, WorldCom, PG&E, United AirLines, Kmart, Bethlehem Steel and LTV are recent examples. Others like Lucent, Xerox, Fleming, AMR and Goodyear hover on the brink. Still others are sold for a fraction of their earlier value or at a slight premium to a long-stagnant stock price—for example, Digital, Compaq, Beatrice Foods, Firestone, Uniroyal, American Motors, Armour Food, Gulf Oil, RCA and Union Carbide.

What's a CEO To Do?

It is clear that many strong forces—ranging from natural limitations and managerial complexity to stakeholder harmony and antitrust concerns—make continuous growth very difficult for already-large companies. Rather than continue to seek growth at any cost, the solution is to seek alternatives to the dilemma—in a sense, to fool the natural limits to growth that large companies face. There are three logical alternatives: Break up the company, create a new corporate form, or make a graceful growth-to-value transition.

Breaking up the company   IBM spun off Lexmark, HP gave birth to Agilent, AT&T divested itself of Lucent, GM launched Delco, Sears separated from Allstate, and 3M broke off Imation. Such spinoffs generally enhance stockholder value both at the time of the announcement and by about 20% in the subsequent 18 months.[20] J.P. Morgan discovered that smaller breakups performed better.[21] It is important, though, that the post-breakup units be small enough (less than $10 billion) to have significant room for growth. Although not all breakups create successful new companies, they do help bring focus to the parent company. J.P. Morgan also found that "the remaining, slimmer parent does materially better than the market following separation."[22]

Nevertheless there is significant resistance to divestiture because it seems "like a tacit admission of failure, evidence of poor management, or in some corporate cultures even . . . treason."[23] The myth of unbounded growth further perpetuates resistance to this seemingly reasonable solution. Indeed, "of the 50 largest divestitures . . . more than three-quarters were completed under pressure, most only after long delays when problems became so obvious that action was unavoidable."[24]

Experimenting with a new corporate form Whereas attempts at internal independence, including tracking stocks and partial spinoffs, may prove not to offer lasting solutions, evolving new organizational forms and management practices over time can afford a company greater scale and scope.[25] Just as the divisional organization (supported by innovations including the telephone and railroads) extended the management capability beyond that of the functional organization in the early 1900s, perhaps an even more decentralized organization (supported by innovations including the Internet and e-commerce) will enable the next growth leap. Also business models that foster competition between different parts of the organization (for example, GM's Chevrolet vs. Pontiac or HP's Inkjet vs. Laserjet) may offer growth advantages. In addition, internal markets for ideas and talent (such as Shell's GameChanger innovation program) that are open to anyone within the organization with a worthwhile contribution to make may provide new routes to growth.[26]

Take Visa, for example, with an estimated 2003 sales volume of $2.7 trillion. It is technically not a company nor does it appear in the *Fortune* rankings. Yet it has a powerful brand, a strategy for growth, and an integrated business system composed of hundreds of card-issuing financial institutions battling for customers.[27] Similarly, electronics firms today outsource manufacturing, integrate supplier design, engage in software alliances, participate in standards bodies and contribute to and benefit from open-source movements.[28] They are integrated ecosystems that compete for ideas, innovation, people and investment. Here the corporation may no longer be the relevant unit of competitive analysis; the new corporate form is a boundaryless organization.

Making a transition from growth to value Using reduced investment to grow earnings can help a company make a graceful transition from a high P/E growth stock to a moderate P/E value stock. Market cap may decline (relative to the DJIA), but this strategy can help avoid the dramatic poststall crash or near bankruptcy that can occur when former growth companies begin delivering neither growth nor profit and are assessed at breakup value. Specific tactics may include increasing earnings stability, balance-sheet strengthening, boosting dividend payout, cost and asset reduction, reductions in marketing and R&D, portfolio adjustments (especially divestitures and spinoffs), and stock repurchase (only if P/E is in single digits). Most companies that survive their growth stall eventually make this transition. It is often delayed, however, due to persistent attempts to recapture growth (for example, IBM in the mid-1980s and early 1990s), or forced after being acquired by a value-oriented firm (for example, Allied Signal's acquisition of Honeywell in 1999). GE, however, shifted focus from growth to profit in the 1950s and transitioned without a crisis. Microsoft's recent decision to begin paying dividends may imply an early recognition of the growth-to-value transition.

This strategy—which requires a shift in corporate culture and investor expectations—may be unpopular because it marks a radical departure from the past. It is thus difficult for any leader to achieve unless precipitated by a crisis. Even when there is a perceived crisis, preliminary case studies indicate that such a transition will take from five to eight years.[29] Denial and short-term incentives create additional barriers because management tends to want to believe they can win the lottery to recapture unbounded growth.

Facing the Liability of Corporate Size

In evaluating their options, the CEO and the board should consider where their company is in its life cycle—growth, stall or poststall. Growth stalls can be anticipated by assessing the natural limits of the company's dominant growth strategy and its pattern of financial performance. Senior managers and board members also have to realistically assess their company's capabilities in innovation and new business creation in order to decide whether their capital and talent would be better spent on core business development than on an increasingly fruitless pursuit of mega-growth. These are not easy decisions to make, especially given the almost unquestioned culture of growth that continues to exist in today's environment. The biggest challenge and first step toward making those decisions, however, is to overcome denial and acknowledge that unbounded growth is indeed a myth.

References

1. C.M. Christensen and M. Raynor, "The Innovator's Solution: Creating and Sustaining Successful Growth" (Boston: Harvard Business School Press, 2003).

2. M.J. Mauboussin and K. Bartholdson, "The Pyramid of Numbers," The Consilient Observer (Credit Suisse First Boston Newsletter) 2, no. 17 (Sept. 23, 2003): 5. See also Christensen and Raynor, "The Innovator's Solution," 22, note 7, regarding methodology.

3. S. Kaplan and R. Foster, "Creative Destruction: Why Companies That Are Built To Last Underperform the Market—and How To Successfully Transform Them" (New York: Doubleday/Currency, 2001).

4. G. Hamel and L. Välikangas, "The Quest for Resilience," Harvard Business Review 81 (September 2003): 52–63. See also Kaplan and Foster, "Creative Destruction," 11, 14. Kaplan and Foster note that the turnover rate among *Fortune* 500 companies has accelerated—reaching nearly 10% in 1998—implying that no more than one-third of today's major corporations will survive in an economically important way over the next 25 years. Further, according to unpublished research done by the Woodside Institute in 2003, the number of S&P 500 companies that have suffered a five-year earnings decline has more than doubled in the last 30 years, suggesting a severe lack of strategic resilience.

5. Corporate Strategy Board, "Stall Points: Barriers to Growth for the Large Corporate Enterprise" (Washington, D.C.: Corporate Executive Board, 1998).

6. The stall range had increased over time slightly faster than inflation (pp. 20–21).

7. This is also true for service companies of equivalent scale.

8. See Corporate Strategy Board, "Stall Points," 13. Wal-Mart, American International Group, Target, and United Parcel Service are still growing; 3M, Hewlett-Packard, PepsiCo and Procter & Gamble now appear to have stalled. In addition, this study by the Corporate Strategy Board cites six companies that stalled but then

restarted growth to 1% over GDP. Of those, Chase, Coca-Cola, Fleming and Motorola appear to have stalled again. Only Johnson & Johnson and Merck are still growing. Thus only six out of 172 *Fortune* 50 (3.5%) are still growing relative to the economy.

9. A.J. Slywotzky, R. Wise and K. Weber, "How To Grow When the Markets Don't" (New York: Warner Books, 2003), 14–15.

10. M.W. Meyer and L.G. Zucker, "Permanently Failing Organizations" (Thousand Oaks, California: Sage Publications, 1989).

11. M.H.R. Stanley, L.A.N. Amaral, S.V. Buldyrev, S. Havlin, H. Leschhorn, P. Maass, M.A. Salinger and H.E. Stanley, "Scaling Behaviour in the Growth of Companies," *Nature* 379 (Feb. 29, 1996): 804–806.

12. R. Gibrat, "Les Inégalités Economiques" (Paris: Sirey, 1933).

13. G. Carroll and M. Hannan, "The Demography of Corporations and Industries" (Princeton, New Jersey: Princeton University Press, 1999). See also Mauboussin and Bartholdson, "The Pyramid of Numbers," which describes mathematical distributions called power laws and their abundance in nature and social systems.

14. Christensen and Raynor, "The Innovator's Solution," 236–243. In this passage, including the section titled "The Death Spiral From Inadequate Growth," the authors state that large targets and large investments paradoxically are "likely to condemn innovators to a death march" and that "capital becomes a poison for growth ventures."

15. Market cap changes are measured relative to the Dow Jones Industrial Average from peak to trough within 10 years of stall.

16. J. Bandler, "Kodak Cuts Dividend by 72% To Finance Digital Shift," Wall Street Journal Europe, Sept. 26, 2003, A4.

17. S. London, "Kodak Aims To Become a Model of Reinvention," Financial Times, Sept. 27, 2003, 8.

18. W.C. Symonds, "Commentary: The Kodak Revolt Is Short-Sighted," Business-Week, Nov. 3, 2003, 38.

19. Kaplan and Foster, "Creative Destruction," 3. However, of the 20 largest U.S. bankruptcies in the past two decades, 10 occurred in the last two years; see Hamel and Välikangas, "The Quest for Resilience."

20. D. Sadtler, A. Campbell and R. Koch, "Breakup! How Companies Use Spin-Offs To Gain Focus and Grow Strong" (New York: Free Press, 1997), 4, 27–31.

21. Ibid., p. 30.

22. J.P. Morgan, "J.P. Morgan's Spinoff Study" (New York: J.P. Morgan, June 6, 1995, updated August 20, 1997 and July 23, 1999); P.A. Gaughan, "Mergers, Acquisitions and Corporate Restructurings," 3rd ed. (New York: John Wiley & Sons, 1997), 414–417; G.L. Hite and J.E. Owers, "Security Price Reactions Around Corporate Spin-Off Announcements," *Journal of Financial Economics* 12, no. 4 (1983): 409–436; K. Schipper and A. Smith, "Effects of Recontracting on Shareholder Wealth: The Case of Voluntary Spin-Offs," *Journal of Financial Economics* 12, no. 4 (1983): 437–467; and J.A. Miles and J.D. Rosenfeld, "The Effect of Voluntary Spin-Off Announcements on Shareholder Wealth," *Journal of Finance* 38, no. 5 (1983): 1597–1606. Each study documents a mean abnormal spin-off announcement return of approximately 3%.

23. L. Dranikoff, T. Koller and A. Schneider, "Divesting Proactively," McKinsey on Finance, summer 2002, 1, http://www.corporatefinance.mckinsey.com_downloads/knowledge/mof/2002_no4/divesting.pdf.

24. Ibid. Also see L. Dranikoff, T. Koller and A. Schneider, "Divestiture: Strategy's Missing Link," *Harvard Business Review* 80 (May 2002): 74–83; and D.J.

Ravenscraft and F.M. Scherer, "Mergers, Sell-Offs and Economic Efficiency" (Washington, D.C.: Brookings Institution Press, 1987), 167.

25. A.D. Chandler, Jr., and T. Hikino, "Scale and Scope: The Dynamics of Industrial Capitalism" (Cambridge, Massachusetts: Belknap Press, 1990).

26. For a description of the GameChanger program, see G. Hamel, "Bringing Silicon Valley Inside," *Harvard Business Review 77* (September-October 1999): 70–84.

27. M.M. Waldrop, "The Trillion Dollar Vision of Dee Hock," Fast Company, October 1996, 75; and D.W. Hock, "Birth of the Chaordic Age" (San Francisco: Berrett-Koehler, 2000).

28. G. von Krogh, "Open-Source Software Development," *MIT Sloan Management Review* 44, no. 3 (spring 2003): 14–18.

29. Refers to ongoing studies of *Fortune* 50 companies conducted by the Billion Dollar Growth Network. The work goes beyond the 50 growth-stall case studies developed jointly with the Corporate Strategy Board in 1997–1998, focusing instead on what happened after the stall—how the companies managed their transition to a lower growth value model. The studies generally examine companies over the past 20-year period, relying on annual reports, Compustat data, secondary sources and follow-up interviews.

POSTSCRIPT

Must Firms Constantly Grow to Be Considered Successful?

Based the two previous selections, it would seem that there are clear reasons to both support and oppose the view that only growing firms are successful firms. Interestingly, the question of whether a firm needs to grow to be considered successful is often overlooked. The primary reason for this is the widespread assumption on the part of business scholars, executives, and other business observers that growth is good and that, therefore, not growing is bad. However, as the article supporting the no side points out, a growth strategy can be both costly and risky. It might, perhaps, prove fruitful if we take a moment and consider a hypothetical example and see if it can shed some light on the question at hand.

Consider a mom-and-pop diner of the type that might be around the corner from you. While enjoying "The Best Burger in the 'Burb!" you ponder the growth question, and ask Bob, the owner, why he doesn't build on his success by opening a new restaurant. Seems like a reasonable question, particularly if we associate success with growth. With pride, Bob replies that three generations of his family have led happy, full lives in the community supported by the income and profits generated by the diner. He has a loyal clientele including a lunch crowd that keeps the place buzzing and his profits steady. He sees no reason to expand and expose his successful business to the risks associated with growth. So, is Bob wrong? It's hard not to admit that his business is successful, at least in the sense Bob suggests. Indeed, it is this sort of response to the growth question that authors Mackey and Välikangas suggest corporations consider. That is, they argue corporations have options other than growth such spinning-off segments of the firm or focusing efforts primarily at becoming a value-driven firm.

Despite costs and risks as well as other options available to companies, growth is typically the focus of most corporate strategy in America. It is highly valued by investors and other stakeholders of the firm and, as Christensen and Raynor argue, can be viewed as an "imperative." Now that you have read both sides of the debate, what are your thoughts? Do you feel that it is "imperative" for firms to grow in order to be considered successful?

Suggested Readings

Clayton Christensen, *The Innovators Dilemma: When New Technologies Cause Great Firms to Fail.* Boston: Harvard Business School Press, 1997.

C.M. Christensen and M. Raynor, *The Innovators Solution: Creating and Sustaining Successful Growth.* Boston: Harvard Business School Press, 2003.

Jim Collins, *Good to Great*. New York: HarperBusiness, 2001.

G. Hamel and L. Välikangas, The quest for resilience. *Harvard Business Review*, 2003, 81: 52–63.

S. Kaplan and R. Foster, *Creative Destruction: Why Companies that Are Built to Last Underperform the Market—and How to Successfully Transform Them.* New York: Doubleday/Currency, 2001.

Chris Zook and James Allen, *Profit from the Core*. Boston: Harvard Business School Press, 2001.

On the Internet . . .

About GlobalWarming.org

The purpose of this organization is "to dispel the myths of global warming by exposing flawed economic, scientific, and risk analysis. Coalition members will also follow the progress of the international Global Climate Change Treaty negotiations."

http://www.globalwarming.org/about.htm

The American Immigration Law Foundation (AILF)

AILF was established in 1987 as a tax-exempt, not-for-profit educational, charitable organization. The foundation is dedicated to increasing public understanding of immigration law and policy and the value of immigration to American society; to promoting public service and excellence in the practice of immigration law; and to advancing fundamental fairness and due process under the law for immigrants.

http://www.ailf.org/

The Ayn Rand Institute

The ARI is a nonprofit educational organization whose goals are to spread the concepts and ideas contained in Ayn Rand's revolutionary philosophy, Ojectivism. Their members appear frequently in the national media and have widespread influence in colleges and universities across America. In staunchly defending capitalism and limited government, ARI provides unique insight into numerous topics of interest to business, including globalization.

http://www.aynrand.org

Globalization Guide.org

This site is the product of the Australian Apec Study Center and is designed to introduce students to the pros, cons, myths, and facts of globalization. Additional resources and access to other globalization links are also provided.

http://www.globalisationguide.org/

PART 4

Environmental and International Management Issues

*I*mages *of young children working long hours in inhumane conditions for less than substance wages were a common sight on television news programs and covers of popular magazines during the 1990s. Major American firms like Nike and The Gap had been accused of running sweatshops in Third World countries as a means of keeping their production costs down. But beyond these terrible images lies a sophisticated defense of sweatshops, one that gets a hearing in the debate on sweatshops presented here. The question of sweatshops is closely related to another topic we debate: whether or not economic globalization is good for humankind. These two issues, along with two others, form the fourth and final section of this text.*

- Is the Condition of the Environment Really as Bad as the Environmentalists Claim?

- Should U.S. Corporations Be Allowed to Hire Illegal Aliens?

- Is Economic Globalization Good for Humankind?

- Are Global Sweatshops Exploitative?

ISSUE 15

Is the Condition of the Environment Really as Bad as Environmentalists Claim?

YES: David Pimentel, from "Skeptical of the Skeptical Environmentalist," *Skeptic* (vol. 9, no. 2, 2002)

NO: Denis Dutton, from "Greener Than You Think," *Washington Post On-line Edition* (October 21, 2001)

ISSUE SUMMARY

YES: In his review of *The Skeptical Environmentalist*, David Pimentel disagrees with Lomborg's optimistic assessment. He also accuses Lomborg of selectively presenting advantageous data while simultaneously ignoring evidence that is damaging to his position.

NO: Denis Dutton, professor of philosophy at the University of Canterbury in New Zealand, agrees with Lomborg that the environment is much better off than the environmentalists would have us believe.

It is standard fare nowadays for introductory-level management textbooks to include a chapter exploring the environmental context in which business management takes place. Among the myriad of topics covered is, inevitably, a discussion on the impact business activities have on the natural environment. In varying degrees, this discussion usually blames business for much of the damage done to the environment and offers guidelines as to what corporations need to do to become more socially responsible. The following quote from a highly respected management text is typical: "[M]uch remains to be done. Companies need to develop economically feasible ways to avoid contributing to acid rain and global warming; to avoid depleting the ozone layer; and to develop alternative methods of handling sewage, hazardous wastes, and ordinary garbage. . . . Companies also need to develop safety policies that cut down on accidents with potentially disastrous environmental results" (Rickey W. Griffin, *Management*, 7th ed., Houghton Mifflin Company, 2002). Some texts argue that management needs to adopt policies of "sustainable development," an approach that emphasizes restricting economic growth to levels that won't outstrip the replenishment rate of our natural resources (Post, Lawrence, and Weber, *Business and Society*, 9th ed., Irwin McGraw-Hill, 1999).

The vast majority of discussions about the state of our natural environment share at least three important assumptions: (1) the earth's environment is in bad shape, (2) it is getting worse all the time, and (3) the primary source of the problem is global business activity. These assumptions are so commonly accepted as true that to question them is to leave oneself open for severe ridicule and criticism. Nevertheless, over the past 20 years or so, a growing number of social commentators, academicians, and environmental movement observers have wondered out loud whether things are really as bad as the environmentalists portray them to be.

The first prominent contrarian voice belonged to University of Maryland professor of economics, Julian Simon (1932–1998). Simon, who argued that human ingenuity was the "ultimate resource," set out to assess the true state of the earth's health in his 1981 tome, *The Ultimate Resource* (Princeton University Press). Using statistics readily available to the public, Simon's startling conclusion was that "Every measure of material and environmental welfare in the United States and in the world has improved rather than deteriorated. All long-run trends point in exactly the opposite direction from the direction of the doomsayers" (quote from Frank Miele, "Living without Limits: An Interview with Julian Simon," *Skeptic*, vol. 5, no. 1, 1997, p. 54). Science correspondent and Society of Environmental Journalists member Ronald Bailey edited a collection of articles by noted environmental scholars addressing various ecological issues. Although not as aggressively optimistic as Simon's work, the consensus of *Earth Report 2000* (McGraw-Hill, 2000) was, nevertheless, a resoundingly positive assessment of the health of our planet. Of all the voices that followed Simon's seminal work, however, that of former Greenpeace-activist-turned-environmental-optimist Bjorn Lomborg has unquestionably been the most controversial.

Lomborg, associate professor of statistics at the University of Aarhus in Denmark, set out to debunk Simon's findings in the late 1990s. Much to his surprise, the data strongly supported Simon's conclusions. Lomborg published his findings in a series of four newspaper articles in 1997 and 1998, thus triggering an intense debate in the Danish media. Ultimately, this debate led to the publication of his highly controversial, *The Skeptical Environmentalist: Measuring the Real State of the Earth* (Cambridge University Press, 2001).

Lomborg contends that the purpose of his book is not so much to attack or provoke the environmental doomsayers but, rather, to provide "a careful democratic check on the environmental debate, by knowing the real state of the world—having knowledge of the most important facts and connections in the essential areas of our world" (p. xx). The crucial point, according to Lomborg, is that we can only make wise and beneficial decisions if we have accurate information and a willingness to act on it.

Denis Dutton, professor of philosophy at the University of Canterbury in New Zealand, agrees with Lomborg that the environment is much better off than the environmentalists would have us believe. In the first selection, Cornell University professor David Pimentel disagrees with Lomborg's optimistic assessment. He also accuses Lomborg of selectively presenting advantageous data while simultaneously ignoring evidence that is damaging to his position.

Skeptical of the Skeptical Environmentalist

Bjorn Lomborg discusses a wide range of topics in his book and implies, through his title, that he will inform readers exactly what the real state of world is. In this effort, he criticizes countless world economists, agriculturists, water specialists, and environmentalists, and furthermore, accuses them of misquoting and/or organizing published data to mislead the public concerning the status of world population, food supplies, malnutrition, disease, and pollution. Lomborg bases his optimistic opinion on his selective use of data. Some of Lomborg's assertions will be examined in this review, and where differing information is presented, extensive documentation will be provided.

Lomborg reports that "we now have more food per person than we used to." In contrast, the Food and Agricultural Organization (FAO) of the United Nations reports that food per capita has been declining since 1984, based on available cereal grains (Figure 1). Cereal grains make up about 80% of the world's food. Although grain yields per hectare (abbreviated ha) in both developed and developing countries are still increasing, these increases are slowing while the world population continues to escalate. Specifically from 1950 to 1980, U.S. grains yields increased at about 3% per year, but after 1980 the rate of increase for corn and other grains has declined to only about 1% (Figure 2).

Obviously fertile cropland is an essential resource for the production of foods but Lomborg has chosen not to address this subject directly. Currently, the U.S. has available nearly 0.5 ha of prime cropland per capita, but it will not have this much land if the population continues to grow at its current rapid rate. Worldwide the average cropland available for food production is only 0.25 ha per person. Each person added to the U.S. population requires nearly 0.4 ha (1 acre) of land for urbanization and transportation. One example of the impact of population growth and development is occurring in California where an average of 156,000 ha of agricultural land is being lost each year. At this rate it will not be long before California ceases to be the number one state in U.S. agricultural production.

In addition to the quantity of agricultural land, soil quality and fertility is vital for food production. The productivity of the soil is reduced when it is eroded by rainfall and wind. Soil erosion is not a problem, according to Lomborg, especially in the U.S. where soil erosion has declined during the past decade. Yes, as Lomborg states, instead of losing an average of 17 metric tons

Figure 1

Cereal Grain Production Per Capita in the World From 1961 to 1999

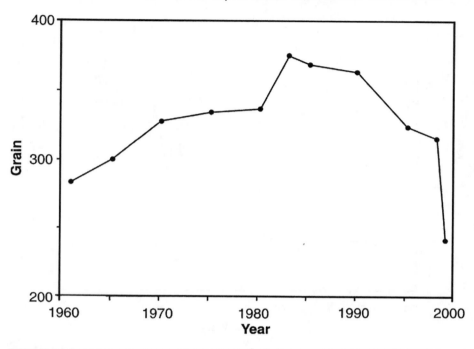

FAO, 1961–1999

per hectare per year on cropland, the U.S. cropland is now losing an average of 13 t/ha/yr. However, this average loss is 13 times the sustainability rate of soil replacement. Exceptions occur, as during the 1995–96 winter in Kansas, when it was relatively dry and windy, and some agricultural lands lost as much as 65 t/ha of productive soil. This loss is 65 times the natural soil replacement in agriculture.

Worldwide soil erosion is more damaging than in the United States. For instance, the India soil is being lost at 30 to 40 times its sustainability. Rate of soil loss in Africa is increasing not only because of livestock overgrazing but also because of the burning of crop residues due to the shortages of wood fuel. During the summer of 2000, NASA published a satellite image of a cloud of soil from Africa being blown across the Atlantic Ocean, further attesting to the massive soil erosion problem in Africa. Worldwide evidence concerning soil loss is substantiated and it is difficult to ignore its effect on sustainable agricultural production.

Contrary to Lomborg's belief, crop yields cannot continue to increase in response to the increased applications of more fertilizers and pesticides. In fact, field tests have demonstrated that applying excessive amounts of nitrogen fertilizer stresses the crop plants, resulting in declining yields. The optimum amount of

Figure 2

Corn Grain Yields From 1910 to 1999

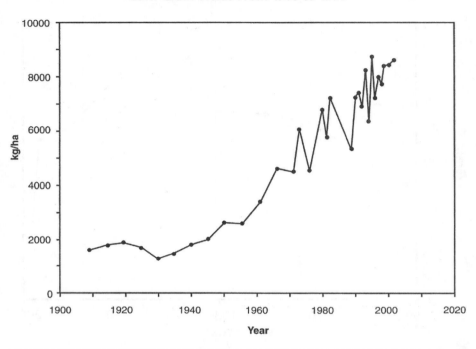

USDA, 1910–2000

nitrogen for corn, one of the crops that require heavy use of nitrogen, is approximately 120 kg/ha.

Although U.S. farmers frequently apply significantly more nitrogen fertilizer than 120 kg/ha, the extra is a waste and pollutant. The corn crop can only utilize about one-third of the nitrogen applied, while the remainder leaches either into the ground or surface waters. This pollution of aquatic ecosystems in agricultural areas results in the high levels of nitrogen and pesticides occurring in many U.S. water bodies. For example, nitrogen fertilizer has found its way into 97% of the well-water supplies in some regions, like North Carolina. The concentrations of nitrate are above the U.S. Environmental Protection Agency drinking-water standard of 10 milligrams per liter (nitrogen) and are a toxic threat to young children and young livestock. In the last 30 years, the nitrate content has tripled in the Gulf of Mexico, where it is reducing the Gulf fishery.

In an undocumented statement Lomborg reports that pesticides cause very little cancer. Further, he provides no explanation as to why human and other nontarget species are not exposed to pesticides when crops are treated. There is abundant medical and scientific evidence that confirms that pesticides cause significant numbers of cancers in the U.S. and throughout the world. Lomborg also neglects to report that some herbicides stimulate the production of toxic chemicals in some plants, and that these toxicants can cause cancer.

In keeping with Lomborg's view that agriculture and the food supply are improving, he states that "fewer people are starving." Lomborg criticizes the validity of the two World Health Organization [WHO] reports that confirm more than 3 billion people are malnourished. This is the largest number and proportion of malnourished people ever in history! Apparently Lomborg rejects the WHO data because they do not support his basic thesis. Instead, Lomborg argues that only people who suffer from calorie shortages are malnourished, and ignores the fact that humans die from deficiencies of protein, iron, iodine, and vitamin A, B, C, and D.

Further confirming a decline in food supply, the FAO reports that there has been a three-fold decline in the consumption of fish in the human diet during the past seven years. This decline in fish per capita is caused by overfishing, pollution, and the impact of a rapidly growing world population that must share the diminishing fish supply.

In discussing the status of water supply and sanitation services, Lomborg is correct in stating that these services were improved in the developed world during the 19th century, but he ignores the available scientific data when he suggests that these trends have been "replicated in the developing world" during the 20th century. Countless reports confirm that developing countries discharge most of their untreated urban sewage directly into surface waters. For example, of India's 3,119 towns and cities, only eight have full waste water treatment facilities. Furthermore, 114 Indian cities dump untreated sewage and partially cremated bodies directly into the sacred Ganges River. Downstream the untreated water is used for drinking, bathing, and washing. In view of the poor sanitation, it is no wonder that water borne infectious diseases account for 80% of all infections worldwide and 90% of all infections in developing countries.

Contrary to Lomborg's view, most infectious diseases are increasing worldwide. The increase is due not only to population growth but also because of increasing environmental pollution. Food-borne infections are increasing rapidly worldwide and in the United States. For example, during 2000 in the U.S. there were 76 million human food-borne infections with 5,000 associated deaths. Many of these infections are associated with the increasing contamination of food and water by livestock wastes in the United States.

In addition, a large number of malnourished people are highly susceptible to infectious diseases, like tuberculosis (TB), malaria, schistosomiasis, and AIDS. For example, the number of people infected with tuberculosis in the U.S. and the world is escalating, in part because medicine has not kept up with the new forms of TB. Currently, according to the World Health Organization, more than 2 billion people in the world are infected with TB, with nearly 2 million people dying each year from it.

Consistent with Lomborg's thesis that world natural resources are abundant, he reports that the U.S. Energy Information Agency for the period 2000 to 2020 projects an almost steady oil price over the next two decades at about $22 per barrel. This optimistic projection was crossed late in 2000 when oil rose to $30 or more per barrel in the United States and the world. The best estimates today project that world oil reserves will last approximately 50 years, based on current production rates.

Lomborg takes the World Wildlife Fund (WWF) to task for their estimates on the loss of world forests during the past decade and their emphasis on resulting ecological impacts and loss of biodiversity. Whether the loss of forests is slow, as Lomborg suggests, or rapid as WWF reports, there is no question that forests are disappearing worldwide (Figure 3). Forests not only provide valuable products but they harbor a vast diversity of species of plants, animals and microbes. Progress in medicine, agriculture, genetic engineering, and environmental quality depend on maintaining the species diversity in the world.

This reviewer takes issue with Lomborg's underlying thesis that the size and growth of the human population is not a major problem. The difference between Lomborg's figure that 76 million humans were added to the world population in 2000, or the 80 million reported by the Population Reference Bureau, is not the issue, thought the magnitude of both projections is of serious concern. Lomborg neglects to explain that the major problem with world population growth is the young age structure that now exists. Even if the world adopted a policy of only two children per couple tomorrow, the

Figure 3

Number of Hectares in Forests Worldwide (x 1 million ha) From 1961 to 1994

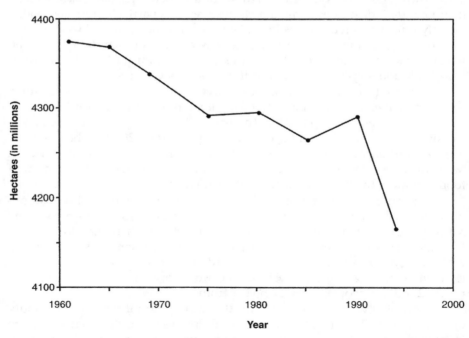

FAOSTAT Database, consulted September 3, 2001

world population would continue to increase for more than 70 years before stabilizing at more than 12 billion people. As an agricultural scientist and ecologist, I wish I could share Lomborg's optimistic views, but my investigations and those of countless scientists lead me to a more conservative outlook. The supply of basic resources, like fertile cropland, water, energy, and an unpolluted atmosphere that support human life is declining rapidly, as nearly a quarter million people are daily added to the Earth. We all desire a high standard of living for each person on Earth, but with every person added, the supply of resources must be divided and shared. Current losses and degradation of natural resources suggest concern and a need for planning for future generations of humans. Based on our current understanding of the real state of the world and environment, there is need for conservation and protection of vital world resources.

Denis Dutton

Greener Than You Think:
The Skeptical Environmentalist: Measuring the Real State of the World by Bjorn Lomborg

That the human race faces environmental problems is unquestionable. That environmental experts have regularly tried to scare us out of our wits with doomsday chants is also beyond dispute. In the 1960s overpopulation was going to cause massive worldwide famine around 1980. A decade later we were being told the world would be out of oil by the 1990s. This was an especially chilly prospect, since, as Newsweek reported in 1975, we were in a climatic cooling trend that was going to reduce agricultural outputs for the rest of the century, leading possibly to a new Ice Age.

Bjorn Lomborg, a young statistics professor and political scientist at the University of Aarhus in Denmark, knows all about the enduring appeal—for journalists, politicians and the public—of environmental doomsday tales, having swallowed more than a few himself. In 1997, Lomborg—a self-described left-winger and former Greenpeace member—came across an article in Wired magazine about Julian Simon, a University of Maryland economist. Simon claimed that the "litany" of the Green movement—its fears about overpopulation, animal species dying by the hour, deforestation—was hysterical nonsense, and that the quality of life on the planet was radically improving. Lomborg was shocked by this, and he returned to Denmark to set about doing the research that would refute Simon.

He and his team of academicians discovered something sobering and cheering: In every one of his claims, Simon was correct. Moreover, Lomborg found on close analysis that the factual foundation on which the environmental doomsayers stood was deeply flawed: exaggeration, prevarications, white lies and even convenient typographical errors had been absorbed unchallenged into the folklore of environmental disaster scenarios.

Lomborg still feels at one with the basic sentiments that underlie the Green movement: that we should strive toward a cleaner, healthier world for everyone, including animals (he's a vegetarian with ethical objections to eating flesh). But his aim in this new catalogue of environmental issues is to counter the gloom with a clear, scientifically based picture of the true state of the Earth and to take a rational view of what we can expect in the next century.

In a massive, meticulously presented argument that extends over 500 pages, supported by nearly 3,000 footnotes and 182 tables and diagrams, Lomborg revisits a number of heartening breakthroughs in the recent life of the planet. Chief among these is the decline of poverty and starvation across the world. Starvation still exists, but there is less of it than ever, as our capacity to produce abundant quantities of food continues to improve. Likewise with other dire scenarios of resource depletion: We are emphatically not running out of energy and mineral resources, the population bomb is fizzling, and, far from killing us, pesticides and chemicals are improving longevity and the quality of life. Neither need we fear anything from the genetic modification of organisms.

For a factual encyclopedia, the book has immense entertainment value, particularly in the way Lomborg traces the urban legends of the Green movement back to their sources. Consider the oft-repeated claim that 40,000 species go extinct every year. Such an annual loss of species, Lomborg points out, would be disaster for the future of life on earth, amounting perhaps to a loss of 25 to 50 percent of all species in the next half century. He manages, however, to locate the source of the story—an off-hand and completely unfounded guess made by a scientist in 1979. It's been repeated endlessly ever since—and in 1981 was increased by arch-doomsayer Paul Ehrlich to 250,000 species per year. (Ehrlich also predicted that half the planet's species would be extinct by 2000.)

Lomborg brings these unhinged forecasts back down to Earth by reminding us that the only actual scientific documentation for species loss is in United Nations figures, which show an actual loss of between a tenth of a percent and 1 percent of all species for all of the next 50 years. This includes beetles, ants, flies, worms, bacteria and fungi, which make up 99 percent of all species, plus a small but unknown number of mammals and birds. Extinction, Lomborg argues, is a problem to be realistically faced and solved, not a catastrophe to be bewailed.

Or consider deforestation. It's been claimed that the world has lost two-thirds of its forests since the dawn of agriculture. The real figure, Lomborg shows, is around 20 percent, and this figure has hardly changed since the World War II. Tropical forests are declining at a small annual rate of 0.46 percent, but this is offset by growth in commercial plantations, which should be encouraged, as their products take the pressure off the tropical forests. In fact, the world's wood and paper needs could be permanently satisfied by tree plantations amounting to just 5 percent of the world's forest cover.

Then there's waste disposal. Are we really running out of landfill space for our garbage? Lomborg shows how the entire trash-dumping requirements for the United States through the whole of the coming century (assuming the country doubles in population) could be met by a single landfill that measures 100 feet high and 18 miles square. That's a lot of trash, but as the total leavings of the increasing U.S. population over a hundred years, it is certainly not unmanageable, and if it's properly dealt with, it need pose no serious pollution threat to air or water.

Speaking of trash, Lomborg favors recycling, but only when it makes sense, and he gives a hilarious analysis of a scheme from Environment magazine to mail used toothbrushes to a plant where they could be recycled as outdoor furniture. This would cost $4 billion to implement for the U.S. population, and that's without taking into account the costs of the postal system handling a billion packages of new and used toothbrushes annually. The recycling cure can be worse than the consumption disease (though I can imagine the U.S. Postal Service might see this idea as a revenue opportunity).

Many well-intentioned environmental policies can have surprising outcomes: Suppose minute pesticide residues have the potential to cause cancer in a tiny number of cases—one estimate would have it around 20 cases per annum in the United States (not very many in a country where 300 people drown in bathtubs every year). So we ban the pesticides. This in turn, Lomborg points out, would sharply drive up the price of cancer-preventing fruits and vegetables. By reducing consumption, especially among the poor, the pesticide ban in the end would cause more cancer (perhaps 26,000 cases annually) than the pesticides would have caused in the first place. Sometimes, as with toothbrushes, the best thing to do about a "problem" is exactly nothing.

Lomborg enjoys placing what look to be serious environmental issues in a comparative context, which can often cause them to diminish considerably in scale. The Exxon Valdez oil spill was portrayed as a disaster of unparalleled magnitude: For example, it killed 250,000 birds. He shows how the long-term effects of the spill were far less damaging than environmentalists predicted, and also puts the avian mortality claim in perspective: Some 300,000 birds are killed by mammals, mostly cats, in Great Britain every 48 hours, and 250,000 birds die from striking plate glass in homes and offices in the United States every 24 hours. How could he know that? I wondered myself, so here as elsewhere, I followed Lomborg's claims back through the footnotes, traced the sources for myself, and found them to be sound. In fact, since The Skeptical Environmentalist was published last month in Britain, an army of angry environmentalists has been crawling all over the book, trying to refute it. Lomborg's claims have withstood the attack.

The book's longest, most detailed chapter is on global warming and the Kyoto Treaty. Lomborg agrees that a warming trend is real but says that the Intergovernmental Panel on Climate Change exaggerates the possible threats and present-day proportions of global warming, while neglecting the benefits of more carbon dioxide in the air and warmer nighttime temperatures. These changes would improve agricultural output in the U.S. and China, and make for vast increases in crop production for Canada and Russia. In any event, Lomborg is promoter of solar energy, which he believes will take over from oil as our major energy source in the next 50 years.

His most stunning conclusion: Even if the Kyoto treaty were fully implemented, it would stave off warming by only about six years—postponing it from 2100 to 2106. So what is the cost to the world economy of this almost invisible benefit we are to bestow on our great-great grandchildren? Anywhere from $80 to $350 billion per annum. Lomborg is very disturbed by these figures, since he sees health improvements as the greatest challenge now facing the human race—especially the enormous gains against disease and poverty that will come from increasing the supply of clean drinking water and the quality of sanitation in the developing world. The costs of Kyoto for one year could give clean water and sanitation to the whole of the developing world, saving 2 million lives, and keeping half a billion people from serious illness. For future, unknown and perhaps nonexistent benefits, Kyoto would squander money that should be applied right now to real, life-and-death human problems. Lomborg's calculations are meticulous, his argument compelling: Implementation of the Kyoto Treaty would be an unforgivable mistake.

Lomborg's original inspiration, the radical Julian Simon, was just a bit too far ahead of his time. This bald, vaguely right-wing economist was on the money, but in the late 20th century, with Green mythology ascendant, no one wanted to know. Paul Ehrlich, as reward for being wrong in all his scary predictions about population and the environment, was showered with prizes, including a MacArthur "genius" fellowship. As Simon cheerfully remarked, "I can't even get a McDonald's." This irrepressible scholar did, however, provoke a young Dane into trying to disprove his claims—a process that led to questioning the factual foundations of the environmental movement itself. Unlike Simon, Lomborg has the correct cultural aura: a young, left-wing European with the looks of a movie star. Simon, who died suddenly in 1998, would have loved to see how things are turning out.

Bjorn Lomborg's good news about the environment is bad news for Green ideologues. His richly informative, lucid book is now the place from which environmental policy decisions must be argued. In fact, *The Skeptical Environmentalist* is the most significant work on the environment since the appearance of its polar opposite, Rachel Carson's *Silent Spring,* in 1962. It's a magnificent achievement.

POSTSCRIPT

vmIs the Condition of the Environment Really as Bad as Environmentalists Claim?

You have just read two articles disputing the relative merits of Danish professor and statistician Bjorn Lomborg's book, *The Skeptical Environmentalist*. Regardless of which side of this debate you agree with, there seems to be no question that it is essential for us to have an accurate accounting of the state of world's environment if we are to utilize our scarce economic resources to best advantage. Most environmentalists argue that there is nothing wrong with maintaining an overly pessimistic view of the environmental situation because it tends to force governments and businesses to act from a preventative rather than from a reactive mindset. In other words, it is safer to be pessimistic. This view has dominated public discussion since the beginning of the modern environmental movement in the 1960s and is responsible for the numerous laws and regulations that affect virtually every aspect of our lives. But, as a growing number of critics have pointed out, in many instances, this view is much worse than a carelessly optimistic attitude where there are no environmental problems at all.

Consider the case of the corporate average fuel economy (CAFE) ratings for automobiles. A 1975 law subjected all cars to fuel-efficiency requirements; currently, new cars must meet a 27.5 mpg standard while larger vehicles such as SUVs must reach at least 20.7 mpg (Robert James Bidinotto, "Death by Environmentalism: What Happens When Humans Must Give Way to Nature," *The Navigator*, The Objectivist Center, March 2004, p. 4). The problem is that these standards have forced automakers to make smaller, lighter, less safe cars. How unsafe? Two reputable studies (1989 by Harvard University and the Brookings Institution; 2001 by the National Academy of Sciences) concluded that the CAFE standards result in 1,200–3,900 additional deaths every year. "In the trade-off between saving gasoline and saving lives, the government rules willingly sacrifice lives" (Bidinotto, p. 4). Given this, it is no surprise that large, safe SUVs are popular with the public; nor is it surprising that SUVs are viewed by environmentalists as major contributors to the depletion of fossil fuels and to global warming.

The point of the above example is that it is just as dangerous to error on the side of extreme pessimism about the environment as it is to be in a state of unfounded optimism. Clearly, then, what is needed is an accurate assessment of the real state of the world.

Suggested Readings

Readings supportive of *The Skeptical Environmentalist:*

Ronald Bailey, Debunking green myths. *Reason,* February 2002.

"Doomsday postponed." *The Economist,* September 6, 2001. http://www. lomborg.com/files/Economist%20review%206-9-01.mht

Jim Peron, Maybe we can smile, the environment is looking pretty good. *The Objectivist Center,* December 19, 2001. http://www. objectivistcenter.org/ articles/jperon_maybe-smile.asp

Readings critical of *The Skeptical Environmentalist:*

Paul R. Erlich, The brownlash rides again. *HMS Beagle,* issue 114, November 9, 2001. http://www.lomborg.com/files/Erhlich%20review.htm

Michael Grubb, Relying on manna from heaven? *Science,* vol. 294, November 9, 2001. http://www.lomborg.com/files/Science%20review%2012-11-01.pdf

Eric Newmayer, Picking holes in the litany of loss. *The Times Higher Education Supplement,* November 16, 2001. http://www.lomborg.com/files/ Times%20Higher%20Educational%20Supplement%2016-11-01.mht

ISSUE 16

Should U.S. Corporations Be Allowed to Hire Illegal Aliens?

YES: Rob Paral, from "Essential Workers: Immigrants Are a Needed Supplement to the Native-Born Labor Force," *Immigration Policy Brief* (American Immigration Law Foundation, March 2005)

NO: Fred Dickey, from "Undermining American Workers: Record Numbers of Illegal Immigrants Are Pulling Wages Down for the Poor and Pushing Taxes Higher," *Los Angeles Times* (July 20, 2003)

ISSUE SUMMARY

YES: Rob Paral, a research fellow with the Immigration Policy Center, believes that the pluses of hiring illegal immigrants outweigh the minuses.

NO: Fred Dickey disagrees. In a detailed exposé on immigration published in the *Los Angeles Times,* reporter Dickey maps out his case against the use of illegal immigrants in the American workforce.

In the months prior to the November 2006 midterm elections, members of the two major political parties faced a bevy of issues important to the American electorate. The war on terrorism in Iraq remained contentious, with many Democrats calling for troop withdrawal and many Republicans calling for patience and support. Although the Republicans provided plenty of evidence to justify their "culture of corruption" label, the Democrats, too, had moral image problems, the result of ongoing criminal and ethical investigations of at least two of their own. The economy, though showing strong, sustained growth, also seemed to be on the verge overheating. Not surprisingly, the Democrats tried to paint the economy black; the incumbent Republicans tried to paint it positive. As important and interesting as those issues were, perhaps the single most important issue of the day involved the topic of immigration. Specifically, the debate centered around two questions: First, what should be done about the 11–12 million illegal aliens already in America? And second, what should be done to stop the river of illegal aliens from entering the country in the first place?

According to the Cato Institute, over the last 200 years, the United States has welcomed 60 million immigrants to its shores (http://www.freetrade.org/issues/immigration.html). Although the vast majority of those immigrants entered the country legally, in recent decades the number of people entering the country illegally has grown tremendously. There is no question that the continued growth of illegal aliens has important ramifications both politically and socially; indeed, one need only observe the behaviors of the two political parties to verify the truth of this statement. But of particular importance to this text is the implication of the growth of illegal aliens on the American workplace. Specifically, we ask, given the current state of affairs, should U.S. corporations be allowed to hire illegal aliens?

An important factor in addressing this question involves determining the impact of illegal immigrants on our economy. Those who believe corporations should be allowed to hire illegal aliens, or at least not be punished for so doing, provide numerous points in support of their position. For example, research has established that immigrants and natives frequently do not compete for the same jobs. In areas where demand for labor is high relative to supply, hiring immigrants results in a complementary outcome rather than a competitive situation. Thus, the view that illegal aliens and other immigrants take jobs from native workers is simpleminded. Indeed, many employers have found that there is a large degree of overlap between the characteristics of an individual willing to accept the risks and dangers of relocating to a foreign land in order to make a better life for himself and the characteristics of a loyal, dependable, and driven employee. Finally, supporters note that illegal aliens contribute mightily to our economy in ways beyond their physical labor; as a group, they contribute billions of dollars to Social Security through payroll taxes. However, owing to fears of being caught and deported, few actually collect payments, thus providing Social Security program with a huge net gain. For example, *The Washington Post* estimated that during the period 1990–98, illegal aliens paid over $20 billion in payroll taxes (Washingtonpost.com).

On the other side of the debate are those who are against corporations being allowed to hire illegal aliens. Central to their position is the argument that illegal immigration disproportionately affects poor American natives since the immigrants are willing to work the unskilled jobs typically held by poor Americans and do so for much less pay. From this perspective, firms that hire illegal aliens are anti-American since they are effectively displacing legitimate American employees. Another charge frequently leveled at supporters is the negative impact on the economy due to illegal immigration, particularly in the area of taxes. On the one hand, critics point out, states loose billions of dollars each year in the form of unpaid taxes. On the other, states are faced with growing demands for governmental services driven by the increase in their populations, much of which is the result of illegal immigration. The net result? States have to raise taxes to meet these needs; thus, the law-abiding American citizen foots the bill for the illegal immigrants.

The question posed here is whether U.S. corporations should be allowed to hire illegal aliens. Rob Paral believes that the pluses of hiring illegal immigrants outweigh the minuses. Fred Dickey disagrees and maps out his case against the use of illegal immigrants in the American workforce.

YES

Rob Paral

Essential Workers: Immigrants Are a Needed Supplement to the Native-Born Labor Force

Introduction

More and more policymakers have come to realize that the U.S. immigration system does not adequately respond to labor shortages in the U.S. economy. However, rational reform of the system is hindered by claims that immigrants "steal" jobs from the native born and drive down wages for native workers by serving as a source of cheap labor. Proponents of restrictive immigration policies, seeking to exploit fears generated by a turbulent economy, attempt to draw parallels between the numbers of recently arrived immigrants and numbers of unemployed native-born workers. Yet the notion that every job filled by an immigrant is one less job available for a native-born worker is inherently simplistic and doesn't account for the fact that immigrants create jobs or that unemployed natives and immigrant workers often do not compete for the same jobs.

Beyond such general considerations, data from the 2000 census permit a quantitative evaluation of the labor market impact of those immigrant workers who entered the United States in the 1990s and were still noncitizens when the census was taken.[1] It is important to consider this group of immigrants because it includes large numbers of undocumented immigrants and large numbers of legal immigrants who have relatively low levels of formal education. Both these types of immigrants compete in the low-wage portion of the economy. Policymakers rightfully worry that the presence of immigrants seeking low-wage work could have a negative impact on natives seeking the same types of jobs.

The impact of noncitizen immigrants who arrived in the 1990s can be examined by comparing the numbers of these immigrants found in specific occupations to the number of unemployed natives who had recent experience working in the same occupations. Two outcomes may result from this comparison:

1. If the number of unemployed natives exceeded the number of employed recent immigrants, then one could conclude, in theory, that the immigrant workers were not necessary. Or,
2. If the number of immigrants in an occupation exceeded the number of unemployed natives, then one could conclude that there were not enough natives to fill all existing jobs. In this latter scenario, removing

Immigration Policy Brief from the Immigration Policy Center, a division of the American Immigration Law Foundation, March 2005. Copyright © 2005 by American Immigration Law Foundation. Reprinted by permission.

those immigrants from the labor force would have lead to a decline in the number of employed persons, with corresponding negative effects on the U.S. economy.

Immigrants in the U.S. Workforce

Immigrants are a critical part of the U.S. labor force. They staff software companies, hospital laboratories, and university engineering departments, as well as filling jobs in factories and fields. In 2003, the foreign born in the United States were 23 percent of production workers, 20 percent of service workers, and 12 percent of professionals.[2] Immigrants are most prominently represented in jobs at both ends of the occupational spectrum—that is, in low-skilled and high-skilled jobs—and are less prominent in jobs requiring a mid-level amount of education.

Recently arrived immigrants are a large portion of all immigrant workers. There were an estimated 33.5 million foreign-born individuals in the United States in 2003, of whom 36.6 percent—or 12.3 million—arrived during the 1990s.[3] Among these recent arrivals were 5 million undocumented immigrants,[4] representing roughly half of the current undocumented population.[5] This migratory wave included many immigrants who were low-skilled and who are the primary focus of recent legislative proposals to "regularize" the entry of immigrant workers into the United States.

Immigrant and Native Workers Are Not Simply Competitors

Some politicians and commentators claim that immigrant workers "steal" jobs from native workers, especially low-skilled jobs that would otherwise go to low-income natives who can least afford to be without employment. At a theoretical level, however, this claim may be disputed. To begin with, distinguishing between jobs merely on the basis of whether they are held by natives or immigrants ignores the fact that many "native" jobs are in immigrant-owned businesses, or are made possible by the purchasing power of immigrants. In other words, many "native" jobs wouldn't exist if not for the presence of immigrants in the labor market.

Even if the fact that immigrants create jobs is overlooked for the sake of analysis, immigrants and natives do not always compete for the same jobs, even within the same occupation. The most obvious reason is geography: unemployed natives and immigrant workers often live in different places. An unemployed native meatpacking worker in Pennsylvania, for instance, is probably not competing for the meatpacking job held by an immigrant in Kansas. In addition, many foreign-born and native-born workers differ in their job expectations. Immigrants often have lower levels of education than U.S. natives and were raised in societies much poorer than the United States. Therefore, immigrants and natives frequently have different views as to what wages and working conditions are "acceptable." Immigrants are sometimes willing to take jobs that natives are not.

Not Enough Native-Born Workers

Leaving aside theoretical considerations, data from the 2000 census indicate that even if native workers could readily have moved to any part of the country in which jobs were available during the 1990s, and even if they had been willing to accept any job offered, there would not have been nearly enough unemployed native-born workers to fill all available jobs. This is illustrated by

Table 1

Theoretical Worker Shortages Due to Loss of 1990s Noncitizen Arrivals

	Noncitizen workers who arrived in 1990s	Unemployed native born	Worker shortage if noncitizens discounted from labor force	Pct by which the category would shrink
Miscellaneous Agricultural Workers	182,082	53,690	108,392	13.4%
Maids and House-keeping Cleaners	161,275	80,825	80,450	6.6%
Sewing Machine Operators	67,917	24,812	43,105	9.2%
Grounds Mainte-nance Workers	132,385	91,884	40,501	4.0%
Construction Laborers	173,874	133,802	40.072	3.2%
Other Production Workers	114.618	81,655	32,963	2.4%
Cooks	194,871	165,458	29,413	1.6%
Painters, Construction and Maintenance	69,053	42,486	26,567	4.7%
Janitors and Building Cleaners	153,872	129,074	24,798	1.2%
Butchers and Meat, Poultry, Fish Processing Worker	39,730	15,381	24,369	8.5%
Other Metal Workers and Plastic Workers	48,138	25,375	22,763	3.7%
Packers and Packages, Hand	63,032	41,419	21,613	5.2%
Packaging and Filing Machine Operators and Tenders	44,769	23,509	21,260	6.8%

A net loss of 108,000 workers would ensue in event of full native employment coupled with loss of recently arrived, noncitizen immigrant workers.

Note: Table includes occupations without extensive formal education requirements, where net loss of workers exceeds 20,000. Persons in this table have been employed within the last five years.

comparing the number of employed immigrants—specifically, the noncitizen arrivals of the 1990s—with the number of unemployed natives for each of the 471 specific occupations categorized by the U.S. Census Bureau in its Public Use Microdata Samples. The analysis includes unemployed natives who had worked in the previous five years, who constituted nine out of ten

Table 2

Theoretical Worker Shortages Due to Loss of 1990s Noncitizen Arrivals

	Noncitizen workers who arrived in 1990s	Unemployed native born	Worker shortage if non citizens discounted from labor force	Pct by which the category would shrink	
Miscellaneous Agricultural Workers	162,082	53,690	108,392	13.4%	
Miscellaneous Personal Appearance Workers	19,362	2,944	16,418	12.3%	Losing recently arrived noncitizen workers while providing full employment for natives leads to net loss of 8.5 percent of butchers nationwide.
Plasterers and Stucco Masons	7,967	2,912	5,055	11.5%	
Jewelers and Precious Stone and Metal Workers	6,634	932	5,702	11.1%	
Pressers, Textile, Garment, and Related Materials	15,480	6,179	9,301	10.0%	
Textile Cutting Machine Setters, Operators, and Tenders	2,571	791	1,780	9.9%	
Sewing Machine Operators	67,917	24,812	43,105	9.2%	
Butchers and Meat, Poultry, Fish Processing Worker	39,730	15,361	24,369	(8.5%)	
Graders and Sorters, Agricultural Products	8,111	4,552	3,559	8.0%	
Tailors, Dressmakers, and Sewers	11,225	2,612	8,613	7.9%	
Taxi Drivers and Chauffeurs	28,316	10,074	18,242	7.5%	

Note: Table includes occupations, without extensive formal education requirements, where loss of workers exceeds 7 percent of labor force. Persons in this table have been employed within the last five years.

unemployed persons. If the number of employed immigrants exceeded the number of unemployed natives in a particular occupation, then there were not enough unemployed natives to fill all available jobs in 2000. It is possible that unemployed native workers might have been willing to switch occupations and take jobs in an area in which they had no experience. For example, an unemployed baker might have become a taxi driver. However, it is unlikely that many natives could have been enticed into the kinds of jobs that immigrants typically hold, such as agricultural labor.

The analysis reveals 167 job categories—or 35 percent of all job categories in the United States—in which the number of noncitizen immigrant workers who arrived in just the 1990s exceeded the number of unemployed natives with recent work experience. Table 1 presents the results of the analysis for those occupations in which the number of immigrant workers who arrived in the 1990s exceeded the number of unemployed natives by at least 20,000. Table 2 presents results for those occupations that would have experienced the greatest percentage reductions in their labor force if immigrant workers had not been present during the 1990s.

The census data indicate that recent noncitizen arrivals comprised tens of thousands of workers in many job categories in 2000. Noncitizen immigrants who came to the United States during the 1990s were 162,000 of the nation's miscellaneous agricultural workers, 194,000 of the nation's cooks, and 153,000 of the nation's janitors. The number of unemployed natives in these job categories was well below the number of employed immigrants, and many industries would have had substantially smaller workforces if not for immigrant workers. For example, the jobs that the native-born unemployed could not have filled accounted for 8.5 percent of all butchers and 6.6 percent of all bakers. In the case of miscellaneous agricultural workers, the 108,000 lost jobs would have represented well over one in ten workers. It is difficult to imagine how a comparable number of unemployed natives with other types of job skills could have been induced to enter agriculture, or how mechanization could have made up for this labor shortfall

Immigrant Wages Increase Over Time

Although immigrant workers were clearly an indispensable part of the labor force in many occupations and industrial sectors during the 1990s, another key consideration is how their wages compared to those of native-born workers. If immigrant workers uniformly earned lower wages than their native-born counterparts in a particular occupation, this might imply that the presence of immigrants in the labor force undercut the earning potential of native workers. However, comparing the wages of native workers with the wages of immigrants who had been in the United States different lengths of time and who had different levels of English literacy reveals that the earning power of immigrants increased with time—and with legal status.

Table 3 uses data from the 2000 census to compare the earnings in 1999 of three groups of immigrants relative to natives: 1.) noncitizens who arrived

Table 3

Ratio of Immigrant to Native Earnings in 1999

	Noncitizens, entered in 1990s	Noncitizens, entered before 1990	Naturalized immigrants
Management, business, and financial operations	0.86	0.95	1.01
Professional and related	1.00	1.14	1.25
Healthcare support	0.96	1.22	1.25
Protective service	0.50	0.63	0.91
Food preparation and serving related	1.33	1.67	1.67
Building and grounds cleaning and maintenance	0.83	1.03	1.17
Personal care and service	0.93	1.20	1.25
Sales and related	0.67	0.95	1.13
Office and administrative support	0.75	1.03	1.17
Farming, fishing, and forestry	0.67	0.87	0.93
Construction and extraction	0.57	0.89	1.00
Installation, maintenance, and repair	0.61	0.85	1.00
Production	0.60	0.79	0.91
Transportation and material moving	0.65	0.87	1.00
Total	0.62	0.92	1.08

Note: Table includes civilian labor force employed during last five years, with earnings in 1999

Earnings increase for immigrants the longer they are in the U.S. and as they naturalize. Earnings of naturalized immigrants exceed those of natives.

in the 1990s, 2.) noncitizens who arrived prior to 1990, and 3.) naturalized citizens. The comparisons are made in 13 employment categories that collectively included all employed persons in the civilian labor force who had earnings in 1999.

Relative wages were lowest among recently arrived noncitizens, who included the most undocumented immigrants and presumably those with the lowest levels of English mastery. Relative wages were highest—in some cases exceeding the wages of the native born—among naturalized citizens, who must have achieved legal status and basic levels of literacy, English ability, and residency in the country.

The pattern of wage improvement holds across all employment sectors. In every employment category—even farming—immigrants earned more the longer they had lived in the country and, by implication, as they acquired legal status and mastered English. The fact that naturalized immigrants earn significantly more than noncitizens implies that legal status translates into higher wages. Immigrants with legal status are freer to move within the economy and sell their skills to the highest bidder.

Immigrants also earned more than natives in some low-skilled employment categories. Surprisingly, even recently arrived noncitizen immigrants out-earned the native born in the category of food preparation and serving (which includes cooks, waiters, and dishwashers). This fact helps to dispel the simplistic notion that employers automatically save money by hiring immigrants instead of natives.

Needed Workers

The United States has long depended on immigrants to compensate for shortfalls in the native-born labor force. The agricultural industry has recognized this fact for decades and relied upon immigrant workers to make up for the shortage of native workers in the fields. The Immigration Reform and Control Act (IRCA) of 1986 created the Special Agricultural Worker program for just this purpose. Other industries in the service and manufacturing sectors rely upon immigrant workers who enter the country through both temporary and permanent visas in categories such as H2A, H2B, and third-preference employment. Organized labor also has accepted the U.S. economy's need for immigrant workers, as exemplified by AFL-CIO's shift to a pro-immigrant stance during the 1990s.

In general, U.S. immigration law has yet to fully acknowledge the economic importance of immigration to the United States. Even though immigrant workers are an essential part of the U.S. labor force, particularly in low-skilled occupations for which fewer and fewer native-born workers are available, U.S. immigration laws continue to impose arbitrary and antiquated numerical limits on how many immigrants may enter the country. These limits have repeatedly proven insufficient to meet actual labor demand, resulting in high levels of undocumented migration. U.S. industries and workers themselves (both immigrant and native) would be far better served if policymakers created a system to ensure that those immigrants who come to fill available jobs do so with legal status and the protection of tough and rigorously enforced wage and labor laws.

President Bush has proposed granting a temporary status to immigrant workers, who would have to leave the United States after a three-year or six-year stay. Although this idea is a useful beginning in the debate over immigration reform, the data in this report suggest that relying exclusively on a temporary worker program may be ill-advised. Immigrants improve their economic status the longer they reside in the United States and as they acquire levels of English proficiency and education associated with the requirements for naturalization. The benefits of this upward economic mobility would be limited under a system that heavily favored temporary workers and that required immigrants to leave the country after a few years. Realizing the full potential of immigrant workers and their contributions to the U.S. economy will require a comprehensive approach that includes improved legal pathways for permanent immigration.

Endnotes

1. The universe of persons in this report includes those individuals in the civilian labor force in 2000 who were either employed or were unemployed but had been employed in the previous five years. Among the unemployed, these persons accounted for 87 percent of the total unemployed population. Data are not available on the types of occupations held by persons unemployed for more than five years. If it were possible to assign these long-term unemployed workers to occupations and include them in the analysis, it would decrease the shortfall of workers resulting from the removal of recent noncitizen arrivals from the labor force. However, the analysis could also remove noncitizens who arrived before 1990, which in turn would increase the shortfall of workers.

2. Bureau of Labor Statistics, Economic News Release: "Labor Force Characteristics of Foreign-Born Workers in 2003," Table 4: "Employed foreign-born and native-born persons 16 years and over by occupation and sex, 2003 annual averages," December 1, 2004.

3. Luke J. Larsen, *The Foreign-Born Population in the United States: 2003*, Current Population Reports, P20-551. Washington, DC: U.S. Census Bureau, August 2004.

4. Jeffrey Passel, *New Estimates of the Undocumented Population in the United States*. Washington, DC: Migration Policy Institute, May 22, 2002.

5. Jeffrey S. Passel, *Estimates of the Size and Characteristics of the Undocumented Population*. Washington, DC: Pew Hispanic Center, March 21, 2005.

Fred Dickey  **NO**

Undermining American Workers: Record Numbers of Illegal Immigrants Are Pulling Wages Down for the Poor and Pushing Taxes Higher

The perils of illegal immigration rattle around in the attic of public policy like a troubled spirit. We pretend not to hear the dragging chains because we don't know how to silence them, but the ghosts will endure, especially in California. Because the nation can't control its borders, the number of illegal immigrants grows by an estimated half-million each year. They come because we invite them with lax law enforcement and menial jobs. Their presence makes our own poor more destitute, creating a Third World chaos in the California economy that we are only beginning to understand.

Patricia Morena has no time for a philosophical discussion on unauthorized immigration. She lives with it, or tries to. She's a U.S. citizen of Mexican descent, and a motel maid in Chula Vista, six miles north of the border. She's short and heavyset, and dresses with care in tasteful thrift shop. She earns $300 before taxes, when she's fortunate enough to have a five-day week. She's a single mom with three children, all stuffed into a ratty little one-bedroom apartment. The eldest, an 18-year-old boy, has taken to stealing; she thinks it's because he's always been poor.

Sitting in the pale yellow kitchen light, she looks resigned rather than angry. She has the fear of anyone who's 39, broke and tired: being replaced. If she didn't have to compete with unauthorized workers in the cheap motels that cluster just north of the border, she thinks, she could lift her wages from $7.50 per hour to maybe $10 and bargain for some health insurance.

But she won't ask for a raise. "If I ask for money, the bosses say, 'I can get a young girl who is faster and cheaper,'" she says. "The bosses have power over illegals. They know they're afraid and not going to ask for overtime, even though I know the law says they should get it." So Morena remains mired, one of 32.9 million people the U.S. Census Bureau says lived in poverty in 2001.

The 1996 welfare reform act was pitched as a means for poor people to elevate themselves through work. President Clinton said at the time that the act was "to give them a chance to share in the prosperity and the promise that most of our people are enjoying today."

Well, seven years later, Morena is still poor. Although she never studied economics, she has learned a fundamental economic truth: The only leverage unskilled workers have is scarcity of labor. Morena can't work her way up the economic ladder because the bottom rungs have been broken off by the weight of millions of new illegal workers. The census bureau says the number of illegal immigrants in the country doubled in the 1990s, from 3.5 million to 7 million, the largest such increase in the nation's history.

So Morena soldiers on at $7.50 an hour, living with a reality that the late Cesar Chavez, champion of the farm worker, understood back in the 1960s. Chavez, says David M. Kennedy, Pulitzer Prize-winning historian from Stanford University, advocated limited immigration to protect the wage levels of the Chicano workers he struggled to unionize. Without such restrictions, demand for labor would fall, and with it the pressure to pay higher wages.

The people who traditionally benefit from the Patricia Morenas and other low-paid workers are farther up the economic ladder—businesses, industries and homeowners. For them, stagnant low wages mean they can hire maids, farm laborers, seamstresses, roofers and carpet cleaners for about the same wages as they paid a quarter-century ago. That helps industries grow cheap lettuce and make down-market shirts. It frees up enough money for homeowners to afford those sports cars whose price tripled even as the cost of getting their lawn mowed stayed the same.

Yet the relentless flow of illegal labor is now changing life for Californians on those higher rungs too.

Apart from the proliferation of workers standing on street corners waiting for jobs, it's difficult to see that migration from Mexico into California during the past two decades is on a scale that astonishes even those who specialize in making sense out of human patterns. One such expert is Victor Davis Hanson, a professor of classics at Cal State Fresno and the author of "Mexifornia," a recent book that reveals the extent of the changing culture and demographics of California. He says that no immigration in American history even remotely compares to the one underway along the southwest border, which, incidentally, is the longest that has ever separated First- and Third World countries.

Today, nearly half of California's residents are immigrants or the children of immigrants, and the state's population is projected to increase by 52%, to 49 million, between 2000 and 2025. An estimated 950,000 Mexicans without papers live in the five-county Greater Los Angeles area, says Jeffrey Passel, a demographer at the Urban Institute public policy center in Washington, D.C. They are mostly nested in communities of the 2.4 million Mexican-born migrants. Statewide, there are 1.6 million undocumented Mexicans, and 4.8 million in the country, Passel says. They make up more than half of the 8.5-million-plus undocumented persons of all nationalities.

The image of migrants popularized by their advocates is of work-tough campesinos who cross the border spitting on their hands and eagerly looking for shovels. That is true to a considerable extent, because a lot of shoveling gets done. As the U.S. Chamber of Commerce says in support of a new amnesty for unauthorized immigrants: "There are approximately 10 million undocumented workers employed throughout the country who are working hard and performing tasks that most Americans take for granted but won't do themselves."

The second half of that sentence has been accepted as a truth for generations. Illegal immigrants are just doing the work Americans won't. But is it true today?

In April, I shopped for a contractor to paint my house trim. I got three bids. One was for $1,600, about $400 less than the others. The only condition was that payment be in cash. That wasn't remarkable. Is there a Californian alive who doesn't know they can pay under the table for cheap immigrant labor? You pay cash. There are no checks. There is no tax record.

But this bargain didn't come from an undocumented worker. It came from an established businessman with good references. I asked why the ethical gyrations.

He vented: "If I'm going to stay in business, I have to do what the illegals do. They never pay taxes, on profits or on their employees' pay. Right there, I'm at a 20% disadvantage. They'll come in here with about six guys with paintbrushes who work for peanuts, do a fair job, and then they're gone." These competitors have driven every American out of gardening, he added, and are doing it to house-painting, roofing and car repair. He concluded in frustration, "What am I supposed to do?"

Roy Beck, executive director of Numbers USA Education and Research Foundation, a Washington, D.C., organization devoted to immigration control, says it's not that millions of unemployed Americans "are too lazy and shiftless to bus tables or wash dishes." What the Chamber of Commerce and like-minded business groups really mean, he says, is that "Americans won't work like slaves, like serfs. Americans want to be paid and treated fairly."

"The National Restaurant Assn., for one, doesn't want their customers to know that this system forces illegal workers to live in abject poverty," Beck says. "It's the serfdom thing. If customers thought about it, they'd say, 'No, I don't want people who are hidden in the kitchen or serving me to be so poor and neglected that they might be TB carriers, and hate my guts for not caring about them.'"

Terry Anderson, a black talk-radio host in Los Angeles, says he sees similar displacement throughout the African American community. "I defy you to find a black janitor in L.A.," Anderson says. "In the '70s, the auto body-repair business in South-Central was pretty much occupied by blacks. Those jobs are all gone now. They're all held by Hispanics, and all of them are illegals. And those $25 jobs that blacks used to hold in the '70s now pay $8 to $10, and a black man can't get hired even if he's expert. It's absolute discrimination, because there's a perception that a Hispanic works better. Well, he works cheaper. They're in the country illegally, so they have no bargaining power, and the wages get driven down."

The point he and Beck make is decidedly not a racial one, not black versus Latino or Mexican versus white. Their point is about money. Illegal, powerless immigrants versus relatively empowered American citizens. Who among us could survive if every day, the streets outside our workplaces were lined with people willing to do our jobs for two-thirds or half the pay because in the world they came from, in the world where their money is sent, half of our pay amounted to riches?

Anderson particularly despairs of the effect the scarcity of low-end jobs has on poor youths. In May, 6.1 million whites and 1.7 million blacks in the country were unemployed. But of those without jobs, young people took the worst hit. The unemployment rate for whites ages 16 to 19 in the labor force was 15.4%, with 892,000 unemployed; for black teenagers, it was 270,000 out of work, at a scary 35% rate.

These kids are the millions of potential burger-flippers and mowers of lawns that Beck and Anderson say employers are bypassing in favor of undocumented migrants. "There was this kid in my neighborhood—good kid, 17 years old, and he goes down to the local McDonald's to get an after-school job," Anderson says. "The manager tells him that because he doesn't speak Spanish, she can't hire him because it would have a disruptive effect on all the other workers who don't speak English. I mean, think of that: Here's a kid trying to get a little ahead—American born, four generations in South-Central—who's told he can't sell French fries because he can't speak a foreign language. You want to talk about disillusionment?"

As cheap, illegal workers flood the labor force, governments and taxpayers are feeling the pinch. Just as one dishonest act often leads to another, illegal labor has led to other illegalities. The most pervasive is the untaxed cash transaction. It has created a surging "underground economy" that has become a hole in society's pocket through which falls many of our democratic values, and a lot of loose cash.

John Chiang of Los Angeles, one of five members of the state Board of Equalization, California's tax oversight agency, says off-the-books businesses can have a "profoundly dislocating effect" on the economy. It pushes some businesses to compete by also cutting legal corners, and discourages other businesses from coming to California.

A study last year by the Economic Roundtable, a Los Angeles research group, found that the underground sector in Southern California probably accounts for 20% or more of the economy, says economist Dan Flaming, author of the report. Nationwide, the International Monetary Fund reported in a 2002 issues paper, underground work amounted to 10% of the total economy.

As the underground sector surged in the '90s, an unpleasant snowball began to gather mass. The amount of tax revenues generated by the economy didn't keep pace with the population growth and accompanying rise in demands for government services. That, in turn, "adds significantly to the tax burden of honest taxpayers," Chiang says. He estimates that the state is losing $7 billion a year in unpaid taxes.

The state Employment Development Department's estimates are somewhat lower, at $3 billion to $6 billion annually in lost income and wage-related taxes. Any way it's counted, that's a pile of money for a state running a

$38-billion deficit that Sacramento is attempting to close by cutting services, raising taxes and borrowing money.

Certainly, not all of the loss is due to illegal immigrants, and the state, with scrupulous political sensitivity, avoids placing blame there. But Jerry Hicks, whose job until recently was to measure the underground economy for the Employment Development Department, reluctantly agrees that common sense would put undocumented workers at the head of the tax-avoidance list. It's anybody's guess how much fault lies with businesses forced to compete by dealing in cash.

That loss of tax revenue is key to understanding why unchecked illegal immigration creates a downward economic spiral. Jan. C. Ting, Temple University law professor and former assistant commissioner of the Immigration and Naturalization Service, says the swelling population of poor people who have little more than manual labor to offer, and who pay few taxes, will inevitably draw heavily on social services. That drain will, in turn, increase taxes on businesses and homeowners, who may depart for other states, which in turn will drive tax rates even higher.

An often-cited National Research Council study in 1997 concluded that each native household in California was paying $1,178 a year in state and local taxes to cover services used by immigrant (legal and illegal) households. The demand for such offsetting taxes undoubtedly has increased in proportion to the numbers of illegal immigrants since then.

What is known is how the tax drain is changing society. As the IMF's issue paper warned last year, the lost revenue can lead to "a deterioration in the quality and administration of the public goods such as roads and hospitals provided by the government."

Hospitals provide a clear warning signal. Here's how it happens: An illegal immigrant, without health insurance, has a serious health problem and goes to a public hospital, incurring a catastrophic medical cost. At bargain basement wages, that patient has as much chance of paying the hospital bill as paying off the national debt. So the patient scribbles out a passable IOU, and disappears.

Someone else pays. America's health system draws its lifeblood from private health insurance, and if large numbers of patients have no insurance or can't pay, the money has to be taken from taxes—siphoned from the state treasury. A robust society can absorb a certain amount of those losses, but if the tax base isn't expanding as fast as the demands placed on it, the system begins to shut down—as Los Angeles County's has.

In 2002, 33% of L.A. County residents were without health insurance or were grossly underinsured. The county thinks that rate is the highest in the United States, which helps to explain why the county prepared to close two hospitals last year because there was too much demand and too little revenue.

Carol Gunter is acting director of county emergency medical services, the person who has to try to run a "business" in which about a quarter of the customers don't have the means to pay for her product, but are entitled to its full service. So just how many emergency room patients are illegal? Federal law prevents her from knowing because hospitals are forbidden to ask about citizenship. What Gunter does know is that, despite billion-dollar federal bail-outs, the number of public L.A. County hospitals recently went from six to five, and another is going to close.

In March, Democratic Sen. Dianne Feinstein announced she had joined other senators in supporting a bailout bill to reimburse state and local hospitals for emergency medical costs incurred by undocumented immigrants. She estimated those costs in California at $980 million in the past year. Celebration over the proposal becomes somewhat muted when we consider that a bailout is—by sinking-lifeboat definition—intended to overcome the effects of a leak, and her statement mentioned nothing about patching the boat. Feinstein declined to be interviewed on the subject.

Jim Lott, executive vice president of the Hospital Assn. of Southern California, puts it bluntly: "We are in a [health-care] meltdown in Los Angeles County to the extent we have never seen before."

The state can't be far behind. An estimated 20% of patients throughout California are uninsured, with hospitals incurring $3.6 billion in uncompensated care. Fifty-one percent of the state's hospitals operated in the red last year.

After the "please pay cash" painting contractor left my house, I put pencil to paper on the bids. Considering that his line of work is labor-intensive, if I accepted the above-board bid of $2,000, probably about $1,500 would go toward wages, and maybe 10% of that would go to the government. If I went for the underground bid, I would get off cheaper—and the government would lose $200. Multiply that by the countless such transactions in California daily, and a lot of hospitals are going to run short, and a lot of potholes are going to grow.

Author Hanson describes the practical effect of the massive immigration numbers: "The unfortunate message we give migrants is, 'You can work here, but only undercover, and you can't join our society.'"

Chiang sees the same ominous divisions. "California is becoming a dichotomy society—high-wealth, low-wealth; educated, undereducated; and the underground economy plays a large role in creating the unregulated atmosphere that tends to widen those social and economic gaps."

So the people on either side of the divide go to their corners. The wealthy to West L.A. and its counterparts around the state. The poor? "We have towns in the Central Valley that are—literally—100% Mexican, and consist mainly of illegal migrants," Hanson says. "In those towns, Spanish is the only language spoken; there is no industry, and the towns are huge pockets of poverty. We can legitimately fear that this is the California of the future."

Two small cities of about the same size in Fresno County underscore Hanson's point. The town of Parlier in 2000 was 97% Latino, with 36% of the town living in poverty, and a per capita income of $7,078, Hanson says. The town of Kingsburg, whose population was 34% Latino, had just 11% living in poverty. The per capita income was $16,137.

The dependence upon agricultural labor, which usually has to be done by hand, puts a low ceiling on what immigrants can earn. That ceiling could be lifted either by stemming the flow of illegal labor, or by mechanizing the farm work. But neither is happening, which suits many farmers just fine.

Philip Martin, professor of agricultural and resource economics at UC Davis, says farmers could quickly mechanize labor-intensive harvesting if it were not so cheap to hire migrants. "Back in the late '60s and '70s, there was a fear there wouldn't be enough farm workers, so that spurred mechanization research," Martin says. "Then there were 70-some subsidized projects at the University of California aimed at figuring out how to pick oranges mechanically. Today, there aren't any, because there is plenty of cheap farm labor. There is probably a machine available to harvest every crop grown in the U.S., but they won't be used as long as the laborers are available at low wages."

Martin's point reveals this turned-around truism: Agriculture in Mexico is modernizing, which forces many laborers off their jobs there. Machines are displacing laborers in the cornfields of Mexico, so they come north to the "advanced" United States to pick fruits and vegetables by hand.

Because the United States makes no real effort to count its undocumented workers, their true impact on the job market is unclear. Common sense does say, however, that if millions of Mexicans are here illegally, they must be working or they would go home. An estimated $10 billion was sent back to Mexico in 2002 by workers in the United States, an increase of $800 million from the year before, says the nonprofit Pew Hispanic Center in Washington, D.C.

The migrants who come north used to be regarded as sellouts or deserters in Mexican society. Now, they're heroes praised by Mexican President Vicente Fox for the money they inject into that faltering economy. That is also a first, Hanson says. "Mexico is a failing society that stays afloat by exporting human capital. If you shut that border down, in five years you'd have a revolution, because Mexico can't meet the aspirations of its own people."

There is no question that illegal immigration greatly troubles Americans. The polls show it, both before and after 9/11. They want them to go home. One poll even showed that almost two-thirds want the military to patrol the border. Of course, they never gripe about the cheap hamburgers or the low-cost gardening that migrants make possible.

Yet, curiously, in a decade of unprecedented illegal immigration, the issue has been put on the back burner by most of society's seers and opinion-formers.

Illegal immigrants are the people we used to call illegal aliens in a coarser time. Now, to some, even "undocumented workers" is too harsh so they've adopted "unauthorized." To many critics of illegal immigration, this tiptoe nomenclature is part of the problem. They say a debate or consensus on the issue is made impossible by a barricade of political correctness, up against which a critic is in danger of that paralyzing accusation—racist.

Most politicians would rather swallow their tongues than talk about illegal immigration, and Dick Morris thinks he knows why. Morris, the former political strategist for Bill Clinton, says both political parties, "especially the Republicans, have to know they're running out of white people to split up. Any major politician is facing dodo bird extinction if he or she fails to reach out to Hispanics. It scares them."

Hanson believes the politics of immigration is about greed and power more than ideology. "It's one of those issues that's backed by strange bedfellows—on the right, you have big business types who want open borders to make money on cheap labor, and don't care about social consequences. On the other side, you have this left-wing racist—I think it's racist—separatist industry of Latino groups and leftist legislators" who want more immigration because it expands their power base.

Quixotically, on the border south of San Diego, the U.S. runs a version of "Checkpoint Charlie" to keep them out. Operation Gatekeeper started in 1994 to stem the flow of illegal immigration north by clamping down on the main ports of entry in the Southwest. In addition to forcing many border crossers to attempt a dangerous trip across the desert, it has had the unintended consequence of transforming a fluid population that used to go back and forth into one that simply stays here.

An unauthorized worker probably would prefer to work in this country and return home as often as possible, preserving his Mexican roots. Gatekeeper, however, has cemented that worker's feet in the U.S. It's not hard to understand his hesitancy to go home for a holiday or family event if he knows there's a good chance he'll be caught on his return. So, he does the obvious thing: He hires a coyote (outlaw immigrant trafficker) to bring his whole family north, often one member at a time.

So, what are the options? close the borders and kick out the undocumented as some arch-conservatives want? Or, on the other extreme, open the borders completely, as libertarians and some Latino groups tend to favor? On both counts, forget about it. Not going to happen. And you can trash amnesty at the present time, too. The War on Terrorism and the tension it has caused between Mexico and the United States, plus a sour remembrance from the results of the 1986 amnesty law, closed the book on "regularization," as Bush and Fox euphemistically called amnesty in the fond days of their mutual affection a couple years ago. A 2002 poll by Zogby International, a polling firm, showed that 65% of Americans opposed a new amnesty.

When the nation tried amnesty 17 years ago, the whole idea was to combine it with a crackdown on hiring illegal workers. Guess what? The amnesty worked for 2.8 million migrants, putting them on the track for citizenship; the crackdown did not, as the rising numbers of illegal crossings demonstrate.

The first amnesty seemed likely to only lead to another, and then another. An advocate of controlled borders is Cecilia Munoz, vice president of the National Council of La Raza, the group considered an arch defender of illegal migration. Munoz says undocumented immigration is bad for both the country and the workers, so she supports amnesty to make them legal, calling it "earned legalization." Her enthusiasm flags, though, when asked if the government should crack down on subsequent illegal immigration that undoubtedly would follow a new amnesty.

But her convictions don't falter. "We are going to ultimately succeed because we're all complicit in this system. We don't like it, but we benefit" from it, and therefore should grant the laborers amnesty.

The last-gasp alternative to amnesty seems to be a "guest-worker program." The guest-worker idea had two antecedents, one from 1917 to 1921, and another, known as the bracero program, from 1942 to 1964. Each was started in response to farmers' complaints of wartime labor shortages. After studying both, professor Martin is convinced that "there's nothing more permanent than temporary workers." He realizes the folly of inviting a poor laborer into a comparative worker's paradise, and then expecting him to run along home when the job is finished.

David Lorey, author of the scholarly "The U.S.-Mexican Border in the 20th Century," says the lesson of the bracero experience "is that guest-worker programs encourage migration." He adds, "There were horrible conditions in the migrant camps, and a lot of abuses that resulted from this neither-fish-nor-fowl program."

In retrospect, the lasting effect of the bracero program was to draw workers north to the border and give them a taste of American wages. For example, in 1940, Mexicali, a Mexican border town south of El Centro, had a population of less than 20,000 people. In 1960, it was 175,000. The programs succeeded in drawing workers, especially in agriculture, but also left a legacy of exploitation and ineffective regulation that has made bracero a dirty word in the lexicon of Mexican migration.

Memories of the abuses leave Hispanic groups skittish to the idea of guest-worker programs. But Brent Wilkes, executive director of the powerful League of United Latin American Citizens, says that his organization might support such a program provided the workers have labor rights equal to those of American laborers, and have an inside-track to eventual citizenship.

However, law professor Ting calls a guest-worker program in any form unworkable. "It's camouflaged amnesty. No one wants to use the word 'amnesty' because the American people recognize it for what it is—admitting defeat of our immigration system. So, they say, 'Let's call it something else. Let's call it a 'guest-worker program.'"

The vacillation over how to effectively control illegal migration drives a senior immigration investigator right up the wall, because he believes the bureaucracy has the answer in its own hands. The investigator has more than 20 years' experience with the INS. Still, he believes he must remain anonymous for fear of retribution.

Currently, he explains, the law requires an employer to make a good-faith effort to ascertain that applicants have valid identification. However, he considers that law a political con job because it gives unscrupulous employers an easy out: They can't be held responsible for not having the expertise to identify illegal or forged documents, so anything short of those being written in crayon can pass muster. The biggest abuses, he says, are of forged immigrant registration cards (green cards) and Social Security cards.

What frustrates him is his conviction that a procedure is already in place that would "immediately identify 70% of the illegal workforce." He explains that as a part of the 1986 immigration law, a voluntary employee verification pilot program was established, and is still operating. Under the program, the validity of Social Security cards and green cards can be quickly checked on all new employees by phone or online. He says the system could easily be expanded into a mandatory nationwide computer hookup by cross-indexing the data bases of the immigration service with the Social Security Administration. The effect would be that honest employers could instantly ascertain the legality of their workforce, and dishonest employers would have no excuse for hiring undocumented workers.

Bill Strasberger, a spokesman for the immigration service, says the pilot program is considered successful. "Employers using it are pleased, and so are we. It provides verification with confidentiality." Asked if it would be expanded or made mandatory by Congress, he laughed briefly, then said, "It really is the direction we need to move in."

Why, then, aren't we doing it? The investigator says that Congress refuses to make the program mandatory so as not to offend big agribusiness and other industries that freely employ illegal workers. These industries then take some of those profits and give generously to members of Congress.

Beck's organization, which advocates immigration control, plans to push for a mandatory employee-verification law. "The American people would not stand for a massive deportation, so what we need to do is use this program to dry up the jobs, then most illegals would gradually go home." If such a law was enacted, he says, the end result would be American workers gravitating to those jobs for slightly higher wages. "You'd end up paying 25 cents more for a hamburger and a dime more for lettuce. Big deal."

This affluent society can certainly afford more expensive hamburgers, but can it afford the hidden costs that currently make those burgers and fries dirt cheap? As Beck asks, "How many unskilled illegal migrants do we allow in? Forty million? Fifty million? What is the end point?"

POSTSCRIPT

Should U.S. Corporations Be Allowed to Hire Illegal Aliens?

In 1986, the Immigration Reform and Control Act was passed with enforcement provided by the Immigration and Naturalization Service. The purpose of this law was, primarily, to discourage American employers from hiring illegal aliens as a source of cheap labor. Employers are required to collect and keep various types of documentation about their employees, including proof of their legality to work. Failing to do so can result in severe financial penalties for the organization. Although the intention of the act may be laudable to many, compliance with the law can be problematic for many firms. University of Washington scholar Wendell French notes that "One of the most difficult aspects of the law is how an employer can actually comply with the law and at the same time avoid violating the Civil Rights Act" (2003: 126–127). By way of example, consider the following case provided by French:

> They [business owners] say they're caught between the governmentís competing demands—fined if they inadvertently hire illegals bearing counterfeit documents, yet risking a Justice Dept. lawsuit if they question workers with suspicious papers too closely. This happened to Monfort, Inc., a beef-packing company with headquarters in Greeley, Colorado. After the INS removed 300 illegals from a Nebraska plant, the company started its own immigration inspections at its other plants and was then fined $45, 576 under the Civil Rights Act for asking "overly intrusive" questions.

Certainly, dealing with the question of whether firms should be allowed to hire illegal aliens or not is complicated enough without organizations having to walk tip-toe on a fine line between stepping on the civil rights of legitimate employees and making sure they don't violate the IRCA of 1986!

Suggested Readings

Wendell French, *Human Resource Management.* New York: Houghton Mifflin Company, 2003.

Mark Krikorian, Jobs Americans wonít do: Voodoo economics from the White House. Center for Immigration Studies, 2004. www.cis.org/articles/2004/markoped010704.html

Open World Conference of Workers, Amnesty for all undocumented immigrants and full labor rights for all workers!. OWC Continuations Committee, 2005. http://www.owcinfo.org/campaign/Amnesty.htm

Jeffery S. Passel, Estimates of the size and characteristics of the undocumented population. Washington D.C.: Pew Hispanic Center, March 21, 2005.

Tom Tancredo, Illegal aliens taking American jobs. House of Representatives, Capitol, Washington D.C. November 17, 2005. www.hireamericancitizen.org/ttscriptcnn.html

Testimony of AFL-CIO President John J. Sweeny before the United States Senate Committee on the Judiciary, September 7, 2001. http://www.judiciary.senate.gov/oldsite/te090701si-sweeney.htm

Robert W. Tracinski, Opposition to Immigration is Un-American. The Ayn Rand Institute, January 15, 1999.

ISSUE 17

Is Economic Globalization Good for Humankind?

YES: Murray Weidenbaum, from "Globalization Is Not a Dirty Word: Dispelling the Myth About the Global Economy," *Vital Speeches of the Day* (March 1, 2001)

NO: Herman E. Daly, from "Globalization and Its Discontents," *Philosophy and Public Policy Quarterly* (Spring/Summer 2001)

ISSUE SUMMARY

YES: Foreign policy expert Murray Weidenbaum, in a reprint of a speech he delivered in 2001, promotes his "yes" response by systematically presenting, and then debunking, the most common "myths" surrounding globalization. He believes that globalization is a force for positive change.

NO: Professor Herman Daly feels that increasing globalization requires increases in political, social, and cultural integration across borders as well. The outcome is a loss of national identity for the countries involved as power is transferred from traditional domestic sources—i.e., governments, domestic businesses, local enterprises—to transnational corporations.

According to a leading textbook on international management, globalization is "global competition characterized by networks that bind countries, institutions, and people in an interdependent global economy" (Deresky, *International Management: Managing across Borders and Cultures,* 4th ed., Prentice Hall, 2003). Globalism is a phenomenon that has its roots in the rebuilding of Europe and Asia in the aftermath of World War II. As a measure of how powerful a phenomenon it has become, consider that the volume of international trade has increased over 3000 percent since 1960 (Griffin, *Management,* Houghton Mifflin, 2002)! Most of this tremendous growth has occurred in the TRIAD, a free-trade market consisting of three regional trading blocs: Western Europe in its current form as the Europe Union, North America, and Asia (including Australia). Increasingly, however, the developing nations of the world are contributing to the expansion in world trade.

Foreign investment has grown at staggering rates as well: three times faster than the world output of goods (Deresky, 2003.) In the early part of the twenty-first century, it is not a stretch to say that virtually all businesses in industrialized nations are impacted to some degree by globalization.

It seems pretty clear that globalization will continue to grow as a dominant force in international relations among countries, particularly as more Second and Third World countries open their borders to international trade and investment. What may be less clear, however, is whether or not this is a positive development. In other words, as we ask in this topic, is economic globalization good for humankind? Foreign policy expert Murray Weidenbaum provides us with a positive response in a reprint of a speech he delivered in 2001. His is an interesting approach to this debate in that he promotes his view by systematically presenting, and then debunking, the most common "myths" surrounding globalization. What is left standing, he hopes, is the realization that globalization is a force for positive change, particularly in the case of poor nations. Weidenbaum believes that the main benefit of globalization is not material in nature; rather, it is the incredible opportunity it provides for the transfer and exchange of ideas between countries. He concludes his argument by asserting that for a country to choose isolationism over globalism is to cut themselves off from "the most powerful of all factors of production—new ideas." While considering Weidenbaum's argument, ask yourself if there are any "myths" he fails to take into account and, if so, consider how damaging they are to his stance.

Professor Herman Daly is strongly against globalization. The foundation for his position resides in his belief that a nation's economic, cultural, social, and political dimensions are intricately intertwined. He feels that increasing economic integration of large corporations across national borders—globalization—requires increases in political, social, and cultural integration across borders as well. The outcome is a loss of national identity for the countries involved as power is transferred from traditional domestic sources—i.e., governments, domestic businesses, local enterprises—to transnational corporations. If left unchecked, these huge, multinational corporate conglomerates will eventually replace national governments as the dominant forces in society. Taken to its logical conclusion, Daly's stance foresees a world where national borders, if they exist at all, are pointless since national identities have disappeared and domestic political structures no longer have meaning.

Daly presents four major negative outcomes he feels are associated with globalization. As you read each, compare it with the "myths" Weidenbaum discusses in his article. Does Weidenbaum address each of these points? If so, does he do so successfully? If not, how much of a threat do you feel Daly's points are to Weidenbaum's position?

YES

Murray Weidenbaum

Globalization Is Not a Dirty Word

Delivered to the Economic Club of Detroit, Detroit, Michigan, January 22, 2001

Today I want to deal with a perplexing conundrum facing the United States: this is a time when the American business system is producing unparalleled levels of prosperity, yet private enterprise is under increasing attack. The critics are an unusual alliance of unions, environmentalists, and human rights groups and they are focusing on the overseas activities of business. In many circles, globalization has become a dirty word.

How can we respond in a constructive way? In my interaction with these interest groups, I find that very often their views arise from basic misunderstandings of the real world of competitive enterprise. I have identified ten myths about the global economy—dangerous myths—which need to be dispelled. Here they are:

1. Globalization costs jobs.
2. The United States is an island of free trade in a world of protectionism.
3. Americans are hurt by imports.
4. U.S. companies are running away, especially to low-cost areas overseas.
5. American companies doing business overseas take advantage of local people, especially in poor countries. They also pollute their environments.
6. The trade deficit is hurting our economy and we should eliminate it.
7. It's not fair to run such large trade deficits with China or Japan.
8. Sanctions work. So do export controls.
9. Trade agreements should be used to raise environmental and labor standards around the world.
10. America's manufacturing base is eroding in the face of unfair global competition.

That's an impressive array of frequently heard charges and they are polluting our political environment. Worse yet, these widely held myths fly in the face of the facts. I'd like to take up each of them and knock them down.

From *Vital Speeches of the Day*, March 1, 2001, City News Publishing. Reprinted by permission.

1. Globalization Costs Jobs

This is a time when the American job miracle is the envy of the rest of the world, so it is hard to take that charge seriously. Yet some people do fall for it. The facts are clear: U.S. employment is at a record high and unemployment is at a 30 year low. Moreover, the United States created more than 20 million new jobs between 1993 and 2000, far more than Western Europe and Japan combined. Contrary to a widely held view, most of those new jobs pay well, often better than the average for existing jobs.

Of course, in the best of times, some people lose their jobs or their businesses fail, and that happens today. However, most researchers who have studied this question conclude that, in the typical case, technological progress, not international trade, is the main reason for making old jobs obsolete. Of course, at the same time far more new jobs are created to take their place.

2. The United States Is an Island of Free Trade in a World of Protectionism

Do other nations erect trade barriers? Of course they do—although the trend has been to cut back these obstacles to commerce. But our hands are not as clean as we like to think. There is no shortage of restrictions on importers trying to ship their products into this country. These exceptions to free trade come in all shapes, sizes, and varieties. They are imposed by federal, state, and local governments. U.S. import barriers include the following and more:

Buy-American laws give preference in government procurement to domestic producers. Many states and localities show similar favoritism. Here in Michigan, preference is given to in-state printing firms; the Jones Act prohibits foreign ships from engaging in waterborne commerce between U.S. ports; many statutes limit the import of specific agricultural and manufactured products, ranging from sugar to pillowcases; we impose selective high tariffs on specific items, notably textiles; and many state and local regulatory barriers, such as building codes, are aimed at protecting domestic producers.

It's strange that consumer groups and consumer activists are mute on this subject. After all, it is the American consumer who has to pay higher prices as a result of all of this special interest legislation. But these barriers to trade ultimately are disappointing. Nations open to trade grow faster than those that are closed.

3. Americans Are Hurt by Imports

The myth that imports are bad will be quickly recognized by students of economics as the mercantilist approach discredited by Adam Smith over two centuries ago. The fact is that we benefit from imports in many ways. Consumers get access to a wider array of goods and services. Domestic companies obtain lower cost components and thus are more competitive. We get access to vital metals and minerals that are just not found in the United States. Also, imports prod our own producers to improve productivity and invest in developing new technology.

I'll present a painful example. By the way, I have never bought a foreign car. But we all know how the quality of our domestic autos has improved because of foreign competition. More recently, we had a striking example of the broader benefits to imports. In 1997–98 the expanded flow of lower-cost products from Asia kept inflation low here at a time when otherwise the Fed could have been raising interest rates to fight inflation. The result would have been a weaker economy. Moreover, in a full employment economy, imports enable the American people to enjoy a higher living standard than would be possible if sales were limited to domestic production.

In our interconnected economy, the fact is that the jobs "lost" from imports are quickly replaced by jobs elsewhere in the economy—either in export industries or in companies selling domestically. The facts are fascinating: the sharp run-up in U.S. imports in recent years paralleled the rapid growth in total U.S. employment. Both trends, of course, reflected the underlying health of our business economy.

The special importance of imports was recently highlighted by the director of the Washington State Council on International Trade: "The people who benefit most critically are families at the lower end of the wage scale who have school-age children and those elderly who must live frugally." She goes on to conclude: "It is a cruel deception that an open system of the free trade is not good for working people."

4. U.S. Companies Are Running Away Especially to Low Cost Areas Overseas

Right off the bat, the critics have the direction wrong. The flow of money to buy and operate factories and other businesses is overwhelmingly into the United States. We haven't had a net outflow of investment since the 1960s. That's the flip side of our trade deficit. Financing large trade deficits means that far more investment capital comes into this country than is leaving.

But let us examine the overseas investments by American companies. The largest proportion goes not to poor countries, but to the most developed nations, those with high labor costs and also high environmental standards. The primary motive is to gain access to markets. That's not too surprising when we consider that the people in the most industrially advanced nations are the best customers for sophisticated American products. By the way, only one-third of the exports by the foreign branches of U.S. companies goes to the United States. About 70 percent goes to other markets, primarily to the industrialized nations.

Turning to American investments in Mexico, China, and other developing countries, the result often is to enhance U.S. domestic competitiveness and job opportunities. This is so because many of these overseas factories provide low-cost components and material to U.S.-based producers who are thus able to improve their international competitiveness.

In some cases, notably the pharmaceutical industry, the overseas investments are made in countries with more enlightened regulatory regimes, such as the Netherlands. "More enlightened" is not a euphemism for lower standards. The Dutch maintain a strong but more modern regulatory system than we do.

5. American Companies Doing Business Overseas Take Advantage of Local People and Pollute Their Environments

There are always exceptions. But by and large, American-owned and managed factories in foreign countries are top-of-the-line in terms of both better working conditions and higher environmental standards than locally-owned firms. This is why so many developing countries compete enthusiastically for the overseas location of U.S. business activities—and why so many local workers seek jobs at the American factories. After all, American companies manufacturing overseas frequently follow the same high operating standards that they do here at home.

I serve on a panel of Americans who investigate the conditions in some factories in China. I wish the critics could see for themselves the differences between the factories that produce for an American company under its worldwide standards and those that are not subject to our truly enlightened sense of social responsibility.

I'll give you a very personal example of the second category of facilities. While making an inspection tour, I tore my pants on an unguarded piece of equipment in one of those poorly-lit factories. An inch closer and that protruding part would have dug into my thigh. I also had to leave the factory floor every hour or so to breathe some fresh air. When I said that, in contrast, the American-owned factories were top-of-the-line, that wasn't poetry.

Yes, foreign investment is essential to the economic development of poor countries. By definition, they lack the capability to finance growth. The critics do those poor countries no favor when they try to discourage American firms from investing there. The critics forget that, during much of the nineteenth century, European investors financed many of our canals, railroads, steel mills, and other essentials for becoming an industrialized nation. It is sad to think where the United States would be today if Europe in the nineteenth century had had an array of powerful interest groups that were so suspicious of economic progress.

6. The Trade Deficit Is Hurting Our Economy and We Should Eliminate It

Yes, the U.S. trade deficit is at a record high. But it is part of a "virtuous circle" in our economy. The trade deficit mainly reflects the widespread prosperity in the United States, which is substantially greater than in most of the countries we trade with. After all, a strong economy, such as ours operating so close to full employment and full capacity, depends on a substantial amount of imports to satisfy our demands for goods and services. Our exports are lower primarily because the demand for imports by other nations is much weaker.

The acid test is that our trade deficit quickly declines in the years when our economy slows down and that deficit rises again when the economy perks up. Serious studies show that, if the United States had deliberately tried to curb the trade deficit in the 1990s, the result would have been a weak economy with high inflation and fewer jobs. The trade deficit is a byproduct of economic performance. It should not become a goal of economic policy.

There is a constructive way of reducing the trade deficit. To most economists, the persistence of our trade imbalance (and especially of the related and more comprehensive current account deficit) is due to the fact that we do not generate enough domestic saving to finance domestic investment. The gap between such saving and investment is equal to the current account deficit.

Nobel laureate Milton Friedman summed up this point very clearly: "The remarkable performance of the United States economy in the past few years would have been impossible without the inflow of foreign capital, which is a mirror image of large balance of payments deficits."

The positive solution is clear: increase the amount that Americans save. Easier said than done, of course. The shift from budget deficits (dissaving) to budget surpluses (government saving) helps. A further shift to a tax system that does not hit saving as hard as ours does would also help. The United States taxes saving more heavily than any other advanced industrialized nation. Replacing the income tax with a consumption tax, even a progressive one, would surely be in order—but that deserves to be the subject of another talk.

7. It's Not Fair to Run Such Large Trade Deficits With China or Japan

Putting the scary rhetoric aside, there really is no good reason for any two countries to have balanced trade between them. We don't have to search for sinister causes for our trade deficits with China or Japan. Bilateral trade imbalances exist for many benign reasons, such as differences in per capita incomes and in the relative size of the two economies. One of the best kept secrets of international trade is that the average Japanese buys more U.S. goods than the average American buys Japanese goods. Yes, Japan's per capita imports from the United States are larger than our per capita imports from Japan ($539 versus $432 in 1996). We have a large trade deficit with them because we have more "capita" (population).

8. Sanctions Work, So Do Export Controls

It is ironic that so many people who worry about the trade deficit simultaneously support sanctions and export controls. There is practically no evidence that unilateral sanctions are effective in getting other nations to change their policies or actions. Those restrictions on trade do, however, have an impact: they backfire. U.S. business, labor, and agriculture are harmed. We lost an overseas market for what is merely a symbolic gesture. Sanctions often are evaded. Shipping goods through third countries can disguise the ultimate recipient in the nation on which the sanctions are imposed. On balance, these sanctions reduced American exports in 1995 by an estimated $15–20 billion.

As for export controls, where American producers do not have a monopoly on a particular technology—which is frequent—producers in other nations can deliver the same technology or product without the handicap imposed on U.S. companies. A recent report at the Center for the Study of American Business showed that many business executives believe that sanctions and export controls are major obstacles to the expansion of U.S. foreign trade.

9. Trade Agreements Should Be Used to Raise Environmental and Labor Standards Around the World

At first blush, this sounds like such a nice and high-minded way of doing good. But, as a practical matter, it is counterproductive to try to impose such costly social regulations on developing countries as a requirement for doing business with them. The acid test is that most developing nations oppose these trade restrictions. They see them for what they really are—a disguised form of protectionism designed to keep their relatively low-priced goods out of the markets of the more advanced, developed nations. All that feeds the developing nations' sense of cynicism toward us.

In the case of labor standards, there is an existing organization, the International Labor Organization [ILO], which has been set up to deal specifically with these matters. Of all the international organizations, the ILO is unique in having equal representation from business, labor, and government. The United States and most other nations *are* members. The ILO is where issues of labor standards should be handled. To be taken more seriously, the United States should support the ILO more vigorously than it has.

As for environmental matters, we saw at the unsuccessful meetings on climate change at the Hague [recently] how difficult it is to get broad international agreement on environmental issues even in sympathetic meetings of an international environmental agency. To attempt to tie such controversial environmental matters to trade agreements arouses my suspicions about the intent of the sponsors. It is hard to avoid jumping to the conclusion that the basic motivation is to prevent progress on the trade front.

I still recall the signs carried by one of the protesters in Seattle, "Food is for people, not for export." Frankly, it's hard to deal with such an irrational position. After all, if the United States did not export a major part of its abundant farm output, millions of people overseas would be starving or malnourished. Also, thousands of our farmers would go broke.

The most effective way to help developing countries improve their working conditions and environmental protection is to trade with and invest in them. As for the charge that companies invest in poor, developing nations in order to minimize their environmental costs, studies of the issue show that environmental factors are not important influences in business location decisions. As I pointed out earlier, most U.S. overseas direct investment goes to developed nations with high labor costs and also high environmental standards.

10. America's Manufacturing Base Is Eroding in the Face of Unfair Global Competition

Unfortunately, some of our fellow citizens seem to feel that the only fair form of foreign competition is the kind that does not succeed in landing any of their goods on our shores. But to get to the heart of the issue, there is no factual basis for the charge that our manufacturing base is eroding—or even stagnant. The official statistics are reporting record highs in output year after year. Total industrial production in the United States today is 45 percent higher than in 1992—that's not in dollars, but in terms of real output.

Of course, not all industries or companies go up—or down—in unison. Some specific industries, especially low-tech, have had to cut back. But simultaneously, other industries, mainly high-tech, have been expanding rapidly. Such changes are natural and to be expected in an open, dynamic economy. By the way, the United States regularly runs a trade surplus in high-tech products.

It's important to understand the process at work here. Technological progress generates improved industrial productivity. In the United States, that means to some degree fewer blue-collar jobs and more while-collar jobs. That is hardly a recent development. The shift from physical labor to knowledge workers has been the trend since the beginning of the 20th century. On balance, as I noted earlier, total U.S. employment is at an all-time high.

If you have any doubt about the importance of rising productivity to our society, just consider where we would be if over the past century agriculture had not enjoyed rising productivity (that is, more output per worker/hour). Most of us would still be farmers.

It is vital that we correct the erroneous views of the anti-globalists. Contrary to their claims, our open economy has raised living standards and helped to contain inflation. International commerce is more important to our economy today than at any time in the past. By dollar value and volume, the United States is the world's largest trading nation. We are the largest importer, exporter, foreign investor, and host to foreign investment. Trying to stop the global economy is futile and contrary to America's self-interest.

Nevertheless, we must recognize that globalization, like any other major change, generates costs as well as benefits. It is essential to address these consequences. Otherwise, we will not be able to maintain a national consensus that responds to the challenges of the world marketplace by focusing on opening markets instead of closing them. The challenge to all of us is to urge courses of action that help those who are hurt without doing far more harm to the much larger number who benefit from the international marketplace.

We need to focus more attention on those who don't share the benefits of the rapid pace of economic change. Both private and public efforts should be increased to provide more effective adjustment assistance to those who lose their jobs. The focus of adjustment policy should not be on providing relief from economic change, but on positive approaches that help more of our people participate in economic prosperity.

As you may know, I recently chaired a bipartisan commission established by Congress to deal with the trade deficit. Our commission included leaders of business and labor, former senior government officials, and academics. We could not agree on all the issues that we dealt with. But we were unanimous in concluding that the most fundamental part of an effective long-run trade adjustment policy is to do a much better job of educating and training. More Americans should be given the opportunity to become productive and highwage members of the nation's workforce.

No, I'm not building up to a plea to donate to the college of your choice, although that's a pretty good idea.

Even though I teach at major research universities—and strongly believe in their vital mission—let me make a plea for greater attention to our junior colleges. They are an overlooked part of the educational system. Junior colleges have a key role to play. Many of these community oriented institutions of learning are now organized to specially meet the needs of displaced workers, including those who need to brush up on their basic language and math skills. In some cases, these community colleges help people launch new businesses, especially in areas where traditional manufacturing is declining. A better trained and more productive workforce is the key to our long-term international competitiveness. That is the most effective way of resisting the calls for economic isolationism.

Let me leave you with a final thought. The most powerful benefit of the global economy is not economic at all, even though it involves important economic and business activities. By enabling more people to use modern technology to communicate across traditional national boundaries, the international marketplace makes possible more than an accelerated flow of data. The worldwide marketplace encourages a far greater exchange of the most powerful of all factors of production—new ideas. That process enriches and empowers the individual in ways never before possible.

As an educator, I take this as a challenge to educate the anti-globalists to the great harm that would result from a turn to economic isolationism. For the twenty-first century, the global flow of information is the endless frontier.

Herman E. Daly

 **NO**

Globalization and Its Discontents

Every day, newspaper articles and television reports insist that those who oppose globalization must be isolationists or—even worse—xenophobes. This judgment is nonsense. The relevant alternative to globalization is internationalization, which is neither isolationist nor xenophobic. Yet it is impossible to recognize the cogency of this alternative if one does not properly distinguish these two terms.

"Internalization" refers to the increasing importance of relations among nations. Although the basic unit of community and policy remains the nation, increasingly trade, treaties, alliances, protocols, and other formal agreements and communications are necessary elements for nations to thrive. "Globalization" refers to global economic integration of many formerly national economies into one global economy. Economic integration is made possible by free trade—especially by free capital mobility—and by easy or uncontrolled migration. In contrast to internationalization, which simply recognizes that nations increasingly rely on understandings among one another, globalization is the effective erasure of national boundaries for economic purposes. National boundaries become totally porous with respect to goods and capital, and ever more porous with respect to people, who are simply viewed as cheap labor—or in some cases as cheap human capital.

In short, globalization is the economic integration of the globe. But exactly what is "integration"? The word derives from *integer*, meaning one, complete, or whole. Integration means much more than "interdependence"— it is the act of combining separate although related units into a single whole. Since there can be only one whole, only one unity with reference to which parts are integrated, it follows that global economic integration logically implies national economic *dis*integration—parts are torn out of their national context (dis-integrated), in order to be re-integrated into the new whole, the globalized economy.

As the saying goes, to make an omelet you have to break some eggs. The disintegration of the national egg is necessary to integrate the global omelet. But this obvious logic, as well as the cost of disintegration, is frequently met with denial. This article argues that globalization is neither inevitable nor to be embraced, much less celebrated. Acceptance of globalization entails several serious consequences, namely, standards-lowering competition, an increased tolerance of mergers and monopoly power, intense national specialization, and the excessive monopolization of knowledge as "intellectual property." This article discusses these likely consequences, and concludes by advocating the adoption of internationalization, and not globalization.

The Inevitability of Globalization?

Some accept the inevitability of globalization and encourage others in the faith. With admirable clarity, honesty, and brevity, Renato Ruggiero, former director-general of the World Trade Organization, insists that "We are no longer writing the rules of interaction among separate national economies. We are writing the constitution of a single global economy." His sentiments clearly affirm globalization and reject internationalization as above defined. Further, those who hold Ruggiero's view also subvert the charter of the Bretton Woods institutions. Named after a New Hampshire resort where representatives of forty-four nations met in 1944 to design the world's post–World War II economic order, the institutions conceived at the Bretton Woods International Monetary Conference include the World Bank and the International Monetary Fund. The World Trade Organization evolved later, but functions as a third sister to the World Bank and the International Monetary Fund. The nations at the conference considered proposals by the U.S., U.K., and Canadian governments, and developed the "Bretton Woods system," which established a stable international environment through such policies as fixed exchange rates, currency convertibility, and provision for orderly exchange rate adjustments. The Bretton Woods Institutions were designed to facilitate *internationalization, not globalization,* a point ignored by director-general Ruggiero.

The World Bank, along with its sister institutions, seems to have lost sight of its mission. After the disruption of its meetings in Washington, D.C. in April 2000, the World Bank sponsored an Internet discussion on globalization. The closest the World Bank came to offering a definition of the subject under discussion was the following: "The most common core sense of economic globalization . . . surely refers to the observation that in recent years a quickly rising share of economic activity in the world seems to be taking place between people who live in different countries (rather than in the same country)." This ambiguous description was not improved upon by Mr. Wolfensohn, president of the World Bank, who told the audience at a subsequent Aspen Institute Conference that "Globalization is a practical methodology for empowering the poor to improve their lives." That is neither a definition nor a description—it is a wish. Further, this wish also flies in the face of the real consequences of global economic integration. One could only sympathize with demonstrators protesting Mr. Wolfensohn's speech some fifty yards from the Aspen conference facility. The reaction of the Aspen elite was to accept as truth the title of Mr. Wolfensohn's speech, "Making Globalization Work for the Poor," and then ask in grieved tones, "How could anyone demonstrate against *that?*"

Serious consequences flow from the World Banks' lack of precision in defining globalization but lauding it nonetheless. For one thing, the so-called definition of globalization conflates the concept with that of internalization. As a result, one cannot reasonably address a crucial question: Should these increasing transactions between people living in different countries take place *across national boundaries* that are economically significant, or *within an integrated world* in which national boundaries are economically meaningless?

The ambiguous understanding of globalization deprives citizens of the opportunity to decide whether they are willing to abandon national monetary and fiscal policy, as well as the minimum wage. One also fails to carefully consider whether economic integration entails political and cultural integration. In short, will political communities and cultural traditions wither away, subsumed under some monolithic economic imperative? Although one might suspect economic integration would lead to political integration, it is hard to decide which would be worse—an economically integrated world *with,* or *without,* political integration. Everyone recognizes the desirability of community for the world as a whole—but one can conceive of two very different models of world community: (1) a federated community of real national communities (internationalization), versus (2) a cosmopolitan direct membership in a single abstract global community (globalization). However, at present our confused conversations about globalization deprive us of the opportunity to reflect deeply on these very different possibilities.

This article has suggested that at present organizations such as the International Monetary Fund and the World Bank (and, by extension, the World Trade Organization) no longer serve the interests of their member nations as defined in their charters. Yet if one asks whose interests are served, we are told they service the interests of the integrated "global economy." If one tries to glimpse a concrete reality behind that grand abstraction, however, one can find no individual workers, peasants, or small businessmen represented, but only giant fictitious individuals, the transnational corporations. In globalization, power is drained away from national communities and local enterprises, and aggregates in transnational corporations.

The Consequences of Globalization

Globalization—the erasure of national boundaries for economic purposes—risks serious consequences. Briefly, they include, first of all, standards-lowering competition to externalize social and environmental costs with the goal of achievement of a competitive advantage. This results, in effect, in a race to the bottom so far as efficiency in cost accounting and equity in income distribution are concerned. Globalization also risks increased tolerance of mergers and monopoly power in domestic markets in order that corporations become big enough to compete internationally. Third, globalization risks more intense national specialization according to the dictates of competitive advantage. Such specialization reduces the range of choice of ways to earn a livelihood, and increases dependence on other countries. Finally, worldwide enforcement of a muddled and self-serving doctrine of "trade-related intellectual property rights" is a direct contradiction of the Jeffersonian dictum that "knowledge is the common property of mankind."

Each of these risks of globalization deserves closer scrutiny.

1. Standards-lowering competition Globalization undercuts the ability of nations to internalize environmental and social costs into prices. Instead, economic integration under free market conditions promotes standards-lowering competition—a race to the bottom, in short. The country that does the poorest job of internalizing all social and environmental costs of production into its prices gets a competitive advantage in international trade. The external social and environmental costs are left to be borne by the population at large. Further, more of world production shifts to countries that do the poorest job of counting costs—a sure recipe for reducing the efficiency of global production. As uncounted, externalized costs increase, the positive correlation between gross domestic product (GDP) growth and welfare disappears, or even becomes negative. We enter a world foreseen by the nineteenth-century social critic John Ruskin, who observed that "that which seems to be wealth is in verity but a gilded index of far-reaching ruin."

Another dimension of the race to the bottom is that globalization fosters increasing inequality in the distribution of income in high-wage countries, such as the U.S. Historically, in the U.S. there has been an implicit social contract established to ameliorate industrial strife between labor and capital. As a consequence, the distribution of income between labor and capital has been considered more equal and just in the U.S. compared to the world as a whole. However, global integration of markets necessarily abrogates that social contract. U.S. wages would fall drastically because labor is relatively more abundant globally than nationally. Further, returns to capital in the U.S. would increase because capital is relatively more scarce globally than nationally. Although one could make the theoretical argument that wages would be *bid up* in the rest of the world, the increase would be so small as to be insignificant. Making such an argument from the relative numbers would be analogous to insisting that, theoretically, when I jump off a ladder gravity not only pulls me to the earth, but also moves the earth towards me. This technical point offers cold comfort to anyone seeking a softer landing.

2. Increased tolerance of mergers and monopoly power Fostering global competitive advantage is used as an excuse for tolerance of corporate mergers and monopoly in national markets. Chicago School economist and Nobel laureate Ronald Coase, in his classic article on the theory of the firm, suggests that corporate entities are "islands of central planning in a sea of market relationships." The islands of central planning become larger and larger relative to the remaining sea of market relationships as a result of merger. More and more resources are allocated by within-firm central planning, and less by between-firm market relationships. Corporations are the victor, and the market principle is the loser, as governments lose the strength to regulate corporate capital and maintain competitive markets in the public interest. Of the hundred largest economic organizations, fifty-two are corporations and forty-eight are nations. The distribution of income within these centrally-planned corporations has become much more concentrated. The ratio of the salary of the

Chief Executive Officer to the average employee has passed 400 (as one would expect, since chief central planners set their own salaries).

3. Intense national specialization   Free trade and free capital mobility increase pressures for specialization in order to gain or maintain a competitive advantage. As a consequence, globalization demands that workers accept an ever-narrowing range of ways to earn a livelihood. In Uruguay, for example, everyone would have to be either a shepherd or a cowboy to conform to the dictates of competitive advantage in the global market. Everything else should be imported in exchange for beef, mutton, wool, and leather. Any Uruguayan who wants to play in a symphony orchestra or be an airline pilot should emigrate.

Of course, most people derive as much satisfaction from how they earn their income as from how they spend it. Narrowing that range of choice is a welfare loss uncounted by trade theorists. Globalization assumes either that emigration and immigration are costless, or that narrowing the range of occupational choice within a nation is costless. Both assumptions are false.

While trade theorists ignore the range of choice in *earning* one's income, they at the same time exaggerate the welfare effects of range of choice in *spending* that income. For example, the U.S. imports Danish butter cookies and Denmark imports U.S. butter cookies. Although the gains from trading such similar commodities cannot be great, trade theorists insist that the welfare of cookie connoisseurs is increased by expanding the range of consumer choice to the limit.

Perhaps, but one wonders whether those gains might be realized more cheaply by simply trading recipes? Although one would think so, *recipes—* trade-related intellectual property rights—are the one thing that free traders really want to protect.

4. Intellectual property rights   Of all things, knowledge is that which should be most freely shared, since in sharing, knowledge is multiplied rather than divided. Yet trade theorists have rejected Thomas Jefferson's dictum that "Knowledge is the common property of mankind" and instead have accepted a muddled doctrine of "trade-related intellectual property rights." This notion of rights grants private corporations monopoly ownership of the very basis of life itself—patents to seeds (including the patent-protecting, life-denying terminator gene) and to knowledge of basic genetic structures.

The argument offered to support this grab is that, without the economic incentive of monopoly ownership, little new knowledge and innovation will be forthcoming. Yet, so far as I know, James Watson and Francis Crick, co-discoverers of the structure of DNA, do not share in the patent royalties reaped by their successors. Nor of course did Gregor Mendel get any royalties—but then he was a monk motivated by mere curiosity about how Creation works!

Once knowledge exists, its proper price is the marginal opportunity cost of sharing it, which is close to zero, since nothing is lost by sharing knowledge. Of course, one does lose the *monopoly* on that knowledge, but then economists have traditionally argued that monopoly is inefficient as well as unjust because it creates an artificial scarcity of the monopolized item.

Certainly, the cost of production of new knowledge is not zero, even though the cost of sharing it is. This allows biotech corporations to claim that they deserve a fifteen- or twenty-year monopoly for the expenses incurred in research and development. Although corporations deserve to profit from their efforts, they are not entitled to monopolize on Watson and Crick's contribution—without which they could do nothing—or on the contributions of Gregor Mendel and all the great scientists of the past who made fundamental discoveries. As early twentieth-century economist Joseph Schumpeter emphasized, being the first with an innovation already gives one the advantage of novelty, a natural temporary monopoly, which in his view was the major source of profit in a competitive economy.

As the great Swiss economist, Jean Sismondi, argued over two centuries ago, not all new knowledge is of benefit to humankind. We need a sieve to select beneficial knowledge. Perhaps the worse selective principle is hope for private monetary gain. A much better selective motive for knowledge is a search in hopes of benefit to our fellows. This is not to say that we should abolish all intellectual property rights—that would create more problems than it would solve. But we should certainly begin restricting the domain and length of patent monopolies rather than increasing them so rapidly and recklessly. We should also become much more willing to share knowledge. Shared knowledge increases the productivity of all labor, capital, and resources. Further, international development aid should consist far more of freely-shared knowledge, and far less of foreign investment and interest-bearing loans.

Let me close with my favorite quote from John Maynard Keynes, one of the founders of the recently subverted Bretton Woods Institutions:

> I sympathize therefore, with those who would minimize, rather than those who would maximize, economic entanglement between nations. Ideas, knowledge, art, hospitality, travel—these are the things which should of their nature be international. But let goods be homespun whenever it is reasonably and conveniently possible; and, above all, let finance be primarily national.

POSTSCRIPT

Is Economic Globalization
Good for Humankind?

According to Freedom House, a non-partisan think tank that monitors the progress of freedom and democracy around the world, the rise in globalization and free trade over the last 30 years has been accompanied by an increase in the percentage of countries whose population enjoys civil and political freedom (Griswold, 2003). Since 1972, the share of those countries where these rights are denied has dropped from 47 percent to 35 percent, whereas the share of those countries enjoying these rights has increased from 34 percent to 45 percent. Freedom House also reports that the most economically open—that is, receptive to the idea of globalization—are three times more likely to enjoy full civil and political liberties than are economically closed countries. Further, numerous studies indicate that nations that are receptive to free trade grow faster and have higher levels of per capita income than nations that resist economic openness.

Facts such as these seem to provide considerable support for Murray Weidenbaum's pro-globalization stance presented here. But recall that Daly doesn't necessarily deny that economically open nations will benefit materially from globalization. His argument is that a country's national and cultural identity will be swept away in the wake of rapid economic growth. And in case you think his fears unfounded, consider the existence of the European Union (EU). There is strength in size, and joining a unified collection of European nations allows each country to better compete in the global marketplace. However, membership in the EU has come at a price: Member countries have to agree to dissolve its currency and adopt a new, single currency, the euro. Across Europe, the history and cultural identity of many countries is intimately tied to its currency, and the decision to disband it for economic reasons was the source of much social unrest. Many critics of the EU agree with Daly and fear that this is merely an early example of the destructive effects globalization—in the form of the EU—has on the national sovereignty of those countries that embrace it.

Suggested Readings

Cato Center for Trade Study Analysis, The benefits of globalization. *Cato Institute,* 2003. http://www.freetrade.org/issues/globalization.html

Vic George and Paul Wilding, *Globalization and Human Welfare.* Palgrave, 2002.

Robert Gilpen, *The Challenge of Global Capitalism.* The Princeton University Press, 2000.

Dan Griswold, Trading tyranny for freedom: How open markets till the soil for democracy. *Trade Policy Analysis, Cato Institute,* January 6, 2003.

Richard Langhome, *The Coming of Globalization: Its Evolution and Contempary Consequences.* St. Martin's Press, 2001.

Edwin A. Locke, Anti-globalization: The Left's violent assault on prosperity. *The Ayn Rand Institute,* September 5, 2003.

William K. Tabb, The amoral elephant: Globalization and the struggle for social justice in the twenty-first century. *Monthly Review Press,* 2001.

ISSUE 18

Are Global Sweatshops Exploitative?

YES: Richard Appelbaum and Peter Dreier, from "The Campus Anti-Sweatshop Movement," *The American Prospect* (September–October 1999)

NO: Radley Balko, from "Sweatshops and Globalization," *A World Connected Web Site* (2004)

ISSUE SUMMARY

YES: The first article, written by scholars Richard Appelbaum and Peter Dreier, chronicles the rise of the grassroots, college campus, anti-global sweatshops movement in the late 1990s.

NO: Columnist and social commentator Radley Balko argues that sweatshops are not exploitative. His article presents several additional points frequently offered in defense of globalization in general, and sweatshops in particular.

Historically, the word "sweatshop" is usually linked with the tremendous industrial growth of the American economy during the mid-nineteenth century. Originally associated with the apparel and garment industries, the use of the term eventually grew to describe any factory position in which employees—frequently, women and children—worked excessively long hours, often in unsanitary or unsafe working conditions, for barely subsistence-level wages. The massive influx of immigrants into the country during this time period resulted in low wage rates and provided corporations with little incentive to improve working conditions in their plants and factories (Matt Zwolinski, "Sweatshops," *Social Issues Encyclopedia*, Entry 167, 2004). Social commentators and union activists at the turn of the century argued that sweatshops were exploitative and called for their abolition. Their efforts resulted in a series of successful labor strikes and legislative actions that helped to dramatically improve worker conditions in the United States. As a result, by the end of the second decade of the twentieth century, sweatshops had become the exception rather than the norm in the manufacturing sector of the U.S. economy.

Recently, the topic of sweatshops has re-emerged as an important social and political issue, this time at the global level. Much of the recent attention on "global sweatshops" is attributed to a series of high-profile investigations into the overseas labor practices of major American and European firms during the 1990s. Newspaper and television news programs reported abusive labor practices and sweatshop working conditions in overseas factories like those owned by contractors hired by Nike, The Gap, and Wal-Mart (through its association with Kathie Lee Gifford). In addition, the Clinton administration pursued several legal lines of attack against firms and industries accused of using sweatshops, and anti-sweatshop activist organizations sprang up on college campuses across America, most calling for boycotts of products made in sweatshop factories. In several instances, campus organizations such as the United Students Against Sweatshops (USAS), buoyed by public outrage and moral indignation, forced multinational firms to close their operations in countries where sweatshops were being employed.

In their current manifestation, sweatshops are portrayed as an inevitable outcome of economic globalization (see issue 16 in this text for more on the subject of globalization) (Zwolinski, 2004). Critics of globalization argue that sweatshops are inherently exploitative since multinational corporations take advantage of the low wages and poor working conditions characteristic of developing countries. The developing countries must compete with each other in order to attract foreign firms; they do this by decreasing their labor standards. Thus, according to critics of globalization, multinational firms use the poverty and desperation of the developing countries to their advantage. Critics also point out that it is not just the workers in the sweatshops who are exploited—jobs in western countries are lost when global firms decide to locate their operations overseas in order to take advantage of the low labor costs.

Proponents of globalization note that most anti-sweatshop efforts actually hurt the very people they intend to help. The reason is simple: workers in developing countries usually have no other alternatives; like it or not, sweatshops represent the best of a bad situation. Shutting down sweatshops takes money out of their hands and sends the workers onto the street where, in many instances, they starve to death or turn to illegal activities, such as prostitution, in order to survive (Radley Balko, "Third World Workers Need Western Jobs," Foxnews.com, May 6, 2004). Proponents of globalization also note that virtually every industrialized first world economy capitalized on cheap labor early in its economic development. For example, consider that the rapid growth of Hong Kong and Singapore over the last quarter of the twentieth century was due in large measure to their willingness to exploit the comparative advantage of cheap labor early in their economic development.

The following articles address the question, are global sweatshops exploitative? The first article, written by scholars Richard Appelbaum and Peter Dreier, chronicles the rise of the college campus, anti-global sweatshops movement in the late 1990s. Columnist and social commentator Radley Balko argues that sweatshops are not exploitative. In addition to those mentioned above, his article presents several additional points frequently offered in defense of globalization in general, and sweatshops in particular.

YES

**Richard Appelbaum and
Peter Dreier**

The Campus Anti-Sweatshop Movement

If University of Arizona activist Arne Ekstrom was aware of today's widely reported student apathy, he certainly was not deterred when he helped lead his campus anti-sweatshop sit-in. Nor, for that matter, were any of the other thousands of students across the United States who participated in anti-sweatshop activities during the past academic year, coordinating their activities on the United Students Against Sweatshops (USAS) listserv (a listserv is an online mailing list for the purpose of group discussion) and Web site.

Last year's student anti-sweatshop movement gained momentum as it swept westward, eventually encompassing more than 100 campuses across the country. Sparked by a sit-in at Duke University, students organized teach-ins, led demonstrations, and occupied buildings—first at Georgetown, then northeast to the Ivy League, then west to the Big Ten. After militant actions at Notre Dame, Wisconsin, and Michigan made the *New York Times, Business Week, Time,* National Public Radio, and almost every major daily newspaper, the growing student movement reached California, where schools from tiny Occidental College to the giant ten-campus University of California system agreed to limit the use of their names and logos to sweatshop-free apparel. Now the practical challenge is to devise a regime of monitoring and compliance.

The anti-sweatshop movement is the largest wave of student activism to hit campuses since students rallied to free Nelson Mandela by calling for a halt to university investments in South Africa more than a decade ago. This time around, the movement is electronically connected. Student activists bring their laptops and cell phones with them when they occupy administration buildings, sharing ideas and strategies with fellow activists from Boston to Berkeley. On the USAS listserv, victorious students from Wisconsin counsel neophytes from Arizona and Kentucky, and professors at Berkeley and Harvard explain how to calculate a living wage and guarantee independent monitoring in Honduras.

The target of this renewed activism is the $2.5 billion collegiate licensing industry—led by major companies like Nike, Gear, Champion, and Fruit of the Loom—which pays colleges and universities sizable royalties in exchange for the right to use the campus logo on caps, sweatshirts, jackets, and other items. Students are demanding that the workers who make these goods be paid a living wage, no matter where in the world industry operates. Students are also calling for an end to discrimination against women workers, public disclosure of the names and addresses of all factories involved in production, and independent monitoring in order to verify compliance.

These demands are opposed by the apparel industry, the White House, and most universities. Yet so far students have made significant progress in putting the industry on the defensive. A growing number of colleges and clothing companies have adopted "codes of conduct"—something unthinkable a decade ago—although student activists consider many of these standards inadequate.

In a world economy increasingly dominated by giant retailers and manufacturers who control global networks of independently owned factories, organizing consumers may prove to be a precondition for organizing production workers. And students are a potent group of consumers. If students next year succeed in building on this year's momentum, the collegiate licensing industry will be forced to change the way it does business. These changes, in turn, could affect the organization of the world's most globalized and exploitative industry—apparel manufacturing—along with the growing number of industries that, like apparel, outsource production in order to lower labor costs and blunt worker organizing.

The Global Sweatshop

In the apparel industry, so-called manufacturers—in reality, design and marketing firms—outsource the fabrication of clothing to independent contractors around the world. In this labor-intensive industry where capital requirements are minimal, it is relatively easy to open a clothing factory. This has contributed to a global race to the bottom, in which there is always someplace, somewhere, where clothing can be made still more cheaply. Low wages reflect not low productivity, but low bargaining power. A recent analysis in *Business Week* found that although Mexican apparel workers are 70 percent as productive as U.S. workers, they earn only 11 percent as much as their U.S. counterparts; Indonesian workers, who are 50 percent as productive, earn less than 2 percent as much.

The explosion of imports has proven devastating to once well-paid, unionized U.S. garment workers. The number of American garment workers has declined from peak levels of 1.4 million in the early 1970s to 800,000 today. The one exception to these trends is the expansion of garment employment, largely among immigrant and undocumented workers, in Los Angeles, which has more than 160,000 sweatshop workers. Recent U.S. Department of Labor surveys found that more than nine out of ten such firms violate legal health and safety standards, with more than half troubled by serious violations that could lead to severe injuries or death. Working conditions in New York City, the other major domestic garment center, are similar.

The very word "sweatshop" comes from the apparel industry, where profits were "sweated" out of workers by forcing them to work longer and faster at their sewing machines. Although significant advances have been made in such aspects of production as computer-assisted design, computerized marking, and computerized cutting, the industry still remains low-tech in its core production process, the sewing of garments. The basic unit of production continues to be a worker, usually a woman, sitting or standing at a sewing machine and sewing together pieces of limp cloth.

The structure of the garment industry fosters sweatshop production. During the past decade, retailing in the United States has become increasingly concentrated. Today, the four largest U.S. retailers—Wal-Mart, Kmart, Sears, and Dayton Hudson (owner of Target and Mervyns)—account for nearly two-thirds of U.S. retail sales. Retailers squeeze manufacturers, who in turn squeeze the contractors who actually make their products. Retailers and manufacturers preserve the fiction of being completely separate from contractors because they do not want to be held legally responsible for workplace violations of labor, health, and safety laws. Retailers and manufacturers alike insist that what happens in contractor factories is not their responsibility—even though their production managers and quality control officers are constantly checking up on the sewing shops that make their clothing.

The contracting system also allows retailers and manufacturers to eliminate much uncertainty and risk. When business is slow, the contract is simply not renewed; manufacturers need not worry about paying unemployment benefits or dealing with idle workers who might go on strike or otherwise make trouble. If a particular contractor becomes a problem, there are countless others to be found who will be only too happy to get their business. Workers, however, experience the flip side of the enormous flexibility enjoyed by retailers and manufacturers. They become contingent labor, employed and paid only when their work is needed.

Since profits are taken out at each level of the supply chain, labor costs are reduced to a tiny fraction of the retail price. Consider the economics of a dress that is sewn in Los Angeles and retails for $100. Half goes to the department store and half to the manufacturer, who keeps $12.50 to cover expenses and profit, spends $22.50 on textiles, and pays $15 to the contractor. The contractor keeps $9 to cover expenses and profits. That leaves just $6 of the $100 retail price for the workers who actually make the dress. Even if the cost of direct production labor were to increase by half, the dress would still only cost $103—a small increment that would make a world of difference to the seamstress in Los Angeles, whose $7,000 to $8,000 in annual wages are roughly two-thirds of the poverty level. A garment worker in Mexico would be lucky to earn $1,000 during a year of 48 to 60 hour workweeks; in China, $500.

At the other end of the apparel production chain, the heads of the 60 publicly traded U.S. apparel retailers earn an average $1.5 million a year. The heads of the 35 publicly traded apparel manufacturers average $2 million. In 1997, according to the *Los Angeles Business Journal,* five of the six highest-paid apparel executives in Los Angeles all came from a single firm: Guess?, Inc. They took home nearly $12.6 million—enough to double the yearly wages of 1,700 L.A. apparel workers.

Organizing workers at the point of production, the century-old strategy that built the power of labor in Europe and North America, is best suited to production processes where most of the work goes on in-house. In industries whose production can easily be shifted almost anywhere on the planet, organizing is extremely difficult. Someday, perhaps, a truly international labor movement will confront global manufacturers. But in the meantime, organized consumers may well be labor's best ally. Consumers, after all, are not as readily moved as factories. And among American consumers, college students represent an especially potent force.

Kathie Lee and Robert Reich

During the early 1990s, American human rights and labor groups protested the proliferation of sweatshops at home and abroad—with major campaigns focusing on Nike and Gap. These efforts largely fizzled. But then two exposés of sweatshop conditions captured public attention. In August 1995, state and federal officials raided a garment factory in El Monte, California—a Los Angeles suburb— where 71 Thai immigrants had been held for several years in virtual slavery in an apartment complex ringed with barbed wire and spiked fences. They worked an average of 84 hours a week for $1.60 an hour, living eight to ten persons in a room. The garments they sewed ended up in major retail chains, including Macy's, Filene's and Robinsons-May, and for brand-name labels like B.U.M., Tomato, and High Sierra. Major daily papers and TV networks picked up on the story, leading to a flood of outraged editorials and columns calling for a clamp-down on domestic sweatshops. Then in April 1996, TV celebrity Kathie Lee Gifford tearfully acknowledged on national television that the Wal-Mart line of clothing that bore her name was made by children in Honduran sweatshops, even though tags on the garments promised that part of the profits would go to help children. Embarrassed by the publicity, Gifford soon became a crusader against sweatshop abuses.

For several years, then—Labor Secretary Robert Reich (now the *Prospect's* senior editor) had been trying to inject the sweatshop issue onto the nation's agenda. The mounting publicity surrounding the El Monte and Kathie Lee scandals gave Reich new leverage. After all, what the apparel industry primarily sells is image, and the image of some of its major labels was getting a drubbing. He began pressing apparel executives, threatening to issue a report card on firms' behavior unless they agreed to help establish industry-wide standards.

In August 1996, the Clinton administration brought together representatives from the garment industry, labor unions, and consumer and human rights groups to grapple with sweatshops. The members of what they called the White House Apparel Industry Partnership (AIP) included apparel firms (Liz Claiborne, Reebok, L.L. Bean, Nike, Patagonia, Phillips-Van Heusen, Wal-Mart's Kathie Lee Gifford brand, and Nicole Miller), several nonprofit organizations (including the National Consumers League, Interfaith Center on Corporate Responsibility, International Labor Rights Fund, Lawyers Committee for Human

Rights, Robert F. Kennedy Memorial Center for Human Rights, and Business for Social Responsibility), as well as the Union of Needletrades, Industrial and Textile Employees (UNITE), the Retail, Wholesale, and Department Store Union, and the AFL-CIO.

After intense negotiations, the Department of Labor issued an interim AIP report in April 1997 and the White House released the final 40-page report in November 1998, which included a proposed workplace code of conduct and a set of monitoring guidelines. By then, Reich had left the Clinton administration, replaced by Alexis Herman. The two labor representatives on the AIP, as well as the Interfaith Center on Corporate Responsibility, quit the group to protest the feeble recommendations, which had been crafted primarily by the garment industry delegates and which called, essentially, for the industry to police itself. This maneuvering would not have generated much attention except that a new factor—college activism—had been added to the equation.

A "Sweat-Free" Campus

The campus movement began in the fall of 1997 at Duke when a group called Students Against Sweatshops persuaded the university to require manufacturers of items with the Duke lable to sign a pledge that they would not use sweatshop labor. Duke has 700 licensees (including Nike and other major labels) that make apparel at hundreds of plants in the U.S. and in more than 10 other countries, generating almost $25 million annually in sales. Following months of negotiations, in March 1998 Duke President Nannerl Keohane and the student activists jointly announced a detailed "code of conduct" that bars Duke licensees from using child labor, requires them to maintain safe workplaces, to pay the minimum wage, to recognize the right of workers to unionize, to disclose the locations of all factories making products with Duke's name, and to allow visits by independent monitors to inspect the factories.

The Duke victory quickly inspired students on other campuses. The level of activity on campuses accelerated, with students finding creative ways to dramatize the issue. At Yale, student activists staged a "knit-in" to draw attention to sweatshop abuses. At Holy Cross and the University of California at Santa Barbara, students sponsored mock fashion shows where they discussed the working conditions under which the garments were manufactured. Duke students published a coloring book explaining how (and where) the campus mascot, the Blue Devil, is stitched onto clothing by workers in sweatshops. Activists at the University of Wisconsin infiltrated a homecoming parade and, dressed like sweatshop workers in Indonesia, carried a giant Reebok shoe. They also held a press conference in front of the chancellor's office and presented him with an oversized check for 16 cents—the hourly wage paid to workers in China making Nike athletic shoes. At Georgetown, Wisconsin, Michigan, Arizona, and Duke, students occupied administration buildings to pressure their institutions to adopt (or, in Duke's case, strengthen) anti-sweatshop codes.

In the summer of 1998, disparate campus groups formed United Students Against Sweatshops (USAS). The USAS has weekly conference calls to discuss their negotiations with Nike, the Department of Labor, and others. It has sponsored training sessions for student leaders and conferences at several campuses where the sweatshop issue is only part of an agenda that also includes helping to build the labor movement, NAFTA, the World Trade Organization, women's rights, and other issues.

Last year, anti-sweatshop activists employed the USAS listserv to exchange ideas on negotiating tactics, discuss media strategies, swap songs to sing during rallies, and debate the technicalities of defining a "living wage" to incorporate in their campus codes of conduct. In May, the USAS listserv heated up after the popular Fox television series *Party of Five* included a scene in which one of the show's characters, Sarah (played by Jennifer Love Hewitt), helps organize a Students Against Sweatshops sit-in on her campus. A few real-life activists worried that the mainstream media was trivializing the movement by skirting the key issues ("the importance of unionized labor, the globalization of the economy, etc.") as well as focusing most of that episode on the characters' love life. University of Michigan student Rachel Paster responded:

> Let's not forget that we ARE a student movement, and students do complain about boyfriends and fashion problems. One of the biggest reasons why USAS and local student groups opposing sweatshops have been as successful as we have been is that opposition to sweatshops ISN'T that radical. Although I'm sure lots of us are all for overthrowing the corporate power structure, the human rights issues involved are what make a lot of people get involved and put their energies into rallies, sit-ins, et cetera. If we were a 'radical' group, university administrations would have brushed us off. . . . The fact that they don't is testament to the fact that we have support, not just from students on the far left, but from students in the middle ground who don't consider themselves radicals. Without those people we would NEVER have gotten as far as we have.

Indeed, the anti-sweatshop movement has been able to mobilize wide support because it strikes several nerves among today's college students, including women's rights (most sweatshop workers are women and some factories have required women to use birth control pills as a condition of employment), immigrant rights, environmental concerns, and human rights. After University of Wisconsin administrators brushed aside anti-sweatshop protestors, claiming they didn't represent student opinion, the activists ran a slate of candidates for student government. Eric Brakken, a sociology major and anti-sweatshop leader, was elected student body president and last year used the organization's substantial resources to promote the activists' agenda. And Duke's student government unanimously passed a resolution supporting the anti-sweatshop group, calling for full public disclosure of the locations of companies that manufacture Duke clothing.

The Labor Connection

At the core of the movement is a strong bond with organized labor. The movement is an important by-product of the labor movement's recent efforts, under President John Sweeney, to repair the rift between students and unions that dates to the Vietnam War. Since 1996, the AFL-CIO's Union Summer has placed almost 2,000 college students in internships with local unions around the country, most of whom work on grassroots organizing campaigns with low-wage workers in hotels, agriculture, food processing, janitorial service, and other industries. The program has its own staff, mostly young organizers only a few years out of college themselves, who actively recruit on campuses, looking for the next generation of union organizers and researchers, particularly minorities, immigrants, and women. Union Summer graduates are among the key leadership of the campus anti-sweatshop movement.

UNITE has one full-time staff person assigned to work on sweatshop issues, which includes helping student groups. A number of small human rights watchdog organizations that operate on shoestring budgets—Global Exchange, Sweatshop Watch, and the National Labor Committee [NLC]—give student activists technical advice. (It was NLC's Charles Kernaghan, an energetic researcher and publicist, who exposed the Kathie Lee Gifford connection to sweatshops in testimony before Congress.) These groups have helped bring sweatshop workers on speaking tours of American campuses, and have organized delegations of student activists to investigate firsthand the conditions in Honduras, Guatemala, El Salvador, Mexico, and elsewhere under which workers produce their college's clothing.

Unions and several liberal foundations have provided modest funding for student anti-sweatshop groups. Until this summer USAS had no staff, nor did any of its local campus affiliates. In contrast, corporate-sponsored conservative foundations have, over the past two decades, funded dozens of conservative student publications, subsidized student organizations and conferences, and recruited conservative students for internships and jobs in right-wing think tanks and publications as well as positions in the Reagan and Bush administrations and Congress, seeking to groom the next generation of conservative activists. The Intercollegiate Studies Institute, the leading right-wing campus umbrella group, has an annual budget over $5 million. In comparison, the Center for Campus Organizing, a Boston-based group that works closely with anti-sweatshop groups and other progressive campus organizations, operates on a budget under $200,000.

This student movement even has some sympathizers among university administrators. "Thank God students are getting passionate about something other than basketball and bonfires," John Burness, a Duke administrator who helped negotiate the end of the 31-hour sit-in, told the *Boston Globe*. "But the tone is definitely different. In the old days, we used to have to scramble to cut off phone lines when they took over the president's office, but we didn't have to worry about that here. They just bring their laptops and they do work."

At every university where students organized a sit-in (Duke, Georgetown, Arizona, Michigan, and Wisconsin) they have wrested agreements to require licensees to disclose the specific location of their factory sites, which is necessary for independent monitoring. Students elsewhere (including Harvard, Illinois, Brown, the University of California, Princeton, Middlebury, and Occidental) won a public disclosure requirement without resorting to civil disobedience. A few institutions have agreed to require manufacturers to pay their employees a "living wage." Wisconsin agreed to organize an academic conference this fall to discuss how to calculate living-wage formulas for countries with widely disparate costs of living, and then to implement its own policy recommendations. [See Richard Rothstein, "The Global Hiring Hall: Why We Need Worldwide Labor Standards," *TAP,* Spring 1994.]

The Industry's New Clothes

Last November, the White House-initiated Apparel Industry Partnership created a monitoring arm, the Fair Labor Association (FLA), and a few months later invited universities to join. Colleges, however, have just one seat on FLA's 14-member board. Under the group's bylaws the garment firms control the board's decision-making. The bylaws require a "supermajority" to approve all key questions, thus any three companies can veto a proposal they don't like.

At this writing, FLA member companies agree to ban child and prison labor, to prohibit physical abuse by supervisors, and to allow workers the freedom to organize unions in their foreign factories, though independent enforcement has not yet been specified. FLA wants to assign this monitoring task to corporate accounting firms like PricewaterhouseCoopers and Ernst & Young, to allow companies to select which facilities will be inspected, and to keep factory locations and the monitoring reports secret. Student activists want human rights and labor groups to do the monitoring.

This is only a bare beginning, but it establishes the crucial moral precedent of companies taking responsibility for labor conditions beyond their shores. Seeing this foot in the door, several companies have bowed out because they consider these standards too tough. The FLA expects that by 2001, after its monitoring program has been in place for a year, participating firms will be able to use the FLA logo on their labels and advertising as evidence of their ethical corporate practices. [See Richard Rothstein, "The Starbucks Solution: Can Voluntary Codes Raise Global Living Standards?" *TAP,* July–August 1996.]

The original list of 17 FLA-affiliated universities grew to more than 100 by mid-summer of this year. And yet, some campus groups have dissuaded college administrations (including the Universities of Michigan, Minnesota, Oregon, Toronto, and California, as well as Oberlin, Bucknell, and Earlham Colleges) from joining FLA, while others have persuaded their institutions (including Brown, Wisconsin, North Carolina, and Georgetown) to join only if the FLA adopts stronger standards. While FLA members are supposed to abide by each country's minimum-wage standards, these are typically far below the poverty level. In fact, no company has made a commitment to pay a living wage.

The campus movement has succeeded in raising awareness (both on campus and among the general public) about sweatshops as well as the global economy. It has contributed to industry acceptance of extraterritorial labor standards, something hitherto considered utopian. It has also given thousands of students experience in the nuts and bolts of social activism, many of whom are likely to carry their idealism and organizing experiences with them into jobs with unions, community and environmental groups, and other public interest crusades.

So far, however, the movement has had only minimal impact on the daily lives of sweatshop workers at home and abroad. Nike and Reebok, largely because of student protests, have raised wages and benefits in their Indonesian footwear factories—which employ more than 100,000 workers—to 43 percent above the minimum wage. But this translates to only 20 cents an hour in U.S. dollars, far below a "living wage" to raise a family and even below the 27 cents Nike paid before Indonesia's currency devaluation. Last spring Nike announced its willingness to disclose the location of its overseas plants that produce clothing for universities. This created an important split in industry ranks, since industry leaders have argued that disclosure would undermine each firm's competitive position. But Nike has opened itself up to the charge of having a double standard, since it still refuses to disclose the location of its non-university production sites.

Within a year, when FLA's monitoring system is fully operational, students at several large schools with major licensing contracts—including Duke, Wisconsin, Michigan, North Carolina, and Georgetown—will have lists of factories in the U.S. and overseas that produce university clothing and equipment. This information will be very useful to civic and labor organizations at home and abroad, providing more opportunities to expose working conditions. Student activists at each university will be able to visit these sites—bringing media and public officials with them—to expose working conditions (and, if necessary, challenge the findings of the FLA's own monitors) and support organizing efforts by local unions and women's groups.

If the student activists can help force a small but visible "ethical" niche of the apparel industry to adopt higher standards, it will divide the industry and give unions and consumer groups more leverage to challenge the sweatshop practices of the rest of the industry. The campus anti-sweatshop crusade is part of what might be called a "conscience constituency" among consumers who are willing to incorporate ethical principles into their buying habits, even if it means slightly higher prices. Environmentalists have done the same thing with the "buy green" campaign, as have various "socially responsible" investment firms.

Beyond Consumer Awareness

In a global production system characterized by powerful retailers and invisible contractors, consumer action has an important role to play. But ultimately it must be combined with worker organizing and legislative and regulatory remedies. Unionizing the global apparel industry is an organizer's nightmare. With globalization and the contracting system, any apparel factory with a union risks losing its business.

Domestically, UNITE represents fewer than 300,000 textile and garment industry workers, down from the 800,000 represented by its two predecessor unions in the late 1960s. In the low-income countries where most U.S. apparel is now made, the prospects for unionization are dimmer still. In Mexico, labor unions are controlled by the government. China outlaws independent unions, punishing organizers with prison terms. Building the capacity for unfettered union organizing must necessarily be a long-term strategy for union organizers throughout the world. Here, the student anti-sweatshop movement can help. The independent verification of anti-sweatshop standards that students want can also serve the goal of union organizing.

Public policy could also help. As part of our trade policy, Congress could require public disclosure of manufacturing sites and independent monitoring of firms that sell goods in the American market. It could enact legislation that requires U.S. companies to follow U.S. health and safety standards globally and to bar the import of clothing made in sweatshops or made by workers who are denied the basic right to organize unions. In addition, legislation sponsored by Representative William Clay could make retailers and manufacturers legally liable for the working conditions behind the goods they design and sell, thereby ending the fiction that contractors are completely independent of the manufacturers and retailers that hire them. Last spring the California Assembly passed a state version of this legislation. Student and union activists hope that the Democrat-controlled state senate and Democratic Governor Gray Davis—whose lopsided victory last November was largely attributed to organized labor's get-out-the-vote effort—will support the bill.

⋅◈⋅

Thanks to the student movement, public opinion may be changing. And last spring, speaking both to the International Labor Organization in Geneva and at the commencement ceremonies at the University of Chicago (an institution founded by John D. Rockefeller and a stronghold of free market economics, but also a center of student anti-sweatshop activism), President Clinton called for an international campaign against child labor, including restrictions on government purchases of goods made by children.

A shift of much apparel production to developing countries may well be inevitable in a global economy. But when companies do move their production abroad, student activists are warning "you can run but you can't hide," demanding that they be held responsible for conditions in contractor factories no matter where they are. Students can't accomplish this on their own, but in a very short period of time they have made many Americans aware that they don't have to leave their consciences at home when they shop for clothes.

Sweatshops and Globalization

"In a village in the Mekong delta in Vietnam a woman and her twelve-year old daughter sit all day in the shade from five in the morning until five in the evening making straw beach mats. For their labour they receive $1 a day."

"In China, workers at Wellco Factory making shoes for Nike are paid 16 cents/hour (living wage for a small family is about 87 cents), 11–12 hour shifts, 7 days a week, 77–84 hours per week; workers are fined if they refuse overtime, and they're not paid an extra rate for overtime hours."

Stories like these are common when we hear talk about "sweatshop" plants in the developing world. We hear worse, too—terrible stories about women and children tricked into bondage, of union organizers getting beaten or killed, of terrible working conditions, long hours, and no bathroom breaks.

And yet American companies still operate low-wage factories—"sweatshops"—in developing countries. And there's still a copious source of labor in those countries eager to take the low-paying jobs western factories offer them.

So what's the story on sweatshops? Are they as bad as globalization critics claim they are? Should we boycott companies that operate them? Can they be stopped? Should they be stopped?

The Race to the Bottom

Globalization critics often cite sweatshops as a prime example of the "race to the bottom" phenomenon. A "race to the bottom" is what happens, they say, when world markets are opened to free, unfettered trade. Without transnational labor guidelines and regulations, big corporations will look to place factories and manufacturing plants in countries with the most relaxed environmental and—for our purposes—labor standards.

Developing countries then compete for the patronage of these companies by lowering labor standards—minimum wages and workplace safety requirements, for example. The result: horrendous working conditions like those described above, and no state oversight to make the factories change them.

Critics of free trade say in some countries it's gotten so bad that companies have begun using slave labor, workers compelled to work unpaid by totalitarian governments eager to entertain western businesses.

In the book *The Race to the Bottom,* author Alan Tonelson describes the process while discussing the 1999 World Trade Organization protests in Seattle:

> Internationally, WTO boosters faced an equally knotty dilemma. Most of the organization's third world members—or at least their governments—opposed including any labor rights and environmental protections in trade agreements. They viewed low wages and lax pollution control laws as major assets they could offer to international investors—prime lures for job-creating factories and the capital they so desperately needed for other development-related purposes. Indeed, they observed, most rich countries ignored the environment and limited workers' power (to put it kindly) early in their economic histories. Why should today's developing countries be held to higher standards?

Tonelson goes on to say that it is workers, then, who must shoulder globalization's burdens, while western companies win cheap labor, western consumers win cheap sneakers and straw hats, and corporate CEOs win eight-figure salaries. And, Tonelson and his supporters argue, it's not just third-world workers. Western workers lose when factories in the U.S. close down, and migrate overseas in search of laborers willing to work for poverty wages.

Critics say sweatshops are a way for corporations to exploit the poverty and desperation of the third world, while allowing them to circumvent the living wages, organization rights, and workplace safety regulations labor activists have fought long and hard for in the west.

What of Sweatshop Workers?

When *New York Times* journalists Nicholas Kristof and Sheryl Wudunn went to Asia to live, they were outraged when they first arrived at the sweatshop conditions Asian factory workers worked under. Like most westerners, the thought of 14+ hour shifts six or seven days a week with no overtime pay seemed unconscionable.

After spending some time in the region, however, Kristof and Wudunn slowly came to the conclusion that, while regrettable, sweatshops are an important part of a developing nation's journey to prosperity. The two later documented the role of sweatshops in emerging economies in their book *Thunder from the East.* Kristof and Wudunn relay one anecdote that helped them reach their conclusion *in the New York Times:*

> One of the half-dozen men and women sitting on a bench eating was a sinewy, bare-chested laborer in his late 30's named Mongkol Latlakorn. It was a hot, lazy day, and so we started chatting idly about the food and, eventually, our families. Mongkol mentioned that his daughter, Darin, was 15, and his voice softened as he spoke of her. She was beautiful and smart, and her father's hopes rested on her.
>
> "Is she in school?" we asked.
>
> "Oh, no," Mongkol said, his eyes sparkling with amusement. "She's working in a factory in Bangkok. She's making clothing for export to

America." He explained that she was paid $2 a day for a nine-hour shift, six days a week.

"It's dangerous work," Mongkol added. "Twice the needles went right through her hands. But the managers bandaged up her hands, and both times she got better again and went back to work."

"How terrible," we murmured sympathetically.

Mongkol looked up, puzzled. "It's good pay," he said. "I hope she can keep that job. There's all this talk about factories closing now, and she said there are rumors that her factory might close. I hope that doesn't happen. I don't know what she would do then."

Globalization's proponents argue that sweatshops, for all their unseemliness, often present developing laborers the best-paid jobs with the best working environment they've ever had; often their other options are begging, prostitution, or primitive agriculture.

Removing the best of a series of bad options, they say, does nothing to better the plight of the world's poor.

Boycotts and Bans

Anti-sweatshop organizations have achieved an impressive level of organization and influence in the last several years. Campus groups have persuaded university administrators at dozens of colleges around the country to refuse to buy school apparel from companies who use sweatshop labor. The activists demand that corporations pay a "living wage" and agree to international monitoring, or face the loss of collegiate licensing privileges—which amount to some $2.5 billion in annual revenue for the likes of Nike, Reebok and Fruit of the Loom.

So far, evidence has shown that boycotts and public pressure do get results, but perhaps not the kinds of results that are in the best interests of sweatshop workers.

Free traders argue that instead of providing better working conditions or higher wages, which had until then offset the costs of relocating overseas, western companies respond to public pressure by simply closing down their third world plants, or by ceasing to do business with contractors who operate sweatshops.

The result: thousands of people already in a bad situation then find themselves in a worse one.

In 2000, for example, the BBC did an expose on sweatshop factories in Cambodia with ties to both Nike and the Gap. The BBC uncovered unsavory working conditions, and found several examples of children under 15 years of age working 12 or more hour shifts.

After the BBC expose aired, both Nike and the Gap pulled out of Cambodia, costing the country $10 million in contracts, and costing hundreds of Cambodians their jobs.

There are lots more examples like that one.

- In the early 1990s, the United States Congress considered a piece of legislation called the "Child Labor Deterrence Act," which would have taken punitive action against companies benefiting from child labor. The Act never passed, but the public debate it triggered put enormous pressure on a number of multinational corporations. One German garment maker that would have been hit with trade repercussions if the Act had passed laid off 50,000 child workers in Bangladesh. The British charity organization Oxfam later conducted a study which found that thousands of those laid-off children later became prostitutes, turned to crime, or starved to death.

- The United Nations organization UNICEF *reports* that an international boycott of the Nepalese carpet industry in the mid-1990s caused several plants to shut down, and forced thousands of Nepalese girls into prostitution.

- In 1995, a consortium of anti-sweatshop groups threw the spotlight on football (soccer) stitching plants in Pakistan. In particular, the effort targeted enforcing a ban on sweatshop soccer balls by the time the 1998 World Cup began in France. In response, Nike and Reebok shut down their plants in Pakistan and several other companies followed suit. The result: tens of thousands of Pakistanis were again unemployed. According to UPI, mean family income in Pakistan fell by more than 20%.

In his book *Race to the Top*, journalist Tomas Larsson discussed the Pakistani soccer ball case with Keith E. Maskus, an economist at the University of Colorado:

> "The celebrated French ban on soccer balls sewn in Pakistan for the World Cup in 1998 resulted in significant dislocation of children from employment. Those who tracked them found that a large proportion ended up begging and/or in prostitution."

In response, several activist groups have stopped calling for boycotts, and have since started calling for pressure from the governments in whose countries the multinational corporations call home. Still, free traders argue, companies make decisions that are in the best interests of their shareholders and investors, and so if locating overseas isn't offset enough by cheap labor to make the investment worthwhile, companies will merely chose not to invest, costing poor countries thousands of jobs.

Are Sweatshops a Stop on the Road to Prosperity?

In his book, Larsson also argues that poor labor standards are usually symptomatic of other problems in a developing country, and that in the long run, they are in fact a *disadvantage* to that country's ability to compete in the international economy. "It is not . . . countries with the worst human rights records that top the annual rankings of national competitiveness," Larsson writes, "and it is certainly not the countries with the lowest wages and least protection for workers that dominate export markets, or attract the lion's share of foreign direct investment."

Every prosperous country today was once mired in "developing" status. And every prosperous country today once employed child labor in its economic adolescence that would today be considered "sweatshop" working conditions.

That includes Britain, France, Sweden, Germany and the United States. Only with the prosperity brought by international trade, globalization's adherents say, can a country then afford to demand better working conditions for its workers.

The economist and syndicated columnist Thomas Sowell writes:

> Half a century ago, public opinion in Britain caused British firms in colo-nial West Africa to pay higher wages than local economic conditions would have warranted. Net result? Vastly more job applicants than jobs.
>
> Not only did great numbers of frustrated Africans not get jobs. They did not get the work experience that would have allowed them to upgrade their skills and become more valuable and higher-paid workers later on.

Today of course, West Africa is still mired in poverty. Contrast Africa to Hong Kong, or to Taiwan, two countries that embraced an influx of foreign investment, and made a leap to prosperity in just 25 years that took most European countries nearly a century.

Kristof and Wudunn likewise point out that fifty years ago, countries like India resisted allowing foreign investment, while countries like Taiwan and South Korea accepted it—including the poor working conditions that came with it. Today, Taiwan and South Korea boast modern, well-educated, first-world econo-mies. India has become more amenable to investment in the last several years—and its economy has shown promise in response. But for decades, India's refusal to accept foreign "exploitation" wrought wide scale poverty and devastation.

In his book *In Defense of Global Capitalism*, Swedish public policy expert Johan Norberg notes that although India still battles poverty, its improving economy has shrunk its proportion of child laborers from 35% in the 1950s to just 12% in the last few years. Norberg further writes that the burgeoning economies in East and Southeast Asia may enable most of the countries in that region to eliminate child labor altogether by 2010.

Globalists also point out that the modern world economy and its inter-connectivity makes it possible for a country to make the transition from an economy where child labor is a necessity to an economy that can afford to ban it in a period of time never before contemplated.

Kristof notes that from the onset of the Industrial Revolution, it took Great Britain 58 years to double its per capita income. In China—where sweatshops are prevalent—per capita income doubles every 10 years. In the sweatshop-dotted southern providence of Dongguan, China wages have increased fivefold in the last few years. "A private housing market has appeared," Kristof writes of Dongguan, "and video arcades and computer school have opened to cater to workers with rising incomes. . . . a hint of a middle class has appeared."

The anti-sweatshop activists response to these arguments says that because the west has wealth and prosperity, it is the west's responsibility to bring the developing world into modernization without exploiting its laborers. Multi-national corporations can still secure comfortable profit margins without paying miniscule wages, forbidding union organization, and forcing long hours with overtime. As Kevin Danaher of the activist group Global Exchange writes, "Should trade agreements be designed largely to benefit corporations, or should they instead put social and environmental concerns first?"

But free trade advocates say that cheap labor is the one commodity developing nations can offer that first world countries can't. Force corporations to pay artificially high wages in those countries, they say, and there's no incentive for a company to endure the costs of shipping, construction, and risk that come with installing plants overseas. If corporations don't invest, those third world laborers again get forced back into the fields, the alleys, the brothels, and the black market. Better to endure the discomfort of poor working conditions in the short run, so that these countries can begin to build the economies that will enable them to demand better working conditions in the long run.

Common Ground?

In the end, there are at least a few areas in which both free traders and anti-sweatshop crusaders can agree. Most free trade advocates agree, for example, that benefiting from slave labor is no better than theft. Sweatshop workers are often the envy of their communities—they make more money than the farmhands or beggars, for example. But it's important that they're working in factories of their own free will. The key to building prosperity is choice, and if workers don't have the option to quit, or to take a job with a factory across town offering better wages, the "free" in "free trade" is a misnomer, and the benefits of globalization are tainted.

Likewise, free traders and anti-globalization activists usually agree that human rights violations should be documented, and that perpetrators of such violations should be publicized and embarrassed. If in its desire to attract foreign investment a government refuses to police a sweatshop factory where women are being forced into sexual favors, or where union organizers get beaten, it's certainly acceptable—in fact it's imperative—that that government be held accountable in the international community.

The fundamental disagreement in the sweatshop debate seems to be whether or not it's fair for big western companies to benefit from cheap labor in the developing world. Globalists say that menial manufacturing labor is the historical first step in a developing economy's first steps toward prosperity. Sweatshop activists say western corporations can afford to pay artificial "living" wages, and that anything less reeks of exploitation. They further argue that if corporations aren't willing to offer better working conditions on their own, western governments should penalize them, and consumers should refrain from buying their products. Globalists argue that if that happens, corporations would have no incentive to invest in the third world in the first place.

As trade barriers continue to fall, developing countries will continue to chose one track or the other—to embrace foreign investment, or to demand wages not proportional to what their national labor market would naturally allow. Which track delivers prosperity and which track produces continued poverty will lend clues as to who's winning the debate.

Further Reading

Global Exchange—An advocacy group that promotes "fair trade" in lieu of "free trade."

Nicholas Kristof—*New York Times* columnist who regularly writes on globalization issues.

Sweatshops.org—Co-op guide to ending America's sweatshops and encouraging "fair trade."

National Labor Committee—is supported by American labor unions to oppose sweat-shops in the developing world

United Students Against Sweatshops—Clearinghouse website for campus anti-sweatshop activists.

www.free-market.net-Free-Market.Net's Globalization Directory—Hosts a litany of articles related to sweatshops and other globalization issues.

David R. Henderson—A Hoover Institution scholar and economist who frequently opposes movements to end sweatshops in the developing world.

Between a Rock and a Hard Place—A Smithsonian Institution history of American sweatshops.

POSTSCRIPT

Are Global Sweatshops Exploitative?

Opponents of global sweatshops argue that they are exploitative in two ways. First, as noted in the introduction to this debate, exploitation occurs when multinational corporations systematically single out countries with favorable labor conditions to produce their products at considerably lower expense than they could in their home country. In addition to this practical position, opponents of sweatshops argue from a moral perspective. In this view, derived from Immanuel Kant's categorical imperative, people are entitled to respect because they are moral beings possessed of dignity. Ethics scholars Denis Arnold and Norman Bowie quote Kant: "In Kant's words, 'Humanity itself is a dignity; for a man cannot be used merely as a means by any man . . . but must always be used at the same time as an end. It is just in this that his dignity . . . consists . . .'" (Arnold and Bowie, "Sweatshops and Respect for Persons," *Business Ethics Quarterly*, vol. 13, no. 2, 2003, p. 222). According to Arnold and Bowie, global sweatshops are inhumane and exploitative because they treat workers as means to an end and not as ends in and of themselves. The below-subsistence wage rates and dangerous, abusive working conditions in sweatshops more than testify to the truth of this assertion.

The standard defense of sweatshops consists primarily of practical observations and arguments, most of which were covered in the article you just read by Radley Balko. But there is a philosophical justification as well. This line of defense argues that workers have a right to do what they want with their labor. Granted, in most developing countries, workers have few options available in terms of deciding how to spend their labor; nevertheless, as long as they decide to work on their own volition, the sweatshops are not guilty of exploiting the workers. Indeed, it is the opponents of sweatshops who are guilty of immoral behavior since they want to take away—through the shutting down of sweatshops and the punishment of multinational firms that use them—the local worker's right to decide how to use his labor. This leads to a difficult question for the sweatshop critics: What right do you (the critic) have to go into another country and tell its people where they can and cannot work?

Suggested Readings

Articles against sweatshops:

Denis Arnold and Norman Bowie, Sweatshops and respect for persons. *Business Ethics Quarterly*, vol. 13, no. 2, April 2003.

Liza Featherstone and United Students Against Sweatshops, *Students Against Sweatshops*. Verso, 2002.

William Greider, No to global sweatshops. *The Nation,* May 7, 2001.

Matt Zwolinski, Sweatshops, Entry 167. *Social Issues Encyclopedia,* 2004.

Articles supportive of sweatshops:

Radley Balko, Third world workers need western jobs. Foxnews.com, May 6, 2004. http://www.foxnews.com/story/0,2933,119125,00.html

Allen R. Myerson, Sweatshops often benefit the economies of developing nations, in *Child Labor and Sweatshops,* Mary E. Williams, ed. Greenhaven Press, 1999.

Thomas Sowell, Third world sweatshops: Multinational opportunity vs. nihilistic indignation. *Capitalism Magazine,* January 28, 2004. http://www.capmag.com/article.asp?ID=3489

Stephen Spath, The virtues of 'sweatshops.' *Capitalism Magazine,* January 18, 2001. http://www.capmag.com/article.asp?ID=151

Contributors to This Volume

EDITORS

DR. MARC. D STREET is currently an assistant professor of management at Salisbury University in Salisbury, Maryland. He received his BA (Economics) from the University of Maryland, College Park (1983); his MBA from the University of Baltimore (1993); and his PhD (Organizational Behavior) from Florida State University (1998). His primary research interests include business ethics and entrepreneurship. Dr. Street's research has appeared in journals such as *Organizational Behavior and Human Decision Processes, Journal of Business Ethics, Journal of World Business,* and *Small Group Research,* among others. He is also the recipient of numerous research and teaching awards. Prior to entering academia, Dr. Street spent 10 years in the private sector, the last four as a financial consultant for Merrill Lynch in Baltimore, Maryland.

DR. VERA L. STREET is currently an assistant professor of management at Salisbury University in Salisbury, Maryland. Her research interests include competitive dynamics, the resource-based view, decision-making, and entrepreneurial strategies. Her research has been published in journals such as *Journal of Management, Journal of Business Venturing,* and *Academy of Management Executive.*

STAFF

Larry Loeppke	Managing Editor
Jill Peter	Senior Developmental Editor
Susan Brusch	Senior Developmental Editor
Beth Kundert	Production Manager
Jane Mohr	Project Manager
Tara McDermott	Design Coordinator
Nancy Meissner	Editorial Assistant
Julie Keck	Senior Marketing Manager
Mary Klein	Marketing Communications Specialist
Alice Link	Marketing Coordinator
Tracie Kammerude	Senior Marketing Assistant
Lori Church	Pemissions Coordinator

AUTHORS

FRITZ ALLHOFF is currently a philosophy doctoral candidate at the University of California, Santa Barbara. He has published numerous journal articles on a wide range of topics including philosophy, history of philosophy, and business ethics.

SARAH ANDERSON is a director of the Global Economy project at the Institute for Policy Studies, a progressive think tank dedicated to a variety of issues.

GREG ANRIG, Jr., a vice president at The Century Foundation, is an expert on the issue of Social Security reform. Additionally, he is a coauthor of the book, *Social Security: Beyond the Basics.*

JUDITH C. APPELBAUM is vice president and legal director at the National Women's Law Center. Ms. Appelbaum participates in litigation, advocacy, and public education activities in many areas of the center's work, including judicial nominations, contraceptive coverage, and child care policy.

RICHARD APPELBAUM is a professor of sociology and global and international studies at the University of California, Santa Barbara. He currently serves as director of the Institute for Social, Behavioral, and Economic Research (ISBER) and as codirector of the ISBER's Center for Global Studies. He is the founding editor of *Competition and Change: The Journal of Global Business and Political Economy,* and he is currently engaged in a multidisciplinary study of the apparel industry in Los Angeles and the Asian-Pacific Rim.

STEPHEN BAINBRIDGE is professor of law at the UCLA School of Law, where he teaches corporate and securities law. He writes the ProfessorBainbridge. com blog.

RADLEY BALKO is a freelance writer living in Arlington, Virginia. Balko publishes his own blog, The Agitator, and writes occassionally for Tech Central Station and Foxnews.com, where he has a regular column.

WILLIAM BOULDING, a graduate of the Wharton School of Business, is a professor of marketing in the Fuqua School of Business at Duke University. His research interests include marketing strategy, customer relationship metrics, and marketing decision making.

JOHN CAVANAGH has been director of the Institute for Policy Studies since 1998. He is the coauthor of 11 books on the global economy, most recently *Alternatives to Economic Globalization: A Better World Is Possible.* He is a graduate of both Princeton University and Dartmouth College.

MARKUS CHRISTEN is an associate professor of marketing at INSEAD in Fontainebleu, France. His research interest focuses on the development of profitable marketing strategies.

CLAYTON M. CHRISTENSEN is the Robert and Jane Cizik Professor of Business Administration at the Harvard Business School, with a joint appointment in the Technology & Operations Management and General Management faculty groups. His research and teaching interests center on the management issues related to the development and commercialization of technological and business model innovation.

ROGER CLEGG writes, speaks, and conducts research on legal issues raised by the civil rights laws. He is vice president and general counsel at the Center for Equal Opportunity, a conservative Washington-based think tank that specializes in civil rights, immigration, and bilingual-education issues.

HERMAN E. DALY is a professor in the School of Public Affairs at the University of Maryland and the author of a classic on the subject of environmental economics, *Steady-State Economics: The Economics of Biophysical Equilibrium and Moral Growth* (W. H. Freeman, 1977). Recently he authored *Beyond Growth: The Economics of Sustainable Development* (Beacon Press, 1996) and *Ecological Economics and the Ecology of Economics: Essays in Criticism* (Edward Elgar, 1999).

FRED DICKEY is reporter for the *Los Angeles Times.* His publications include articles on the topics of immigration and Indian gaming in California.

PETER DREIER is the Dr. E. P. Clapp Distinguished Professor of Politics and director of the Urban & Environmental Policy Program of the Urban & Environmental Policy Institute at Occidental College in Los Angeles, California. Prior to joining the Occidental faculty in 1993, he served nine years as director of housing at the Boston Redevelopment Authority and as senior policy adviser to Mayor Ray Flynn of Boston, Massachusetts. He has also taught at Tufts University.

DANIEL W. DREZNER is assistant professor of political science at the University of Chicago and the author of *The Sanctions Paradox.* He keeps a weblog at www.danieldrezner.com/blog.

DENIS DUTTON is a professor of philosophy who lectures on the dangers of pseudoscience at the science faculties of the University of Canterbury in New Zealand. He is also editor of the Web site Arts & Letters Daily (http://www.aldaily.com).

DR. JOSEPH T. GILBERT teaches strategy and management ethics at the graduate level, and his research has been published in a number of journals.

EDMUND R. GRAY is professor and chair of the department of management at Loyola Marymount University. He has authored or coauthored five books and over 70 articles and other scholarly publications.

LARRY GROSS, CPCU, is an account executive with Insurance Services Office, Inc. (ISO) and has been with ISO for 15 years. He was chair of the Research Committee for the CPCU Society's Philadelphia Chapter at the time of this publication.

ROBERT D. HAY is a professor of management at the University of Arkansas. He retired in 1990 after 41 years of teaching, research, and service. He is the author of 11 books as well as numerous articles and cases.

IRA T. KAY is the practice director in charge of Watson Wyatt Worldwide's compensation practice. He has written and spoken widely on executive compensation issues. He is also the author of several books on the subject.

BRIAN H. KLEINER is a professor of management at California State University, Fullerton. Dr. Kleiner has published over 500 articles and publications and has served as an expert witness in numerous court cases.

NANCY R. LOCKWOOD is a human resource expert for the Society for Human Resource Management. She is certified as a senior professional in HR management and a Global Professional in Human Resources by the Human Resource Certification Institute.

NAOMI LOPEZ is director of the Center for Enterprise and Opportunity at the Pacific Research Institute in San Francisco. She has written extensively on issues of gender discrimination.

YING-TZU LU has published work on drug testing and related issues in publications including *Management Research News.*

JIM MACKEY is the managing director at the Billion Dollar Growth Network, a research consortium focused on large-company growth and innovation.

ALEXEI M. MARCOUX is assistant professor of management at Loyola University in Chicago and sometime contributor to the Cato Institute.

JOHN H. McWHORTER, a senior fellow at the Manhattan Institute, earned his PhD in linguistics from Stanford University in 1993 and became associate professor of linguistics at University of California, Berkeley after teaching at Cornell University. He writes and comments extensively on race, ethnicity, and cultural issues.

SUNGWOOK MIN studies the effects of first moving on firm performance. Min is currently an assistant professor of management in the College of Business, California State University, Long Beach.

JAMES MORRISON, PhD, a veteran of three presidential administrations, is the principal of Morrison and Associates, a Washington-based business consulting firm. The firm provides government relations services for major corporate clients.

LISA H. NEWTON is a professor of philosophy and director of the Program in Applied Ethics at Fairfield University in Fairfield, Connecticut. She is coauthor, with Catherine K. Dillingham, of *Watersheds 3: Ten Cases in Environmental Ethics,* 3rd ed. (Wadsworth, 2001) and coauthor, with David A. Schmidt, of *Wake-up Calls: Classic Cases in Business Ethics* (Wadsworth, 1996). She is also the author of numerous articles in journals of business and health care ethics.

ROB PARAL is a research fellow with the Immigration Policy Center and is also affiliated with the Sargent Shriver National Center on Poverty Law in Chicago.

DAVID PIMENTEL, a professor at Cornell University in Ithaca, New York, holds a joint appointment in the Department of Entomology and the Section of Ecology and Systematics. He has served as consultant to the Executive Office of the President, Office of Science and Technology, and as chairman of various panels, boards (including the Environmental Studies Board), and committees at the National Academy of Sciences, the United States Department of Energy, and the United States Congress.

CHRIS PROVIS studied and taught philosophy and now is associate professor in the School of International Business at the University of South Australia.

His work has appeared in numerous journals including the *Australian Journal of Labour Law* and the *Negotiation Journal.*

MICHAEL E. RAYNOR (D.B.A., Harvard University) is a director in Deloitte Research, the thought leadership arm of Deloitte, the global professional services firm. His client work, research, writing, and speaking focus on the fields of corporate and competitive strategy.

ALAN REYNOLDS is a senior fellow at the Cato Institute. A former columnist with *Forbes* and *Reason,* Reynolds has been a frequent contributor to such publications as *The Wall Street Journal, American Spectator, National Review,* and *Harvard Business Review.*

WILLIAM T. ROBINSON is associate professor of management, Krannert School of Management, Purdue University. He received a PhD in business administration from the University of Michigan in 1984. His current research examines how order of market entry influences ongoing product development strategies.

STEPHEN J. ROSE, formerly a senior economist at the Educational Testing Service, is now with ORC Macro.

STEVEN E. RUSHBROOK is a senior consultant in the compensation practice in Waston Wyatt Worldwide's New York office. He has degrees from Trinity College and Vanderbelt University's Owen Graduate School of Management.

JACOB SULLUM, a graduate of Cornell University where he majored in economics and psychology, is a senior editor of *Reason* magazine.

ROBERT B. THOMPSON is the George Alexander Madill Professor of Law at Washington University, St. Louis, Missouri. His work has been published in numerous law journals across the country including the *Case Western Reserve Law Review.*

LIISA VÄLIKANGAS is the managing director at the Woodside Institute, a research laboratory that develops new management practice for corporate resilience.

BERNARD WASOW is an economist and senior fellow at The Century Foundation. He is an expert in Social Security reform and has written and published numerous articles on the topic.

MURRAY WEIDENBAUM is the chairman of the Weidenbaum Center at Washington University in St. Louis. He is also the author of *Business and Government in the Global Marketplace,* 6th ed. (Prentice Hall, 1999) and *Looking for Common Ground on U.S. Trade Policy* (Center for Strategic and International Studies, 2001).

Index

Note: Italicized letters f, t and n following page numbers indicate figures, tables and endnotes, respectively.